VICTIMS AND SURVIVORS

VICTIMS AND SURVIVORS

The Nazi Persecution of the Jews in the
Netherlands 1940–1945

BOB MOORE

A member of the Hodder Headline Group
LONDON • NEW YORK • SYDNEY • AUCKLAND

First published in Great Britain in 1997 by
Arnold, a member of the Hodder Headline Group
338 Euston Road, London NW1 3BH
175 Fifth Avenue, New York, NY 10010

Distributed exclusively in the USA by
St Martin's Press, Inc.
175 Fifth Avenue, New York, NY 10010

British Library Cataloguing in Publication Data
A catalogue record for this book is available from the British Library

Library of Congress Cataloging-in-Publication Data
Moore, Bob. 1954–
    Victims and survivors : the Nazi persecution of the Jews in the
Netherlands, 1940–1945 / Bob Moore.
        p.   cm.
    Includes bibliographical references and index.
    ISBN 0-340-49563-4 (hardbound) – ISBN 0-340-69157-3 (pbk.)
    1. Jews–Netherlands–History–20th century.   2. Holocaust, Jewish
(1939–1945)–Netherlands.   3. Netherlands–Ethnic relations.
I. Title.
DS135.N4M664   1977
940.53' 18'09492–dc21   97-4209
                                                                                    CIP

ISBN 0 340 69157 3 (pb)
ISBN 0 340 49563 4 (hb)

Typeset in 10/12pt Sabon by Saxon Graphics Ltd, Derby
Printed and bound in Great Britain by J W Arrowsmith Ltd, Bristol

For Susan, Elizabeth and James

Contents

Preface

It is now more than 50 years since the end of the Second World War. In that time, historians have learned a great deal about all aspects of Nazism and its attempted domination of Europe. In this respect, the history of the Holocaust is no exception. No other single issue has generated as much literature or so much debate as this most heinous of Nazi crimes. Even after half a century, it continues to occupy a central place in contemporary culture. Yet in spite of all the words, many debates and many facets of the Holocaust in Europe remain confined to the languages of the countries in which they took place. Scholars in those countries have tended to see the persecution of the Jews as a national tragedy rather than one which is of direct interest to the outside world. This is certainly true of the Netherlands, where only a few of the major works on the subject have appeared in translation. Thus while Anne Frank has become an icon for the literature and remembrance of the Holocaust, the circumstances in which her particular tragedy was played out are much less widely known or understood.

It is now almost 30 years since Jacob Presser's book, *Ashes in the Wind*, appeared in English. To date, it has been the only work which has tried to tell the whole story of the Holocaust in the Netherlands. Since its appearance, there has been a whole canon of scholarly literature which has re-examined both the sources and his conclusions. Essentially, *Victims and Survivors* is intended to update the debates by synthesising the more recent scholarship on the subject. Although references are made to archival collections in the Netherlands, Britain and the United States, this work makes no claims to be based on primary research. The sources for some of the key documents have, however, been included because neither Presser nor Louis de Jong, in his comprehensive history of the Netherlands in the Second World War, have given precise locations.

No book of this nature could be completed without the help of others. I gratefully acknowledge the financial assistance given by the British

Academy and the Twenty-Seven Foundation (Scouloudi Fund). During my tenure at Bristol Polytechnic (University of the West of England, Bristol) the Humanities Faculty Research Committee also provided funding for visits to the Netherlands. More recently, the Department of History at Manchester Metropolitan University has made available both research time and resources to allow the project to be completed. Similarly, research would be far more difficult without the assistance of archivists and librarians. In this respect, I would particularly like to thank the staffs at the Wiener Library (London), the *Koninklijke Bibliotheek* (The Hague), the *Rijksinstituut voor Oorlogsdocumentatie* (Amsterdam), the UWE St Matthias Library (Bristol) and the MMU All Saints Library (Manchester) for their efforts on my behalf.

On a personal note, I owe a debt of gratitude to a number of people who have helped bring this book to fruition. Some eight years ago, long conversations with Irène van den Berghe helped to shape my ideas. During the preparation of this book, I was given the opportunity to read drafts of an anthology of literature on the Holocaust in the Netherlands, *Anne Frank and After*, compiled by Dick van Galen Last and Rolf Wolfswinkel. In many respects our two books are complementary and I am delighted to find that they will appear in print at more or less the same time. More recently I have exploited my friends, Ian Kershaw and Joe Harrison. They have both painstakingly read versions of the manuscript and made many invaluable suggestions. Likewise, Henry Mason, Barbara Hately-Broad and Dick van Galen Last have also commented on drafts of the text. Their collective effort has undoubtedly improved the final version immensely, but any errors and omissions remain entirely my responsibility. In addition, I can only marvel at the patience of my publisher, Christopher Wheeler, who has been prepared to tolerate my procrastinations and prevarications.

However, my final words of thanks must go to my wife, Susan, and my children, Elizabeth and James. They could not have been more supportive or understanding and it is to them that this book is dedicated.

Saddleworth
November 1996

NORTH SEA

TEXEL

Waddenzee

Afsluitdijk

Den Helder

Schagen *Wieringermeer*

Schoorl
Alkmaar

NOORD
HOLLAND

Leeuwarden

FRIESLAND

Sneek
Joure
Heerenveen

Steenwijk

Blokzijl

Delfzijl

GRONINGEN
Groningen

Nieuw Beerta

Assen
Westerbork

DRENTE

Hoogeveen
Meppel Coevorden

Zwolle

Heemse
Ommen

OVERIJSSEL

Almelo
Hengelo

Ijmuiden
Zandvoort
Haarlem
Niew Vennep
Noordwijk

Zaandam
Amsterdam

Santpoort

Bussum
Hilversum
Loosdrecht
Wassenaar

Laren
't'Gooi
Soest

Bloricum

Putten
Barneveld

Vierhouten

Soeren

Amersfoort
Bilthoven

Deventer
Apeldoorn

Enschede

Zutphen

Scheveningen
Leiden
The Hague
Delft ZUID-

Utrecht
UTRECHT

Ede GELDERLAND

Lek R
Lexmond

Hoek van Holland
Rotterdam

Oosterbeek Winterswijk
Arnhem

HOLLAND Dordrecht

Tiel

Nijmegen

Heusden

Maas R

Moerdijk
Middelburg
Roosendaal Breda Tilburg
Bergen op Zoom

ZEELAND

s'Hertogenbosch
Vught

NOORD-
BRABANT

R. Rhine

Vlissingen
Sluis

Eindhoven

Venlo

Roermond

LIMBURG

Echt

BELGIUM

Heerlen
Maastricht Vilt

GERMANY

The Netherlands

Kilometres
0   50   100

|1|

Introduction

Historians and the Holocaust in the Netherlands

In his introduction to Werner Warmbrunn's survey of the Netherlands under German occupation published in 1963, Louis de Jong, at that time director of the Netherlands State Institute for War Documentation (RIOD), noted that innumerable people had been moved by reading the diary of Anne Frank, or seeing the play or the film based on the book. His purpose was to point out that the Nazi persecution of the Jews in the Netherlands was only one aspect of the German occupation and that the experience for the Dutch population as a whole was more extensive and complicated.[1] This is undoubtedly true, but the underlying assumption, that the Anne Frank story had brought with it an understanding of the Holocaust in the Netherlands to these millions of readers, may well remain open to doubt.[2]

The publication of the diary in the summer of 1947 was certainly instrumental in bringing the innumerable individual tragedies of the Holocaust home to a world still struggling to come to terms with the sheer scale and enormity of the Nazi crimes committed during the five and a half years of war. This one girl's recorded thoughts and description of her experiences in hiding from the Germans in Amsterdam went a long way beyond the immediate context of the 'Final Solution' in the Netherlands and became a symbol for all Jewish suffering under the Nazis throughout occupied Europe. The Dutch edition, *Het Achterhuis. Dagboekbrieven van 12 juni 1942–1 augustus 1944* went through six editions in three years and translations into German, English and French were prepared and published in the early 1950s. By the 1980s, the book had been translated into more than 50 languages, been published in umpteen editions and sold millions of copies.[3] The diary was given added poignancy by the knowledge of what had ultimately befallen this

young Jewish girl, but the popularity of this one book did not lead to anything more than a superficial understanding of the specific context in which
the tragedy of the Frank family and so many others had taken place. Perhaps
because the sentiments in the book were so universal, the specific Dutch context of the story was seldom afforded much attention.

As a result, the historiography of the persecution of the Jews in the
Netherlands has remained primarily a domestic issue. Essentially, it has
mirrored the attempts of Dutch society to come to terms with the enormous tragedy played out in its midst during the German occupation. For a
country proud of its tolerance and liberal traditions, it was almost inconceivable that a whole section of its citizenry could have been sacrificed to
Nazi ideological imperatives with so little protest or opposition. Yet this
seemed the only conclusion. The raw statistics tell a chilling story. Of more
than 140,000 Jews living in the pre-war Netherlands, approximately
107,000 were deported to the East and at least 102,000 were murdered or
worked to death in the Nazi camps.[4] Horrific enough on their own, the
impact of these figures was compounded by two other statistics. Firstly
there was the fact that the deported Jews constituted around 40 per cent of
the total civilian casualties for the country as a whole.[5] This made it abun-
dantly clear that the Jews had suffered out of all proportion to their non-
Jewish compatriots. While this could be partly explained by the low levels
of mortality suffered by Dutch civilians as a result of German occupation
policies and the relatively short periods of fighting on Dutch soil in 1940
and 1944–45, a far more telling comparison emerged when the 73 per cent
Jewish mortality of the Netherlands was compared with the figures for
Belgium (40 per cent) and France (25 per cent).[6] How could such a huge
difference have arisen between apparently similar states, and more importantly, how could the Netherlands compare so unfavourably with her nearest Western European neighbours?

The need to recognise the scale of the tragedy in the Netherlands and
then to explain how and why it happened has thus formed the basis of academic and popular writing on the subject. To understand how the debate
has developed in the Netherlands since 1945, it is essential to begin with a
survey of the published works and the ways in which authors have
approached the central questions involved. The main academic historiography has gone through a number of phases, beginning with narratives which
explained what happened, progressing through publications which detailed
how the tragedy had taken place, and finally giving rise to studies which
recognised the atypicality of the Dutch case when contrasted with other
Western European states. These more recent works have been able to
engage with the new lines of enquiry engendered by comparative research
on the Holocaust as a whole and the attempts to provide overall syntheses
of the main problems of interpretation. Interdispersed with these analytical
texts have come a whole canon of memoirs, local narrative histories and

even novels on the subject which have all contributed in some way to produce a clearer picture of the Holocaust in the Netherlands.

The immediate post-war years produced two monographs written by eyewitnesses which have had a lasting impact on the interpretation of events during the German occupation. The first attempt to provide a detailed chronicle of events came in 1947. Heinz Wielek's *De Oorlog die Hitler Won* (The War that Hitler Won)[7] mixed narrative history with personal and collected memoirs and combined them with some of the key documentary evidence. Although written before the first archival and eyewitness collections became available, the book remains highly influential and formed a central text for all later authors. Wielek was a refugee German Jew, active in left-wing circles, who had survived primarily because he was the partner in a mixed marriage. After the war, he was commissioned by publishers to complete the work started by two other Jewish journalists who had been deported. Other survivors also began to write histories of the persecution. Three came from prominent Zionists, Pick, Taubes and de Wolff, who had obtained Palestine certificates late in the occupation and one from Berkley, the son-in-law of a leading functionary of the *Joodse Raad* (Jewish Council).[8] All these authors had reasons to be grateful to the Amsterdam Jewish Council. Wielek had been an employee and the others had benefited from the Council's active help in obtaining their certificates. Perhaps as a result, their conclusions were relatively sympathetic to the Council. Their juxtaposition with the accounts from those who had not been so favoured began what was to become one of the central debates in the historiography, namely the culpability of the Council and its leadership in the deaths of over 100,000 of their co-religionists. They were accompanied by the first of the camp memoirs, most notably de Wind, *Eindstation ... Auschwitz* (Terminus ... Auschwitz, 1946), Vogel, *Dagboek uit een kamp* (Diary from a Camp, 1946) and van Doorn, *Vught: Dertien Maanden in het Concentratiecamp* (Vught:Thirteen Months in the Concentration Camp, 1945).[9] Each of these contained further specific details on aspects of the persecution and how it had been carried out.

In addition, this period saw the publication of four books which attempted to defend the role of the major churches during the occupation. Touw, *Het Verzet der Hervormde Kerk* (The Resistance of the Reformed Church) and Buskes, *Waar Stond de Kerk?* (Where did the Church Stand?) dealt with the Dutch Reformed Church; Th. Delleman (ed.), *Opdat wij niet vergeten* (Lest We Forget) dealt with the Calvinist *Gereformeerde* Church; and Stokman, *Het Verzet van de Nederlansche Bisschoppen tegen Nationaaal-Socialisme en Duitsche Tyrannie* (The Resistance of the Dutch Bishops against National Socialism and German Tyranny) discussed the Roman Catholic Church.[10] While their focus was on resistance activities, none of these authors could avoid addressing what the churches as institutions had or had not done for the Jews. Given the limited nature of the help which had come from that quarter, the books tended to concentrate on official protests and how attempts had been made to protect baptised Jews from the Nazis. By taking a fairly defensive stance, none of them really did justice to the role of individual churchmen or to church-based rescue networks in helping to save Jews from Nazi persecution, either because the authors were unaware of their activities, or because they did not consider it as part of their remit.[11] Whatever the reason, the fact that these became the standard texts on church resistance meant that the whole story of what individual churchmen and women had done for the Jews was initially left untold.

The first attempt to produce a researched history of the persecution in the Netherlands came in 1950 with the publication of *Kroniek der Jodenvervolging 1940–1945* (Chronicle of the Persecution of the Jews 1940–1945) by Abel Herzberg, initially as part of a series, *Onderdrukking en Verzet* (Oppression and Resistance), and then as a single volume.[12] Like Wielek, Herzberg was another survivor of the events he described and connected with the Jewish Council. As such, he used his personal experiences to help interpret events, and his narrative was the first to address the central issue of why so many Jews from the Netherlands had fallen victim to the 'Final Solution'. Chronologically arranged, the text attempted to place events in the Netherlands in the wider context of Nazi policies against the Jews. Again, the work became a central text for later authors and opened the debate on the role of the Jewish Council in earnest by defending aspects of its conduct.[13] Although the book was not at odds with other published works at the time it appeared, by 1950 many of the Dutch war crimes trials had taken place and a clearer view of the occupation period was beginning to appear. Moreover, in 1947 the former joint-chairmen of the Jewish Council, Professor David Cohen and Abraham Asscher, had been heavily censured by a Jewish Court of Honour for their behaviour during the occupation and also become the subjects of court proceedings. Herzberg had acted as legal counsellor to both men, and his book was in large part the result of his researches in conducting their defence. His personal involvement with both Asscher and Cohen undoubtedly helps to explain his more conciliatory line over their behaviour. Many subsequent writers were to take a less charitable view and virulent condemnations of the Council and its leadership have continued to appear from many quarters, thus perpetuating a debate which has lasted to the present day. Herzberg's work also broke new ground by being able to use the secondary and archival collections of the *Rijksinstituut voor Oorlogsdocumentatie* (State Institute for War Documentation, RIOD).[14] This highlights a second facet of the debate on the Jewish Council and on the persecution of the Jews in the Netherlands as a whole, namely the existence of large quantities of written archival material and post-war testimony.[15] This is in stark contrast to Jewish Councils in Eastern Europe where many records have been lost or destroyed in the wartime and post-war occupations.

The publication of Herzberg's book marked the end of the first phase of writing on the persecution in the Netherlands. The Dutch war crimes trials were over and public attention had returned to other, and more pressing matters, such as domestic economic reconstruction and the Indonesian conflict. The existence of the RIOD, charged with researching all aspects of the occupation, left little scope for other authors, and there were plans to produce a special study of the persecution of the Jews almost immediately. The same year that Herzberg's work first appeared, the RIOD commissioned a book from Jacques (Jacob) Presser, a leading Dutch historian and himself a survivor of the persecution. Although intended to take only two years, the project did not appear until 1965, 15 years after its inception. Presser's book broke new ground in a number of ways, by having access to much more of the documentary and eyewitness material assembled by the Institute, and by using interview material from surviving persecutors, bystanders and victims of the tragedy. In that regard his work still represents the most complete, and indeed the only attempt to tell the whole story in its own right.[16] In the meantime, public awareness had been reawakened by the trial of Adolf Eichmann in Jerusalem in 1961. Herzberg had been one of the journalists covering the trial and the Institute's director, Louis de Jong, now began using Presser's material to make part of a 21-episode television documentary on the occupation.[17]

Presser's work had an enormous impact on the Dutch public[18] and set the agenda for future discussions. His text divided the persecution into three distinct phases. The first, isolation, from May 1940 to September 1941, began with the invasion and encompassed the early measures against the community. He regarded the point at which Jews were segregated in education and forbidden to use public amenities, restaurants, cafés and concert halls as the watershed into the second phase, towards deportation. This second phase of gradual restriction, forced removal from the provinces and concentration in Amsterdam, ended when the first deportations began in July 1942. The final phase encompassed the 15 months to September 1943 during which time the Jews were deported from the Netherlands to the death-camps in Poland. In dealing with the subject in this staged way, Presser was able to chart the development of German policies and the reactions and responses of the Jewish community. His characterisation of the process as a game of cat-and-mouse, where the German functionaries played with their Jewish 'prey', undoubtedly fitted the facts of the situation, but it remains arguable whether the occupiers whose task it was to deal with the 'Jewish question' in the Netherlands always had a precise knowledge of the ultimate objectives of their masters in Berlin.[19] His detailed investigation also began the discussion on Jewish resistance, the various ways in which the Jews themselves managed to survive, both legally and illegally, inside the Netherlands. Finally he charted the fate of those who were deported and who became victims of the 'Final Solution'

in the camps of Eastern Europe. Published as *Ondergang* (Destruction), the
book was often emotive, and no one could fail to be moved by the stories
of human tragedy which Presser used to underscore his narrative. It was
rapidly made available in both Britain and the United States (and remains
the only substantial work on the subject translated into English).[20]

Given its high-profile reception, the book did not go uncriticised. While
informing a general readership about the fate of Dutch Jewry, it also drew
some less favourable comments. For example Schöffer, in an extensive
review, observed that Presser had written from the perspective of the victims, which meant that the structures and organisation of Nazi rule in general and the persecution policies in particular did not come across clearly.
Nor, it was argued, were certain individuals, perceived by others as central
to the story, given the attention they deserved.[21] Some reviewers commented that Presser's perspective drew too heavily on his own experiences
as a survivor, and felt that these had informed the narrative to the exclusion of other important elements. Boas, for example, criticised the choice
of Presser as the author of this book on account of his distance from
Jewish life before the occupation. (This is in complete contrast to those
who thought the task should have been entrusted to a non-Jew who would
have been perceived by the Dutch public as more 'objective'.) She argued
that he was ignorant of many aspects of Jewish life which would have otherwise informed his judgements, and more seriously, that he brought his
own particular prejudices to bear on both the analysis and content of his
work to the point where it was 'subjective ... and highly egocentric'.[22] This
included the apparent double standard which Presser adopted in condemn-
ing the Jewish Council while having requested and indeed received help
from the organisation.[23] She also felt that there was too much information
which was undifferentiated, and that this had blurred any analytical purpose which the book might have had. Moreover, he was accused of having
written exclusively about the experiences which led to the destruction of
the Jews and this approach was criticised, by Herzberg among others, for
being too pessimistic.[24]

In spite of these criticisms, Presser's work formed the basis for the extensive chapters on the persecution of the Jews contained in de Jong's magisterial
official history, *Het Koninkrijk der Nederlanden in de Tweede Wereldoorlog*
(The Kingdom of the Netherlands in the Second World War),[25] and almost all
the subsequent general works on the Holocaust which included material on
the Netherlands. His study also inspired further work on the subject by other
members of the RIOD staff such as A.J. van der Leeuw, and above all Ben
Sijes. Both made major contributions to knowledge on the subject in the
1970s and 1980s.[26] While most of their work was specifically about the
Netherlands, van der Leeuw is widely credited with having been the first to
take an overtly comparative approach to the high levels of mortality among
Jews from the Netherlands when compared with Belgium and France. His

analysis suggests that the Netherlands lacked a 'favourable factor', an element or set of circumstances which in some way favoured Jewish survival, when compared with the other countries of Western Europe.[27] If this served to open the door for more comparative research, de Jong's work highlighted one of the problems in Dutch historiography on the occupation period, namely the categorisation of individuals, institutions and their actions as either *goed* (correct) or *fout* (false). This vision of everything being either black or white imparted a more or less moral judgement on every aspect of behaviour and gave little scope for judgements about the 'grey' areas in between. While this crude mechanism for apportioning blame for what took place during the occupation period may have suited a general Dutch readership, it was rapidly challenged by scholars both inside and outside the country.

This challenge to orthodoxy came from a number of quarters, most notably from Blom, 'In de ban van goed en fout? Wetenschappelijke geschiedschrijving over de bezettingstijd in Nederland' (Under the Spell of 'goed' and 'fout'? Academic Historical Writing on the Occupation Period in the Netherlands)[28] and from Hirschfeld, *Nazi Rule and Dutch Collaboration: The Netherlands under German Occupation, 1940–1945.*[29] Both rejected the idea of simple categorisation in favour of a more nuanced approach which allowed for a wider variety of interpretations. Of more direct importance to the study of the Holocaust in the Netherlands were the first attempts to place the national experience in a comparative context. This had been done implicitly in many of the general European survey works on the 'Final Solution', but although these studies have often noted the unusually high mortality of Jews from the Netherlands, the contrast with the rest of Western Europe is almost invariably lost when Eastern Europe is included in the analysis.[30] For the most part, explanations tended to stress the speed and intensity of German persecution, the difficulties of hiding in the Netherlands or the influence of the Schutzstaffel (SS) and the relative efficiency of its apparatus when compared with other occupied countries.[31] The few attempts at overt comparative analysis have also been criticised for their flaws. For example Helen Fein, in *Accounting for Genocide,* has tried to produce a precise methodology for the comparative study of the Holocaust in the whole of occupied Europe, yet her conclusions are highly generalised and qualified and take no account of the differences in German administrations or the speed of the deportation process across occupied Europe.[32] This may be due to the size of the task she has undertaken, yet in an important article, Marrus and Paxton suggest that even generalisations confined to their more limited subject of Western Europe 'break apart on the stubborn peculiarity of each of our countries'.[33]

While it may ultimately be the case that attempts at comparative analysis will founder on the particularities of individual national examples, there are a number of reasons to remain optimistic. One of the problems for all scholars working in this field has been the language barrier. Several authors have been able to employ both primary and secondary texts in German, French and English, sometimes with the addition of Hebrew or Polish. However, this has still served to exclude works published in other languages such as Dutch. For the most part, the comparative surveys have therefore continued to rely primarily on the few works published or translated into English or German. In the Dutch case, this has been compounded by the continued assumption that the fate of the Jews, alongside many other aspects of the German occupation, was essentially a national (as opposed to an international) issue, with the result that until the last decade only a very few texts, and with the exception of Presser certainly not the most important ones, have appeared in translation. This has now begun to change. Perhaps prompted by the appearance of comparative analyses of the Holocaust, a new generation of Dutch historians has started to look again at the central debates on the fate of the Jews in the Netherlands. Moreover, since the early 1980s, more of their conference papers and publications have appeared in English or German, making their findings far more accessible.[34]

In directly addressing the problem of why a greater proportion of Jews from the Netherlands were killed than from other countries in Western Europe, Blom sets out a comparative framework within which to discuss the experiences of the Netherlands in relation to the other occupied Western European democracies. The basic structure is a familiar one, based on the models created by Hilberg and others which divide the subject into three specific parts: the behaviour of the German occupiers, the behaviour of the victims, and the circumstances and setting in which the events took place. Having looked at the statistical comparisons, Blom begins with the most important determinant, namely the German plans for Western Europe and the character and activities of the occupying regimes. From this follows a survey of the general setting and the specific elements of German rule which had a direct or indirect impact on the persecution of the Jews. Finally, he examines the behaviour of the victims themselves and questions whether there were differences in their community organisations or reactions to German occupation which might account for the wide variations in mortality.[35] By highlighting what is untypical in the Dutch case, Blom has effectively set out much of the agenda for further new research on the Netherlands.

In the first place he notes that in comparative terms, nationality or country of origin made little or no difference to an individual Jew's chances of survival once he or she had been deported to the East.[36] Thus the focus of explanation has to be on the processes, structures and circumstances which allowed the Jews to be deported from the countries of Western Europe. Moreover, while there were few differences in the German plans for the occupied territories in the West, some small variations may have served to generate a disproportionate effect when it came to the implementation of policies against the Jews. For example, the

Netherlands had a civilian regime under *Reichskommissar* Arthur Seyss-Inquart which differed from the military governments in Belgium and France, especially in the greater scope it allowed for the SS, German police and Nazi Party to operate unhindered. The influence of competing jurisdictions within the Netherlands might have been expected to produce conflicts and inefficiencies within the German administration, but it appears that in regard to the Jews there remained a singularity of purpose among all the agencies involved. The nature of the German functionaries employed in the Netherlands might also have been significant. Blom does not engage in a comparison of the German personnel in Western Europe, but does stress the fact that the German administration of the Netherlands had a preponderance of Austrians, including Seyss-Inquart himself, three of his four *Generalkommissare,* and several lower-ranking functionaries. This may have served to assist contacts between them and the key functionaries working in Berlin such as Adolf Eichmann and Ernst Kaltenbrunner who were also from Austria. However, conclusions of this nature are inevitably impressionistic and rely on a wider analysis of whether the minor German functionaries dealing with Jewish affairs in the Netherlands were any more assiduous or efficient than their colleagues elsewhere.

One other factor related to German planning of the 'Final Solution' in Western Europe might have had a crucial bearing on the high levels of mortality suffered by Jews from the Netherlands. A comparison of the scale of deportations from France, Belgium and the Netherlands shows that there is a general correlation except for the months between March and July 1943. In this period, the deportations from France and Belgium to Auschwitz were more or less halted, yet those from the Netherlands continued as approximately 35,000 Jews (nearly 35 per cent of the victims from that country) were taken to the extermination centre at Sobibor.[37] This raises the question of why transports from the Netherlands were continued to a different location, while those from France and Belgium were halted. Blom suggests a combination of German satisfaction with their machinery in the Netherlands compared with internal difficulties elsewhere. This is certainly likely, but should not be seen as an explanation in itself for the higher mortality rate in the Netherlands. Even if transports had been suspended in line with those from France and Belgium, the very fact that the deportation process in the Netherlands ran so smoothly would have allowed it to resume functioning and still ensured the removal of as many Jews, albeit at a slightly later date.

Assessment of the setting and the nature of German rule also provides some factors which mark out the Netherlands. The geographic position of the country, bordering on Germany and distant from any neutral havens, made escape more difficult than from France, Norway or Denmark. Even the landscape militated against survival in the Netherlands, with few sparsely populated areas or suitable topography to provide hiding places.

More important was the reaction of the Dutch bureaucracy to German rule. Its 'quality, effectiveness and efficiency'[38] may have been crucial to German 'success' in the Netherlands. Blom highlights the almost perfect registration of the population and the production of forgery-proof identity cards as prime factors in assisting German plans. Yet this begs a further question, namely why was the bureaucracy prepared to be so compliant? Antisemitism was probably less prevalent in the Netherlands than in France or Belgium during the 1930s. A traditional deference to authority (however constituted) on the part of civil servants and population alike may have been a crucial factor which differentiated the Dutch from their European neighbours. The structure of Dutch society also contrasted with the rest of Western Europe. Its segmentation into four vertical *zuilen* or pillars, comprising three clearly identifiable groups, Roman Catholic, Protestant and social democratic, together with a fourth, more nebulous, neutral or liberal group, was more or less unique. While some individual Jews were associated with the two non-religious *zuilen*, the organisation of society in this form did have the effect of isolating the Jews from the mainstream and may have influenced the Dutch population's reaction to the plight of its fellow citizens during the occupation. Deference to authority clearly limited the development of resistance to German demands until later in the occupation – when it was too late to save the Jews from deportation – and the predisposition of the population as a whole to accept segmentation as a norm prevented any widespread protests over the gradual isolation of the Jews from the rest of Dutch society. The exception to this is, of course, the strike in February 1941 against the first arrests of Jews in Amsterdam. Often cited in comparative analyses as one of the few gentile protests against Nazi antisemitism in Western Europe, its significance may be more as an exceptional event which temporarily fused the organisational structures of another group outside mainstream society, the communists, with popular indignation, but one which at that time could not be sustained politically in the long term, and in any case collapsed under German pressure within a matter of hours.

In considering the victims, Blom also raises a number of points. First of all, he asks if the integration and assimilation of the Jews into Dutch society coupled with the lack of virulent antisemitism in the Netherlands in the 1930s gave its Jewish community a false sense of security before, and indeed for some months after, the invasion of 1940. He also wonders if the deferential attitude of the Dutch population as a whole helps to explain the widespread Jewish compliance with German ordinances and the lack of any real organised resistance. It has often been suggested that 'foreign' Jews were more vulnerable to the German persecution than their native co-religionists. This certainly holds good for Belgium and France, but not for the Netherlands. Here there is reason to suppose that 'foreign' Jews (numbering around 20,000 or 14 per cent of the total Jewish population) had a

better chance of survival than their Dutch counterparts.[39] Unconvinced by
the security offered by neutrality and the liberal nature of Dutch society,
less deferential to authority and more suspicious of German motives as a
result of first-hand experience of state-sponsored antisemitism in Germany,
Poland or even Tsarist Russia, these refugees may have been better prepared for what was to come, and thus more likely to find ways of survival.
Other factors in the Netherlands which may have been at variance with
France and Belgium include the structure and concentration of the Jewish
community. Was the high proportion of proletarians among the Dutch
Jews or their concentration in Amsterdam relevant to their fate? Moreover,
did the behaviour of the Jewish religious and secular elite have a bearing
on events? Certainly, the role and co-operative behaviour of the Jewish
Council in Amsterdam was in contrast to that of its counterparts in France
and Belgium where Jewish organisations took a less compliant stance.

The importance of this comparative research has been in raising new
questions about the history of the Holocaust in the Netherlands. It has been
taken up by Pim Griffioen and Ron Zeller, who have attempted a comparison of all the factors germane to the Holocaust in the Netherlands and
Belgium.[40] In addition, there has also been further work on specific debates.
For example, one of the main indictments levelled against the leadership of
the Amsterdam Jewish Council has been its co-operation with the Germans.
This has been taken up and analysed extensively by two Israeli scholars,
Joseph and Dan Michman, who have both contributed important monographs and analytical articles on aspects of the Dutch Jewish community
before and during the occupation, and on the activities of the Jewish
Council.[41] A specific charge against the Council leadership was that they had
sacrificed the Jewish proletariat in order to save themselves from deportation. The charge is a complicated one and based on the way the Amsterdam
Jewish Council handed out exemption stamps which (temporarily) protected their holders from deportation. This aspect of the Council's role has
been recently re-examined,[42] as has the behaviour of other local Jewish
Councils in the country. Another new and contentious area for research has
been the role of Dutch civil servants, and especially the police, in the persecution of the Jews. Aided by the newly available archive material and the
publication of diaries and memoirs, historians are now able to give a clearer
picture of the behaviour of these key personnel.[43] One of the leading scholars in this field, Johannes Houwink ten Cate, has also made an important
contribution on another key area, a detailed demographic survey of the
effects of the deportation on the structure of the Jewish population in the
Netherlands.[44] Finally, the whole question of Jewish resistance to the
Germans has become a major topic in recent Holocaust historiography, and
while this was clearly never a major feature of the persecution in the
Netherlands, it cannot be ignored completely and attempts have been made
to carry out research into its extent and effectiveness.[45]

Another debate focuses on Jewish survivors of the Holocaust and the people who helped them. One strand of this research centres on the attempts of sociologists Samuel and Pearl Oliner to identify the existence of pure altruism among those who sheltered Jews in occupied Europe.[46] This has produced a trend towards the interviewing or re-interviewing of survivors and their hosts. Inevitably, the investigators have had to work against the diminution of memory on the part of their subjects, but the results have added to the historical record as well as providing some thought-provoking conclusions in their own right, albeit of a general character rather than specifically related to individual countries. The authors have been able to call on a good deal of material collected from survivors and their hosts in the Netherlands, although a disproportionate amount seems to have come from people who subsequently left the country to live abroad. Their collection of material also precludes the use of contemporary or near-contemporary written accounts of the events and relationships they are trying to analyse. While this is wholly understandable given the particular methodology they are employing, it has served to preclude from their studies a good deal of evidence readily available in the Dutch, Israeli and other archives.

Historians have also come to give more attention to children as victims and survivors of the Holocaust, most notably Deborah Dwork in her comparative European survey *Children with a Star: Jewish Youth in Nazi Europe*. Again, her conclusions are more general than country-specific, but work by Dutch sociologists sheds light on one particular area of enquiry, namely the relationships between Jewish children hidden in the Netherlands during the occupation and their temporary 'foster' parents. While directed towards developing contemporary guidelines for individuals and institutions to help war victims, the research has thrown some interesting light on the particular nature of these relationships through a series of case studies where both child and hosts were interviewed about their experiences and interrelationship.[47] The whole question of the Jewish orphans who survived in the Netherlands or who came back from the camps became a major issue in the post-war Netherlands. The remnants of the Dutch Jewish community fought to gain custody of these children, and in so doing created conflict with government-sponsored agencies. Yet even in cases where the agencies ruled in its favour, there were some foster-parents who refused to hand over their charges. Normally their reticence was inspired by a desire to prevent the child whom they had converted to Christianity, from returning to Judaism. While there were only a handful of such cases, at least one became a *cause célèbre*. The Anneke Beekman affair involved a young girl hidden by two sisters and brought up as a Catholic during the occupation. Having refused to hand her over after the war, the foster-mothers then contrived to hide the child, in defiance of

Dutch law, in the Netherlands and Belgium until she reached the age of majority.[48]

The experiences of Jews in hiding have also come under closer scrutiny. Both interviews and archival material have been used to portray what life was like for the minority of Jews who, like the Frank family, attempted to evade capture by the Germans. They demonstrate the huge variety of experiences of those who attempted to live 'underground' between 1942 and the liberation, and also provide essential evidence in the debates about the motivation and conduct of rescuers, and their relationships with the victims they sheltered.[49] Another facet of the recent literature has been to escape from the persecution of the Jews in the Netherlands as being exclusively contextualised within the history of the Second World War. Neither Herzberg, nor Wielek, nor Presser gave any attention to the history of the Jews before 1940 as a factor in explaining the victims' responses to events during the occupation. This had been remedied to some extent by Louis de Jong, but has recently been reinforced by two general histories of the Jews in the Netherlands which allow a longer-term perspective on the Jews, their communities, and their place within Dutch society.[50]

These two volumes also encompass the post-war history of the Jews in the Netherlands, a period which has also been the subject of research on specific problems. In't Veld has examined the creation and proceedings of the Jewish Court of Honour, set up to investigate the role of the Jewish Council leadership, and Houwink ten Cate has assessed the wider issues of Dutch judicial action against the same 'defendants',[51] while A.J. van Schie has made important contributions to the debate on the restitution of Jewish assets.[52] Finally, there is also the work of Hondius who has examined the whole issue of people returning from the camps during and after 1945 and the re-emergence of antisemitism in post-war Dutch society.[53]

Concentrating on the contribution which general academic and comparative studies have made to an understanding of events in the Netherlands should not be allowed to obscure a parallel trend, namely the continued publication of memoirs and remembrances of survivors and their helpers, and of local studies on particular Jewish communities. Of the memoirs, pride of place has to go to journalist Philip Mechanicus, whose posthumously published diary covering his imprisonment in the Westerbork transit camp was the first of its kind to reach a wide audience.[54] It has been followed by many more, some like that of Mechanicus written by those who died in the camps,[55] and others from Jews who survived in the Netherlands and those who helped them. While each account has its own personalised style and approach, almost every one contains details which help to build a picture of life for the persecuted during the occupation period.[56] There are also memoir collections, for example the excellent compilation on German Jews in the Netherlands by Jakob and van der Voort, *Anne Frank war nicht allein* (Anne Frank Was Not Alone).[57] Apart from being important in their own right, these accounts draw attention to the specific experiences of the refugees in the Netherlands. The local studies on Jewish communities are numerous. Perhaps the most extensive and best researched is van Dam, *Jodenvervolging in de Stad Utrecht* (The Persecution of the Jews in the City of Utrecht). This is based primarily on the surviving records of the community and interviews with survivors. When so much attention has been given to the far more numerous Jewish community in metropolitan Amsterdam, this study provides an important insight into how the persecution affected provincial cities. Having said this, Amsterdam was the centre of events during the occupation and it has produced its own local historians and commentators who have chronicled the destruction of the centuries-old Jewish quarter of the city.[58] All this material has been supplemented by magazine and newspaper articles on specific aspects of the persecution, usually prompted by an anniversary or commemoration, by the discovery or publication of new material, or when a particular issue has become of major public interest, such as the case of the Jewish orphans during the 1950s, or the prolonged debate on the presumed Jewish collaborator Friedrich Weinreb in the 1970s and 1980s.[59] The role of Dutch news magazines and periodicals such as *Vrij Nederland, De Gids* and *De Groene Amsterdammer* should not be underestimated. Their high profile in Dutch cultural life has meant that journalists as well as professional academics have continued to play a major role in the debates.[60]

Structure

The inference to be drawn from this selective historiographical survey is that research and understanding of the persecution of the Jews in the Netherlands has moved on a long way since the appearance of Presser's monograph in the mid-1960s and even since the publication of the relevant volumes of de Jong's history. Old controversies have been re-examined and new ones have emerged as both comparative studies and specifically Dutch research have shed fresh light on areas of doubt and debate.

The comparative statistics on the fate of European Jewry have highlighted the abnormality of the Dutch case for all scholars working in the field, but the language barrier and the concentration on events in France and in Eastern Europe have meant that specialist research and publication on the subject have been carried out almost exclusively by Dutch and Israeli scholars. As already suggested, although some of the major works on the *Jodenvervolging* (persecution of the Jews) in the Netherlands have appeared in English translations, the publications in Dutch have not gained a wider audience and thus have not been extensively used by scholars attempting to construct comparative analyses of the Holocaust. The primary purpose of this book is twofold: firstly to provide a history of the

Holocaust in the Netherlands, and secondly to draw together all the recent scholarship using the agenda suggested by the comparative studies carried out to date.

To achieve this end, the structure is essentially chronological. Chapter 2 places the Dutch Jews into the social, economic and political context of the Netherlands as a whole, highlighting their long history in the country and their social and organisational structures and divisions. From this follows an analysis of two specific problems faced by the Dutch Jews in the 1930s, namely the effects of the economic depression and the arrival of Jewish refugees from Germany. The chapter also attempts to compare the Jewish communities in the Netherlands with those of Belgium and France on the eve of the German invasion, with a view to highlighting differences which might have had some impact on their ability to survive the occupation and the mechanics of the 'Final Solution'.

Chapters 3–5 cover the stages of identification (May 1940–January 1941), isolation (January 1941–July 1942) and deportation (July 1942–September 1943) of Dutch Jewry. This is an adaptation of the chronological divisions used by both Presser and de Jong, but one which employs slightly different time periods. Moreover, their focus on the extermination of Dutch Jewry in Poland as a further stage has been left out of this narrative. As with most other Jewish deportees to the East, few actually survived the war to return home and this book is concerned primarily with the German success in deporting so many Jews, and the difficulties for the minority who did manage to survive, legally or underground, inside the Netherlands. These three chapters outline the development of German policies towards the Jews in the first three years of the occupation, but also address a number of specific debates.

Firstly, there is the question of why so few Jews managed to escape from the Netherlands when the invasion began on 10 May. While the speed with which the country was overrun provides one answer, a number of other complicating factors can also be identified.

Secondly, there is the question of the gradual introduction of antisemitic legislation. To understand this, it is essential to see the complex relationships which determined the scope and timing of events. These can be summarised as the German occupying administration's relationship with the Dutch bureaucracy and people, its relationship with the various central authorities in Berlin and its own lack of cohesion and the preponderance of in-fighting and competition between institutions and between individuals.

Thirdly, there is the debate surrounding the existence of a German-sponsored Jewish Council, which was unique in Western Europe. These organisations were common in the Eastern occupied territories of Poland, Lithuania and the Soviet Union, and have been a focus for scholars concerned with Jewish responses to Nazi persecution and extermination policies. Their researches have exposed the practical and moral dilemmas, both for the participants faced with German demands, and for historians trying to understand the pressures and the realities for Jews living under Nazi rule. Many of the publications have been influenced by the experiences of writers who were themselves survivors, and who saw the existence of the Jewish Councils either as a positive element in their survival, or merely a form of Jewish collaboration which worked against their interests. For the most part, the major texts on the various *Judenräte*[61] take little account of the Amsterdam Jewish Council, and still less of those in the Dutch provinces, yet the same debates with the same moral and methodological agendas occurred there too. The intention is to summarise these debates and to address the central questions of whether the co-operative attitude of the Jewish Council in the Netherlands was defensible, implying at least some investigation of its alternatives, and whether its role in assisting the Germans was of major importance to the ultimate fate of Dutch Jewry.

A fourth question which arises from this period is to try and explain the compliant attitude of the Dutch Jews faced with deportation. While it is true that only a minority actually gave themselves up for deportation when summoned, most waited quietly at home for the police to fetch them or lived in constant fear of the arbitrary raids which might carry them away. Inevitably, this leads into discussions about Jewish resistance to deportation and the whole vexed question of how people avoided capture, but while we have a good deal of information about life in hiding from survivors and those who helped them, there is very little archival material to help us understand the majority who did not actively resist deportation.[62]

Chapters 6 and 7 look at the ways in which Jews did manage to survive inside the Netherlands. Houwink ten Cate has divided the Jewish population into six groups. These divisions were essentially created by the occupying Germans and the systems they instituted. The six groups were those who went underground (*c.*25,000), those who were in mixed marriages (*c.*12,600), members of specially exempted groups (*c.*8,500), those who worked for the Germans in some capacity (*c.*16,000), the staff of the Jewish Council (17,500) and the vast majority who were unprotected by any such special status (*c.*85,000). As he points out, with hindsight it was those in the first three categories who had the greatest chance of surviving the occupation.[63] To show how and why this was the case, this study adopts another approach to the question of survival, by differentiating between those people who gained some form of protection *within* the German system – through official legal exemptions or other forms of preferential treatment – and those who sought to survive *outside* the system by living illegally underground. These are by no means mutually exclusive categories, but do provide a starting point for an analysis of how survival was possible in the Netherlands.

Chapter 8 examines another major issue raised by the Holocaust in comparative perspective, namely the place of Jewish self-help and the role of rescuers and bystanders in the Dutch context. Was the survival of relatively few Jews in the Netherlands the fault of the Jews themselves for their lack of resistance to the Germans or was it the responsibility of Dutch society in failing to protect one group of its citizens from the murderous intentions of the occupying power? Finally, was there a collective failure of the Dutch people to help their Jewish fellow citizens in their hour of need? Were the Dutch less likely to help or shelter Jews on the run than the Belgians or the French?

Chapter 9 turns to the debates on some of the specifically unfavourable factors for the Jews in the Netherlands, such as the functioning of the German administration, the co-operative attitude of specific branches of the civil service and the role of the Dutch police. Once again, these factors need to be seen in a comparative context, but collectively they are perhaps the most important elements in understanding the high levels of mortality among Jews in the Netherlands.

Chapter 10 addresses a particular, and largely unquantifiable, feature of Jewish survival in the Netherlands suggested by comparisons with the rest of Western Europe. There is evidence that, unlike for example in France, foreign (and specifically German) Jews had a better chance of survival than their Dutch counterparts. From relatively inauspicious positions on the eve of the occupation, some refugee Jews managed to carve out privileged positions for themselves and their families. This can be seen partly as luck, partly as a function of their heightened sense of self-preservation, and partly owing to the Nazi predilection for dealing with other Germans in preference to other nationalities. While the numbers of survivors may have been small, examination of the refugee minority in the Netherlands also provides a comparative perspective on the fate of the majority of Dutch Jews.

The last chapter examines the end of the war and the treatment of those Jews who did return from the camps, together with some of the issues which emerged in the post-war era. Only three have been highlighted here, namely the arguments about the culpability of the Jewish Council leadership, the vexed question of Jewish children orphaned by the Holocaust, and the legal and administrative complications surrounding the restoration of Jewish property. If nothing else, this serves to demonstrate that the end of hostilities and the liberation of the Netherlands did not bring an end to the problems for the few surviving Jews and their attempts to rebuild their shattered communities. Moreover, it also suggests that many Dutch people had not really come to terms with, or even recognised, the tragedy which had taken place in their midst. Perhaps because everyone had their own experiences of occupation and their own stories of discomfort and deprivation, few people were particularly concerned about the fate of the deportees. Their continuing absence could be explained in many different ways. To some extent it could be argued that the Holocaust had very little effect on Dutch society. In the immediate post-war years, society re-established itself in a form not so dissimilar from before the occupation. There were new social, political, economic and international problems associated with the end of hostilities which allowed the events of the war to be compart-mentalised and then marginalised. Dutch men and women continued with their lives within their own social, religious, or political milieu. The same social and religious prejudices continued to be aired against the Jews, even though most of them had disappeared from the Netherlands for good. Only occasionally was the early post-war world forced to confront the issues left unresolved when the courts or the media brought them back into the public gaze.

|2|

The Jews and the Netherlands before 1940

The pre-war history of the Jews in the Netherlands has received a good deal of critical attention from historians since 1945, inevitably conditioned by the wholesale destruction during the occupation period. At the heart of this critique is the view that the structures of the Jewish communities in the Netherlands and the behaviour of their leadership in some way contributed to their vulnerability when the Germans arrived in 1940. Many publications take a very critical view of the pre-war period and are often openly condemnatory of the Dutch Jews and their leaders. Survivors and Jewish historians of the post-war period are often overtly critical from at least three different perspectives. A class-based analysis seeks to show that the destruction of the mass of Dutch Jewry was predicated on their victimisation by an irresponsible and self-seeking Jewish bourgeoisie. Zionists criticise the Dutch Jews for having lost their Jewish identity and failing to see the threat posed by racially based antisemitism. Finally, there is also a perspective which claims that the Jews and their leaders failed to live up to their religious obligations and allowed belief and ritual to become 'empty' and 'formalistic'.[1] A variant of this is the idea that the Jews came to believe in their integration into Dutch society[2] and failed to see that they were neither part of mainstream Dutch society nor sufficiently self-contained or socially self-sufficient to combat the isolation imposed on them by the German occupation. The dangers inherent in these approaches are that the victims of Nazi persecution are judged for their pre-war conduct on the basis of hindsight, and that blame for their destruction is placed, at least partially, at the door of the victims.

While rejecting the condemnatory aspects inherent in some of these works, it is important to recognise that the structures of Jewish life prior to 1940 did have some bearing on subsequent events. Their history in the post-emancipation (after 1795) Netherlands has been characterised as a period 'when an alien community living in the Netherlands transformed itself into a disparate group of Jewish Dutchmen, with little affinity to either each other or to world Jewry'.[3] The implication here is that the fragmentation process experienced by Dutch Jewry was not combined with full assimilation of all groups and classes into mainstream Dutch society, leaving them psychologically and organisationally unprepared when they were redefined into a single racial category by the incoming Germans and isolated from their 'Dutch' fellow-citizens.

The development of Jewish communities in the Netherlands

During the later medieval period, there had always been a small number of Jews in the Netherlands, but they tended to come and go, never establishing a permanent community in any one city. This situation began to change after the creation of the Dutch Republic when in 1579 the Union of Utrecht abolished the Inquisition, introduced freedom of worship and removed much restrictive legislation. Although they were never intended as the primary beneficiaries of this liberalisation, Jews found the changes an encouragement to the establishment of formal Jewish communities. As a result, the Seven Provinces became something of a haven, being outside the jurisdiction of the Spanish Habsburg Empire. By 1600 there were reportedly a few hundred resident Jews, mainly in Amsterdam, many of whom had migrated northwards from Antwerp and the Spanish-controlled southern Netherlands. By 1610 Amsterdam could boast around 400 resident Sephardi (Portuguese) Jews, and by the 1630s Ashkenazi (Eastern European) Jews also began to arrive from the German states and Poland. By 1675 there were 2,500 Sephardim in the city and 5,000 Ashkenazim, figures which had expanded to 5,000 and 19,000 respectively by 1795. It can be argued that this expansion was due in part to the liberal character of the Dutch Republic, but it should also be remembered that the Sephardi Jews became increasingly important to the Republic through their banking and commercial activities. This economic importance, which helped to bolster the liberal attitude adopted towards Jews from the rich Sephardi community, may thereby also have facilitated the immigration of many poorer Ashkenazi Jews from the East.[4]

For the Jews in the Netherlands, conditions varied from place to place. Although they were free to move within the boundaries of the Republic, every Dutch city retained certain restrictions. In Amsterdam, which had by far the largest Jewish population, Jews were allowed free access to the city but were denied rights of citizenship. Elsewhere, some towns such as Utrecht and Deventer excluded them altogether, while others had fewer restrictions even than Amsterdam. The insistence that Jews should live in a ghetto, an area of the town set aside for them, was common. Yet even in Amsterdam, where there was no such restriction, the Jews more or less created their own ghetto by congregating in a particular part of the city. Many towns also had restrictions on Jews marrying non-Jews, a prohibition which also found support from Jewish religious leaders who were anxious to defend against the dilution or diminution of their communities. Until the end of the eighteenth century, this situation remained virtually unchanged. The Netherlands' increasing economic importance and its need for labour encouraged foreign immigration. Jews arriving in the country still found restrictions imposed on their employment. While they were able to establish themselves in retailing and commerce, trades controlled by the guilds remained firmly closed. Even in mundane forms of employment, the Jews continued to be marked out by their dress, dietary laws and religious observance, and while many other foreign immigrants were assimilated, the Jews continued to be treated as a group apart.

This situation was further complicated by relations between the Sephardi and Ashkenazi Jews. Even in Amsterdam, there were few points of contact between the two groups. Their cultures and traditions were very different, a difference compounded by the fact that the Sephardi Jews spoke Portuguese and the Ashkenazim spoke Yiddish. The Sephardim chose to avoid any contact with their Eastern European co-religionists, which necessitated the continuance of separate religious and secular organisations by each community. By the end of the eighteenth century, the elite of the Sephardi Jews formed a rich and powerful, but numerically very small, group in Amsterdam. By contrast, the Ashkenazim were far more numerous, but also far more socially and economically diverse, with a large proportion of them being numbered among the poorest inhabitants of the city.

The great watershed for the Jews came during French rule when, after a considerable struggle, they were legally emancipated by the first National Assembly of the Batavian Republic on 2 September 1796. This gave them full civic rights in common with all other Dutch citizens and ended much legal discrimination. Although the decree was passed unanimously by the Assembly, there were people who remained firmly opposed to the measure. Many Dutchmen continued to regard the Jews as an alien group unfit for citizenship. Others, who adopted a federalist stance, opposed the measure on the grounds that it attacked the autonomy of town corporations. Even the Jewish communities' leaders voiced their disquiet, fearing that emancipation would weaken their autonomy.[5] During the first half of the nineteenth century, some of the leadership's fears were justified. While emancipation did not put an end to social and economic antisemitism in the Netherlands,[6] there was an identifiable movement of Jews out of Amsterdam and the other big cities into the provinces, and also an increase in the number of 'mixed' marriages, frequently resulting in the Jewish partner leaving the community. This dispersion of the Jews throughout the

Netherlands was paralleled by the continuing decline of the Sephardi community. In spite of retaining a more coherent identity, its numbers remained static and while its outward organisation and appearance remained impressive, by the twentieth century it was no more than an empty shell.[7]

If the Sephardi community was in terminal decline, the same could not be said about the Ashkenazim. While their communities also suffered from dispersion and disarray in the first half of the nineteenth century, the second half saw the advent of something approaching a religious revival led by Chief Rabbi J.H. Dünner and underwritten by an increasingly prosperous bourgeoisie. Dünner transformed the religious life of the community, altering rabbinical training and restoring religious institutions.[8] While he is often credited with saving Jewish religious life in the Netherlands, there were a number of adverse effects to his policies. For example, the changes to rabbinical education, a refusal to recognise qualifications obtained elsewhere and curtailing the use of Yiddish all served to detach Dutch Jewry from the great centres of Jewish learning in the East. More importantly, its new generation of 'intellectual' rabbis became increasingly divorced from their congregations. What emerged was a core of highly orthodox community members who took pride in their religious observance, surrounded by a much larger group whose observance of religious obligations varied from neo-orthodoxy to the celebration of only the most important feast-days. This trend was mirrored in falling attendances at synagogues, and a decline in Jewish education as parents sent their children to the newly established state schools after 1857.[9]

The second half of the century also witnessed some notable demographic and social changes. Poverty remained endemic among many sections of both the Ashkenazi and Sephardi communities. The proportion of Jews in the country as a whole increased slightly as a result of immigration from Eastern Europe in the 1870s and 1880s, but this was undermined by a falling birth rate which helped to create an ageing Jewish population in comparison with the national trend. The period was also characterised by the rapid urbanisation, mainly to Amsterdam, of Jews from the provinces, thus reversing the trend of the previous half-century. Marriages between Ashkenazim and Sephardim increased, as did 'mixed' marriages of Jews and non-Jews. City life and industrial employment undoubtedly played a role in weakening the bonds between Jews and their religious communities. Moreover, the closely knit Amsterdam Jewish quarter was uprooted and dispersed by slum clearance schemes and a general movement to the suburbs which meant that by 1930 only 18 per cent of the Jewish community still lived in the old district.[10] Industrial employment also brought Amsterdam's Jews into contact with new ideas and philosophies. Many members of the Jewish proletariat were attracted to socialism and gave up even a nominal adherence to Judaism.[11] In turn, the attractions of socialism and the opposition of the religious establishment and the Jewish press made sure that neither orthodox nor socialist-based Zionism had little more than a tenuous hold in the Netherlands.

The Jews and Dutch society

This fragmentation of the Jewish community from the later nineteenth century through to the 1930s is often contrasted with developments within other sections of Dutch society. During this period, the liberal control over the Dutch state was challenged by the increasing social and political organisation of the major religions in the country. Both the Roman Catholics and the Calvinists began to see social organisation and political representation as the best way of protecting their interests against the demands of the 'liberal' state, finally breaking into government themselves as coalition partners in the late 1880s.[12] This began the process of *verzuiling* or pillarisation in Dutch society where integrated subcultures (*zuilen*) emerged which cut across class lines, uniting disparate economic and social groups on the basis of their religious affiliation. The Calvinists and the Roman Catholics were followed by a social democratic *zuil* which emerged after the 1880s, and while never so clearly visible, there was also evidence of a liberal or neutral *zuil* creating the foundations for a vertically integrated society. These four 'pillars' encompassed a large proportion of the Dutch population and were bound together by a common adherence to what might essentially be termed bourgeois precepts and beliefs, namely capitalist production, parliamentary democracy, order and authority, national interests and a set of rules for civility and proper conduct.[13] Characterised as *burgerlijk-verzuild* (bourgeois-pillarised), this form of societal organisation was more or less unique to the Netherlands. At a political level, it allowed for co-operation between disparate confessional groups and came to dominate many aspects of social life as well. Other minority groups also developed some of the structures of the four main *zuilen*, but the mere existence of these large blocks tended to exclude smaller groups from any real participation in mainstream Dutch society.

This situation would have created complications even for coherent Jewish communities in the Netherlands, but their problems were compounded by the fragmentation taking place just at the moment when other groups, both religious and secular, were organising to protect their interests. The Jewish financial and commercial bourgeoisie was becoming partially assimilated into liberal institutions. At the same time, the elitist views of the religious leadership precluded unity or organisational strength among the Jews based on belief or observance. This in turn weakened many individuals' commitment to their religion, even to the point of apostasy, and facilitated the 'conversion' of sections of the proletariat to social democracy. Yet these are only two elements among many which have been put forward to explain the behaviour of the Jews in the Netherlands. It has been suggested that the divisions within the Jewish community were already too pronouced, between Ashkenazim and Sephardim, and between elite and proletariat, to create the basis for any common identity. A second factor was the pre-existence of Jewish religious institutions which provided a sense of security without making great demands on the individual. However hollow and impotent these institutions may have been, they provided a justification not to engage in further organisation to combat the changes taking place in the rest of Dutch society. Fear of antisemitism may also have played some part in explaining the lack of a potent Jewish political force. Even allowing for the relatively favourable 'liberal' environment within the Netherlands, there was the defensive view that any prominent Jewish organisation was likely to engender antisemitic feeling among other sections of Dutch society. This is linked to the view that the Jews were never able to muster a 'critical mass' large enough to make a success of such an organisation. They were never more than a small minority within Dutch society and had the problems of losing potential supporters to other creeds and ideologies, and to apostasy, without the possibility of being able to increase the size of their constituency. This draining of resources was compounded by the processes of social modernisation which increased geographical and social mobility.

Certainly by the 1930s it was impossible to perceive the Jews in the Netherlands as a homogenous group. The religious and economic divisions which emerged in the late nineteenth century had been exacerbated rather the healed. It is true that neither liberal Judaism nor Zionism had any great effect in further fragmenting Dutch Jewish opinion, the former because it was perceived as an alien German import and the latter because it ran counter to the majority assimilationist tendency. The liberal community never had more than a thousand members (and many of these were German refugees), and the Zionists could claim only 3 per cent support from Dutch Jewry as late as 1940.[14] Nonetheless, the crucial factor seems to have been the chasm between Jewish elite and proletariat. The exclusive and smug orthodox observance of the few alienated the remainder who saw little reason to remain within the religious community. Moreover, class differences between Jewish employers and employees became far more important in shaping social interaction than any shared religious belief or common background. These conflicts actively encouraged people to move away from religious observance, even away from regarding themselves as Jewish at all, and also opened their minds to new ideologies such as social democracy. This trend could also be seen at a different level, where Jewish professionals and certain sections of the merchant class found it socially and professionally advantageous to play down their Jewish origins.

It is important, however, not to overstate the case. It has been shown that of the 79,400 Jews in Amsterdam in 1941, only around 500 (0.6 per cent) had been baptised and a further 5,700 (7.18 per cent) were described as being outside the community. In real terms, the vast majority of the Jews were still affiliated in some way to Judaism, and there is other evidence to support this. As many as 92 per cent of all Jewish marriages were still held in synagogues (compared to 76 per cent for Roman Catholics and 31 per cent for Protestants in their respective churches) and although 16.9 per cent of Jews in Amsterdam who married had non-Jewish partners, the proportion of 'mixed marriages' was much higher among Roman Catholics and Protestants.[15]

The net effect of all these forces can be summarised as two parallel trends within Dutch Jewry: of increasing assimilation, and increased secularisation highlighted by declining regular synagogue attendance and observance of anything except major festivals and celebrations.[16] This has been characterised as a Jewish communal structure in decline, a picture which is reinforced by available evidence. The census for 1930 showed that the Jewish population of the Netherlands had actually declined by 3 per cent since 1920, having previously experienced gradual but unspectacular growth since the mid-nineteenth century.[17]

Table 2.1 Jewish population of the Netherlands, 1909–30[18]

Census	Ashkenazim	Sephardim	Total	Percentage of total Dutch population
1909	99,785	6,624	106,409	1.81
1920	109,293	5,930	115,223	1.68
1930	106,723	5,194	111,917	1.41

While the communities had benefited from some Eastern European immigration, there is no doubt that the overall decline was symptomatic of the fact that a marked number of people born into the Jewish community no longer recognised it as their religious home.

Of the 111,917 Jews enumerated in 1930 (1.41 per cent of the Dutch population), 65,523 (or 58.5 per cent of the total) lived in Amsterdam, representing 8.65 per cent of the city's population. Most of the rest lived in the other two large cities of Western Holland, Rotterdam (c.10,000) and The Hague (c.10,000). In all, 80 per cent lived in the seven largest cities with a further 10 per cent in the smaller towns and 10 per cent in the countryside.[19] Each city had its 'Jewish areas' where the Jews had traditionally lived and worked. These 'voluntary ghettoes' were usually in the poorer quarters of the old city, centring on the synagogues, and they remained intact even after the Jewish middle class had moved away to the suburbs. However, it is important to note that these concentrations *were* 'voluntary' rather than forced, and that there was not a single neighbourhood, even in the 'Jewish quarter' of Amsterdam, where the Jews actually formed the majority of the population.[20] Portrayals of the district also present something of a contradiction. Several well-known writers in the postwar period such as Gans and Sluyser take an almost nostalgic line on the sense of community which existed there before the war, whereas other sources dwell on the filth, degradation, poverty and social problems which were as bad as anywhere in the country.[21]

Jews and the economy in the 1930s

The social and economic structures of Dutch Jewry before the German occupation are also worthy of consideration as a factor in their vulnerability. While emancipation had opened up most trades and professions, it remained the case that the Dutch Jews tended to be concentrated in specific economic sectors. The 1930 census revealed an overrepresentation of Jews in some occupations, as shown in Table 2.2.

Table 2.2 Jews in the Dutch economy, 1930[22] (where 100 = national participation in the sector)

Occupation	No.
Banking	195
Business people	268
Clothing trade (rag trade)	332
Wholesale traders	465
Warehouse and retail traders	510
Pedlars and hawkers	513
Commercial travellers	1,141
Market traders	1,556
Diamond cutters	4,055

Not only was there a marked overrepresentation of Jews in certain occupations, but the majority of these occupations were at the lower end of the national earnings scale. While there were some very prosperous Jewish bankers and diamond merchants, and a layer of middle-class merchants and well-off professionals,[23] the vast majority were either engaged in lower-middle-class or proletarian occupations. Yet even this description may be misleading when applied to the 1930s. While pedlars and hawkers might theoretically be 'independent' traders and therefore entitled to be counted among the middle classes, in reality they were often more impoverished than their working-class neighbours. A report on the earnings of Amsterdam Jewry carried out in 1937 revealed that half of those surveyed earned less than fl.500 per year and 69 per cent less than fl.1,000 per year. Similar results were obtained for the Jewish community in The Hague where 72 per cent earned less than fl.1,000.[24] To give an idea of what this meant in real terms, in 1934 a fully employed harbour worker in Amsterdam or Rotterdam was likely to receive around fl.30 per week or fl.1,500 per year.[25]

In part, the poverty of the Jews had been due to the general downturn in the economy during the 1930s, but some sectors had been hit harder and earlier than others, and these were often the ones in which many Jews earned their livings. The diamond and tobacco industries were the most obvious examples of this trend, and this points to an unusual facet of the Jewish community in Amsterdam, namely the existence of a Jewish industrial proletariat. Even before the 1930s, employment in these declining industries was decreasing, with more and more people being reduced to peddling, unemployment and poverty, yet the traditions of a working-class culture remained. Adherence to social democracy was strong, and it was pressures brought to bear by the Social Democratic Party on the City Council which helped to break up the old Jewish slum districts by providing new housing for the workers in different areas. This had the effect of helping to loosen family and neighbourhood ties and at the same time furthering the process of Jewish assimilation into the working class as a whole.[26] It has been argued that this process created a crisis of identity among Amsterdam's Jewish working class. Cut loose from their ghetto neighbourhoods, networks and traditions, they were caught in a no-man's land where the underlying antisemitism within gentile Dutch society prevented their wholehearted integration. Some did make the transition and were happy in their new environment, but for many others the picture is one of disorientation, attempting to conform to changed circumstances while at the same time hanging on to elements of their Jewish traditions. Women were often in the forefront of trying to maintain old networks and family ties, but their efforts foundered as people were rehoused and systems of mutual help broke down. This in itself created a more pressing problem for the Jewish community as a whole, namely the need to extend and expand Jewish charities and welfare agencies in order to fill the gaps in care and mutual support left when neighbourhoods were dismantled.[27]

The collapse of international trade after 1929 hit almost every sector of the Dutch economy. The structure of the Dutch economy and the policies of successive governments have both been blamed for this, but whatever the root cause, the impact on marginal businesses was particularly severe. A disproportionate number of Jewish rag merchants, street and market traders were receiving some form of financial help even by 1929 and this worsened as the crisis deepened. Larger Jewish concerns also felt the squeeze and often cut back on production and employment. This could be seen in the Jewish-dominated Amsterdam diamond industry where by 1935 unemployment levels among the 5,000 skilled diamond workers (cutters and polishers) exceeded 50 per cent.[28]

The conclusion to be drawn here is that while Jews suffered disproportionately because of their leading role in the diamond industry and in the field of marginal (street) trading, with these two exceptions, the Jews in Amsterdam were probably no better and no worse off than their non-Jewish neighbours. Moreover, in working-class districts Jews probably looked to class ties rather than Jewish ties when faced with adversity. However, it is also true to say that the historic position of the Jewish majority among the poorer sections of society did make them vulnerable, both to the effects of the economic depression of the 1930s and what was to follow after the German occupation.

Social developments in the 1930s

It has been argued that the Jews in the Netherlands, even if they had been able to construct a coherent identity, were numerically too small to have constituted a viable *zuil* within Dutch society.[29] As a result, the social, economic and religious divisions which had developed since emancipation cannot be held primarily responsible for the position of the Jews in the 1930s. For the most part, they were perceived by other sections of Dutch society as a separate group, increasingly so as the major religious denominations and ideological blocks sought to strengthen their internal ties. To some extent Jewish assimilationism had been a response to this and an attempt to counteract its effects on a personal level, but the events of the 1930s, the economic crisis and the emergence of virulent National Socialism across the border in Germany were also to have a marked impact on the fragmentation of Jewish life and the social processes of the previous hundred years.

The appointment of Hitler as Chancellor of Germany had both a psychological effect and practical consequences for the Jews in the Netherlands. Hitler's speeches and the activities of National Socialists before and after January 1933 propounded the existence of a 'Jewish question' in Germany. This had no direct consequences, but the arrival of the first refugees from Nazi persecution in the spring of 1933 did highlight a critical problem. On the one hand, the Dutch Jews were honour-bound to help their fellow co-religionists in need with financial and material assistance. On the other hand, there was the question of how far this help should extend. Should it just be to provide temporary shelter and financial help while the refugees looked for a more permanent home, or should it extend as far as assisting their permanent settlement in the Netherlands and pressing the state for liberalisation of immigration and aliens' restrictions to allow even more of the persecuted to escape from Germany? Apart from the philanthropic and humanitarian motives, there was also another factor which framed this response, namely the fear of what effect unregulated and uncontrolled Jewish refugee immigration might have on the position of the Dutch Jews. Increasing antisemitism among the Dutch population remained a real concern for all those involved.

To meet both humanitarian and defensive needs, the Jewish communities sought to establish secular organisations which could undertake the charitable and organisational needs of the tasks involved. Material help for refugee Jews from Eastern Europe had been a feature of Jewish welfare in the Netherlands since the turn of the century.[30] However, most of this had been directed towards help for transmigrants, the vast majority of whom left for destinations in the New World. The organisation of this help was along paternalistic lines, with the officials, most notably (Raphaël) Henri Eitje, operating a system which differentiated the worthy poor from beggars and swindlers. In 1933 the main task was to provide support for refugees without funds who had arrived in the Netherlands with no further planned destination. To this end, the *Comité voor Bijzondere Joodse Belangen* (Committee for Special Jewish Interests, CBJB) and the *Comité voor Joodse Vluchtelingen* (Committee for Jewish Refugees, CJV) were created in March and April 1933. The initiative behind both of these committees came from Professor David Cohen, chair of Ancient History at the University of Amsterdam and, more pertinently, a member of the Permanent Commission of the Dutch-Jewish (Ashkenazi) Congregation. He was well aware that the bureaucracy of the religious communities would be incapable of dealing with the manifold problems of refugees and thus decided to promote separate organisations to meet the specific needs of the situation.[31] To expedite this, he invited his friend, the acknowledged secular leader of Dutch Jewry and leading diamond merchant Abraham Asscher,[32] to be chairman of the CBJB while he acted as secretary and presided over the CJV, which became responsible for the day-to-day running of relief work. In addition, he brought other members of the Jewish elite on to the board of the CBJB, notably S. van den Bergh (a member of the First Chamber of the Dutch Parliament), A.C. Josephus Jitta (professor of the Technical University in Delft) and *mr.* L.E. Visser (at that time, vice-president of the Dutch Supreme Court).[33]

In spite of its own best efforts to remove the need for its existence, the CJV not only continued to function throughout the pre-war period, but also grew in size and scope as the refugee crisis deepened in the later

1930s. All this time, the organisation struggled to raise funds for its work while trying to minimise the number of refugees settling in the Netherlands. In this respect, its founding principles were meeting two objectives set out by the Dutch state, firstly that refugees were not the responsibility of government, but of private charitable efforts, and secondly that the Netherlands was not to be treated as a country of settlement, but only as one of transmigration. While receiving almost absolute compliance in these matters from the CJV, the government steadfastly refused to accord the CJV leadership any special consultative status on refugee matters. This was undoubtedly a status sought after by David Cohen, whether out of a genuine desire to try and influence affairs or out of personal ambition it is impossible to say.

There is no question that the CBJB and the Jewish elite in general was primarily concerned about an influx of refugees from Germany stirring up antisemitism in the Netherlands. Whether their fears were justified can be no more than a matter for speculation. In comparison with the rest of Western Europe, antisemitism in the Netherlands had never been particularly virulent. Its appearance could be categorised under three headings. The first was the religious anti-Judaism which portrayed the Jews as Christ-killers. This was most prevalent in Roman Catholic teaching but could also be found in Calvinist circles. A variant of this was the critique mounted by the hyper-rationalist secularists who condemned Judaism in the same way that they condemned all religions. The second category might loosely be termed cultural antisemitism. This manifested itself in seeing Jews as purveyors of capitalism or Bolshevism but also created some glass-ceilings within society, preventing Jews from holding high office or joining certain clubs and societies. While both these features could be seen as evidence of antisemitism, the segmented organisation of Dutch society meant that other minority groups were likely to suffer similar discrimination, suggesting that this was a function of minority status rather than peculiarly directed towards the Jews. The third category was the virulent and deliberate antisemitism espoused by National Socialist and other extreme right-wing groups.[34] It would be wrong to suggest that this had no appeal in the Netherlands, but it should be noted that the Dutch *Nationaal-Socialistische Beweging* (National Socialist Movement, NSB), having made a huge gain (8 per cent of the vote from nothing in the provincial elections of 1935) found its vote halved in 1937 after it espoused a far more overtly antisemitic programme.[35] Whatever the realities of the situation, the fear of increasing antisemitism played a crucial role in determining both government policy and indigenous Jewish reaction to the refugee influx of the 1930s.

The CJV did its best to dissuade refugees from settling in the Netherlands, but this also created a contradiction. Opportunities for settlement overseas were limited and some refugees had to be helped to become self-supporting in the Netherlands, if only to reduce the burden on CJV funds. Yet by finding opportunities for refugees to find work or establish businesses, they were often doing more for 'foreigners' than was being done for the (Jewish) unemployed, either by the state or private Jewish charities. This was the source of much internal tension, with even Dutch Jewish employers complaining about the CJV deliberately helping new refugee businesses establish themselves in sectors of the economy which were already under severe pressure.[36]

To a large extent, the criticisms of the CJV have centred on its deference to Dutch government wishes and its inability to make a stronger case for a more liberal construction and interpretation of Dutch immigration policy. While this deference may have been in pursuit of some influence within government circles, there has also been a more sinister construction placed on CJV behaviour, namely a strong antipathy towards the refugee Jews from Germany. Perceived as arrogant and alien by many Dutch Jews, the refugees were not well-liked. They were accused of treating their Dutch co-religionists with contempt while continuing to praise everything German to the detriment of conditions in the Netherlands. Dutch Jews found these attitudes hard to digest from people who had often lost everything in their flight from Nazism. They were 'ill-mannered', 'took all the best places', and 'spoke so loudly'.[37] Equally resented was the apparently arrogant attitude of the German Jews towards the Dutch, whom they seemed to regard as their social inferiors. Even those refugees who were self-supporting, and in some cases comfortably well-off, also came in for criticism. In 1935 it was estimated that there were about 34,000 empty dwellings in Amsterdam, with local people unable to afford the rents being demanded by the landlords, yet this did not prevent some Jewish refugees from settling in the leafy suburbs of Amsterdam-South.[38] Indeed, the refugee enclaves became so well-known that in some quarters the number 24 tram was re-christened the 'Berlin express', and the number 8 reputedly had a sign that the conductor also spoke Dutch.[39] This apparent affluence was resented by local Jewish and gentile populations alike, and made it more difficult for the relief organisations to collect money for those who did need help. One of the practical problems for the CJV was the settlement of 82 per cent of refugee Jews in the major cities of North and South Holland,[40] but even more serious was their concentration in specific districts of Amsterdam. They had undoubtedly been drawn by the existence of a large Jewish community and the opportunities for work and welfare support which the city might hold, but their presence in such numbers was seen as detrimental both to minimising the impact of refugee immigration on public opinion and to obtaining popular sympathy for the plight of the German Jews. For their part, many refugees from Germany found it difficult to adjust to their changed circumstances. From being well-off and respected members of established communities in Germany, many were reduced to near penury and recipients of aid from charitable organisations in an alien country.

There is no doubt that the CJV (and the Dutch Jewish communities in general) would have much preferred the refugees to be passive and grateful rather than aggressive, demanding and less than gracious recipients of aid. David Cohen excused their attitude by arguing that the government also feared a growth in popular antisemitism if the refugee influx was not checked,[41] but many Dutch Jews were not entirely unhappy with the government's restrictive attitude. An extreme critic, Jaap Meijer, commented on the fears engendered by the refugees.

> The shaky structure of their own position was set against the even weaker one of the their German co-religionists, who had little to expect from either side [Dutch Jews or Dutch government]. They irritated the Jews, who understandably took out their own problems on these unfortunate refugees of their own race; and they irritated the non-Jews (as Germans? as Jews?) who disliked meeting them in Amsterdam-South just as much as Americans dislike meeting negroes.[42]

Herzberg went so far as to describe the feeling between German and Dutch Jews as one of hatred, although de Jong describes it more as varying gradations of aversion.[43] Whatever the precise nature of the relationship, it is clear that there was little love lost between the refugees and their hosts. Many of the donors to the CJV undoubtedly hoped that their money would make the 'problem' go away by assisting in the re-emigration of the refugees with as little fuss as possible. Thus they were doubly upset if the refugees behaved in such a way as to draw attention to themselves or, worse still, tried to establish themselves as business competitors in already depressed sectors of the Dutch economy.[44] The antipathy between Dutch and German Jews went deeper than the latter's position as ungrateful recipients of aid. Although described as co-religionists, the largely liberal German Jews had little in common with the orthodox Dutch. Their traditions and histories were very different. Moreover, the more aggressive stance of the Germans sat ill with the more defensive attitudes adopted by their Dutch counterparts towards Dutch society. Finally, as Meijer indicated, the refugee Jews were resented for being 'Germans' or 'foreigners' just as much as they were for being Jews. Anti-alien feeling was as strong as antisemitism in the Netherlands at a time of crisis when national (economic) interests were considered paramount.

The refugees themselves were a far from homogenous group. Although around 33,000 had arrived in the Netherlands between 1933 and 1939, several thousand had re-emigrated overseas leaving around 20,000 still resident when the occupation began.[45] They included both Germans and a substantial number of Eastern European nationals and stateless persons, primarily so-called *Ost-Juden*, who had been resident in Germany but had lost their former nationality and not sought to acquire a new one.[46] This latter group were regarded by the Dutch government and immigration officials as a particular liability – as bearers of an 'alien' and 'non-western' mentality and culture, and because it would be almost impossible for them to re-emigrate.[47] The refugees also came from a full range of class and occupational backgrounds, from left-wing, working-class activists to the highest echelons of the German Jewish bourgeoisie. People with readily accessible assets outside Germany found it fairly straightforward to settle in the Netherlands. Some individuals were also able to transfer their business enterprises out of Germany or to set up new firms using their expertise in particular economic sectors.[48] At the other end of the scale were people who had no chance of being self-supporting in the Netherlands, because Dutch immigration restrictions forbade their employment, because their skills were peculiar to Germany, or because they were ill or too old to look after themselves. People who were not self-supporting were usually given some limited financial help, either by the CJV or one of the left-wing refugee relief organisations, but these organisations were always trying to reduce the burden on their meagre funds either by finding ways of making individuals capable of supporting themselves or by finding emigration opportunities for them.[49] It has been estimated that the CBJB and CJV raised in excess of fl.6 million for refugee relief work in the period 1933–40, of which around a third came from major Jewish charities abroad, but that the organisation was still supporting 4,821 refugees at the beginning of 1940.[50]

Socially, culturally and linguistically, the Dutch Jews had little in common, either with the German-speaking, westernised, liberal Jews from metropolitan Germany, or with the Yiddish-speaking, Central European, orthodox *Ost-Juden*, and close proximity in the years 1933–40 did nothing to bring them closer together. Even the liberal Jewish community in the Netherlands, which grew substantially as a result of incoming refugees from Germany, was soon riven by disputes. By 1935 these had become so contentious that the Dutch Jews, feeling themselves 'taken over' by the Germans, decided to secede and form a separate community.[51] Although only one example, this animosity between the 'hosts' and their 'guests' was set to continue throughout the occupation period.

After the *Anschluss*, and then the November 1938 *Reichskristallnacht* pogrom, the pressure on all European countries to take refugees from Germany increased, as did the desperation of those trying to leave. In the Netherlands, the government convinced itself that stricter controls would have to be placed on immigration and closed the border to most incoming refugees. It gave permission for the admission of a further 7,000 refugees on the understanding that they should be accommodated in camps rather than live freely in the community. Initially, those who had entered the country legally and who had resident relatives were allowed to live with them. The remaining Jewish male refugees were sent to camps in Rotterdam and Amsterdam, while baptised Catholics were housed at Sluis and Protestants at Bilthoven and Schoorl.[52] The large number of refugee children who had been brought to the Netherlands without their parents could not be put into camps and had to be spread around orphanages and other suitable homes. By May 1939 there were a total of eight camps for legal refugees and a further 24 institutions housing children. In addition, there were four camps for illegal refugees – those people who had managed to cross the border without the necessary papers but who could not be sent back to Germany. Although women and children in this category were allowed to live in private accommodation, adult males were placed in separate camps. These 'illegal' camps were under military control and administered by the Ministry of Justice.[53] Conditions were harsh and lacking comfort, prompting complaints from inmates about their treatment. Only the demoralisation of the refugees and the fact that the Dutch government allowed illegal entrants to be 'legalised' after six months in these camps prevented this simmering unrest from escalating.

Although the Dutch government was committed to the idea of housing refugees in camps, the arrangements made in the months after December 1938 were only temporary. Discussion took place between the authorities and the relief agencies about the creation of a central refugee camp. A number of sites were rejected, mainly on the grounds of cost.[54] In the end, land at Westerbork near Assen in Drenthe was earmarked for the project. An isolated and bleak spot in the middle of heathland and not far from the German border, the intention was to build a series of barracks for both legal and illegal refugees, with living quarters for families as well as individuals. In siting and planning the camp, the authorities were anxious to minimise the cost, but also to show that they were not favouring the refugees by placing them inside 'fortress Holland', nor giving them living conditions better than those of the poor native inhabitants of Drenthe. This camp, begun with the help of refugee labour, had been partly occupied in the early months of 1940 but the transfer of refugees living freely in the Netherlands had barely begun when the war began on 10 May. The proximity of the camp to the frontier had caused a good deal of disquiet among the refugees housed there – a disquiet which was fully justified when the camp was overrun by the Germans on the first day of the invasion. Conditions were far from ideal. Apart from the damp climate and windswept nature of the area, the accommodation was inevitably much less attractive than living in an Amsterdam apartment.

There were also some organisational changes in the way refugees were handled during this last peacetime year. There was increasing collaboration between the CJV and the smaller denominational committees set up to help Protestant and Catholic (Jewish) refugees. This began as a centralised fund-raising effort but grew into a more permanent *Centrale Raad* (Central

Council).[55] It is worthy of note that from their inception, these respectable bourgeois organisations all shared the government's antipathy towards foreign 'red elements', and distanced themselves from any contact with (left-wing) political refugees. Anyone with a 'political' background or suspected of remaining active whilst in the Netherlands was shunned and directed towards the Social Democrat or Communist help-organisations. By 1939 the Dutch government had also adopted a more streamlined approach to the refugee problem by setting up the *Centrale Commissie Vluchtelingenvraagstukken* (Central Committee for Refugee Questions). This was designed to set out and co-ordinate clear policy and demarkation guidelines for the various departments dealing with refugees. In the event, these changes in structure came too late to make much difference to the treatment of refugees and in any case did little to improve the lot of those concerned.

The shabby treatment (as they saw it) handed out to the refugees by the Dutch government and the Jewish relief organisations helped to sour relations between Dutch and German Jews on the eve of the occupation. Certainly, the German Jews felt that more could have been done for their welfare and the thought of being housed in barrack blocks in the middle of the Dutch countryside far away from the main conurbations and relatively close to the German border was anything but an appealing prospect. The Dutch government was not willing to be seen doing any more for the refugees than it would do for the Dutch unemployed, but it may also have been the case that the conditions were designed to 'encourage' the refugees to re-emigrate if at all possible. Certainly the conditions in some other camps were less than adequate, although it seems more likely that this was due to a lack of proper organisation and resources than deliberate policy.[56]

The role of the CJV has also come under scrutiny. One conclusion is that the readiness of the Jewish elite to organise and finance relief work itself indicated a desire to reaffirm its commitment to the Netherlands, and to show how it could protect Dutch interests while at the same time discharging the obligation to help its German co-religionists. At the same it represented an important statement about the position of the Jews within Dutch society. In attempting to make its aims acceptable to the state, the CJV leadership reacted to the refugee crisis in the way it thought the authorities wanted it to react, by putting Dutch interests first and avoiding any 'political' involvement.[57] This deferential and compliant attitude has been cited, above all by de Jong, as a link between the pre-war behaviour of Asscher and Cohen and their later leadership of the Amsterdam Jewish Council.[58] The continuity of their tenure in pre-war and wartime positions of importance and influence cannot be denied, but their conduct before 1940 has to be judged on its own merits and not with the benefits of hindsight. Faced with limited funding and a government determined not to allow large-scale immigration or preferential treatment for refugees, the CJV achieved a good deal within the parameters it set for itself. There was no resort to illegal actions, or to direct confrontation with the government. Indeed, the CJV's ultra-correct behaviour going beyond what was required made it the staunchest upholder of state policy, in an ultimately fruitless attempt to obtain 'influence' within the decision-making structure. In this respect, the CJV leadership was acting in exactly the same way as any non-Jewish bourgeois group in the Netherlands of the 1930s might have done.

Finally, it is worth reflecting on the Frank family as a illustration of refugee life in the Netherlands. In many respects its story is atypical. Otto Frank had previous contacts with the country, in his case dating back to 1923 when the family bank had established a branch in Amsterdam. This collapsed in 1924, and was followed into insolvency by the German parent bank in the spring of 1933. This latter disaster, coupled with the events of 1 April, encouraged the family to consider emigration. One brother had already moved to Paris and another to London, Otto had at least one good friend in Amsterdam, access to funds from Switzerland via his brother-in-law and access to commercial information which allowed him to establish a business selling pectin and other fruit products under licence. Existing contacts in the Netherlands and access to funds and information made him unusual among the first cohort of Jewish refugees who arrived in the Netherlands in the summer of 1933. The business, like many refugee-run enterprises, was not particularly successful and by 1939 had still not recouped its initial losses. However, the firm did survive, ultimately employing six people including A. Dunselman, an Amsterdam lawyer, Victor Kugler, an Austrian businessman but long-time Amsterdam resident, and Hermine (Miep) Santrouschitz (later Gies) who had been brought to the city as a child in 1919 with many thousands of others to recuperate from the appalling conditions in Vienna and then been adopted by her Dutch foster-parents.[59] The firm thus contained an interesting mixture of Jewish and non-Jewish, and Dutch and non-Dutch employers and employees. This may not have been unique but it was certainly unusual among refugee-owned businesses. Moreover, the firm had other strengths: it was not confined to a niche market but operated by selling to the population at large, and not just in a particular locality, or to a particular group, or within the Jewish community.

By 1940, if not booming, the firm was well-established, able to pay its way and support the members of the Frank family comfortably in their *Amsterdam-Zuid* flat. Given this self-sufficiency, it seems unlikely that Otto ever had any contact with the refugee relief organisations. All these factors place Otto Frank and his family among the minority of refugee Jews in the Netherlands. The majority were not nearly so well placed, especially those who arrived in the Netherlands during and after 1938. As a result, the Franks' story cannot be taken as typical. Indeed, many of the factors referred to above, such as having Dutch partners and friends, were to be crucial in allowing the family to protect its financial interests and ultimately to facilitate its move into hiding in 1942.

International comparisons

In conclusion, it seems appropriate to reflect on the comparisons and contrasts between Jews in the pre-war Netherlands and her nearest European neighbours. In overall terms, the Dutch, French and Belgian Jewish populations were never more than tiny minority groups within their respective countries.[60] Nevertheless, there were notable differences between them. The Dutch were a long-established community with roots in Amsterdam going back several centuries. By contrast the numbers of Jews in Belgium were much smaller, perhaps 2,000 towards the end of the nineteenth century. (Trans)migration from Eastern Europe during and after the 1880s brought the total to around 10,000 by 1914. These immigrants were made up primarily of Jews who chose or were forced to stay in Europe rather than continue their journey to North America. A similar pattern occurred after the First World War, but the imposition of United States immigration quotas meant that many more of these migrants settled in Belgium and France. By 1930 the total Jewish population in Belgium stood at around 50,000. German statistics based on racial rather than religious criteria put the total Jewish population in 1940 as 65,696, but crucially only 4,341 (6.6 per cent) were Belgian nationals. Put another way, 93.4 per cent were either foreign nationals or stateless.[61] In France, a massive wave of immigration from post-revolutionary Russia after 1921 increased the size of the total Jewish population from a post-First World War 90,000 to its 1939 level of 260,000, an almost threefold increase in less than 20 years. On the eve of the German invasion, more than half of the Jews in the country were foreign born and only 25 per cent could claim French ancestry.[62] In contrast, only around 17 per cent of the Jews in the Netherlands were not Dutch citizens. In terms of settlement, the magnetic effect of Amsterdam as a centre for the Jewish community in the Netherlands was mirrored by Antwerp which was estimated to contain two-thirds of all the Jews[63] in Belgium, and Paris which was home to half the Jews in France.[64]

The 'layering' of the various Jewish communities in each country is also an important characteristic. None of them could be described as homogenous. In the Netherlands there was a basic division between Sephardi and orthodox Ashkenazi Jews, the latter having been reinforced by immigration from Eastern Europe after 1881. While there had been some apostasy, there had also been the emergence of a small group of adherents to liberal forms of observance and worship. The Jews who came as refugees from Nazi Germany in the 1930s were also far from being a homogenous group, except insofar as they were considered as foreign. They ranged from highly assimilated liberal Jews from urban Germany to orthodox *Ost-Juden* whose origins lay in the small towns and cities of Poland and Russia. In Belgium there seems to have been a similar tripartite division (albeit in completely different proportions) between the established Jewish community, the recent immigrants from Eastern Europe, and the refugees who arrived after 1933. Steinberg notes the parallel development rather than integration between the Belgian Jews and the incomers from Eastern Europe after 1880. Moreover, he also demonstrates the national diversity of the Jews in Belgium, encompassing 43 different nationalities by 1940, albeit that 75 per cent were either Belgian, Dutch or of German or Polish origin.[65] In France the situation was more complicated, with nineteenth-century French Jewry being supplemented by refugees from Alsace-Lorraine after 1870. These two groups provided most of the affluent Jewish middle class and members of the liberal professions. Unlike those in Belgium, the huge influx of immigrants from Eastern Europe did show a tendency to regard their settlement as permanent by acquiring French citizenship for their children, but the levels of assimiliation undoubtedly depended primarily on how long they had been resident in the country. Like the rest of Western Europe, France played host to refugees from Nazi Germany after 1933, and to a limited number of Jews from Belgium and the Netherlands who arrived in advance of the German armies in the spring of 1940.[66]

Insofar as the information exists, the occupational distribution of the Jews in the three key cities shows some similarities. The diamond industries in Amsterdam and Antwerp were dominated by Jews as employers, but the workforces differed. In Amsterdam the Jews also formed the vast majority of the workforce, whereas in Antwerp the cutters and polishers were mostly non-Jews. While the industry declined in Amsterdam during the 1930s, it underwent a period of sustained growth in Antwerp. In both countries some Jews could be found in the liberal professions, but most were concentrated in specific sectors of commerce and trade. In Belgium this included morocco-leather (handbags), furs and certain elements of the textile and fashion trades. These were sectors in which the newer immigrants had been able to gain a foothold. In Amsterdam where the Jews had been resident for much longer, there was greater diversification, but similar sector specialisations remained, perhaps reinforced by the employment policies of Jewish entrepreneurs and the family-oriented nature of many businesses. In Paris there were marked divisions in the occupational distribution of French and non-French Jews, with the latter being far more heavily concentrated in industrial/proletarian and marginal lower-middle-class sectors of the economy.[67] In addition, all three cities contained the essential 'Jewish' service sector made up of rabbis, schoolteachers, kosher food producers and retailers, whose function was to provide for the particular needs of the community.

In the Netherlands, as in Belgium, there was a clear social division between the established Jewish community and the newcomers. Moreover, there seem to be similarities between the two countries in the distribution of wealth. While we have apparently precise figures for the Amsterdam Jewish community, the more impressionistic pictures of Belgium and

France suggest similar patterns, with many lower-middle-class producers and traders working at the margins of their particular sector. Retailers were in many cases market traders or hawkers. Producers often employed only themselves and their families, and frequently used their home as a 'factory'. Paris and Amsterdam seem to have had more Jews employed in the industrial sector than Antwerp, and these workers were likely to have suffered from the general increase in unemployment during the recession of the 1930s, and also from the increasing discrimination against foreign labour brought in by desperate governments to assuage nationalist opinion. All this leads to the conclusion that the proportion of pauper Jews in Belgium and France was as high, if not higher, than the Netherlands, given the larger percentage of recent arrivals.[68]

The available evidence suggests that there was little espousal of Zionism in any of the three countries. Jews who considered themselves settled and assimilated into Western European society were unlikely to envisage emigration to Palestine, and even the more recent immigrants from Eastern Europe were, by their very movement *within* Europe, effectively rejecting a Zionist alternative. While some minds would be changed by adverse social and economic conditions in the 1930s, the limited membership of Zionist organisations throughout Western Europe testifies to its continuing lack of appeal. The same is true of the refugees after 1933. Herbert Strauss stresses that more Jewish refugees from Germany went to Palestine in 1933–36 than to any other country,[69] but those who moved to other European countries made a decision to stay in Europe. (Although this should be qualified by the fact that many people left Germany hurriedly and that arranging an emigration to Palestine involved a good deal more preparation and paperwork than crossing the nearest available frontier.) Emigration to Palestine did represent a possible escape route for refugees in the Netherlands, Belgium and France, but was never as popular as resettlement in North America, and was in any case limited after the British mandate power imposed new immigration restrictions after the Arab disturbances of 1936.[70] Emigrant training schemes were established in both France and the Netherlands to teach potential settlers agricultural and horticultural skills, but the numbers involved remained low.[71] However, this evidence may be misleading as the Jewish Agency increasingly targeted its immigration certificates towards people still inside Germany or Austria on the grounds that they were under greater threat. As a result, there were fewer opportunities for those coming from other countries.

The patterns of Jewish emancipation in the three countries were also similar. In Belgium emancipation had come with the Constitution of 1830 and a specific organisation, the *Centraal Israëlitisch Consistorie*, had been created in 1832 to represent the religious community to the government. For most Jews, religious affiliation was the only factor that marked them out from their fellow citizens and these Belgian Jews regarded themselves as fully assimilated.[72] This could not be said of the immigrants from Eastern Europe after 1880 who retained their separate traditions, culture and identity, both from their co-religionists and from the population at large. This continued division remained strong until the occupation. Even the far right Rexist movement attempted to exploit it by linking anti-foreign feeling with antisemitism, but distinguishing between Belgian Jews who were entitled to the same rights and liberties as other citizens, and the 'ghetto Jews' who were not.[73] Some attempts were made in the 1930s to combat the growth of antisemitism, most notably by Max Gottschalk, who founded the *Foyer Israélite* in May 1937. While directed at the political threat, this organisation was open to all, and thus provided the beginnings of a gangway between the 'consistorial' Belgian Jewish elite and the rest of the Jews in Belgium.[74]

France had been the first country in Europe to grant full civil rights to Jews under the Emancipation Act of 27 September 1791. This legislation encouraged immigration in the nineteenth century, from Belgium, the Netherlands, and from Spain. Later this was supplemented and then swamped by refugees and immigrants from Eastern Europe. A much higher proportion of these recent immigrants adopted French nationality than their Belgian counterparts, and it was primarily the later refugees from Nazi Germany and Austria who suffered from legislation which denied them work and residence permits. Moreover, they were also viewed with distrust by their co-religionists, faced by increasing popular antisemitism, who regarded the newcomers as 'a threat to those already established'.[75] In this respect, the response of French society was no different from that in the Netherlands or Belgium, but is perhaps slightly more remarkable in the sense that it represented a reversal of the strong support given to French Jewry by government, liberal opinion and the Left during the Dreyfus affair.[76] In comparative terms, it seems that there was little material difference in the responses of the three states or their established populations to the influx of refugees during and after 1933. Immigration laws, while based on differing legal premises, were tightened in each country to reduce the numbers who were entitled to enter and settle. All governments, popular opinion and the existing Jewish populations supported these moves to a greater or lesser extent. Refugees perceived France as more welcoming in 1933, and this meant that it took the lion's share of the exodus from Germany in 1933–35. However, this relatively lenient approach was soon modified by restrictions imposed in early 1936 and augmented by the Daladier government in the aftermath of the assassination of German Third Secretary vom Rath at the Paris Embassy on 7 November 1938.[77]

While one can point to differences between the histories of the Jews in France, Belgium and the Netherlands, they all experienced much the same events and pressures: emancipation, immigration from Eastern Europe, increasing antisemitism and economic pressures in the 1930s, and finally the refugee influx after 1933. All three 'communities' were divided in different ways, between Ashkenazim and Sephardim, between established families and newcomers, between nationals and non-nationals, between orthodox and liberal observance, and along class lines. Yet the most compelling factor which differentiates the Jews in the Netherlands from their French and Belgian counterparts may be not in the existence of these divisions, but rather in their relative proportions. The percentage of long-established Jews was much higher in the Netherlands than elsewhere. The immigration from Eastern Europe in the 40 years 1880–1920 had had much less impact. This greater degree of long-term integration and assimilation, it has been argued, may have given the Dutch Jews a far greater feeling of security in their environment, but conversely also made them more complacent and less prepared for ensuing events.[78] Certainly, this apparent complacency has been used to criticise the Jewish leadership, and the population as a whole, for their responses both to the crisis of the 1930s and to the German occupation. It is doubtful whether the economic composition or demographic distribution of the Jews in the Netherlands in 1940 made them more vulnerable to the Germans since these statistics are not particularly dissimilar to those of Belgium and France. More problematic are the traditions and patterns of Jewish leadership. Was the structure which provided David Cohen and Abraham Asscher with the task of representing Dutch Jewry, first to the Dutch government in the guise of the CJV, and then later to the Germans as chairmen of the Jewish Council, materially different from those in Belgium and France? In all three countries, it had been the Jewish elite which had organised refugee relief,[79] yet only the Dutch organisation developed into a Jewish Council. Could the key lie in the personalities? Were, for example, the leading members of the *Consistorie* better able to see that their role *vis-à-vis* the Belgian government in the 1930s could not be continued once the Germans had arrived? Is the key to understanding the fate of the Jews in the Netherlands less dependent on differing histories and structures than on the fact that the Netherlands produced a leadership which ultimately proved incapable of the task it was given? Reducing such a complex question merely to the role of personalities will scarcely provide a satisfactory answer. As the succeeding chapters will demonstrate, both the political, economic and social structures of the Jews in the Netherlands, and the attributes and actions of their leaders, played some role in the question of survival.

|3|

Invasion and occupation: the first months

War and invasion

The first months after the Dutch armed forces had surrendered to the invading Germans on 14 May were remarkable, not because the German occupation brought so many changes to everyday life in the Netherlands, but precisely because there were so few changes. Initial German policy was designed to minimise the effect of the occupation and retain as much normality as was practical. The Dutch were, after all, fellow 'aryans' and there were no specific plans for the occupation of the country. Moreover, the war against France was continuing, and even after victory in the West, the planners in Berlin were anxious that the occupation of the Low Countries and France should use as few German resources as possible. In spite of this general policy, the ideological aims of the occupying power did begin to be implemented in 1940, albeit in an apparently piecemeal rather than structured form.

The events of the year 1940 provide three issues which need to be addressed: firstly, the problem of why so few Jews managed to escape before the capitulation; secondly, how the early measures against the Jews in the Netherlands were conceived and implemented by the Germans; and thirdly, how the victims and the Dutch population at large reacted. In different ways, each of these debates provides part of the answer as to why so many Jews in the Netherlands fell victim to the 'Final Solution' in the following years.

Of the estimated 140,000 Jews in the Netherlands in 1940 (see Appendix),[1] only a small minority managed to escape from the country before it was overrun. To understand why this was the case, a number of elements need to be considered. The simplest, but by no means entirely erroneous explanation is the sheer speed of the Germans' success in forcing a surrender of the Dutch armed forces in five days. This gave very little time for anyone to react at all, let alone plan and execute their permanent departure from hearth and home. That said, there were other influential factors at work. As has already been shown, the Jewish community in the Netherlands had a long and well-established history within Dutch society. Dutch Jews saw themselves primarily as Dutch citizens and therefore just as bound up with the fate of *their* country as anyone else. The idea of leaving was only considered as a last resort. Their decision-making was undoubtedly influenced by what they thought a German occupation might mean for them, with refugee Jews, not surprisingly, far more afraid of the future than their native counterparts. In addition, access to finance, transport and other resources played a crucial role in determining opportunities for escape, and personal considerations served to keep many individuals from trying to flee from the Nazis.

On Friday 10 May 1940, the German armed forces attacked the Netherlands along a broad front. Although the Dutch government had been warned of German intentions in the days leading up to the invasion, its policy, outwardly at least, remained stoically wedded to the principles of neutrality and the avoidance of anything which might annoy its German neighbour. This attitude was reflected in, or perhaps mirrored, the general public mood. Confidence that a policy of strict neutrality would save the Netherlands from the Nazi menace was widespread and the news of German aggression therefore came as a shock. Few people were psychologically prepared for the blow when it came.[2] Having escaped the direct effects of hostilities during the First World War, the attack by the Germans was a singular and catastrophic event.

On hearing the news, every Dutch man and woman, theoretically at least, had the chance to make a decision – to go or to stay. To stay meant the possibility of living under German occupation but to leave meant abandoning home, security, assets and even family for an uncertain future on the road in order to escape. Yet this begged a further question: where could safety be found? Certainly the Dutch defensive plan to fall back behind inundated farmland and defend 'fortress Holland' provided the incentive for many people from the eastern provinces to flee westwards in the first days. Relatives and friends in the towns of Utrecht, Holland and Zeeland could, hopefully, be relied upon to provide at least temporary shelter, but they too were thinking of the future. As Dutch war refugees travelled westwards, their potential hosts were often fleeing south towards Belgium and the supposed greater security of France, or further westwards with the possibility of a sea-borne escape to England. The picture painted by contemporary chroniclers and by historians is one of chaos and disorder, of people fleeing in all directions on the basis of individual decisions. This was certainly the case as the Dutch military commander Winkelman surrendered the country to the Germans on 15 May, although some earlier planned evacuations had been carried out by the authorities to facilitate military operations.[3]

For the Jews in the Netherlands, the choices of what to do in the event of a German invasion were much the same as for their non-Jewish counterparts. Insofar as they can be talked of as a group, they seem to have shared the views of the rest of the population, hoping against hope that neutrality would protect them and their country from the Nazi menace. Herzberg describes their mood as 'a little prayerful and very hopeful, with pounding heart[s] and closed eyes'.[4] He also observed that the Dutch Jews were afraid, 'and like all fearful people, they retreated into illusions'.[5] Their fear of what might be in store for them if the Germans *did* invade was probably heightened by the knowledge of what had happened in Germany, Austria and the Sudetenland over the previous seven years – a fear which was even more strongly expressed by the refugees from those countries who had experienced it first-hand, although they were seldom thanked for their warnings. Indeed, some Dutch Jews clung to the belief that the persecutions in Germany were the result of misdeeds and misdemeanours committed by the Jews. This view implied not only that the German Jews had brought the catastrophe on their own heads, but also that such measures were specific to Germany and would not be repeated against the law-abiding and respectable Dutch Jewish population.[6]

Although small in number, the Jewish communities near the German border had little or no chance at all to react.[7] Many people awoke to find enemy troops in the streets, and by mid-morning on 10 May, towns such as Venlo, Roermond and Enschede had already been overrun. For them, German occupation was already a reality. Only those who fled westwards immediately had any chance of outrunning the German advance. A young German Jew who had lived with his family in Hengelo since 1936 managed to escape by bicycle as far as Amsterdam with a friend, crossing rivers by boat (as the bridges had all been destroyed).[8] Even then, these two youths got no further than Amsterdam. Penniless and deprived of their bicycles, they were caught by the surrender, and with further flight impractical, they returned home. By 11 May, Dutch forces had fallen back to the *Ijssellinie* (the military defensive line on the Ijsselmeer and River Ijssel) and had more or less evacuated Drenthe, Groningen and Friesland.[9] The Jews of these northern provinces also had little or no time to leave their homes, even if they had wanted to do so.

Further west, there was more time to react. Yet in the first hours of the war, there was no immediate panic. The bulk of the Dutch Jewish community lived inside 'fortress Holland' which was to be defended to the last. In any case, travel was difficult. Few families had their own cars and most public transport had been suspended.[10] In addition, the fear of fifth columnists and military action against German parachutists around Rotterdam and The Hague made it almost impossible to reach the coast in those areas.[11] As a result, Ijmuiden became the focal point for people seeking to escape by sea. During the first three days of hostilities, ships continued to leave the port of Amsterdam via the *Noordzeekanaal* to Ijmuiden and the open sea. Some took German prisoners-of-war out of the country but others did take civilians and a few Jews managed to find passage on these ships. Only on Monday 13 and Tuesday 14 May did the trickle of would-be refugees become a flood. By this stage it was clear that the Dutch army was unable to hold the German advance and many thousands of Jews, fearing the worst, were part of the estimated 30,000 men and women who fled to the coast on the off-chance of finding a boat to take them to England.[12] Ijmuiden and Hoek van Holland became swamped with people. Huge sums were reputedly paid for places in fishing boats. Pearls and jewellery also became a medium of exchange as German aircraft strafed boats in the harbour. Bicycles and even cars, some of which had been purchased the same day just to reach the coast, were abandoned on the beach as their owners searched frantically for some means of escape.[13] While the fears of an imminent capitulation had exacerbated the rush to the ports, rumours of ships waiting to sail for England were also rife. On 14 May Professor Cohen, as chairman of the CJV, announced that he had been told by The Hague that there was a boat at Ijmuiden waiting to take all the Jews who so wished to England. While most of the committee's functionaries decided that they could not give up their work and flee, the committee attempted to spread the word in Amsterdam insofar as this was possible in a city with regular air-raid warnings and no telephone service.[14] Yet even before news of this ship had circulated in Amsterdam, rumours that the British consulate was issuing visas for England created a crowd of hundreds outside its offices in spite of the fact that there were no consular officials there.

The roads also became crammed with refugees, yet the Dutch authorities maintained strict pass controls and many would-be escapees never even made it as far as the coast.[15] The 'drama of Ijmuiden', of official intransigence in the face of a desperate population, created bitter recollections for many who were there. Soon after midday on 14 May, an order had been issued by the Dutch authorities that all refugees should be diverted into a park just outside the town.[16] While the object of this order was to prevent vast numbers of people crowding on to the docks and creating chaos, there was no time to arrange an orderly evacuation to the shipping which was available. The lucky ones were those who had arrived in the port before the ban was imposed. In many cases they were able to find places on coasters and fishing boats still in the port. However, the flood of Jews and others from Amsterdam and places further east did not arrive until the afternoon of that day, by which time it was too late. Unfortunately, the closure of the port by the Dutch military authorities proved so effective that the last few coasters and the steamship *Bodegraven* (presumably the ship referred to by the authorities in their

communication with Professor Cohen) left port without being able to take
on a full complement of passengers.[17]

For those trapped outside the town or still on the road, there was no
choice but to return home as the Dutch forces capitulated. There were
rumours that a few brave souls had managed to find boats and escape days
after the surrender,[18] but they were undoubtedly very small in number. The
vast majority who made some attempt to leave the country had to remain
behind.[19] While it is easy to see how the victims of this chaos could interpret it as deliberate obstruction and ill-will on the part of the authorities,
Presser, for one, remained unconvinced,[20] and it is the British sources
which may hold the key to the closing-off of the ports. Even before the
invasion, the British had intended to deprive the incoming Germans of
Dutch assets and port facilities if the country were overrun. Thus on 10
May, detachments of Royal Engineers were sent to the ports of Rotterdam,
Amsterdam, Hoek van Holland and Ijmuiden to destroy oils stocks and
harbour installations. By 13 May, with the full knowledge of the Dutch
military authorities, the Engineers had laid charges to harbour installations
in Ijmuiden, and the need for these demolitions to be carried out may well
have prompted the closure of the port to incoming refugees.[21] In this light,
the actions of the Dutch military authorities seem far more logical. By
keeping civilians away from an area which might have to be destroyed at
any moment, they were preventing an immediate loss of life while at the
same time ensuring that the intended destruction of the harbour could be
carried out according to plan. In the event, the demolition was held up for
as long as possible, leading to the charge that more people might have been
given the opportunity to escape, but given the *ad hoc* way in which orders
were transmitted and then rescinded to those on the ground, it is difficult
to see how the local military commanders could have been more flexible in
their approach.

In spite of the difficulties, some Jews did manage to circumvent the confusion and escape by sea to England. Presser estimates the number at a few
hundred.[22] They included a group of 75 Jewish children from the orphanage in Amsterdam who had previously been rescued by Gertrude
Wijsmuller-Meijer from Germany and Austria with the *kindertransporte*.
After the meeting of the CJV on 14 May which discussed the Dutch government's provision of a ship for Jews, she managed to 'conjure up' five
vehicles and a travel permit from the Amsterdam garrison commander.
With these essentials, she transported the children to Ijmuiden. By this
stage, the order preventing any further refugees from entering the town
was already in force, and it was only this remarkable lady's chance meeting
with an acquaintance at the control point which allowed her to see the
Dutch commander and persuade him to permit the buses to enter the dock
area. The children were embarked on the *Bodegraven* which finally left at
about 7.00 that same evening.[23] There was also at least one Jewish family

which spent a week in a small boat on the North Sea before reaching England. Four students managed to gain control of the Scheveningen lifeboat and with a group of (mainly German) Jews set out for England, only to suffer engine failure in mid-voyage. They were lucky enough to be picked up by a tugboat making the same journey from Ijmuiden.[24] Others were less fortunate. There were individual tragedies, as in the case of J. Goudstikker, the Amsterdam art dealer who found passage on a ship only to fall to his death in the hold while it was dark.[25] Other escapees who set sail often could not complete the voyage and had to return to the Dutch coast, or were sunk by German aircraft or mines.[26] Their numbers went unrecorded.

In addition to the Jews who attempted to escape the Germans by fleeing to the coast, others joined the exodus of refugees southwards. Here again, some form of transport was at a premium, providing the means to outrun the speed of the German advance. How many succeeded in this enterprise, let alone how many attempted it, will remain a mystery as only those who succeeded in reaching England or one of the neutral states were likely to have found more than temporary respite from the Germans.[27] Some Dutch refugees progressed no further than France – to be caught by the Franco-German armistice. Others were recorded among the estimated 50,000 people who crossed into Spain from France in the summer of 1940.[28] Spain in the aftermath of civil war was never considered as a haven, and the refugees either moved on to Portugal in an attempt to escape across the Atlantic, or eventually chose to return to the unoccupied zone of France once a degree of stability had been restored.

In assessing the ability of Jews in the Netherlands to expedite a last-minute escape from the Nazi menace, one has to draw the conclusion that money and influence were important ingredients in successful escape. Several authors comment on the thousands left behind when the privileged few, both Jews and non-Jews, were able to make their way to safety. This is best summed up by the perhaps rather jaundiced phrase from Wielek: 'Money without luck can make things possible, but luck without money seldom prevails on such occasions.'[29] To counter this, it should also be said that prompt action was also important. By the Monday and Tuesday of the invasion, even the possession of wealth or influence was no guarantee of success. This begs the question of how many Dutch Jews had planned their escape in expectation of a German attack? Judging by the small number who did manage to escape and the chaos which the deteriorating military situation created at the coast, the answer is probably not very many.

While the preponderance of Amsterdam Jews in the rush to the coast reflected their geographic proximity and numerical superiority, the experiences for Jews in provincial towns were very similar. For example, many of the Jews in Utrecht attempted to get to the coast and a few succeeded in escaping, but most came back. The impulse to flee was very strong, but few had the money or the contacts to make such a step anything more than a forlorn hope. An alternative form of 'escape' was to remain in the city but stay with non-Jewish friends. In the event, many Jewish households tried to do something to save themselves, but the net effect was not very great and the prevailing atmosphere in the city remained one of fear.[30]

It should not be forgotten that the majority did not join the rush to the coast. A large section of Dutch Jewry made a conscious decision to stay put and not to leave home and family for the dangers and uncertainties of being a refugee. The difficulties of finding transport and the dangers of being on the road when there was military activity all around would have undoubtedly deterred many from venturing beyond their front doors. Yet not all the reasons for staying at home were negative. There were many positive reasons for remaining. While individuals without family commitments could make almost a free choice,[31] others were bound by their family ties and obligations. Leaving meant giving up home and employment. Was it physically possible to move large or extended families, and if not, then who was to be left behind? Anyone with aged parents or dependent relatives would have to think very carefully before opting to leave. Equally important was the fact that many Dutch Jews were either in the armed forces[32] or involved in some form of ancillary service such as air-raid wardens.[33] It would have been unthinkable that these men should have left their posts to flee the country. They were just as patriotic as their non-Jewish colleagues and most probably never considered flight. Their parents, wives and children were equally unlikely to consider leaving without them. Thus the majority of Dutch Jews had neither the resources nor the opportunity to flee the country, but for some a more extreme and final option could still be considered – suicide.

There are no precise figures on how many people took this form of escape, but there was talk of a 'suicide epidemic'. From personal experience, Sophie Citroen recalled being told that two of her closest friends, their child and grandmother had all gassed themselves.[34] Herzberg recounts going to a *pension* which was home to a number of German Jews and finding a man and his wife dead in their room.[35] The servant recalled that the man 'had always said that he would not go through it all a second time'.[36] It took an inordinate length of time for an ambulance to arrive. While the numbers of war wounded may have accounted for some of the delay, there were potentially a large number of suicides and attempted suicides which had to be dealt with as well. The Jewish cemeteries contain a disproportionate number of headstones dated 15 May or soon afterwards. Graves often contained whole families and not just individuals. Herzberg speaks of simple, ordinary, middle-class people drinking tea, eating biscuits and calmly discussing how to save their children from the Nazi menace by killing them on the grounds that it was better that they should do it than Hitler.[37] While there are no detailed statistics for the number of suicides, the annual figures for Amsterdam increased threefold from 1939 to 1940 and most of this might be attributed to Jews taking their own lives. There are only guesses at the number of Jews who succeeded in taking their own lives in the days during and after the German invasion, still less the numbers who attempted this step. Some prominent persons were included among the dead, notably Emanuel Boekman (Amsterdam alderman), Paul May (banker), Jacob van Gelderen (member of parliament) and Michel Joëls (city councillor in The Hague).[38] Various sources cite 30 successful suicides in The Hague, 100 in Amsterdam.[39] Even in the small Jewish community of Utrecht, four people took their own lives.[40] Warmbrunn estimates the total number at approximately 200 for the week beginning on 14 May,[41] but this does not account for the numbers who tried and failed to kill themselves. Even after the capitulation, there were rumours that exit permits could be obtained and Presser refers to Jews queueing at the offices of the *Bevolkingsregister* (the population register) with bandaged wrists and throats.[42]

Most susceptible to suicide as a way of escape were the refugees from Germany and Austria.[43] Apart from the realisation that their persecutors were catching up with them again, there was the lack of association with their host country. Germans were particularly suspect after the invasion and the Dutch government's response was to insist that such people should not leave their houses. If they did, they were liable to be arrested as enemy aliens.[44] Thus, isolated and unable to play any part in defence of their adopted country, many of them could only fear the worst. Yet, in some respects, the refugees in Amsterdam and the other cities were in a privileged position. Jewish refugees who had arrived in the last year of peace had often been interned and the lack of a coherent government response to an invasion was particularly manifest in the case of these German, Austrian and stateless refugees. A few of these recent arrivals were held in a purpose-built camp at Westerbork in the north-eastern province of Drenthe. In the event of danger, there was a plan to evacuate the inmates by train to Dordrecht and then by ship to Zeeuws Vlaanderen in the far south-west of the country. The *Commissie Afvoer Burgerbevolking*, which was responsible for organising the evacuations in tandem with the military authorities, had asked the government on several occasions to make sure this particular group were moved to safety in good time, but the government, trapped by its political stance on neutrality, refused to countenance sanctioning the move until the German invasion had actually begun.[45] The fear was that allowing the movement of refugees away from the German border would be a tacit admission to the Dutch population and the world at large that something actually *was* wrong and that even the government no longer believed in the safety of neutrality.

In the morning of 10 May, the national evacuation plans were put into action. For the refugees at Westerbork, a train was provided at the nearby station of Hooghalen, and most of the camp inmates were moved at very short notice with little more than the clothes they stood up in.[46] Sixteen refugees, together with the Dutch staff, were left in the camp. Rather than stay put, they took shelter in a nearby farm.[47] By 8.45 a.m., all the evacuees had arrived at the station. However, the original plan to take them south and west was rendered impractical as the railway bridge at Zwolle had already been blown up. Through the intervention of Rabbi Levisson, who had taken a keen interest in the welfare of the refugees, the train took its passengers north to Leeuwarden, presumably with a view to transporting them across the *Afsluitdijk* which dammed the *Ijsselmeer* (see map, p. xi). Here, the evacuees were caught by the Dutch military withdrawal and had to be billeted with civilians in the town.[48] When the Germans arrived on the following day, some citizens put their 'guests' out on the street, fearing German reprisals for having given shelter to German Jews. Only by using small hotels, pensions and the Jewish school was the housing difficulty overcome.[49] On 27 May the refugees were moved back to the camp by the Germans.[50]

Other German Jewish internees fared little better. British forces at Hoek van Holland reported the attempted evacuation of refugees held there on 13 May. These unfortunates were bombed and machine-gunned by German troops during the battle for the town but suffered no casualties, only for some of them to be wounded the following day when the town was evacuated and the Germans mounted a further raid from the air.[51] The 115 Protestant German Jews who had been held at Sluis in Zeeuws Vlaanderen were put under the protection of a Captain Molenaar, whose main task was to transport 18 prominent Dutch National Socialists and three Communists southwards away from the German advance. Molenaar managed to find buses to transport the Protestant Jews and the group ended up in Dunkirk, where Molenaar was arrested as a suspected fifth columnist. His 'crime' had been to be heard talking in German to one of his charges – a German Jewess who was heavily pregnant. Although he was released, most of the group were taken to Calais in the forlorn hope that they could be shipped to England. In the event, all of them were caught in Calais by the German advance on 26 May. The 18 National Socialists were set free, the three Communists handed over to the Gestapo and 82 of the Protestant Jews found their way back to Sluis.[52] For no readily apparent reason, Molenaar was not given charge of the 260 Catholic German Jews who were also interned at Sluis. De Jong thinks it may have had something to do with the availability of transport,[53] but in the event it made little difference as the vast majority ultimately fell into German hands, irrespective of whether they they had been evacuated from Sluis or not.[54]

Occupation and first restrictions

After the panic of the war, experiences in the days following the capitulation did not correspond with the expectations of the Jews in the

Netherlands, or the majority of the Dutch population. The German army arrived in those areas not already taken by military action, but the soldiers obeyed orders in adopting a wholly 'correct' attitude towards the civilian population. 'Everyday life quickly regained its normal rhythm [and] very little seemed to have changed.'[55] This was the case even for the Jews, who had most to fear from the occupiers.

> Nothing happened. No pogrom and no persecutions. The dead were buried, there was grief, there was mourning and there were certainly problems in respect to departed family members and friends whose possessions, insofar as it was possible, were taken to safety, or what appeared to be safety. There were widows, orphans, abandoned husbands, wives and children, albeit more than usual, but people made the best of it and went back to work.[56]

This leads into the second element for discussion, namely to explain the development of anti-Jewish measures during the course of 1940. To do this, it is important to look at the structures of German rule before placing events in the Netherlands in the wider context of the debates on the development of the 'Final Solution' in Western Europe.

During May the country remained under military control, but from the 29th this was superseded by a German civilian government led by Arthur Seyss-Inquart. He was appointed *Reichskommissar* (Reich Commissioner) by Hitler to head the Dutch administrative apparatus which had been left in place. The secretaries-general (the chief civil servants in each ministry) had been instructed to stay at their posts by the government as it fled into exile, and told to continue with their functions provided that these remained within the terms of the existing Dutch constitution and laws. Thus the Germans inherited a fully operational and highly efficient administrative system to which they had only to provide a limited number of 'managers'. In the event, there were four *Generalkommissare* (general commissioners) appointed for the Netherlands: Hans Fischböck (Financial and Economic Affairs) and Friedrich Wimmer (Justice and Administration) were nominated by Seyss-Inquart himself while Hanns Albin Rauter (Higher SS and Police Leader) and Fritz Schmidt (Party and Special Affairs) were Hitler's personal choices.[57]

The appointment and installation of this new regime took some time and this may help to explain why there were no immediate steps taken against the Jews in the Netherlands. However, it was also the case that the war against France was still in progress. For the time being at least, the main German objective was to keep the Netherlands quiet and free from disturbance with the minimal use of resources. The 'correct' behaviour of the soldiers of the occupying *Wehrmacht* (German armed forces) had been the first stage in this process, and was reinforced by Seyss-Inquart's reassuring speech in the *Ridderzaal* (Dutch parliament building) on the day he

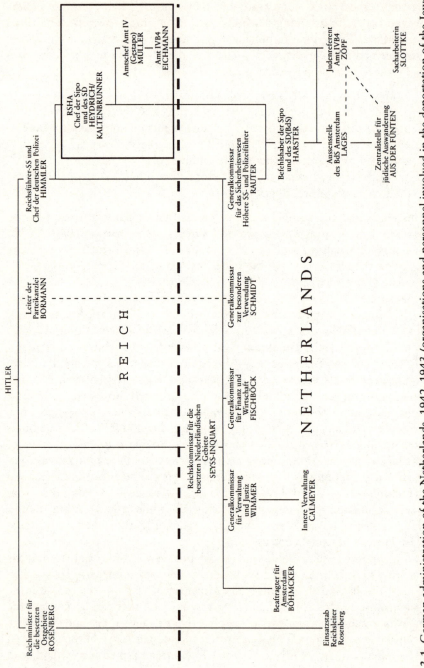

Fig. 3.1 German administration of the Netherlands, 1942–1943 (organisations and personnel involved in the deportation of the Jews)

took over. Dutch Jews gleaned from various sources that the Germans did not consider the Netherlands to have a 'Jewish problem' and *Generalkommissar* Schmidt was perfectly happy to reinforce an assurance from the German military commander that Dutch Jews would not be molested. As Presser points out, can the Jews in the Netherlands really be blamed for accepting these signs and reassurances at face value? It was, after all, exactly what they wanted to hear.[58]

What the Jews in the Netherlands could not possibly have foreseen were the consequences of some of the decisions taken at this early stage. Initially, the Germans had intended to install a military government in the Netherlands, but this was rapidly re-thought as the war in the West progressed. The appointment of Josef Terboven as Reich Commissioner for Norway provided the blueprint for dealing with countries whose administration did not appear to require a large military presence, but which were populated by racially pure 'aryan' stock which might be persuaded as to the benefits of National Socialism.[59] Seyss-Inquart was therefore brought in to undertake a similar role in the Netherlands. It is possible that the early assurances received from German military personnel about the lack of a 'Jewish question' in the Netherlands were given in good faith. What neither the German soldiers nor the Dutch Jews knew at the time was that the whole administration was about to be turned over to a civilian government which would allow a much greater influence for the SS and the Nazi Party in the running of the country when compared with countries such as Belgium, where the military remained in charge.

Yet even after the civilians had taken over, the first months gave little direct indication of what was to come. In a pattern which had parallels with the Jews' experience in Germany after 1933, but in contrast to the immediate imposition of legislation which took place in Austria and the Sudetenland, the process of identifying, marginalising and finally isolating the Jews in the Netherlands was undertaken gradually and by bureaucratic means. This began in a relatively innocuous fashion on 1 July, with a letter to the Dutch civilian air-raid protection service from the office of the *Höhere SS- und Polizeiführer für die besetzten niederländischen Gebiete – Befehlshaber der Ordnungspolizei* and signed by *Generalmajor* Schumann, which stated that all Jews, nationals of states at war with Germany and all Dutchmen with anti-German sentiments were to be dismissed from the service by 15 July. This first German imposition set the pattern for future events. There was a threat of further measures if the orders were not carried out. A protest from the effective head of the Dutch civil service, *mr.* K.J. Fredericks (Secretary-General at the Ministry of the Interior), as to whether this new regulation was compatible with the German undertaking that there was no 'Jewish problem' in the Netherlands was dealt with 'personally' by *Generalkommissar* Wimmer, but the import of his conversation with Fredericks went unrecorded. As Presser points out, it might have been

more appropriate for Fredericks to ask *how* such a measure could be
squared with previous German pronouncements.[60]

Further measures did then follow, albeit in a somewhat haphazard and
apparently unstructured form. On 2 July a regulation insisted that all Jews
were to be excluded from labour drafts to Germany. There had been a tradition, stretching back into the 1930s, of the Dutch government forcing
the unemployed to take up work in Germany or lose entitlement to benefits in the Netherlands. On 21 June the Ministry of Labour had issued a
circular stating that all unemployed Dutch males were to register for
labour service in Germany. Good pay and fringe benefits were offered, but
the carrot was quickly replaced with a stick four days later when those who
refused to register were threatened with loss of benefits for themselves and
their dependants.[61] Not surprisingly, the Germans were unwilling to have
Dutch Jews brought into the Reich, and thus took the appropriate action
to prevent it happening.

The steps to identification

Both measures required the authorities to identify Jews. In the case of the
air-raid protection service, this was done via an attestation which all staff
had to sign, namely that they did not belong to any of the three 'undesirable elements'. Although there were minor differences in the execution of
this order in different cities, the overall effect was the same, with Jews
being excluded from the service. Presser notes that reports show persons in
the other two categories being allowed to stay.[62] From this he deduces that
the real victims of the measure had always been the Jews. In certain areas,
there was resistance to the idea of signing the attestation and some people
resigned in protest. In Amsterdam, after an appeal by the mayor, the
authorities even had to concede that some Jews would have to be retained
to maintain the service in areas of the city where they formed a large proportion of the population.[63] Following hard on the heels of this legislation
came yet another German favourite, namely the restriction of ritual slaugh-
ter. It was enacted on 31 July amid a whole series of otherwise unremark-
able administrative measures introduced by the Department of Social and
Economic Affairs. While the Dutch College of Secretaries-General
undoubtedly tried to dissuade the Germans from this measure, there was
very little they could do and after consultation with 'the Dutch Rabbis' the
legislation became law on 5 August.[64]

Far more serious were the measures taken in the autumn of 1940 to
exclude the Jews from education, public office and the economy. Again,
the progress towards these ends was implemented only gradually. A law of
20 August (VO 108/1940) which allowed *Reichskommissar* Seyss-Inquart
to dismiss civil servants at will was not considered as a particular threat to

the Jews, but eight days later the College of Secretaries-General was instructed by *Generalkommissar* Wimmer to ensure that no one of 'Jewish blood' was appointed, elected or promoted to public office. This was not intended as a published ordinance but merely an internal instruction. Protests that indignation would be aroused when this policy inevitably became public knowledge were reinforced by the 'discovery' that such provisions would violate at least two articles of the Dutch constitution. All the agonising within the College of Secretaries-General and the protests lodged with the Germans were to no avail, and the Dutch civil servants were soon reduced to asking Wimmer for a definition of who precisely was of 'Jewish blood'. Circulars were sent out to provincial and local authorities on 30 September defining a Jew as anyone with one Jewish grandparent who had been a member of the Jewish community. From this, it was only a small step to the implementation of the so-called aryan attestation, sent to all government departments in mid-October. This required all civil servants, including teachers, to attest to their racial origin. Either a Form A (aryan) or Form B (non-aryan) had to be returned by 26 October. In effect, Jewish civil servants were being asked to identify themselves. While there was a great deal of soul-searching about these forms in both academic and bureaucratic circles, most of them were returned.

Protests came from the universities where Professor Telders of Leiden University asked that 'these despicable forms' be returned uncompleted. Professor Scholten of Amsterdam organised a petition signed by academics to be sent to Seyss-Inquart, and there were other petitions from the students at various universities. Presser records that the staffs of the Amsterdam Lyceum and the Christian High School in The Hague refused to sign *en bloc*.[65] However, nearly all the teachers and academics did eventually sign the declarations. In the civil service, there were a few individuals prepared to resign rather than complete the forms, but most did so. Elsewhere, protests were limited. The Roman Catholic church leadership failed to find the right moment to launch a pastoral letter against the measures. The Dutch Reformed Church did organise a proclamation which was read from the pulpits of many churches on 27 October, and the theologian Koopmans published a pamphlet which went further by criticising the church leadership for not doing more to oppose the aryan attestation.[66] Presser makes the point that none of these protests ultimately achieved very much or deflected the Germans from their objectives. Yet it should not be ignored that in an environment where the press was censored and the general population unaware of the precise import of impenetrable legislative prose, any commentary on measures which the Germans were trying to keep as low-key as possible could only help to heighten public awareness of what was happening.

In spite of the protests, the receipt of the forms allowed the Germans to proceed by dismissing all the Jews in government service. To that end, they employed a statute which was already in existence. The decree (VO 137/140), published on 13 September, did not mention the Jews directly but stipulated that the 'legal and financial status of public servants, and especially the conditions of their employment and dismissal may, if necessary, be amended in disregard of the existing laws'. This was enough to sanction the wholesale expulsion of Jews from government service at the beginning of November. Again the College of Secretaries-General fought a rearguard action to defend their Jewish colleagues, but to no avail. A palliative of 'temporary suspension from duty' was initially agreed by the Germans in mid-November, but the 'temporary' was almost immediately rescinded and in late 1940 it became clear that they would settle for nothing less than dismissal. For the secretaries-general, the ground on which the battle was being fought changed from trying to protect the suspended civil servants' jobs to negotiating some degree of adequate compensation for them. Threats that the College would refuse to carry out any further German measures against the Jews did produce a better financial settlement for those dismissed, but by this stage the secretaries-general were becoming increasingly worried about their own position within the legislative and executive system. Moreover, Presser believes that the apparent improvements on the terms for dismissal were just part of the German tactics when dealing with the Dutch civil servants – to make totally unreasonable demands so that enforcing their real wishes then appeared to be a concession.[67]

Presser is particularly critical of the leading Dutch civil servants, seeing their lack of resistance to the German measures as capitulation. Certainly they were culpable in being drawn into using the Nazi vocabulary when discussing the exclusion of the Jews from Dutch public life. Should they have tried harder to resist the German measures? What could they have hoped to achieve? Presser makes the point that in 1940 it was conceivable that Seyss-Inquart still needed a compliant Dutch bureaucracy, and was prepared to make some concessions, even if they were only short-lived. In defence of the secretaries-general, they had been charged by the elected government with overseeing the administration of the Netherlands during the German occupation and could not therefore desert their posts at the first provocation. They did at least try to defend the position of 'non-aryans' within the civil service as demonstrated by the number of times the topic appears in the minutes of the College. In addition at this early stage in the occupation, they were acting on the basis, however naïvely, that Seyss-Inquart and his colleagues, as the *de facto* government, would honour the promises they made. In so doing, they made the mistake of assuming that they were dealing with men who adhered to the same norms of behaviour as themselves. They would soon realise the error of their ways. It would be wrong to exonerate the Dutch civil servants for their traditional deference to authority and 'correctness' in dealing with the

Germans.[68] The policy gave no scope at all for obstructing the wishes of the occupier, but it should be remembered that at the time when these first, crucial pieces of legislation were being enacted, the bureaucrats were still trying to come to terms with their new role under German tutelage. De Jong notes that it is clear from the minutes of the College of Secretaries-General that many of these leading bureaucrats were concerned that their subservience to the occupying power was going beyond their instructions and obligations as civil servants,[69] but in the event only two chose to resign in these early months.[70] It has also been argued, probably with justification, that this 'characterless' attitude by most of these leading civil servants had a 'disastrous' effect on all other Dutch institutions' attitudes towards the Jews – an effect which was manifested in the lack of protests when further measures were enacted.[71]

The full effect of this stance became apparent in the last week of November when government departments, local authorities and educational institutions were told that their Jewish staff were to be dismissed. Although the press had been instructed not to mention the matter, there were protests and strikes in some schools as pupils reacted to the departure of their Jewish teachers,[72] but by far the loudest protest came from the universities. Leading academics spoke out against the measure, the most famous being Professor Cleveringa's speech to the Law faculty at Leiden University on 26 November in honour of his Jewish colleague Professor Meijers. Students in several institutions organised strikes, most notably in Delft and Leiden. This can be considered remarkable in itself insofar as Dutch university students traditionally came from bourgeois backgrounds and were notoriously apolitical prior to 1940. The results were predictable. Student leaders were arrested or went underground, Cleveringa himself was detained and many universities were ordered to be closed by the Germans. A few brave academics and many of their students had been prepared to stand up and be counted in the protest which followed the dismissals, but the Jewish teachers and lecturers still had to leave.[73] At best, the protests had drawn attention to what might otherwise have gone unnoticed by the rest of Dutch society.

Elsewhere in the civil service, the departure of 'non-aryan' staff was not marked in the same way. Jewish employees of the Amsterdam telephone exchange were not permitted to enter the building to say goodbye to their former colleagues. Mayors in several towns were reported to have carried out the German orders without demur, but perhaps the most telling incident took place in the Dutch High Court where its president, *mr.* Lodewijk Visser, was suspended and then dismissed by order of the Germans. When debating the issue, his former colleagues voted in favour of his dismissal by a majority of 12 to 5.[74] A good deal of justified criticism has been levelled at the High Court, not only because of its behaviour towards its former president, but also because no word of protest came from this body which was charged with upholding the very principles of Dutch law against which the 'aryanisa-tion' of the civil service so grossly offended.[75] In many cases, victims of the legislation received their dismissal notices at home and then chose, or were specifically instructed, not to return to their former workplace.

While the psychological effects of this expulsion of Jewish civil servants may have been far-reaching, only about 2,000 of the 200,000 state employees were directly affected. This was little consolation to those involved, yet even before the civil servants had received their dismissal notices, the Germans had embarked on a process which would affect a much larger section of the Jewish community. On 22 October a now infam-ous decree (VO 189/1940) had been promulgated. For the first time, the Jews were mentioned by name and the criteria set out in this decree were used as the basis for deciding who should be expelled from the civil ser-vice. While the definitions used to expel Jews from the air-raid protection service had been relatively narrow, these were far more comprehensive:

Article 4

Definition of Jews

1. Jews are all persons whose grandparents included three or more full Jews by race. (And see 3 below)
2. Persons with only two fully Jewish grandparents are deemed to be Jews if they either
   a) belonged to the Jewish religious community on 9 May 1940 (or subsequently joined it);
   b) or were married to a Jew on 9 May 1940 or after that date.
3. A grandparent is deemed a full Jew if he was at any time a member of the Jewish religious congregation.

However, the decree had a much wider purpose, namely the compulsory registration of all Jewish enterprises and economic activities. This involved firms and businesses owned by Jews, funded by Jewish capital or share-holders, or having Jewish directors. The one Jewish director of the *Nederlandse Bank* was enough to compel its registration. The term Jewish capital was very widely interpreted so that even firms which had as little as a quarter of their capital supposedly belonging to Jews were included, but to make sure nothing fell through the net there was a catch-all clause to include an enterprise under predominantly Jewish 'influence'. It should come as no surprise to find that this 'influence' was never defined. All the evidence suggests that the bankers, businessmen, investors and street traders caught by the definition complied with the instruction and sent their quintuplicate forms in to the newly established *Wirtschaftsprüfstelle* (Bureau of Economic Investigation).

In surveying the events of 1940 as they affected the Jewish community in the Netherlands, it would be wrong to assume that the bureaucratic measures enacted by the state were the only things to infringe on everyday life. For some people life changed very little, while for others the new laws and restrictions had a profound effect. On the one hand, foreign Jews forced to move away from the coast were faced with finding new lodgings and, if at all possible, some form of employment. Civil servants found themselves suspended, then dismissed, but not yet without salary. On the other hand, unemployed Jews were excluded from labour drafts to Germany and thus remained on state support in the Netherlands. Jewish businesses and enterprises continued to function more or less normally, even after the registration process. Nevertheless, there were some more sinister happenings which could be seen taking place in the latter half of 1940.

It is undoubtedly true that certain Dutch institutions and organisations were very quick off the mark in trying to anticipate future German demands. The Dutch air-raid protection service was certainly guilty in this regard,[76] but other organisations also took steps to demote or exclude Jews. The *Nederlandse Bioscoopbond* (Dutch Cinema Union) was first to act, forcing its Jewish members to resign in May. Cinemas were also in the forefront early in January 1941 when the Germans used the pretext of protests during performances to ban Jews from all cinemas and ultimately to bring about the dismissal of all Jewish employees.[77] Under German pressure, the *Concertgebouw* and *Residentie* orchestras moved their Jewish musicians from the front row to the back and in the autumn dropped all works by Mendelssohn from their repertoire. Two Jewish publishers were forced to withdraw from membership of the *Uitgeversbond* (Publishers' Association). The *Nederlandse Verbond van Vakverenigingen* (NVV) trade union organisation sacked all its Jewish employees in the summer and autumn, and the Social Democrat publishing house *De Arbeiderspers* did likewise with its editors and distributors.[78] When the *Nederlandse Journalistenkring* (Dutch Journalists' Circle) became the *Nederlandse Journalisten Verbond* (Dutch Journalists' Union) on 23 November, Jews were no longer accepted as members.[79] At a different level, the Germans began purging libraries and bookshops of undesirable literature, albeit not on a very systematic basis. School textbooks, especially those for history, were 'amended', with the Germans insisting that certain sections were expurgated and replacement chapters inserted.

More visible were other steps taken by the Germans to identify and isolate Jews. In some localities, they demanded that Jewish shops have signs in the windows saying 'Jewish business'. This began in Zandvoort as early as the end of May. Towards the end of 1940, coffee houses, cafés and restaurants began to have signs in their windows saying 'Jews not welcome'. Herzberg gives no reason for this sudden change of policy, but Presser intimates that it was in large measure due to the intimidatory tactics of the NSB, WA (the paramilitary wing of the NSB) and other National Socialists, especially in the big cities.[80] In spite of the German authorities' desire that there should be no disturbance to public order, there were cases of Jewish-owned shops or cafés patronised by them having their windows broken. Jewish actors and actresses were barracked and molested in the theatres and there were recorded cases of Jews being robbed of money, either by German soldiers, members of the WA or of the NSNAP (*Nationaal Arbeiderspartij-Socialistische Nederlandse*). Jewish graves at Assen in Drenthe were desecrated and on the night of 4/5 August the synagogue in Zandvoort was blown up.[81]

In trying to gauge the impression all these measures made on the Dutch Jewish population, and their reaction to them, it has to be said that most accounts spend little time on these early months. Yet even if people could avoid the antisemitic press, hang on to stable employment and preserve a degree of normality in their everyday existence, the signs of segregation and isolation from the rest of Dutch society were already beginning to appear and there was a potential threat of violence from the Dutch National Socialists. After 14 May, escape from the country was almost impossible, although some individuals did manage to buy their way out using funds held abroad. One of the more spectacular escapes foiled by the Germans involved five German Jews attempting to fly to safety from an airfield near Arnhem.[82]

If it appears that the Dutch Jews were unsure of their future in the Netherlands, it is worth questioning if the German authorities themselves were certain where their anti-Jewish measures were leading. The rapid capitulation of the Western European states had created something of a problem. German policies on many matters were still being developed on an *ad hoc* basis, and the 'Jewish question' was no exception. More to the point, even the various offices in Berlin which claimed competence over such matters had no clear or uniform design during 1940. As a result, while remaining within the broad guidelines determined by the *Reichssicherheitshauptamt* (RSHA), much was left in the hands of officials inside the countries concerned.[83] This might have led to radically differing approaches, but it seems that similar patterns of bureaucratic restriction and compulsory registration were followed throughout occupied Western Europe. In France, and without apparent German pressure, the Vichy regime passed the *Statut des Juifs* on 4 October 1940, which excluded Jews from certain sectors of public life. Less than two weeks later, a law was passed which allowed for the internment of foreign Jews and the Germans ordered a census of Jews in the occupied zone and a special census of Jewish commercial enterprises, properties and economic activities.[84] In Belgium there was also an attempt to make all Jews register with the police after 28 October, although this appears to have met with widespread resistance and non-compliance. In both these countries, it appears that the Jews were less compliant than their Dutch counterparts, showing much less deference towards authority, and a healthy disregard for its orders. This trend towards non-compliance, even at this early stage in the occupation, was almost certainly helped by the knowledge that the Germans would find it difficult to identify evaders through other governmental records.

The events of 1940 in the Netherlands suggest a policy which was a combination of measures designed to parallel the pattern of Jewish segregation which had been carried out in Germany in the years 1933–39 – but with the important provision that everything was introduced gradually and nothing was to be done precipitately which might lead to outright protests or civil unrest. Thus it was similar to the course of events in the rest of Western Europe, but unlike Austria in 1938 or occupied Eastern Europe in 1939 when legislation and restrictions were introduced almost overnight. In addition, some measures were taken merely to plug gaps in existing legislation or to make sure that new laws did not run counter to the 'spirit' or intention of the Nazis in marginalising and isolating the Jews. The prohibition of unemployed Jews being drafted for labour service in Germany is a good example of such a measure. The comparison with events in pre-war Germany can be taken further when assessing the disruption caused by radical antisemitic elements, both German and Dutch. De Jong suggests that the instances of unsanctioned, arbitrary or localised action against the Jews was prompted by the bureaucratic way in which Seyss-Inquart was dealing with the 'Jewish question'.[85] The radicals wanted more action – and more quickly. Whether their activities served to speed up the process in 1940 is open to some question. On the whole, the German administration was able to keep control of events and even stifle or suppress the excesses of the more virulent antisemites, but at least one commentator has suggested that there were just as many tensions *within* the German leadership. Joseph Michman, in surveying the origins of the 'Final Solution' in the Netherlands, makes the point that there were conflicts between Seyss-Inquart and other German officials whose prime loyalty was to the SS leadership in Berlin.[86] While this type of conflict should not surprise us, given our knowledge of the way in which the Nazi state functioned, its existence undoubtedly influenced the radical changes in policy which took place in the early part of the following year.

4

Isolation

The period from the turn of the year in 1941 to the summer of 1942 could be regarded as the most important in determining the fate of Dutch Jewry. In these 18 months, the Nazi leadership in Berlin moved from the vague and ill-defined notion that there had to be an *Endlösung* (Final Solution) to the 'Jewish question', through the development of the *Kommissarbefehl* (Kommissar-order) and homicidal policies towards partisans and civilians to a genocidal policy against the Jews which became 'mechanised' and streamlined after the Wannsee Conference in January 1942. The issue here is not to debate the precise genesis of the 'Final Solution' in the minds of the Nazi leadership, but to examine the impact of its decisions on the Netherlands. Charting the gradual isolation of the Jews from the rest of Dutch society in this period does serve to raise a series of questions which this chapter will address. These can be grouped under two main headings. Firstly, was it the case that all the measures taken against the Jews came about through orders from the top, or were there local initiatives and circumstances which served to alter the nature and the pace of legislative isolation? Certainly, it appears that both the German administrators in the Netherlands and even indigenous National Socialists played some part in determining the course of events. Secondly, how did the Dutch population, the state bureaucracy and the Jews themselves react to these measures? The protest in Amsterdam at the end of February 1941 against the first mass arrest of Jews is invariably cited in comparative European works as an unusual example of popular solidarity with the plight of the Jews, but this begs the question of whether it was also unusual in the context of the Netherlands. Even more contentious is the behaviour of the Jews who purported to lead the people in their hour of need, namely the men of the Amsterdam Jewish Council. Much opprobrium has been heaped on this organisation and its leaders for having co-operated, and perhaps even collaborated, with the occupying Germans, but there are conflicting views on their motivation and conduct, and these also bear closer examination here. Finally, it seems appropriate to reflect on the impact of these measures on their intended victims. How did ordinary Jewish families, without money or influence, deal with the progressive removal of economic existence and civil and personal rights? Their testimony is scant because most were deported and killed, but evidence of their plight and their reaction does remain, in their contemporary writings and in the memories of the few who did survive.

The formation of the Jewish Council and the February strike

It is widely accepted that January and February of 1941 represent a watershed in the persecution in the Netherlands. The beginning of compulsory registration for all Jews is often regarded as the last element in the first stage of the German 'plan' of identification, isolation, deportation and extermination, but there were other events which can now be seen as having been signposts for the future. The beginning of 1941 saw the first steps towards the creation of a 'Jewish ghetto' in Amsterdam, the establishment of a Jewish Council and the first punitive round-ups and deportations. With hindsight, it is easy to see how these events fit into a pattern, but it remains open to question if such a coherent plan actually existed at the time, and whether either the German authorities or the victims were aware of the ultimate consequences which these steps might have.

At the turn of the year, the legislation to exclude Jews from Dutch society began to increase in volume. Jews were no longer allowed to employ non-Jews as domestic servants, they were excluded from cinemas and new Jewish students were barred from the universities.[1] The introduction of these new restrictions in such a short space of time does require some explanation. While it may well be that the German authorities were attempting to increase the pace of anti-Jewish legislation in the country – either in line with directives from Berlin or on their own initiative – the measures can also be explained at an individual level. The exclusion of 'aryans' from Jewish households was a favourite German decree based on Nazi fears of racial 'contamination', thus its introduction at this stage should not come as any great surprise. The exclusion of the Jews from the universities can also be seen as a logical step after the removal of Jewish teachers and lecturers. Both measures were an integral part of the identification and isolation process, but the exclusion from the cinemas was rather different. During the summer and autumn of 1940, there had been many instances of German luminaries being barracked and jeered by the audience when they appeared on the screen. In an attempt to provide both an explanation and a scapegoat for this, the

German authorities in the person of *Generalkommissar* Schmidt leant heavily on the Dutch Cinema Union to ban all Jews from their premises, a ban which was imposed on 7 January.[2]

Three days later followed the final stage in the identification of the Jews in the Netherlands. Decree VO 6/1941 of 10 January ordered the formal registration of all Jews. This measure had been signposted by *Generalkommissar* Schmidt the previous August but the timing of its introduction appears to have had no particular significance. Using the widest possible definition of the term 'Jew', the Germans insisted that all those who might be included in such a definition register and complete a questionnaire. Local authorities were charged with setting up offices in every community and the process was carried out in the early months of 1941.[3] Registration was done in writing, and on payment of a guilder the person concerned received a yellow card. Doubtful cases were to be referred to *Generalkommissar* Wimmer's office where they were adjudicated by a lawyer from Osnabrück, Dr Calmeyer. The significance of this process lay not in its implementation, but in the very high levels of compliance it produced. Presser could not find a single case of Jews who had deliberately avoided registering. Subsequent to his researches, one or two cases did come to light, but the total numbers involved remained extremely small.[4] While those who registered could not have known precisely how this information might ultimately be used, they were nevertheless effectively betraying their existence and whereabouts to an occupying power which was becoming increasingly malevolent in its behaviour towards them.

Explaining this level of compliance is complicated. Many of those involved reasoned that their names and addresses already existed in the local population registers, or in the records of the synagogues to which they belonged. Not only would avoiding the registration process be a waste of time, but non-compliance could be easily identified and those involved punished. Non-registration carried a prison sentence of up to five years. This apparently rational, if ultimately dangerous, response has been linked to a wider explanation for the docility of the Jews in the Netherlands. This centres on the traditional deference to authority and respect for the rule of law exhibited by the Dutch population as a whole which transcended the German occupation, and continued to exercise an enormous power on non-Jews and Jews alike, even when 'authority' became increasingly at odds with the norms of Dutch society.[5] There was a strong and perhaps natural desire to remain within the law and to comply with a regulation which had no immediate practical consequences, rather than become a lawbreaker who could expect severe punishment. Only those who already lived outside the law, like illegal immigrants, Communists, or those who had a fear of any dealings with authority (such as Eastern European Jews), or those who thought they did not fall within the definitions used by the Germans, were likely to have evaded the registration process in any numbers. Certainly, the total of around 157,000 registration forms received by the authorities suggests that compliance had been more or less complete. All of these factors could be used to justify registering, but there was a positive side as well. In the wake of this measure, many people who had never been a part of the Jewish community in the Netherlands chose to join it, possibly out of pride, or defiance, or a need to belong to a community when danger threatened.[6]

Table 4.1 Jewish population in the Netherlands, January 1941[7]

	No.	Percentage
'Full Jews'		
Dutch	118,455	74.1
German	14,495	9.1
Others	7,295	4.6
Subtotal	140,245	87.8
'Mischlinge'	19,561	12.2
Total	159,806	100.0

Table 4.2 Religious affiliation of 'full Jews', January 1941

Religious affiliation	No.	Percentage
Jewish	125,657	89.6
Roman Catholic	700	0.5
Protestant	1,245	0.9
None	12,643	9.0
Total	140,245	100.0

As we are now aware, the registration of the Jews in the Netherlands was the first step to isolation and eventual deportation and extermination. Most of the Dutch Jews in the Netherlands do appear to have registered and only a very few avoided this fatal step. While some with Jewish ancestors chose to associate themselves more closely with the Jewish community at this time, others with Jewish grandparents and parents tried just as hard to dissociate themselves. Their pleas to the authorities to consider them on the basis of upbringing and/or religious belief rather than racial origin invariably fell on deaf ears. A few individuals, whose parents or grandparents had lived abroad and who could not, therefore, be identified as Jews, were able to avoid registering altogether, safe in the knowledge that they were unlikely to be betrayed by the existing population registers. Finally, there was also a trade in 'aryan' ancestors whereby individuals with Jewish parents could hire an 'aryan father' who was prepared to certify that he was the progenitor of the son or daughter, rather than the father given on the birth certificate. This last attempt at deceiving the authorities increased when the full implications of registration became clear.[8]

For the non-Dutch Jews, the situation may have been slightly different. In theory, all resident foreigners had to register with the police, but the levels of illegal immigration, especially in the period after November 1938, made it certain that there were some Jews who had entered the country but had evaded registration. Unlike their Dutch counterparts, the Jewish refugees from Germany and those of Polish or Eastern European extraction were far more distrustful of bureaucracy and avoided it wherever possible. Thus while people who had been discovered entering the country illegally, or had given themselves up to the authorities, had usually been consigned to a camp before the occupation began, there were others who escaped detection and could therefore avoid the German ordinances as well. It was also possible that when foreign Jews were ordered away from the coastal areas, they might avoid being recognised in another town. To be successful, the people undertaking a 'disappearance' would still need outside help or some access to false identity papers.[9] Militating against this form of escape was the obvious 'foreignness' of the Eastern European Jews in terms of language, dress and ritual. While some people did manage to 'disappear' at this early stage, their numbers were undoubtedly very small.[10]

The next stages in the process of identification and isolation came, not from this planned administrative process, but from the provocative activities of Dutch National Socialists against the Jews in Amsterdam. De Jong notes that in December, *Generalkommissar* Schmidt had given permission for the paramilitary NSB *Weerafdeling* (WA) and the *Sturmabteilung* (SA) of the NSNAP to take action against Jews and supporters of the *Nederlandse Unie* in cafés, restaurants and in the streets.[11] There were incidents in Utrecht and The Hague. In mid-January WA men and German civilians plundered a number of Jewish shops in Arnhem. The WA in The Hague, Rotterdam and Amsterdam began forcing hotels and restaurants to display signs stating that Jews were not wanted as customers. In Amsterdam this action had been specifically sanctioned in mid-December by Böhmcker, Seyss-Inquart's special commissioner for the city of Amsterdam and his deputy in charge of anti-Jewish measures.[12] At that time, the WA with the co-operation of the *Sicherheitspolizei* (Sipo) and *Sicherheitsdienst* (SD) (i.e. the Security Police and the Security Intelligence Service of the SS) had placed signs in nearly every café and restaurant in the city. Most were subsequently removed by the owners, but the campaign was recommenced at the beginning of February. On Saturday 8 February the activities of the WA led to fighting around the Rembrandtplein. Next day, the violence increased and the 'Alcazar' café in the nearby Thorbeckeplein was attacked and wrecked.[13] Other cafés and dance halls also fell victim to this indiscriminate violence. At that stage, some German troops were involved, but the activities of the Dutch police in trying to maintain order ultimately brought their withdrawal to prevent a confrontation between the various forces of 'order'.[14] The police were rapidly losing control of the situation as the Jews inside the Jewish quarter of Amsterdam, reinforced by non-Jewish neighbours and workers from other districts, took steps to protect themselves from the WA provocations. The violence persisted in the following days until Tuesday evening when a group of 40 WA men fought a pitched battle with a newly formed Jewish action group (*knokploeg*) and were forced to withdraw in disarray, leaving one of their number seriously injured. The man, 45-year-old Hendrik Koot, was to die three days later,[15] but long before this, new measures were enacted against the Jews of Amsterdam.

Within hours of the incident, the Dutch police had been given orders to seal off the 'Jewish quarter'. Böhmcker had been advocating this step since December. He also wanted a complete clearance of all non-Jews from the area, but this was never carried out and the closure lasted only a few days. Subsequently the area was marked out with signs saying *Juden Viertel, Joodsche Wijk* (Jewish quarter) creating what de Jong describes as an 'optical ghetto'.[16] The only people who did move from the Jewish quarter at that stage were members of the NSB, WA and NSNAP. Böhmcker's role here is interesting. As Seyss-Inquart's deputy in charge of anti-Jewish measures, he had apparently been content to sanction actions against Jews in public places in December and January, and had been in the forefront of suggesting new restrictions on the Jews. However, he had apparently ordered the WA commandant in Amsterdam to keep his men out of the Jewish quarter prior to the Koot incident.[17] Was this a case where Böhmcker began to feel that matters were getting out of hand, that measures against the Jews could not be allowed to conflict with wider concerns about public order? Whatever his reservations, he remained an enthusiast for the idea of a ghetto. Both he and Schmidt had been pressing for action at meetings of the *Reichskommissariat*, against the opposition of Rauter and the caution of Seyss-Inquart. The disturbances, coupled with Rauter's absence on sick leave and Seyss-Inquart's imminent departure on a skiing holiday,[18] provided the ideal excuse for the two men to put their plan into operation, even if it was abandoned shortly afterwards.

This interpretation of events has prompted some criticism, based on the lack of hard evidence for a long-standing plan for the ghettoisation of Amsterdam Jewry. A letter from Böhmcker to the Amsterdam City Council on 16 January, asking for information on the location of Jews in the city, is often cited as evidence for a plan, but even if he received a reply on 29 January,[19] was this time enough to formulate a practical idea for a future ghetto? Moreover, as the figures he was sent demonstrated, even the

'Jewish quarter' contained only a minority of the city's Jewish population. Certainly, this and the absence of more telling evidence counts against the idea of a coherent and thought-through plan for a ghetto on Eastern European lines, but does not invalidate the possibility that the sealing-off of the Jewish quarter was in part an immediate practical response to the disturbances themselves, and in part a method by which Böhmcker and Schmidt could be seen as active in formulating and executing policies against the Jews. In this context, there is no reason why either Böhmcker or Schmidt should have had any hand in directing the WA, but were merely reacting to the consequences of its actions in the 'Jewish quarter'.

The following day, apparently at the behest of Schmidt, Böhmcker summoned the leaders of the two Jewish communities in Amsterdam[20] and insisted on the formation of a 20-strong *Judenrat*.[21] There is some doubt as to his precise intention in calling these men together. De Jong, Presser and Herzberg all assume that there was a plan to create an organisation to represent all the Jews in the Netherlands which would be headed by the civil and religious leaders of the two communities. This is indeed what actually emerged, but Knoop claims that Böhmcker originally had in mind only a group to represent the Jews from the Jewish quarter, and that the idea of a fully fledged *Judenrat* actually came from Abraham Asscher, who insisted that the Jews should be represented by notables, of whom there were none in the Jewish quarter.[22] This allowed Asscher and his colleague from the Jewish Refugee Committee, Professor David Cohen, to assume the joint-chairmanship of this new body and co-opt a group of leading Jews to fill the remaining places. Only one representative from the Jewish quarter was asked to join, a butcher from the Jodenbreestraat named Quiros. He remained only a few weeks. Likewise, the one member of the Jewish working class, I. Voet (a former chairman of the Dutch General Diamond Workers' Union), lasted only until mid-April 1941 before retiring for health reasons.

In demanding the creation of a Jewish representative body in Amsterdam, Böhmcker effectively ignored an existing Jewish organisation, namely the *Joodse Coördinatie-commissie* (Jewish Co-ordination Committee, JCC). This had been created under the aegis of Dutch Zionists and on the joint authority of the Netherlands Israelitic Congregation and the Supreme Committee of the Portuguese Community to provide a national representative organisation for all Jews in the Netherlands. Its establishment was designed to overcome the fragmented and often divisive relationships between different branches of Dutch Jewry: Zionist and assimilationist, orthodox and liberal, Ashkenazi and Sephardi, left- and right-wing. Although the JCC contained many leading Zionists, it was chaired by a non-Zionist, *mr.* Lodewijk Visser, the recently suspended president of the High Court and activist within the Jewish community. In spite of having worked alongside both Cohen and Asscher in the Committee for Special Jewish Affairs before the war, it was clear that there was a long-standing animosity between Visser and the two joint-chairmen of the newly formed Jewish Council. They did not invite him to become a member of the Council, although a number of other JCC members were invited and accepted. Visser had taken a stand on the principle that Jews of Dutch nationality should be represented and protected by the Dutch authorities and not by specially created organisations which would imply a difference between Jews and other Dutch citizens.[23] Consequently, he was inherently opposed to the idea of a special 'Jewish Council'.

The establishment of the Jewish Council, therefore, had a number of effects. First of all, it created a second organisation to represent Jewish interests, at least initially just for Amsterdam, and directly at the behest of the Germans. This in turn created a conflict between the two bodies, one of which was working closely with the German authorities and the other refusing any direct contact with the occupiers. Moreover, although the Jewish Council was supposedly responsible only for Amsterdam, the fact that the city contained more than half the country's Jewish population and the headquarters of most of its leading organisations and institutions, made it difficult to see how the supposedly national JCC, operating from The Hague, would exercise any real control. Indeed, it soon became apparent that the chairmen of the Jewish Council were not prepared to accept Visser's authority as chairman of the JCC.[24] In the end, the JCC was entirely marginalised, and then finally dissolved on 10 November 1941 by the very organisations which had founded it less than a year before. There is no doubt that the leaders of the Jewish Council conspired in its demise. By setting up parallel organisations and using their contacts with the Germans to assist in empire-building, the Jewish Council was able to spread its influence and control to include all matters pertaining to the Jewish communities throughout the country by the autumn of 1941. Yet even in defeat, Visser remained adamant that co-operation with the Germans was the road to ruin, and he continued his principled opposition until his death in February 1942. Whether his approach to the problem of dealing with the German authorities would have brought different results for Dutch Jewry it is impossible to say,[25] but his opposition to both the occupying power and the Jewish Council in Amsterdam does show that there were some individuals within the Jewish community prepared to respond in more robust ways to the Nazi threat.

The first meeting of the future Jewish Council took place on the after-noon of 13 February. Even at this stage, Asscher and Cohen had been warned by Izak Kisch, one of Visser's closest associates, that the Council would be hated by the Jewish community and be seen as laughable by the non-Jews.[26] In spite of the warning, the organisation was formally estab-lished and a precedent was set later that day when Asscher spoke to a meeting of some 3,000 Jews in the great hall of the Diamond Exchange. There, he announced the formation of the representative body and insisted that, on account of the recent disturbances, all weapons held in the Jewish quarter be handed in to the police. Most accounts have assumed that this second step was taken at Böhmcker's behest, but again the precise circumstances are open to debate. In the same way that Asscher expanded the role of the representative body, he may also have taken its remit to include steps to maintain peace and order – including measures to 'disarm' the civilian population.

In effect, the first steps towards Jewish collaboration with the Germans had begun, with the self-appointed elite of the Jewish Council acting as a conduit for Nazi demands. The behaviour of this Jewish elite, and Asscher and Cohen in particular, has been the subject of much debate. The actions of these two men have been heavily censured by the post-war Jewish community, historians and Dutch society. One of their most virulent critics, Knoop, makes the point that the Jewish Council was *their* creation, *they* recruited the members, and *they* were aware of where their actions might lead. He seems to regard their assumption of the mantle of community leaders without any mandate save that of the Germans as no more than arrogance.[27] This turns the duty (*plicht*) felt by the Jewish upper bourgeoisie to lead the community into an act of betrayal. Certainly, every author on the subject notes that the Jewish Council was not representative in any real sense. The overwhelming majority of Jews in the Netherlands were from poor or working-class backgrounds which were far removed from the lives and lifestyles of the Council members. Nevertheless, this should not invalidate the motives of Asscher, Cohen and all who joined them. Any post-war utterances by those involved were inevitably coloured by what happened in the years after 1941, but the fact that the leading members of the community *did* see it as their duty to provide some leadership should not be dismissed lightly. In the words of David Cohen, 'many of them had dedicated their lives to the community, either in the religious, or the philanthropic or social fields. For them, there was no question that they should take this [task] on.'[28] De Jong does at least raise the problem of what else the self-appointed representatives of Dutch Jewry could have done when faced with Böhmcker's demands.[29] Go back on the promises already made to the Germans, leave Asscher and Cohen isolated, take effective responsibility for German reprisals? This begs the question of the extent to which the Jewish Council leadership was in fact responding to demands, or merely using the vaguely expressed wishes of the German authorities to create organisations of its own choosing.

Asscher's demand that the Jews should hand in all their firearms and other weapons to the police undoubtedly began a trend. In passing on this German order, the embryonic Jewish Council was tacitly admitting that the Jews had some responsibility for the disorders rather than portraying them as victims of Nazi terror who acted only in self-defence. While the Germans were keen to lay the blame for any and all disturbances at the doors of the Jews, even they realised that they had a serious problem on their hands. If the NSB and WA were allowed to continue their campaign of vandalism and violence, it was clear that the police were unwilling to intervene against them. Even Rauter finally accepted that the vandalism had to stop so that order might be restored, but he also wanted the *pro-cureurs-generaal* to find opponents of the NSB who could be blamed for the disturbances.[30] In the aftermath of the Koot incident, men from the Jewish quarter had been arrested and then photographed with weapons in their hands. These photographs were then given as 'evidence' to the press and as reinforcement of the German claim that they were dealing with an outbreak of terrorism.

The situation in Amsterdam remained uneasy. On the afternoon of Saturday 15 February the *Dam* had to be cleared by the authorities. On Sunday there were further incidents and on the Monday the WA man Koot was buried and there were further minor outbreaks of violence in the city. It is possible that the disorder might have died down had it not been for a series of events the following Wednesday. A detachment of German *Ordnungspolizei* led by the Sipo-SD chief in Amsterdam, Lauhus, sur-rounded an ice-cream parlour 'Koco' owned by two German-Jewish refugees, Ernst Cahn and A. Kohn, which had been used as a base by one of the *knokploegen* (action groups). The parlour had had its windows smashed the previous Saturday and when men in uniforms appeared out-side, those inside assumed that the WA had returned and one of the own-ers deployed a bottle of ammonia gas against the intruders. The Germans began firing, stormed the building and chased those inside to an adjoining building where they were apprehended. The owners had managed to escape, but were also arrested later the same evening. Kohn was sentenced to ten years in gaol but died after being deported. His partner Cahn was sentenced to death in The Hague on 27 February and executed on 3 March 1941.[31] The commander of the firing squad had also been part of the original SD detachment, a certain *SS-Untersturmführer* Klaus Barbie.[32] In German eyes, the events at the ice-cream parlour not only reinforced their view that they were dealing with terrorists, but also represented a major escalation of the violence. Attacks on Dutch National Socialists were one thing, but when the 'terrorists' had the temerity to use violence against the police force of the occupying power, that was something else entirely. Certainly Himmler, who had a detailed report from Lauhus, chose to see it in that light and ordered immediate reprisals through the arrest of at least 425 Jews between the ages of 20 and 35 from the Jewish quarter.

The German raid on the Jewish quarter took place on the afternoon of Saturday 22 February. Some 600 men from the *Ordnungspolizei* sealed off the area and began dragging people off the street and breaking down doors to find suitable victims. Women and children were mishandled and beaten, as were any others who tried to resist. Those arrested were taken to the

Jonas Daniël Meyerplein where they were forced to run the gauntlet through rows of policemen who beat them, and then squat down with their arms outstretched. The first raid failed to produce enough men and it was repeated the following day. All were taken to an internment camp at Schoorl from where a few who were sick were returned to Amsterdam. The remaining 389 were transported by train to Buchenwald on 27 February and some months later to Mauthausen. None of them survived the war.[33] As would be the case in many occupied countries in the following four years, German reprisals were met with further resistance. For the first time, the Germans had shown their hand. The mask had been removed and the tactics of the oppressor which had been so evident in Germany since 1933 were now being applied in the Netherlands. The arrests in Amsterdam may have taken place in the Jewish quarter, but in broad daylight and (in the case of the Sunday raid) in front of hundreds, if not thousands, of non-Jews who used the shops and markets in that district. As a result, the news of the raids spread like wildfire through the city.

Since the last months of 1940 there had been a number of strikes, supported but not necessarily initiated by the illegal Dutch Communist Party (CPN).[34] Those employed on public works schemes had struck against the lowering of their weekly wages and on 17 February metal workers in Amsterdam-North had struck when it was feared that the Germans intended to send some of them to work in Germany. In each case, these actions against the Dutch authorities had achieved their aim and had not resulted in arrests. However, when the news of the arrests reached the illegal CPN leadership, they decided on a far more dangerous course of action. As de Jong points out, striking against the Dutch authorities in one's own interests was one thing, striking against the Germans' actions in support of fellow Jewish workers was quite another. The strike was planned for Tuesday 25 February and initially involved municipal employees but soon spread to other sectors throughout Amsterdam. The metal and shipyard workers who had been involved in the strike the previous week had also stopped work by mid-morning and the absence of some of the city's trams on the streets provided an indication to the rest of Amsterdam's labour force that a protest was in progress. From a narrow base of Communist-orientated workers' groups, the strike wave grew to encompass many who were not Communists. Both Social Democrats and patriots generally were happy to endorse this protest and lend their support to the street demonstrations which followed.

The Germans were surprised by the strike and its extent. Seyss-Inquart was in Vienna. Böhmcker tried to persuade the Mayor and Acting Police Commissioner in Amsterdam to take decisive action, and he also threatened Abraham Asscher with more arrests of Jews if the strike was not halted immediately. Rauter began to mobilise German police units and some patrols used firearms against demonstrators. Although a 7.30 p.m.

curfew was generally obeyed, the strike did not end. While most municipal employees did return to work under threat of dismissal, others joined in, both inside Amsterdam and elsewhere. By the afternoon German police and SS troops had been deployed in the city's streets and a state of emergency declared. Several people were wounded by German use of firearms and at least seven were killed on the second day. By midday on Thursday, the strike had ended everywhere. It had been both a protest against German anti-Jewish policies and against German rule in general, garnering support from many sections of Dutch society. Its success in mobilising the people on to the streets probably convinced the Communists that they had a major weapon at their disposal. Only time would show this to be false. At the same time, the upheaval had shown the power of the Germans to control the Dutch population, and the fact that they would not tolerate public displays of dissent. Moreover, while the heroism of the strikers and the 'particular dignity' of the action cannot be denied, it has to be said that it failed to deflect the Germans from their task and merely taught them that they would have to proceed more circumspectly in future.[35]

At the same time, the events of February had warned the Germans that they needed to think carefully about the way in which policies against the Jews were pursued. The activities of Dutch National Socialists on the streets had to be curbed, but there was also the question of how relations with the Jewish community might be regularised. It appeared that the policy of merely introducing directives concerning the Jews without prior consultation was not working, and a new system needed to be found. The demand for the establishment of a Jewish Council in Amsterdam had been an unplanned step taken in response to the disorders in the city and the perceived need to communicate with the Jewish community directly. The lack of planning is evidenced by the fact that the Germans first proposed to call in the religious leaders of the two communities, and it was they who directed an approach to Abraham Asscher as best placed to deal with secular political matters.[36] The establishment of a direct relationship between the German administration and the Jewish community in Amsterdam was designed to act 'as a conduit for applying pressure'[37] and also as a means whereby the publication of such directives could be limited to the Jewish community alone and not be made available to the public at large.

Power struggles within the German administration

The German administration undoubtedly used far more coercive power to put down the February strike than it would have preferred, given the overall desire to keep the Netherlands (and the rest of Western Europe) as quiescent as possible and to bring the Dutch 'with a firm but very gentle hand' back to the 'Germanic community'.[38] At the same time, events in the

Netherlands and decisions being made in Berlin forced all the authorities concerned to consider their policy on the Jews. What emerged was a conflict of interests and jurisdiction which was not peculiar to the 'Jewish question', the German administration of the Netherlands, or indeed to any sphere of Nazi government. In this particular instance, the competition for control was between Seyss-Inquart, who as Hitler's personally appointed Reich Commissioner relied directly on the *Führer*'s support, and Rauter, who as *Generalkommissar* for Security Matters was nominally subordinate to Seyss-Inquart, but as Higher SS and Police Leader he took orders from Heydrich and his chief Himmler. In the months following the February strike, these two men vied for primacy in control over Jewish affairs, and were joined in the competition by *Generalkommissare* Schmidt and Fischböck, each with his own agenda, plans and vision of the future. Interestingly, for all the SS claims to competence in measures related to the Jews, its senior representative in the Netherlands, Rauter, had had little impact in the period before and during the establishment of the Jewish Council. For the most part, it seems to have been the non-SS leaders, Schmidt and Böhmcker, who made all the running.[39]

The early months of 1941 saw attempts by Heydrich and the RSHA to gain complete control of the Jewish question throughout the occupied territories. This suited Rauter and his subordinates who were anxious to break free from the *Reichskommissar*'s control. Heydrich proposed the establishment of a *Zentralstelle für jüdische Auswanderung* (Central Office for Jewish Emigration) on the same lines as those already established in Vienna, Berlin and Prague. He was said to perceive this as 'an example for the solution of the Jewish question in all European countries'.[40] The timing of this decision, and of Seyss-Inquart's agreement, have never been precisely determined, so it is impossible to say if Heydrich's plan was in response to the events of February or drafted independently and perhaps before the disturbances. Nevertheless, what is clear is that the Netherlands was to be used as a model to be followed in other occupied territories, at least in the West.[41] Heydrich wanted the *Zentralstelle* in Amsterdam for two reasons. Firstly, it was where the vast majority of the Jews were living, and secondly, it would be geographically removed from Seyss-Inquart's administrative power base in The Hague. Michman argues that Seyss-Inquart could not object to the creation of the *Zentralstelle* because of Heydrich's power in these matters,[42] although he did voice some objection to the name, preferring the 'Central Office for Jewish Affairs'. While the reasoning behind the objection is unclear – and it seems a weak point on which to raise an objection about jurisdiction – he may have felt that reference to emigration, when opportunities were so restricted and some Jews from Greater Germany were already known to have been moved eastwards into Poland, could only imply deportation. This was something which would unsettle rather than reassure the Jewish communities and their leaders and thus be counter-productive. More likely, the objection was one more manifestation of the ongoing battle for competence and control within the German hierarchy.[43]

The *Zentralstelle* as originally intended was set up in the van Eeghenstraat in Amsterdam at the end of March 1941. Run by *SS-Obersturmführer* Dr Erich Rajakowitsch, who had previously been employed at the RSHA in Berlin and before that with Eichmann in Vienna,[44] the organisation's first task was to win the confidence of the Jewish Council and to convince them that the possibilities for emigration were real and that the *Zentralstelle* would protect their interests. To this end, Eichmann also sent Jakob Edelstein and Richard Friedmann, two well-known Zionist Jews from Prague who had been extensively involved in the emigration of Jews under the aegis of the *Zentralstellen* in Vienna and Prague.[45] Their visit to Amsterdam was remarkable for a number of reasons. Here were two committed Zionists being given unrestricted access and movement in Amsterdam by the SS, ostensibly in order to win over the Jewish leadership to working with the *Zentralstelle*. Although they did win the confidence of the Jewish Council, their attempts to warn the joint-chairmen Asscher and Cohen about co-operating with the Germans fell on deaf ears. In spite of being told what these men had seen in the East, Asscher and Cohen remained convinced that the Germans would never dare to do in the Netherlands what they had done in Eastern Europe. Moreover, they were apparently convinced that there would be an imminent Allied invasion which would drive the Germans out within a short space of time.[46] In fact, little came of the visit and the Jewish Council was ultimately ordered by Eichmann to set up a so-called *Expositur* as a liaison office between itself and the newly formed *Zentralstelle*.

At this stage, both Seyss-Inquart and the combined forces of the SS in Berlin and The Hague were on parallel but potentially competitive courses. Rauter was clearly determined to increase his control in this sphere by building on Heydrich's establishment of the *Zentralstelle*. In a letter to Seyss-Inquart dated 18 April 1941, he announced his intention to use his authority as *Generalkommissar* to transfer all the 'handling of all the relevant matters' to the Chief of the Security Police and SD (Harster) who was acting on the orders of *SS-Gruppenführer* Heydrich, and had been appointed as authorised Deputy for Jewish Affairs. This was clearly an attempt to move all aspects of the Jewish question in the Netherlands into the ambit of the SD and SS. For Seyss-Inquart, the problem was to find a means to counter this SS attack on his position. By the end of March, *SS-Hauptsturmführer* Willi Zöpf, a friend of Harster, had arrived to take overall control of the *Zentralstelle*, and he was now actively encouraging contacts with the Amsterdam Jewish Council. Against this, Seyss-Inquart had appointed Senator Böhmcker as the Commissioner for Jews. To try and resolve matters once and for all, he called a meeting of all the *Generalkommissare* and several security police officials. No precise details of what took place at this meeting have survived, but other references give a reasonable indication of what was discussed. By this stage, all the participants knew and agreed that the prime objective was the removal of all Jews from the Netherlands. The discussion, as was to be the case at Wannsee early the following year, centred not on the policy itself, but how and under whose control it should be implemented.

Seyss-Inquart managed to win one major victory at this meeting with the help of Hans Fischböck, *Generalkommissar* for Finance and the Economy. As part of their plans, the SS had suggested setting up a fund for Jewish emigration whose capital would come from confiscated Jewish assets and would be used to fund the work of the *Zentralstelle*. However, Fischböck reproduced a staged plan for the gradual exclusion of the Jews from the economy, combined with a series of structures which would allow for the centralised collection of Jewish businesses into a single holding company and Jewish assets into an exclusive bank. He had suggested this to Goering after the *Reichskristallnacht* as a means of avoiding the widespread corruption which had followed from the 'aryanisation' and sequestration of Jewish assets in Germany and Austria. Rajakowitsch and the *Zentralstelle* had no answer to this comprehensive plan and were forced to concede.[47] Denied access to these funds, and outnumbered by his opponents, Rauter was forced to defer to Böhmcker's authority and the importance of the *Zentralstelle* was limited until the deportations began in the summer of 1942.[48]

Not all issues were straight disputes between Seyss-Inquart and the SS. For example, on the question of establishing Jewish ghettoes in the major towns and cities, *Generalkommissar* Schmidt and Senator Böhmcker both spoke in favour of such a measure and Seyss-Inquart would have found it hard to resist the proposal had it not been for Rauter's objections. He adopted Heydrich's line that concentrating Jews did not necessarily mean the establishment of ghettoes. Although Jews were ultimately concentrated in Amsterdam during 1942 and 1943, there was never any attempt to create a formal ghetto in the city. Lines of dispute were therefore not always clearly drawn between the *Reichskommissar* on the one hand and the SS on the other.[49]

The meeting in May 1941 did, however, establish a series of mutually agreed targets for all those involved, namely steps to be taken to facilitate the removal of the Jews from the Netherlands. The disputes over competence, although not entirely settled, were pushed to the background in the short term. However, if the original discussions about policy had arisen out of a crisis in the Netherlands itself, by the summer of 1941 this was no longer the driving force behind further decision-making. The origins of Nazi genocidal policies in the spring and summer of 1941 coupled with the planning and execution of the invasion of the Soviet Union have been discussed at length in all the literature concerned with the debate on the origins of the 'Final

Solution'.[50] The advance into Russia and the first stages of the war of annihilation against the Jews in Eastern Europe brought the possibility of deporting the Jews from the Netherlands that much closer. This enabled the SS leadership in The Hague to make a further attempt at undermining Seyss-Inquart's position. Harster, as Chief of the Sipo and SD, set up *Sonderreferat J*, a department under his command to deal with Jewish affairs. The intention was that it should dictate policy to the *Zentralstelle* and this structure would then dominate all aspects of the Jewish question in the Netherlands.[51] Seyss-Inquart's response was a face-to-face meeting with Hitler on 25 September which gained approval for the measures taken to date.[52] On the strength of this, Böhmcker was asked to compile a memorandum on the steps taken against Dutch Jewry, their implications and the measures needed to complete matters.[53] This formed the basis for another plenary meeting on 8 October 1941 which led to a series of further compromises by the competitors. The idea of having a country-wide organisation to represent the Jews was finally dropped and the Amsterdam Jewish Council subsequently informed that it would take up this responsibility. The *Zentralstelle* and the Security Police were to reach agreement with Böhmcker on all basic problems and co-ordinate their spheres of activity. Any idea that the *Zentralstelle* should expand its functions and be used as an agency to control the entire process was quashed by Seyss-Inquart. Nevertheless, its practical role did begin to increase as deportation of the Jews became more of a possibility. By this stage, Heydrich had abandoned the idea of the Netherlands *Zentralstelle* as a model for other countries and the RSHA had established in The Hague a branch of its *Referat IVB4*, the section of the Gestapo–SD led by Adolf Eichmann and responsible for the execution of deportation and extermination policies. Surprisingly, leadership was given to the idle Zöpf (presumably because of his friendship with Harster) rather than the assiduous Rajakowitsch. The *Zentralstelle* was thereby downgraded in importance and became merely an executive agency in the process of deportation. It was nominally under the command of Willi Lages but the day-to-day running was left in the hands of *SS-Hauptsturmführer* Ferdinand Hugo Aus der Fünten.[54]

While the role of the *Zentralstelle* may have been constrained, Rajakowitsch moved to take up a new role heading *Sonderreferat J*. The discussion in August 1941 about the creation of this organisation had included the first written link between the term 'Final Solution' (*Endlösung*) and 'Deportation' (*Aussiedlung*) in a circular from Harster.[55] It was clear to those involved that from this point onwards any idea that the 'Jewish question' could be solved by emigration had been abandoned and that deportation to the East was now the preferred option. Sijes also reflects on Rajakowitsch's role here. Although far from being the most powerful functionary in the system, and subordinate to the 'indolent' Zöpf,[56] he was another Austrian with direct links to, and a friend of, Eichmann. Moreover, he was a convinced antisemite and saw the Jews as 'one of the most destructive elements in central Europe'.[57] After the war, he always maintained that during 1941 the term *Endlösung* was applied to the Madagascar Plan and changed only after the Wannsee Conference in January 1942. Sijes doubts the veracity of this claim, not least because Rajakowitch had had first-hand experience of the 'Jewish reservations' at Nisko (Poland) during 1939, and had subsequently been in close contact with Eichmann. There was a good chance that he knew what the real import of the change of terminology from *Auswanderung* ('Emigration') to *Aussiedlung* in the summer of 1941 really entailed. Moreover, it was clear from his actions that he had no qualms about a policy of extermination. In this respect, he may have been ahead of, and better informed than, some of his superiors.[58]

De Jong has argued that the debates about structures which took place during 1941 were not just arguments about competence but also about the way in which policy against the Jews was to be carried out. Certainly, there were many schemes which were put forward and then dropped. Schemes to put Jews in work-camps, to introduce ghettoes, yellow stars, or the full provisions of the Nuremberg Laws were all suggested by various functionaries but then dropped, usually at Seyss-Inquart's insistence. Was he trying to delay actions against the Jews to prevent unnecessary disturbances or because the suggestions would have meant others undermining his position as *Reichskommissar* and thus in overall charge of the Netherlands? It is difficult to believe that competence conflicts did not play an important role in the creation, content and speed of anti-Jewish measures in this period, both accelerating some elements and retarding others. Whatever the conclusion, de Jong is clear that the higher echelons of the *Reichskommissariat* knew that deportation was now the solution to the question of the Jews in the Netherlands – at least 15 months before it was begun. He also claims, without citing any direct evidence, that they 'at least knew or supposed that the majority of the Jews would not long survive the deportation'.[59]

This meeting in October may have put an end to the immediate power struggle between competing German authorities, but it did not preclude the possibility of further disagreements or the continued existence of overlapping and conflicting functions. Harster was being asked to co-ordinate and reach agreements with Böhmcker. Whether this would work in practice was another matter. At the same time, two of the other *Generalkommissare* continued to have some control over matters related to the Jewish question, with Fischböck still having primacy in economic matters and Wimmer retaining powers, for example, on questions of race and mixed marriages.[60] Houwink ten Cate has argued that the arrangements established in September 1941 worked 'rather well' in practice, with the various authorities having decided and agreed on their areas of competence.[61] However, although it is important to understand this competition for control which took place in the spring and summer of 1941, the crucial question must be what impact this power struggle had on the development and execution of policies against the Jews.

The isolation of the Jews

The period between February 1941 and the first deportations in July 1942 is usually described by historians as the period in which the Jews in the Netherlands were systematically isolated and excluded from the rest of Dutch society. During this period, the Germans enacted a whole series of decrees and orders, each one placing greater restrictions on the economic and social life of the intended victims. The fact that this legislation was introduced piecemeal led Presser to characterise the relationship as a game of cat-and-mouse, with the Germans making demands or introducing new restrictions while the Jewish Council and sometimes individual Jews attempted to find loopholes or exclusions in the drafting of decrees to minimise their impact, only for the Germans then to issue further 'clarifications'. The question then arises whether this was part of a deliberate plan to keep the Jewish community guessing about German intentions, or mere sadism on the part of those involved – enjoying their victims' continued discomfort. Another possible explanation for this continuing flow of legislation may have been the result of competition between elements of the German administration, with each one trying to outdo the other with yet another order or yet another limitation, or alternatively just an inability to see or think through the complex ramifications of apparently simple measures.

In fact, this pattern of behaviour had begun even before the February strike. On 11 February severe restrictions were placed on Jews attending universities and sitting examinations. This was enacted by the Dutch Department of Education, Science and Culture, but under orders from Seyss-Inquart. Presser notes that the *Reichskommissar* was wont to get compliance from the Dutch civil servants by proposing far-reaching measures and then allowing them to be watered down, thus making it seem as though the bureaucrats had gained some concessions and forestalled something worse. In this particular case, students were allowed to sit examinations or enrol for the academic year 1941–42 only with the special permission of the Secretary-General, van Dam.[62] This method of dealing with the Dutch civil service, designed to make it appear that there was some point to negotiation and therefore some point to the Dutch officials staying at their desks, may also explain the somewhat incomplete and apparently ill-thought-through nature of the legislation enacted against the Jews in these early months.

After the February strike, the Germans stepped up their campaign by making the Jewish Council in Amsterdam wholly responsible for all Jewish organisations in the city. This 'co-ordination' was complemented by the suppression of all Jewish newspapers except one, the *Joodse Weekblad*, a paper started by a young revisionist-Zionist (wanting a Jewish state on both side of the River Jordan), Jacques de Leon. One interpretation is that the German intention was to make this the organ of the Amsterdam Jewish Council and also the conduit for future German decrees which would effectively screen them from non-Jewish circles.[63] However, both Herzberg and Presser point out that German antisemitic decrees were not restricted to the *Joodse Weekblad* and some were not published in its pages at all, suggesting that 'insulation' was not the prime motive. They also note that the newspaper was also welcomed in Jewish circles as a means of bringing the Jews together as a community and for acting as an organ for pastoral and social messages. In retrospect it has been argued that its existence may have helped cohesion inside Jewish circles but only at the expense of increasing isolation from the rest of Dutch society.[64]

De Leon's fleeting celebrity in all this has also been closely examined. Little is known about him before the occupation, but he undoubtedly ingratiated himself with the Germans by suggesting a scheme for placing the Jewish unemployed in special camps to clear heathland, with a view to their later mass emigration to Palestine. This, together with his role in the *Joodse Weekblad*, made him a traitor in many eyes. The Germans did for a time champion his cause,[65] perhaps thinking that if his scheme was widely accepted it would make the task of concentrating the Jews even easier. They may even have considered him as an alternative leader for the Council instead of Asscher and Cohen. In the event, they dropped the idea, probably thinking that he could not command the level of support from the Jewish community which they required. Their insistence on his salaried editorship of the paper when it became the official organ of the Jewish Council may have been in the nature of a reward for services rendered, although de Leon played little or no part in the running of the *Joodse Weekblad* and ultimately became one of the early victims of the deportation programme in July 1942, deliberately placed on the list by Asscher and Cohen.[66] In assessing his role, Herzberg has no doubt that the Germans saw de Leon as some kind of 'rat-catcher' who would play Zionist tunes on his flute and lead the converted into the camps. This was clearly why the Jewish Council leadership were so worried about his potential role as a 'false messiah' and the credence given to him by the Germans. His fall into anonymity was the result of the occupiers' lack of confidence in him, although both Presser and Herzberg are moved to speculate whether the Jews could have fared any worse under his leadership than in the hands of Asscher and Cohen.[67]

Another pattern in the persecution of the Jews recurred in the spring of 1941. On 2 April S.L.A. Plekker, NSB leader and newly appointed mayor of Haarlem, published a series of by-laws which prohibited Jews from moving to or within the municipality, and excluded them from a wide range of public facilities.[68] Here again it seems that the indigenous NSB were setting the agenda for the isolation of the Jews, or at least acting in advance of the German administration, whether out of a commitment to antisemitic action or just to please their Nazi masters remains unclear. A matter of days later, the Germans began the process of concentrating the Jews in Amsterdam by banning any removals out of the city.

Further measures against the Jews followed thick and fast. They were ordered to surrender radio sets on 15 April and banned from owning them after 1 May. Jewish doctors, apothecaries, lawyers, translators and a range of other professional groups were forbidden to work for non-Jews and Jews were also banned from the stock and other commodity exchanges on the same day. Less than a week later, certain streets in Amsterdam were designated as 'Jewish streets', although this is as close as the Germans came to declaring a ghetto in the city. In mid-May orchestras were 'aryanised', and at the end of the same month all Jews were banned from using public parks and swimming baths in designated holiday areas. Beaches were also subject to segregation.[69]

The beginning of June saw the first restrictions on movement for Jews, but more serious was the first Jewish hostage-taking by the Germans through a *razzia* (raid) in Amsterdam on 11 June. In the previous four weeks there had been sporadic attempts at sabotage by resistance groups. A bomb attack on a house in the Schubertstraat used as a club by German *Kriegsmarine* officers in Amsterdam on 14 May had not produced any casualties, but a similar attack which destroyed the *Luftwaffe* telephone exchange at Schiphol on 3 June resulted in the one soldier being seriously injured. This prompted German retaliation. Lages was ordered to arrest 300 Jews between the ages of 18 and 35 for removal to Mauthausen. Carrying this out did pose some difficulties. Lages was afraid to use street raids for fear of provoking a response similar to that in February, and using the information available from the Jewish registration process might only lead to other future victims being forewarned. The solution was devious in the extreme. In March 1941 just over 200 trainees (mainly German refugees) from the Jewish agricultural college at Wieringermeer had been ordered back to Amsterdam by the Germans. Boarded out to families in the city, David Cohen had already approached the Germans to see if they could be sent back. In this way, he came into contact with Klaus Barbie, and it may have been the *Obersturmführer*'s idea to ask Cohen and Gertrud van Tijn (as leaders of the college's executive) to provide him with a list of addresses, ostensibly to facilitate the trainees' return to Wieringermeer.[70] Not suspecting the worst, van Tijn handed over the list. Lages and Barbie knew that the list would not furnish enough hostages on its own, and the police were therefore ordered to arrest not just the trainees, but all men falling within the given age range at the addresses they had been given.

On 11 June the Jewish Council sent word to the trainees that the Germans were coming to fetch them. Some became suspicious and did not return to their lodgings, but the Germans were still able to arrest 61 and the quota was made up with small street raids in Amsterdam-South, on cafés and on Jewish sports clubs.[71] From Amsterdam, the victims were taken to a camp at Schoorl and a few days later transferred to Mauthausen where all of them perished. By this time, death notices had started arriving in Amsterdam from the first group to be sent to Mauthausen via Buchenwald in February.[72] There could be little doubt that this second group would suffer the same fate. The Jewish Council met on 12 June to discuss the crisis, realising that Cohen had been duped into handing over the trainees. Asscher suggested closing down the Jewish Council altogether if the Germans were to act in this way. Cohen responded by asking who would be there to help the community if the Council disbanded. He also suggested that such a step might rebound to the detriment of those already in German camps and might lead to fresh reprisals. Ultimately, only the lawyer, Kisch, voted for dissolution and the rest against, including Asscher who had apparently been convinced by Cohen's arguments.[73] The College of Secretaries-General was also aware of the arrests, but felt it could do little itself, and suggested that only a Jew would be able to represent the interests of the hostages with the Germans. Neither was it prepared to negotiate an introduction to Rauter for the chosen intermediary. Lodewijk Visser expressed himself willing to intervene, even though he might suffer severe consequences for his actions. In the event, his attempt to see Rauter ended with an adjutant and the intervention came to nothing.[74]

Cohen and Gertrud van Tijn have been heavily criticised for their conduct in this affair and condemned as naïve for believing that the Germans really intended to return the trainees to the Wieringermeer. However, evidence suggests that the Germans did have plans for the training farm to be reoccupied prior to the bombings.[75] Moreover, when Gertrud van Tijn had been asked by Barbie on 9 June to furnish a list, she replied that the Gestapo already knew where the trainees lived because, as foreigners, they had been registered on their arrival in the city. Her view was that the list could only duplicate information which the Germans already had.[76] This rather different slant on circumstances does make the behaviour of Cohen and van Tijn more explicable. Nevertheless, the list undoubtedly made the Germans' task a good deal easier and also served to implicate the Jewish Council in the hostage-taking.

In many respects, this event can be seen as a turning point. The discussion and vote within the Jewish Council effectively set its course for the future, of co-operation rather than resistance through dissolution. The obvious German duplicity was also exposed, at least to the Council and its members. However, the main impact was to set a benchmark for the future. No one could be in any doubt what the term 'Mauthausen' meant when linked to the Jews.[77] This was always the threat which the Germans could bring into view when there was any hint of non-compliance with their wishes, and this was the fate from which the Jewish Council felt it was trying to defend the rest of Dutch Jewry.

The summer and early autumn brought a whole series of new regulations and restrictions on the Jews. In August all Jews were required to register their assets with Lippman-Rosenthal, a former Jewish bank taken over by the Germans to deal with the financial affairs of the Jews. Cheques and money had to be deposited in specially created accounts and all other stocks, shares and other deposits also had to be declared and handed over. On 15 September this registration was extended to include all land and property.[78] Jewish children were ordered to be schooled separately from 1 September onwards (1 October in Amsterdam). Protests came from the Catholic and Protestant schools when some 200 of their baptised pupils (whom the Germans regarded as full-Jews) were also included in the legislation. Rather than take on their protest, the Germans advised the Jewish Council to persuade the parents to back down lest reprisals were taken. As a result, the parents 'voluntarily' removed their children from the schools. A very small number of protests also came from the state schools, but usually from individual teachers, and the net result was that some 10,000 Jewish schoolchildren were henceforward educated separately. At the same time, the ability of Jewish university students to finish their studies were further curtailed.[79]

September also saw further restrictions with signs saying 'Forbidden for Jews' appearing in parks, zoos, hotels, cafés, guest houses, theatres, cabaret and concert halls, libraries and reading rooms. Herzberg notes the particular impact of library closures which excluded the Jews from the source of their culture.[80] In addition, their travelling was made subject to permit. It appears that, in line with the restrictions on Jews in holiday areas and resorts, the Germans and their NSB allies were increasingly unhappy about coming into contact with Jews in places of public recreation. At the same time, economic restrictions were hardened. An order of 22 October 1941 (VO 198/1941) decreed that all Jewish business employment could be subject to permits and conditions. Employers were also given permission to dismiss Jews at three months' notice and alter their pension provision. In practice this meant that any Jew in employment could be made redundant after 31 January 1942, and many Jews were dismissed without compensation while others had their pensions reduced or stopped entirely by employers keen to save money. At an early stage, on 1 November 1941, the Germans used the legislation in VO 198/1941 to rescind some 1,600 permits for Jews working in the textile and clothing trades. Stamp and antique dealers, together with all but two Jewish printing firms, were also shut down, with their stock and equipment being sold off to third parties. In mid-1942 the same decree was used to extend the exclusion of Jews from a whole raft of trades and professions.[81]

On 14 September a raid took place in *Twente* (the area close to the German border around the town of Enschede). A series of sabotage actions in that area served as a pretext for the Germans to order the local police to effect the arrest of 110 victims.[82] After two days, the whole group was deported to Mauthausen. Three weeks later, on 7–8 October, similar raids took place in the *Achterhoek*, Arnhem, Apeldoorn and Zwolle, again ostensibly because of sabotage actions in the region. This time, the authorities were less successful as many of the intended victims were warned in advance, by the police themselves, or by their own misgivings, into staying away from home. These raids require some further explanation. As a means of bringing home to local populations the reprisals which would be carried out for acts of sabotage, they were a great success.[83] Yet these were innocent people being victimised for crimes they had not committed. Was this a case where the Germans deliberately targeted the Jews because they were (to National Socialists) the obvious suspects, and that actions against others would admit that sections of the Dutch population no longer accepted German rule? While this pretence had probably been abandoned in Amsterdam after February 1941, could the same be said about the provinces? More likely, it was another example of Rauter and his subordinates attempting to demonstrate their strength in matters concerning the Jews.[84] Subsequently, the shooting of a German soldier in Haarlem prompted the Germans to seize and execute ten hostages, of whom three were Jews, the chairman of the town's Jewish community, the chief rabbi for *Noord-Holland* and the local representative of the Jewish Council.[85]

For the Germans, these raids demonstrated that local police and *Marechaussee* (Dutch state police) could not necessarily be relied upon to carry out measures against the Jews. For the Jews, this renewed victimisation made it clear that they would always be the targets when the Germans took reprisals. Moreover, they could look for little or no help from the Dutch state, its functionaries, or the Jewish Council, all of whom seemed powerless to stop or even ameliorate German actions. The process of isolation was already well under way. Whether such a clear pattern was apparent to the Jews in the Netherlands at the time cannot be directly ascertained, but inaction on their part may have been conditioned more by a lack of viable alternative responses than ignorance of what was being done.

One example of this was the German demand in September that all 16,000 German Jews should register for emigration with the *Zentralstelle*, even though very few of them were actually in possession of visas. The motive for this step had come from Seyss-Inquart's meeting with Hitler of 25 September, when the *Führer* had made it clear that the German refugees should be the first to be deported from the Netherlands.[86] Those involved had to complete over 30 separate forms, yet at the end of November, of 400 who had submitted their papers, not one had received an exit visa. In response to an enquiry from David Cohen, the Germans confirmed that the intention was to facilitate emigration overseas rather than deportation, though they gave no indications of where emigrants might be permitted to go, except to exclude Poland as a destination. While this had some effect, other reports created greater uncertainty. The first systematic mass deportations of Jews from Germany to Poland had begun on 16 October, and word of this was beginning to reach the Netherlands. German Jews also became aware that they had been stripped of their German citizenship. On 5 December all non-Dutch Jews were ordered to register for 'voluntary emigration'. Some panicked and there were a few suicides,[87] yet in the following months there were neither emigrations nor deportations and most non-Dutch Jews continued to set great store by registering for emigration.[88] Approximately one in eleven of the foreign Jews chose not to register, presumably to avoid any dealings with the Germans, and it appears that no further action was taken against them.[89]

In the same period, the Germans decided that unemployed Jews would be sent to work-camps. Since the summer of 1940, the Germans had attempted to entice Dutch workers to take up employment in Germany. This had quickly become coercive as the unemployed were informed that they and their families would lose any claim on state benefits if they refused a job offer in Germany without good cause. In some respects, this was nothing new as some previous Dutch governments had used employment opportunities in Germany in the later 1930s to force workers off state unemployment registers.[90] After the German occupation, there may have been as many as half a million unemployed workers in the country. Freed from political constraints, a number of the secretaries-general began a complete reorganisation of state controls over the labour exchange and benefit system, bringing in many provisions which had been politically unacceptable before the war. The net effect was to drive the unemployed into work in Germany, or into job-creation programmes in the Netherlands.[91] However, for the Germans, this created something of an anomaly, as the Jews were excluded from conscription to Germany and *Generalkommissar* Schmidt's scheme for work-camps in the summer of 1941 had been dropped.[92] In effect, the Jews were the only group who could continue to claim benefit without being enlisted for a job-creation programme, although in fact some unemployed Dutch Jews had already been deemed fit enough for the heavy labouring involved and drafted into the system. Nevertheless, this acted as a rehearsal for the resurrection of the scheme in October–November of the same year.

On 27 November the Jewish Council was informed that henceforward all unemployed Jews would be liable for compulsory transfer to separate labour camps and the health and fitness of those called up would be certified by Jewish doctors.[93] Apart from the fact that German decrees were increasing the numbers of Jewish unemployed by the day, there was little which the Jewish Council could do to protest against the measure. After all, labour service in job-creation programmes (mainly clearing heathland and working on land reclamation) had been an obligation for the unemployed for a number of years. The Jews could not argue that they were above something which was being inflicted on every other Dutch citizen. Strangely, nothing followed immediately from this meeting. Then, suddenly, six weeks later, the Jewish Council was informed by one of Böhmcker's subordinates, the fanatical antisemite Rodegro, that on Saturday 10 January at 10.00 a.m. precisely they should have 1,402 unemployed Jews present at Amsterdam Central Station for transport to work-camps in Drenthe. This gave them five days to organise suitable candidates and have them medically screened. The Jewish Council fell into line, although protesting long and hard about having to transport workers on the Sabbath.[94]

To find this number of workers, the Council called up 2,200 Jews in Amsterdam who were in receipt of state benefits, and a further 400 unemployed who were not. This, it was hoped, would provide the full quota. The requests to attend the medical examinations were sent out by the Municipal Social Affairs Department, but produced a very poor response. As a result, the authorities rounded up a large number of Jewish street traders and brought them to the screening centre at the Diamond Exchange building. Two Jewish doctors involved in the medical screening threatened to stop work and on the Friday *Het Joodse Weekblad* published a plea for all those who had been called up to attend and, if found fit, to go to the work-camps which were under Dutch control. Those who disobeyed were threatened with the most serious consequences.[95] In the end, only 1,075 men were passed fit and, of these, 170 did not come to the station on the Saturday morning.[96] The ones who did were transported to eastern Netherlands, then in the grip of winter. Two days earlier, all the workers in other camps had been sent home because the frost had made the ground unworkable.[97] The frost lasted until April, but this did not prevent further call-ups of unemployed Jews and their transmission to camps. In March, Rodegro indicated that he wanted Jews still in work to be conscripted for labour service as well.[98] The head of the Amsterdam labour exchange made it clear that he had no legal right to do this and could only call people up for screening. In any case, he did not have the addresses of working Jews. It was therefore a question of whether the Jewish Council was prepared to hand them over.[99]

Again, this was a moment when the joint-chairmen of the Jewish Council might have halted their course towards total co-operation with German demands. The minutes of the Council meeting of 5 March indicate yet another compromise. In order to 'forestall disruptions as far as possible', it was agreed to hand over the names of unmarried men between the ages of 18 and 40 with the exception of religious leaders, teachers, doctors and skilled technicians.[100] With this help, the Germans were able to go on increasing the numbers of Jews in the work-camps during the spring and summer of 1942. The Jewish Council had been assured that conditions in these camps would be the same as for all other work-camps in the Netherlands, yet the experiences of the first inmates – sent out in the worst of the winter – should have alerted them that the Germans were to apply a different standard to the Jews. After two months, the quantity of the rations was reduced, the sick were not sent home and the wages paid were 25 per cent lower than elsewhere.[101] By September, between 7,000 and 7,500 Jews had been conscripted for 37 camps spread all over the eastern and southern Netherlands. The camp population reached a peak in that month with a total of 5,242 inmates.[102] The civil servant charged with inspections described them as 'in reality, concentration camps run by the *Rijksdienst voor de werkverruiming* [State Employment-Creation Office]'.[103] By this stage, the Jewish doctors charged with screening those called up had been replaced by National Socialists. The Germans had become concerned by the numbers of Jews being exempted from labour service by the doctors, who tended to take specialists' certificates (which the rich found easier to obtain than the poor) at face value and tried to find fault with as many candidates as possible. This all changed when the Jewish doctors were dismissed. The Nazis who replaced them passed nearly everyone and took no notice either of medical notes or of genuine incapacities and afflictions.[104]

Not surprisingly, the Jewish Council was held responsible for this treatment, both by the (working-class) victims and by their dependants. They were referred to as the Jewish treason (*verraad*) or trouble (*onraad*). Certainly, the fact that the Jewish professional classes appeared to be excluded did not help matters. Men called up were in some cases being hauled away from perfectly good jobs, given no home leave and paid a paltry 14 guilders a week. There were also delays in dependants receiving money from their breadwinners' new employment. When a group went to complain to the Jewish Council that they had no money for food or rent, they were left to wait while the chairmen finished their food and smoked their cigars.[105] Even Rodegro, who was in charge of commissioning labour drafts on behalf of the German authorities, had protested that there were no rich Jews on the lists called up for labour service.[106] The Council was also widely criticised in the illegal press for its attitude to the German demands. According to de Jong, Cohen was uninterested in what Jewish proletarians or lower-middle-class traders thought of his actions, but was sufficiently concerned about the views of his peers to convene a meeting in the spring of 1942 to discuss the criticisms. Here he put forward the rationale for the Council's actions, that basic compliance, coupled with attempts to sabotage the system from within, would draw out the proceedings much longer, while rejection would provoke a quick and brutal German response.[107] In effect, Cohen argued his case on the basis that it was the best available option and that the potential alternatives were far worse. This point has also been cited by Herzberg, as a partial defence for the Council's attitude to work-camps. He argues that as the numbers of Jewish unemployed increased, the Council was informed by the Dutch authorities that there was no chance that the Germans would allow these people to remain at liberty indefinitely (as other non-Jewish unemployed workers were placed in Dutch camps or sent to work in Germany). Since October 1941, the Nazis had been deporting the Jews from Germany into the ghettoes of Eastern Europe, therefore the only way to prevent the Germans from doing the same to Dutch Jews was to co-operate in the work-camp scheme and thereby at least keep them in the country.[108]

While the unemployed Jews were being conscripted to work-camps, the Germans introduced a new series of measures. These involved the removal of all non-Dutch Jews to the camp at Westerbork, and the concentration of all Dutch Jews in Amsterdam. At the beginning of 1942, the Germans commissioned the building of 20 new barrack blocks at Westerbork and informed the Jewish Council of their plans. The chairmen could not sway the decision. De Jong argues that Cohen and Asscher must have known that even with the new accommodation, Westerbork could not hold the approximately 20,000 non-Dutch Jews then living in the Netherlands, and therefore that they must also have known that the Germans intended to deport those involved. Was it the case that they hoped this was just directed against German Jews, or that the process would take so long that the Dutch Jews would never come into the reckoning for future action? Certainly, Cohen and Asscher had no opposition within the Council simply because the non-Dutch Jews were not represented there.[109]

Both this and the concentration of the Jews in Amsterdam began with the removal of all Jews from certain provincial towns.[110] The victims were informed that, on a certain day, they would be required to hand over their house keys to the Dutch police. They could take with them only what they could carry, and a list of the house contents was to be left with the police.[111] The Germans also set up a special section of the *Zentralstelle*, the *Hausraterfassungsstelle*, to provide a complete registration of the property. The collection of effects and house clearing was carried out by yet another office, the *Einsatzstab Rosenberg*. Inevitably, the relocation of so many people, either to Westerbork or to specific neighbourhoods in Amsterdam, was a bureaucratic nightmare. The Jewish Council and its various subsidiaries co-operated fully in trying to find accommodation, initially by asking Jewish house-owners in Amsterdam to take in new arrivals. This proved less than successful and the City Council set up a special office to investigate spare capacity in Jewish dwellings, but in April and May its inspectors only found 360 spare beds in nearly 2,700 houses.[112]

Even if the pace of rehousing was determined by the shortage of space (Westerbork was deemed full in May, and some German Jews from

Hilversum were brought to Amsterdam as a result), the Germans had established most of the bureaucratic institutions they would require to deprive the Jews of their remaining property and effect their deportation. In the spring and early summer of 1942, the Germans also continued the isolation of the Jews from the rest of the Dutch population. In February their identity papers (*persoonsbewijs*) were stamped with a letter 'J' or 'B'.[113] Henceforward, any Jew stopped by the authorities would immediately be marked out by his or her documents. On 23 March Seyss-Inquart decided that the remaining elements of the Nuremberg Laws should be introduced in the Netherlands. Many of their provisions had long since been superseded by other restrictive legislation, but the main effect was to prohibit marriage and sexual relations between Jews and non-Jews.[114] This step was never the subject of a formal decree and Seyss-Inquart merely instructed the authorities to act as though the laws had been formally introduced. Four days later, *Het Joodse Weekblad* carried an article outlining what the new policy meant and Jews betrothed to non-Jews had to report to the Sipo. Those who complied with this latter stipulation were arrested. The women were sent to Ravensbrück and the men, after fearful mistreatment at the camp in Amersfoort, to Mauthausen where they all died.[115] The late and rather obtuse introduction of this measure may have been due to the complications it would have caused if a formal decree had been drafted. Using racial definitions to legislate might well have brought into question the many marriages between Dutch 'aryans' and Indonesians.[116] This was one can of worms which the German authorities preferred to keep closed.

Further restrictions and prohibitions followed. For example, Jews were forbidden to use private cars, and at funerals only the coffin could be carried by the hearse.[117] In 1940 and 1941 the WA and NSB had encountered public protest when they enthusiatically attempted to place signs saying 'Forbidden for Jews' in cafés, restaurants and public places. However, in the spring of 1942 the same task was carried out by the Dutch authorities at the behest of the Germans, and with very little open protest. This may have been a function of the increasing NSB influence within the Dutch administration. Certainly, the *Procureur-Generaal* in Leeuwarden, an ardent NSB member, tolerated no exceptions and even had signs placed outside vestries.[118] However, enforcing these bans was difficult if the Jews could not easily be identified. As a result, the end of April brought a far more dangerous obligation for all Jews in the Netherlands, namely the requirement to wear a yellow six-pointed star on all outer clothing. In line with previous behaviour, the Germans gave the Jewish Council precisely three days to implement the measure. Some latitude was grudgingly given by Aus der Fünten when it became clear that distribution at such short notice was impossible, but after 4 May the regulations against Jews not wearing stars were rigorously enforced.[119]

The introduction of the star gave renewed impetus to implement measures designed to further restrict Jewish interaction in Dutch society. Now that they had been rendered easily visible, Jews were excluded from a number of streets around the parliament and government buildings in The Hague. The Germans also verbally forbade the Jews from engaging in sports activities in public, but made this clear only by organising a raid to arrest Jews at sports clubs and then sending them to Westerbork. Jews were banned from the fish-market, forbidden to buy or eat fruit and forced to buy their greengroceries from Jewish vendors in fixed Jewish markets. Later they were to be excluded from all non-Jewish shops except between 3.00 p.m. and 5.00 p.m. Their ability to travel was also severely curtailed and after 12 June all bicycles and other vehicles had to be handed in to the authorities. The expropriation of bicycles was extended to the entire population in the following month as the Germans attempted to turn the Dutch 'from a cycling nation to a walking nation'.[120] However, if this latter measure was directed more towards acquiring transportation for German use, its earlier application to the Jews was deliberately designed to limit their ability to travel. All of these measures were enforceable because the Jews could now be easily identified.

By this stage, it must have been apparent to the Jews in the Netherlands that there was to be no halt to German measures against them. Many of the restrictions such as those on bicycles and radio sets were ultimately also inflicted on the population at large. Conscription to work-camps was the fate of both non-Jewish and Jewish unemployed. This made it difficult for Jews to make a case for staying away, even though conditions for them were worse and the schemes were rapidly extended to include those who were still in work. Jewish reactions to the gradual process of their isolation between January 1941 and the summer of 1942 cannot be considered as homogenous. Decrees and restrictions had differing effects on individuals, depending on their circumstances. At each stage, the person had to make a decision whether to comply or to disobey. Compliance would lead from minor inconveniences through major disadvantages to an ultimate surrender of personal liberty, yet the alternative was almost inconceivable. Disobedience to 'officialdom' was alien to most Dutch Jews – as it was to the rest of the population. Moreover, refusing to register oneself, surrender property or comply with the numerous antisemitic decrees would bring down the full weight of both German and Dutch legal and executive bureaucratic apparatus on an individual who had no resort to any form of organised support. With the exception of those Jews who were closely tied to the (clandestine) left-wing political parties, the only body to fulfil this role was the Jewish Council, and its policy was invariably one of compliance with German wishes. The isolation of the Jews in the Netherlands was all but complete by the summer of 1942, yet it remains almost impossible fully to comprehend the true nature of this isolation in the minds of ordinary Jewish families.

|5|

Deportation and extermination

The deportations

The deportations of Jews from the Netherlands began in the high summer of 1942. By this stage, there was no question that the whole process was being governed by orders from Berlin. On 27 May the Chief of the Sipo and SD, Reinhard Heydrich, was mortally wounded by assassins in Prague and died eight days later. It has been argued that this provided the impetus for accelerating action against the Jews in Western Europe. Certainly it was the case that the planning for the deportations from France, Belgium and the Netherlands took place before Heydrich's successor had been appointed, which suggests that at this point Eichmann was taking orders directly from Himmler. On 22 June Eichmann informed *Legationsrat* Rademacher at the German Foreign Office that it was intended to 'evacuate' 40,000 Jews from occupied France, 10,000 from Belgium and 40,000 from the Netherlands to Auschwitz at the rate of 1,000 per day. Sijes points out that these quotas had been altered from an original meeting at the RSHA on 11 June when the figure demanded from the Netherlands had been only 15,000.[1] This radical change may have been the result of doubts expressed by functionaries such as *Judenreferent* Theodor Dannecker in Paris about his ability to meet the original figure for France (50,000 each from the occupied and unoccupied zones), especially if it meant widening the net to include French Jews in addition to the foreigners who had been the sole targets of the deportations begun in March. By June, meeting quotas was already proving problematic.[2] Conversely there had been few problems in identifying and isolating the Jews in the Netherlands, with the result that the country was probably considered capable of rendering a larger proportion of its Jews than had been originally stipulated.[3]

News of this new order was given to the members of the Jewish Council on 26 June by Aus der Fünten who informed them that men and women between the ages of 16 and 40 years of age would have to be registered for 'police-controlled labour contingents' to work in Germany. The Council was told that it would be asked to say how many people it could process each day.[4] This new request, to collaborate in deportations to the East, again led to soul-searching amongst the members of the Council when it met the following day. Some, at least, suggested ending all co-operation, but none resigned when the majority decided that continuing to work might delay the implementation of new measures and that they should press for exemptions for leading Jews to retain a strong core for the rebuilding of Jewish society in the Netherlands. It was also argued that shutting down the Council would play into the hands of the more radical Germans and provide them with a pretext for even harsher measures. Once again, the Council chose the path of co-operation rather than confrontation, but it is questionable whether this was a real choice. By trying to meet German demands, the Council members would be among those who were protected, while to disobey would make them and their families the prime targets for reprisals. To sweeten the medicine, Aus der Fünten confirmed that the labour camps were all in Germany and that all the executive work would be done by the German police and the Council staff would only be registering those to be sent eastwards.[5]

Getting the Council to co-operate was only one of the Germans' tasks. Up to this point, the measures against the Jews had been dictated primarily by internal conditions and subject to timescales which could be altered or amended by Seyss-Inquart, Rauter or Böhmcker. Now the timetable was being set by Berlin and it was Himmler and Eichmann who were dictating both the dates of the deportation and the numbers involved. From this point onwards, the German leadership in the Netherlands had to meet targets or face the consequences. This imperative – to meet the needs of the deportation process as dictated by the killing capacity of the extermination centres in the East – became the central objective and can explain the often duplicitous behaviour of the lower-ranking functionaries like Lages, Zöpf and Aus der Fünten. All their actions were geared towards having a sufficient number of Jews in the transit camp at Westerbork to fill the twice-weekly trains. How this was achieved and who was deported could only be of secondary importance.

In many respects, they were well prepared for the task. The Jewish Council had shown itself compliant and in some respects positively helpful in the processes of identification and isolation. The complete registration of the Jews in the early months of 1941 had been used to compile a detailed card index of names and addresses. This had been done by the *Zentralstelle* with help from Jewish Council personnel. This access to detailed information coupled with the Jews' concentration in Amsterdam and the presence of several thousand males in work-camps and German 'refugees' in Westerbork gave the Germans a large 'reserve' supply of victims to make good any shortfalls in the numbers required for deportation. However, the initial victims of deportation were to come from Amsterdam itself and the first 4,000 were required for transport from 14–17 July. The staff of the *Zentralstelle* made the initial selections from the card index. The first letters were sent out to those 'selected' for deportation on 4 July and delivered the following day. Each of those summoned had to report to the offices of the *Zentralstelle* where they would be given forms to be completed and returned with the help of Jewish Council staff.[6] This made it essential to insist on the Council meeting minimum targets for registrations before the trains left Amsterdam for Westerbork. Many of the first victims selected were from the refugee community (and in line with overall German policy to begin by targeting the non-nationals in the countries concerned).[7]

The first two weeks of July saw feverish activity in a number of quarters. The Jewish Council worked to help process the paperwork of those to be sent eastwards. It was at this stage that the individual had to make the decision of whether to comply or not. Whether the German authorities became aware of a potential for non-compliance from non-attendance at the *Zentralstelle*, or saw the reaction to the possibility of exemption as a sign that most Jews would not willingly give themselves up for labour service in Germany, it is impossible to say. Whatever the cause, they were sufficiently worried to take pre-emptive action. From 12 July, orders to register for deportation were no longer sent by post, but delivered personally by the police. Even this seems to have had little effect as many people ordered to report on 13 July did not appear.[8] Therefore, on the day the first tranche of deportees were due to report to Amsterdam Central Station some 700 Jews were taken from the streets in all parts of the city and held at the German Security Police Headquarters as hostages against the appearance of those called-up.[9] The threat was that they would be sent to Mauthausen if the quotas were not met. The Jewish Council was prepared to use this threat to try and ensure compliance and sent out a circular to all those called up, 'we feel obliged to impress on you the gravity of the situation. Think carefully. The fate of 700 fellow-Jews is at stake.'[10] In the event, 962 people reported to the station and were conveyed in two trains to Hooghalen (at that time the nearest station to Westerbork). This was a considerably smaller number than the Germans had hoped for, and the quota of deportees sent to Auschwitz by train on 15 and 16 July had to be made up with inmates from Westerbork camp.[11] Even at this stage, the German authorities in the Netherlands were having to dip into their 'reserves' in order to meet their quotas.

When the first call-up letters had been received, their impact was enormous, not just on the recipients but also on their families and neighbours. When it was discovered during and after the *razzia* of 14 July that the possibility of exemption existed, the premises of the Jewish Council were swamped. At this stage, the Council merely removed its own workers from

the lists in line with an agreement reached with Aus der Fünten on 30
June. Later on the system was to become far more formalised and controlled in every aspect except total numbers, by the Council itself. It could
be argued that this also indicated a change in the Council's behaviour.
From having tried to protect the majority by conniving at the sacrifice of
the minority for labour service inside the Netherlands, the Council's efforts
were now specifically directed at saving a minority 'essential to the life of
the Jewish community in the Netherlands',[12] at the expense of the majority
who would be unprotected and therefore liable for deportation as and
when they were called up.

The rest of July saw a further seven transports from Amsterdam to
Westerbork and the deportation of a further 3,948 people from there to
Auschwitz. Some minor changes were made to the systems used to call up
Jews and the criteria for those eligible. First of all, the age range was
increased to include all those up to 50 years old. Secondly, it became
apparent that the *Zentralstelle* offices were simply not large enough to
accommodate the work involved, and the Portuguese synagogue in the
Jonas Daniël Meyerplein was pressed into service. It was also decided to
move the collection point away from the Central Station to the former
Hollandse Schouwburg theatre building, subsequently referred to as the
Joodse Schouwburg.[13] This may have been for 'cosmetic' reasons, to take
the process of deportation away from a very public place and therefore out
of sight of the citizens of Amsterdam, even though the trains departed in
the middle of the night. Alternatively, it may have been done to provide an
enclosed holding area so that once people had been registered they could
be held without fear of non-attendance when the time came for their train
to leave.

These first call-ups and deportations set the pattern for what was to follow over the next 15 months. From the beginning, it was clear that quotas
were unlikely to be met entirely from those selected by the *Zentralstelle*.
This was confirmed by the the poor attendance for the transport of 3
August and prompted a further raid on *Amsterdam-Zuid* by the German
police on 6 August, this time reinforced by the *Politiebataljon Amsterdam*,
a specially trained force of Dutch policemen. Cordoning off a series of
streets, the men then began house-to-house searches, often with great brutality. This action yielded around 1,600 Jews, of whom approximately
1,000 seem to have been released after being screened at the *Zentralstelle*,
apparently by Aus der Fünten personally, and only the remaining 600 were
sent on to Westerbork and then to Auschwitz.[14] A day later, the Germans
continued their threats against those who had not reported when
instructed. A special edition of *Het Joodse Weekblad* made it clear that they
would be sent to Mauthausen, as would any Jews caught not wearing a star
or changing their address without notifying the authorities. These new regulations seem to have had little effect as a further raid was instituted on 9

August, carried out this time by members of the Sipo in civilian clothes on a more prosperous part of the city.[15]

Again these raids provide evidence that the local German bureaucracy was now tied to quotas ordered by Berlin. Cohen records a meeting with Aus der Fünten on the morning of 6 August where the latter made it clear that the trains had to be filled and that he 'had no alternative'.[16] Whether Aus der Fünten was genuinely upset about what he was being asked to do, as Cohen suggests, remains open to question, but the results of his actions are incontrovertible, the trains were filled and the transports went on. The Jewish Council, unable to stop the pace or extent of the round-ups, extended their bureaucratic activities to providing for those being deported. Staff were transferred to Westerbork to deal with the day-to-day problems of those in transit or being held in the camp, others still were employed at the *Joodse Schouwburg* or in providing basic necessities for those who had not been given time to prepare for their departure. All of this reinforced the impression that the deportation for labour in Germany was real and that the deportees would have to establish themselves in a new environment.

None of the threats, nor the experience of the German raids in Amsterdam, encouraged people to report voluntarily for 'labour service' and deportation. As a result, the Germans stepped up the process of terror against the Jews still further. Raids and house searches were increased to the point where the Jewish Council suggested that people had their 'bags packed at all times' and recorded that call-ups and deportations were taking place so quickly that people should bear in mind that there would not be sufficient time to put their affairs in order.[17] By this stage, any pretence of retaining the age limits for deportees had been dropped as many elderly people were seized, along with entire families.[18] Meetings with the German authorities, such as one on 8 September, failed to produce any changes in the system. The only concession obtained was a formalisation of the exemption system. The Council had complained that the speed of the round-ups and subsequent deportation had made it impossible to investigate individual cases and apply for exemptions. The one concession made by the Germans was to allow those who were supposedly exempted from labour service, like Jewish Council staff, schoolteachers, Jews in mixed marriages and those working directly for the war effort, to carry a special stamp on their identity papers.

The system of exemptions became quite complex. It had started in the summer of 1942, when after 30 July a list of Council staff and other 'indispensable' people in both Amsterdam and the provinces was drawn up and they were issued with safe-conducts signed by the General Secretary of the Jewish Council, Bolle. With German agreement, this system was extended so that protected people received a numbered stamp on their identity papers, the number indicating the reason of the exemption: thus foreign

Jews were given numbers in the range 10,000–20,000, baptised Protestant Jews, 20,000–30,000, and so on. By far the largest group were the 17,500 exemptions granted to the Jewish Council for distribution to its employees. The Council chairmen had originally asked for 35,000 but this had been halved by Aus der Fünten.[19] Having agreed to the idea, the Council was then placed in the invidious position of having to make choices about whom to protect. The stamps were therefore issued to what the Council leaders regarded as the 'core' of Jewish society. Lists were drawn up based on the original work of Bolle and updated. A list of 11,000 Jews from the provinces was largely disregarded as they were about to be forcibly moved to Amsterdam.[20] Few, presumably, received any form of exemption and the vast majority were thereby immediately rendered vulnerable to deportation on their arrival in Amsterdam.

The issue of exemption stamps began on 16 September, with the first of the Jewish Council exemptions being made some 12 days later. The lists of those exempted also included names of wives and children under 16. The stamps merely said that the holder was 'exempted from labour service [in both Germany and the Netherlands] until further notice'. This was hardly a cast-iron guarantee of security, but given the experience of continued round-ups by the Germans in the streets and houses of Amsterdam, it is hardly surprising that anyone with real or imagined influence struggled to get their names, and those of their family, on to the lists of those protected by stamps. Presser quotes from Gertrud van Tijn's memoirs.

> When the first stamps were issued, the scenes at the Jewish Council were quite indescribable. Doors were broken, the staff of the Council was attacked, and the police had often to be called in .... The stamps quickly became an obsession with every Jew.[21]

While the granting of most exemptions rested on practical grounds of religious affiliation, nationality or employment in war industry, the 17,500 stamps allocated to the Jewish Council were essentially in the gift of the Council's leadership and its so-called 'exemption committee'. Both at the time and subsequently, the way in which stamps were allocated has led to charges of favouritism and corruption: that the Council saved itself and those people closest to it, at the expense of all others. The Council's perception of protecting a 'core' of Jewish society was based on the idea that its staff, and the (Amsterdam) class they represented, were that core. Most of the indictments against the Council for its handling of the issue (and there were many who thought it should have never reached the position of making such selections) came from those who were left unprotected, but charges of favouritism also came from within the organisation itself. The head of an important section of the Council wrote to the 'exemption committee' to ask why he was not being allocated enough exemptions to protect his staff, while the parents and parents-in-law of other employees, and even trainees and people who had done little or nothing for the work of the Council, were getting exemptions every day.[22] Presser is equivocal on the subject. He maintains that it would have been amazing if corruption and nepotism had not played some role in the allocation of exemptions. Quoting Cohen's justification for the inclusion of so many of the 'elite' among the 17,500 that discrimination was unavoidable because the Council's work required administrative training, he also points out that if the 'proletarians' were not so trained, neither were so many sons or brothers of more influential Jews.[23] The charges are difficult to refute.

The background to the scramble for protection, even though this was ultimately an illusion, was the continued nightly cycle of police raids. For those without a stamp, each night became a torment, listening for the sound of cars in the street after curfew or waiting for the knock on the door. There are relatively few records of the fears and horrors experienced by those left unprotected in their homes. Those which have survived have been often retold[24] and paint a harrowing and almost unimaginable picture of people under terrific strain, not knowing the full import of what 'labour service' meant, but realising that it would be much worse than their present circumstances and in any case afraid of the untrammelled power which the German authorities and their police 'servants' were able to wield. At the same time, the possibility of salvation was extremely limited as most escape routes had long since been closed. Paper protection through stamps was confined to a fortunate few, who may have been lulled into a false sense of security precisely because they did possess a stamp. The only alternative was to go underground, but for the majority this step into illegality was as impractical as it was unthinkable.

The scale and ferocity of the raids in the summer had convinced almost every Jew that there was no point in volunteering to report when called up by the *Zentralstelle* as the Germans were going to meet their quotas anyway. In practice this meant that almost all the transports from Amsterdam were being filled by people seized by the German police and their Dutch counterparts. This system was, in itself, imprecise, as the police had no idea how many people they were likely to arrest in house searches and raids on the 'Jewish' areas of Amsterdam. As a result, some of those taken spent days or even weeks held at the *Joodse Schouwburg* before being escorted to the Central Station for conveyance to Westerbork and beyond. This sometimes provided for the possibility of escape or temporary protection, but only for a very few. It also produced horrendous living conditions when hundreds or even thousands of people were seized and held there until the next scheduled transport. This was a theatre building, largely unreconstructed and unadapted for its new role. Inmates slept where they could and suffered in the heat when the plumbing and water supply was inadequate. In the meantime, the Germans had turned their attention to other concentrations of Jews which provided easy targets. During the day, they began to target Jewish old-people's homes. The occupants, old, sick and defenceless, were all carried away indiscriminately. This finally gave the lie to the idea that deportees were being selected primarily as a labour force.[25] In similar fashion, the Germans also began to clear out the Jewish orphanages. Just like adults, the children were sacrificed to meet the unremitting imperative of the quota.

The other main group of captives were the Jews already held in work-camps in the Netherlands. In the autumn, the German authorities took steps to increase the pace of arrests. This was to include the families and dependants still at large of men in the work-camps, but also a further 5,000 Jews from Amsterdam. To do this, they required the services of all the available agencies. German and Dutch police, NSB, Dutch SS and German Nazi Party functionaries and the personnel of the *Zentralstelle* were all drafted in for a series of mass raids which took place on 2–3 October.[26] The only Jews safe from this action were those with exemptions, baptised Protestants, and people suffering from diphtheria, scarlet fever or typhoid. Even some foreign Jews were now ordered to be arrested.[27] Between 13,000 and 15,000 Jews were apprehended in this short period.[28] Presser notes that although the Dutch police had more men involved than any other agency, they managed to arrest a mere 700 people.[29] This suggests that they warned many of the intended victims or gave them time to escape if this was practical. The action also covered the provinces where there were examples both of Dutch bureaucratic co-operation with the Germans and of attempts to undermine the efficiency of the operation.[30] Certainly, in Amsterdam, the Jews had had advance warning of what was about to happen. Apart from the probability that some individuals had been tipped off by contacts in the police, there was the presence of so many policemen in the streets and the appearance of many extra trains at the Central Station. Although the rumours and then the actuality of the raids filled the Jewish population with panic, there was little they could do to stop the arrests or save themselves. All the victims of these raids were sent directly to Westerbork, where at least 3,000 had to sleep on the ground as the camp buildings were too small to hold all the new arrivals.[31]

It appears that this new action was carried out at the behest of Rauter, who had boasted in letters to Himmler on 10 and 24 September that the work-camps had 7,000 or 8,000 Jewish inmates, no longer referred to as volunteers, who could be sent to the East. Moreover, he claimed they had around 22,000 dependants who could also be caught and deported.[32] While these figures were exaggerations, there seems little doubt that Rauter was trying to impress his superior with his diligence. This view of the major round-up as a local initiative is reinforced by the fact that the transports from Westerbork to Auschwitz did not increase in frequency or size in the following weeks and months. The raids of 2–3 October had provided a large 'reserve' to make up the transports for subsequent weeks which more or less removed the need for further captures. They had also demonstrated that while large sections of the Dutch population were unlikely to protest openly about the deportations – as they had done in February 1941 – they were equally unshaken in their support for the Jews. In August a group of 50 Jews held outside the *Zentralstelle* in the Adema van Scheltemaplein were given food by the locals[33] and an October report by the *Wehrmacht-kommandantur* in The Hague noted Jews taken to stations accompanied by local townspeople with tears and with fond farewells. In Gouda even the local police apparently took part in this passive protest and declaration of solidarity.[34]

Some Jewish workers who had received temporary exemption from deportation because of their economic importance also became targets towards the end of the year. Their story demonstrates clearly the tensions between the German economic exploitation of the Netherlands and the fulfilment of the 'Final Solution' against the Jews. In the summer of 1942, the officials of IVB4 and the *Zentralstelle* had agreed to exempt 2,250 Jewish workers, but the *Rüstungsinspektion* (Office for German Military Economic Affairs) and *Zentralauftragsstelle* (Office for German Civilian Economic Affairs) were met with strong protests from Dutch employers in certain sectors of the economy that this limited distribution of exemptions would rob them of large sections of their workforces. At this stage, neither Aus der Fünten nor the head of the *Rüstungsinspektion*, Rear-Admiral Reimer, were prepared to compromise, but when it became clear that more than 3,000 workers in the clothing industry were left unprotected and advertisements for replacements had generated only 16 replies, the German economic agencies realised that there was a problem. At that time, large sections of the industry were taken up with providing clothes for the German domestic market, and the Hollandia works in *Amsterdam-Noord* was working exclusively on contracts for Rommel's *Afrika-Korps*. When in August the *Zentralstelle* tried to cut the numbers exempted still further, the *Rüstungsinspektion* and *Zentralauftragsstelle* mobilised all their influence and succeeded in having the number of exempt workers raised to 4,300. Given that each exemption also covered wives and children, the number of people protected by stamps represented a considerable group within Dutch Jewry.

In the event, the protection afforded to this group was short-lived. De Jong describes it as a thorn in the flesh for IVB4 and the *Zentralstelle*. On 11 November the Hollandia works was raided on the pretext that it was being used as a base for underground Communist activity. The victims were deported some three weeks later.[35] Against this type of charge, the economic organisations had no real defence and had to concede the gradual reduction of exemptions for those considered economically important. By March 1943, the number of workers with exemptions had been reduced to 1,842 and Seyss-Inquart had meanwhile insisted that all exemptions should be rescinded by the end of May.[36] Although the numbers of Jews deemed to be important for the German war effort was substantial, these events suggest that neither the organisations charged with overseeing German economic interests nor the military commanders had the will or the power to withstand Rauter's power when backed by Himmler. This does seem to be a contrast with other Western European countries where Jews considered economically important were afforded greater protection by these agencies and where the influence of the SS was commensurately smaller.[37]

By the end of the year, *c*.40,000 Jews had been transported from the Netherlands to the East, but the work went on.[38] From the beginning of 1943, Jewish hospitals, orphanages and sanatoria were targeted.[39] The Germans had obtained figures for the end of December which suggested that there were around 8,000 Jewish patients in hospitals around the country. By far the largest single concentration was in the Jewish psychiatric hospital *Het Apeldoornse Bos*, just outside Apeldoorn in the Veluwe. There had been rumours earlier in the autumn that the hospital was to be cleared and the inmates deported in order to make room for patients from Germany, but in spite of their respectable provenance, the director had refused to believe them, or to take any possible precautions.[40] There is evidence that a number of German and Dutch agencies had their eyes on the site and its buildings, and this seems to have been the motivation for the final decision to clear the hospital. At the beginning of January, Rauter issued orders to have the site investigated for its suitablity as an SS facility. Aus der Fünten was sent to investigate and on 20 January a squad of *Orde Dienst* men from Westerbork arrived. They were used to help organise the departure of the inmates. Some members of staff and patients drew the appropriate inference from this and went into hiding, but for the majority of patients, and many of the staff who refused to leave their charges, this was not an option. Then on the night of 21–22 January a detachment of *Schutzpolizei* arrived to escort the deportees to Apeldoorn station. Led by Aus der Fünten, the man who six months earlier had apparently been regretful for the deportations, the German police ransacked the building and horribly beat and maltreated many of the (defenceless) inmates. In a catalogue of crimes against the Jews in the Netherlands, this is regarded by authors as the most cowardly and reprehensible. The deportees were thrown into lorries and transported to the cordoned-off station. The same 'horrible and bestial behaviour' befell the children who were also taken to the station and loaded on to the cattle wagons. The train with the patients and 50 nurses was sent directly to Auschwitz where nearly all were gassed immediately on arrival and none of the remainder survived the war.[41]

While this action was apparently instigated by Rauter, it is clear that officials in Berlin were directly involved. According to Harster, because of the difficulties involved with this particular transport, Eichmann had been consulted and had given permission for the hospital to be cleared. He had also provided the train and (presumably) the order that it should proceed directly to Auschwitz rather than via Westerbork.[42] Moreover, this was one of a number of similar actions against other Jewish institutions, suggesting that acquiring the premises of *Het Apeldoornse Bos* was not the primary, or even the main reason for its clearance. In the following two months, all the Jewish hospitals, sanatoria, old-people's homes and orphanages were cleared and their patients and children sent to Westerbork, irrespective of their state of health. On 1 March the large Jewish hospital in Amsterdam, the *Joodse Invalide,* was raided. The staff had been forewarned and many had fled before the Germans arrived. However, the patients, most of them old and infirm or sick, could not escape and were rounded up by the SS who then proceeded to ransack the building. Two days later, the *Nederlands-Israëlitisch* Hospital was also raided. After the attack on the *Joodse Invalide*, many of the staff and patients had taken fright and left. Even those who were not fit to be moved were collected by relatives and taken away on handcarts. When the raid took place, there remained only a small core of staff and a few very ill patients.[43] In this raid, the Germans were able to apprehend 130 pensioners and 50 from the hospital itself. No one who witnessed the nature of these particular raids and transport of children and the sick in body or mind, or the brutal way in which the victims were treated, could have been left in any doubt that deportation for labour service was anything more than a façade.

In the early months of 1943, there were also some changes to German policy. Until then, the occupiers had relied primarily on the gaol at Amersfoort to hold political and punishment cases arrested by the German police. This facility clearly had its limits and it was decided to create a new 'proper' concentration camp at Vught (near 's-Hertogenbosch) in Brabant. This would act both as a labour and a holding camp for political undesirables, criminals and Jews, with the latter carefully segregated from the rest. The first 250 inmates arrived from Amersfoort in the middle of January, followed almost immediately by a further 450 from Amsterdam, many of whom had been in possession of exemptions for war-work. The Jewish population of the camp grew rapidly as more people were sent there from Amsterdam, and then from the rest of the country when Rauter banned all the remaining Jews except those in mixed marriages from the provinces. On 2 May the population of this new camp had reached 8,700.[44] The general initiative for this change seems to have come from the RSHA in Berlin where Himmler had ordered that concentration camps should be more effectively utilised to meet the needs of the war effort. This allowed the Germans in the Netherlands to contemplate the idea of moving Jews exempted from deportation as useful to the war economy to specially built factories inside Vught. These included a satellite from the Philips factory in Eindhoven, clothing, fur and rag-sorting enterprises, and there were also plans to bring diamond cutting and polishing machines from Amsterdam.[45] The Jewish Council leadership were prepared to see this change in a positive light as it seemed to suggest that Jews were now going to be kept in the Netherlands rather than all be deported. The economic functions in Vught also suggested to the Council that this was an attempt to create a more or less permanent ghetto alongside Westerbork and Auschwitz.[46]

The second change to German policy also emanated from Berlin, but this time from the Foreign Office which wanted some Jews held back for possible exchange with Germans held overseas. To this end, they wanted all Jews with immigration certificates for Palestine, and the estimated 1,300 with remaining substantial capital assets, to be kept out of the deportation process but ultimately conveyed to the 'exchange camp' at Bergen-Belsen. De Jong describes these two changes as 'complications' to the process of removing the Jews from the Netherlands. This may be overstating the case, as it could also be argued that placing Jews in a camp, whether it was Westerbork or Vught, made them more vulnerable to future changes in German plans than if they had been allowed to remain at liberty in Amsterdam or elsewhere in the country.[47]

The months between March and July 1943 also saw another change in German actions, if not in policy. Until March, every transport from Westerbork (and the ones direct from Amsterdam and Apeldoorn) had been sent to Auschwitz. Suddenly on 2 March, the destination was changed and 19 of the following 20 transports were sent to Sobibor extermination camp in Lublin district.[48] These 19 transports carried off a total of 34,313 people, of whom only 19 survived.[49] Explaining the halting of transports to Auschwitz is relatively straightforward, as the camp was almost entirely taken up with the extermination of the Jews from Salonika (March–May) and then beset by a typhus epidemic.[50] More difficult to explain is why transports from the Netherlands were switched to Sobibor when those from other Western European countries were suspended. It has been pointed out that the Dutch victims of Sobibor more or less account for the percentage difference in mortality rates between the Netherlands and its nearest neighbours. Both before and after this period, the level of deportations from all three countries are broadly comparable. Blom has suggested that German satisfaction with the conduct of affairs in the Netherlands compared with the problems being encountered in France and Belgium may have played some part in the decision.[51] Of more marginal importance to the overall survival of Dutch Jewry is the fact that Sobibor was purely an extermination camp, with no function as a labour camp. Thus the survival rate among Dutch Jews of 0.05 per cent compares unfavourably even with the 1.75 per cent of Auschwitz.[52] Whatever the reason for the temporary change of destination, the end result for the deportees was the same. With the exception of two Wednesdays in June, the transports left weekly with chronological precision[53] until 20 July. After a break of exactly five weeks, transports were resumed to Auschwitz on 24 August as the last Jews still living legally in Amsterdam were rounded up.[54]

By May 1943, the process of removing the Jews from Amsterdam was reaching its climax. In March the Jewish Council had already recorded that the rounding up of Jews had taken on an 'alarming range' and by April there was some recognition of the scale and scope of the impending disaster. The trains to the East were now composed of goods wagons and people were being moved from Vught to Westerbork,[55] indicating that the hopes for a permanent Jewish settlement in the Netherlands had proved entirely illusory. By far the greatest number of Jews still at large in the city were those protected by Jewish Council stamps. On 11 April David Cohen had provided the *Zentralstelle* with a complete list of the people being protected by Council exemption stamps.[56] A breakdown of these people is given in Table 5.1.

Table 5.1 Holders of Jewish Council exemption stamps, April 1943

	Employees	Wives	Children	Total
Amsterdam	8,000	3,800	2,750	14,550
Provinces	564	221	297	1,082
Total	8,564	4,021	3,047	15,632

On 21 May Aus der Fünten told Asscher and Cohen that they had to select 7,000 holders of Council exemption stamps for deportation. Such a large staff was no longer required for a diminishing Jewish population. The chairmen were given 20 minutes to decide whether to comply. In the event, the full Council met some four hours after the ultimatum had been given, and once again unanimously agreed to comply.[57] Finally having to choose from amongst their own created even more tensions within the Council bureaucracy than before. Some departments drew lots, while a 'commission' was set up to 'do the hangman's work'[58] and re-categorise people according to new criteria about indispensability. The effect on morale in general, and on those now deemed surplus to requirements, can only be imagined. In the event, fewer than 7,000 call-up papers were sent out,[59] and only around 3,000 complied with the summons. As a result, the Germans mounted yet another mass raid in the Jewish quarter on 26 May, arresting approximately 3,000 people.[60] This more or less emptied the area of Jews altogether. For the next month, there were no further actions until the last mass raid on 20 June which caught the remaining Jewish Council staff, whose stamps were rendered invalid. The Germans mobilised all their available men for this final sweep through south and east Amsterdam, including men from the *Orde Dienst* at Westerbork imported specially for

the occasion. Some 5,550 people were arrested and shipped to Westerbork via the Amsterdam Muiderpoort station. After this, Aus der Fünten insisted that the Council could make do with a much smaller staff as there were only 14,000 Jews left. He suggested a figure of 1,700 but then put it down as 170 and refused to correct the error. Pressure for a further 35 exemptions succeeded in producing a concession of 2,800 from Wörlein in Aus der Fünten's absence, but his return resulted in another raid and a new wave of arrests.[61]

A night raid on 23 July removed still more members of the Jewish Council bureaucracy.[62] Of those who remained, a large number were in possession of a '120,000' stamp, the most exclusive and inviolable protection of all. It encompassed the leadership of the Jewish Council and all those Jews whom the Germans found it expedient to protect from summary deportation. This included people who might be useful for exchanges such as those with relatives, friends or contacts with enemy states, as well as the rich or those who were still economically useful, such as diamond merchants. The issue of these stamps increased rapidly in summer of 1943, although ultimately it did not prevent their holders' removal to Westerbork during the last raid on 29 September, when Amsterdam was finally deemed clear of Jews. Right to the bitter end, the Council continued to try and protect a few by re-categorising those who remained according to their supposed indispensability. Given the fact that the vast majority of Jews had already been deported, this attempted selection from the few who remained does not make an edifying spectacle.[63] Interestingly, the departure of this last privileged group did not mean the end of the Jewish Council. Four or five functionaries were kept on, housed in the *Expositur* building, ostensibly to file records. They managed to make this last until September 1944, at which point they and their families went into hiding. There were still 14,000 Jews at liberty in the city consisting mainly of Jews in mixed marriages (8,000–9,000), Portuguese and foreign Jews, those whose ancestry was still being examined, and a few with special exemptions.[64] It was possible to justify a Council 'contact section' for them and for the Jews still in Westerbork, but Wielek cynically thought it more likely that Aus der Fünten was trying to preserve his existing function within the Netherlands and 'still did not want to go to the Eastern Front'.[65]

Even if the '120,000' stamps could not keep their 1,500 holders in the Netherlands, they did serve to mark them out for preferential treatment. Many, including the chairmen of the Jewish Council, were sent to the 'model' camp of Theresienstadt on account of their work. This privileged few were joined by others selected by Harster, who wanted men decorated by the German armed forces in the Great War, those who had been of service to the German state in peacetime, and those with relatives in the *Protektorat* of Bohemia-Moravia to be similarly favoured.[66] Others were shipped to Bergen-Belsen to await exchange negotiations. In the event, neither camp was a guarantee of safety and at least half the Dutch Jews in Theresienstadt were ultimately sent to Auschwitz. Nonetheless, mortality rates among Dutch Jews in these camps were much lower, with 40.5 per cent (Theresienstadt) and 58.7 per cent (Bergen-Belsen) surviving the war.[67]

The removal of the Jews from the Netherlands allowed the Germans to plunder all the remaining assets of their victims. Jews who reported to the *Zentralstelle* had to surrender the keys to their property, those who were arrested in raids had their doors sealed by the police. After their departure, officials from the *Hausraterfassung*[68] inventoried all the possessions and representatives from Lippmann-Rosenthal took away any valuables. This process became even more co-ordinated when raids became the norm. These were often carried out by squads (*Kolonne*) containing two police-men, two *Hausraterfassung* staff members and one from the Lippmann-Rosenthal Bank.[69] There had been some debate about what should happen to the Jewish assets seized in this way. In December 1941 Hitler had decreed that they should be made available to people in German cities who had had suffered losses in Allied bombing raids. However, he had also apparently given custody of these belongings to the *Reichsminister* for the Eastern Territories, Alfred Rosenberg, a view he confirmed in March 1942. In the meantime, other German agencies also began to stake claims and Seyss-Inquart was beset on all sides. The compromise was that the goods would be transferred to the so-called *Einsatzstab Rosenberg*, but that the Gauleiter of Cologne and Münster would be given what he needed to make good losses suffered in bombing raids. In fact, as de Jong points out, transport to the East was so unreliable that most of the Jewish assets seized in the Netherlands went no further than western Germany.[70]

After the house contents had been inventoried, the keys were handed over to the *Einsatzstab Rosenberg* which employed Abraham Puls, a Dutch removal and storage firm, to empty the houses and flats. Their activities soon brought a new verb into the Dutch language. In total, some 29,000 Jewish dwellings were '*gepulst*' and their contents conveyed to the docks or railway stations for transport out of the country. The contents of 25,000 dwellings filled 666 barges and 100 goods wagons. A small quan-tity was kept in the country for use by the *Wehrmacht*, while poorer qual-ity furniture was sold off in the Netherlands. Some of the more desirable houses and flats were occupied by the Germans themselves or Dutch Nazis. Others were used by the municipalities to house evacuees, but many less well-appointed residences, especially in the Jewish quarter, remained per-manently empty.[71] Nothing of any value was left untouched or unclaimed by some German agency, from the smallest item of furniture to the price-less collections of books and artefacts seized by the *Einsatzstab Rosenberg* and stored in the Portuguese synagogue on the Jonas Daniël Meyerplein in Amsterdam.

The process of stripping the Jews of all their remaining assets allowed scope for widespread corruption. The sheer numbers of dwellings meant that many were left unattended for some time, providing scope for unofficial 'Puls-ers' to remove the contents.[72] All the officials involved had the opportunity to enrich themselves in some way or other. No controls were strong enough and Lages went as far as disbanding the squads working for the *Zentralstelle* when the scale of their corruption became too great.[73] Nonetheless, a number of favoured people did make a great deal of money from the system. In The Hague, 12 Dutch policemen were arrested and their commissioner worried that any further investigations might implicate a hundred or more for the same offences. The 12 were let off with a disciplinary punishment.[74] Even if the system was not free from corruption, it was nevertheless extremely efficient in its prime purpose, of collecting and disposing of all the assets owned by Jews.

Reflections on the Jewish Council

As the Jews were being more and more isolated from the rest of Dutch society, so the functions of the Jewish Council increased. The Council itself was underpinned by a whole series of departments, including Finance and a Treasury with various sub-sections. As the Germans gradually reduced the ability of Jews to trade or buy food in open markets, so the Council took over the task of provisioning and feeding the population, necessitating another whole series of subsidiary departments. There was also a Social Affairs department which dealt with employment, accommodation and special services; another department helped provide for those being sent away or living in Westerbork. In fact there was no aspect of Jewish life under the Germans which did not have a responsible Council department or office.[75] When the arguments took place over the numbers of stamps which the Jewish Council were requesting, the officials countered German claims by pointing out that more and more functions were being transferred from the Dutch bureaucracy to the Council, which had effectively become 'a state within a state'.[76] This development has been seen positively, most notably by Herzberg, and the Council's archives demonstrate just how extensive the welfare and support systems had become. Feeding and clothing the poor, helping to house and look after the elderly and infirm all became part of the Council's remit as responsibility for the Jews was gradually removed from the Dutch civil authorities.

Although often portrayed as a hierarchical structure, with all power concentrated in the hands of the presidents, there were other spheres of influence and power bases within the structure and at least two other people who had a special position. One was the head of the so-called *Expositur*, a former Viennese advocate, Dr Edwin Sluzker. His office acted as the sole liaison with the German authorities. This gave Sluzker the ability to talk directly with Aus der Fünten and his colleagues, who also seem to have preferred dealing with Germans rather than the Dutch. The result was that Sluzker could often obtain some concessions when all other avenues had failed.[77] He was also able to keep his department open much longer than any other and succeeded in spinning out the work of the *Expositur* until September 1944 when he went underground with his family.[78] The other influential person was Gertrud van Tijn. As head of the Department of Emigration and Displaced Persons' Aid Bureau, her formal status within the Council was not particularly high, but her previous work with David Cohen on behalf of refugees in the 1930s undoubtedly gave her added influence, as did her department. After 1941, emigration was seldom a practical possibility for any Jews in the Netherlands, but she was used by the Germans to investigate mass emigration schemes and later the possibility of exchanges. Thus she had been allowed to travel to Lisbon in 1941, and was ultimately released from Bergen-Belsen in July 1944.[79]

The role played by the Jewish Council in the fate of the Jews has perhaps been the most hotly debated issue within Dutch Jewish circles ever since the organisation was created in 1941. The Council and especially its two co-chairmen, Asscher and Cohen, have come in for severe moral censure from some contemporaries and from later historians. The debate has been both heated and more or less unremitting with Presser devoting an entire chapter to the workings of the Council and referring to it extensively elsewhere, and de Jong also affording it a great deal of space. This attention shows the importance given to the issue, but it should always be borne in mind that the Council, whatever its faults, played only a subordinate practical role in the fate of Jews. Certainly, it collaborated by engaging in dialogue with the Germans and helping to draw up lists for those to be deported, consistently making 'selections' which had the effect of removing individuals' protected status, but however reprehensible this may have been regarded, it was only a contribution to the smooth running of the deportation process and probably not a fundamental one. Certainly, the Germans would have been faced with greater difficulties if there had been no co-operation from the Council, but no one has been able to argue that these problems were insurmountable, given the prevailing circumstances. At most, the behaviour of the Council saved the occupiers a great deal of administrative work. In so doing, it also facilitated the isolation of the Jews, and may thereby have removed the possibility of the Germans having to engage in more high-profile actions against the Jews which might, in turn, have provoked public disquiet and even disorder. This can only be conjectural, but a more damning charge can be made from a psychological angle. It is undoubtedly the case that many Jews vested a good deal of trust in their leaders and therefore in the Council and its ability to mediate with the Germans. Only gradually was this trust undermined as restrictions increased and the selections and deportations began. In effect, many were lulled into a false sense of security by the mere existence of the Council and the tone of its early statements, leading to a belief that they did have some protection. Consequently, by the time it was clear that this protection was illusory it was too late to change, though for the vast majority there were few viable alternatives at any time.

The debate has been extensively summarised by Michman,[80] who traces the development of opinions and the ways in which judgements have been passed on the behaviour of the Council and its leadership. During the deportation period, the leadership was widely reviled and despised by those who had never had, or had lost, its protection. Michman cites Mechanicus as referring to the 'malicious glee' of those still in Westerbork in September 1943 when the leadership was brought there,[81] but it is interesting that in the same entry Mechanicus also cites some who sought to excuse them. 'They're just weak men who did what they could and wanted to save their own skins too.'[82] Even in the transit camp and amongst the victims there were already differing views about the Council and its leadership. The immediate post-war literature can also be divided into two schools of interpretation: those who condemned the Council for its actions and even its establishment, and those who had worked for the Council or in some ways benefited from its existence. In this latter category, Michman cites three books by prominent Zionists who had obtained Palestine certificates with the active help of the Council, and also the work of K.P.L. Berkley whose father-in-law had been chairman of the Council's finance committee.[83] This did not mean that there was no criticism from within the ranks of the Council. The opinions of Kisch and Visser have already been noted, but Gertrud van Tijn, who occupied a leading position in the Council and had worked with Cohen on refugee relief for years before the occupation, also fell out with the leadership and resigned.

Perhaps inevitably, the joint-chairmen, Asscher and Cohen, became the focus of the debate on the Council. It was often assumed that they had more or less dictatorial powers over their fellow Council members and the various heads of departments within the organisation, although Michman questions this by pointing out the influence exercised by departmental heads and the relative autonomy of Council representatives elsewhere.[84] He cites the special relationship of the Council representative in The Hague with the SS High Command, and the work of the Enschede Jewish Council in hiding Jews, against orders from Amsterdam. Assessing the level of 'influence' exerted in a meeting is inevitably problematic even when minutes exist, as they seldom provide indications of when individuals are swayed by arguments. Certainly there were occasions where David Cohen seems to have persuaded the members of the Council to accept his views, but the Council's minutes do not provide a complete picture of precisely what happened at its meetings. In the post-war era, Cohen did nothing to try and spread the responsibility for what the Council had done to other surviving members.

The facts of what the Jewish Council did are not disputed. Having been established at the behest of the German authorities in February 1941, it acted as a conduit for orders and regulations. Each time it was asked for a concession in the form of co-operation or the compilation of lists or choices of who should be eligible for labour service or deportation, the Council complied. Small concessions made by the Germans acted as a spur to maintaining the illusion of a negotiating position, though these minor victories were invariably undermined by the next demand. The discovery of legal loopholes in German ordinances was also invariably countered with further legislation or just by summary *diktat*. In some respects this did have the appearance of a game of cat-and-mouse, but that would imply that the Germans were playing with their Jewish victims. The truth was more pragmatic. By asking for more than they needed, the Germans always had the ability to concede some ground. Wielek put it quite succinctly. If Aus der Fünten wanted 80 people, he asked for 100 and when the Jewish Council protested, he allowed them to claw back 20. He achieved his purpose while the Council believed it had also won a victory.[85] Moreover, it guaranteed that the Council continued to think it had a vested interest in the system and would thus go on co-operating. In the final analysis, it was this co-operation which the Germans valued most of all and wished to maintain for as long as possible. In that respect, they were remarkably successful. The co-operation continued until the very end: to the point where all the Jews had been transported out of Amsterdam. Time and again, the Jewish Council leadership responded to German threats with compliance for fear of something much worse, which they interpreted as a breakdown of order and a free-for-all in which there was no safety for anyone. Moreover, there was the view which followed from the Council's belief that the Jews were being taken to the East for resettlement: that disobedience might lead to more severe treatment (the threat of Mauthausen) for those being deported, and for the rest still in the Netherlands.

The failure of the Jewish Council's policies was plain for all to see as the occupation came to an end. It had failed to prevent the deportation of more than a few dozen of the people whom the Germans wished to see deported, and had failed to recognise the murderous import of the term 'resettlement in the East'. However, there remain debates on the Jewish Council and its behaviour which have to be addressed. Michman places them under three headings. Was it absolutely necessary to organise the Jewish Council? Were there any alternative strategies? Were the actions of the Jewish Council leadership criminal, or merely errors which nevertheless had fatal consequences?[86] He cites Cohen's defence of the Jewish Council as being that power rested with the Germans and not with the Dutch authorities so that only negotiation with the occupiers would have any effect on policies against the Jews. There was an assumption that the war would end in a German defeat and that this would not be long in coming; therefore the main aim had to be procrastination in order to save the elite of the Jewish population. Michman points out that even the policy of procrastination was a failure, as there is no evidence that any Council action served to delay the process of deportation. However, his greatest condemnation is reserved for the policy of protecting the elite as the core of the Jewish community.

> Cohen's argument that he had to protect and preserve a nucleus of the elite for the eventual rehabilitation of the community, and if necessary leave the others to their fate, is unacceptable – an excuse for saving members of a protected class to which the heads of the Council themselves belonged. Indeed, the results show that to the extent to which matters depended on the Council, it was the rich and the intellectuals who were saved.[87]

Herzberg carefully ignored the arguments about the Jewish elite in his defence of Asscher and Cohen. In assessing the alternatives to the Jewish Council he points out the marginal and completely ineffectual nature of the Jewish Coordination Commission which refused to have any dealings with the Germans.[88] A principled stand was taken by Visser, but one which was to be of little value in the face of the occupiers' overwhelming power. Asscher and Cohen were not perceived as men who would defend a principle, but pragmatists who would compromise in order to obtain concessions and agreements. It was their fate that no amount of negotiation or compromise could alter the Germans' ultimate purpose. Moreover, these two above all others had to take responsibility for the actions of the Council. Certainly Herzberg seems keen to defend the two as men caught up in events which they could not ultimately control. He, and most other commentators, do not question their goodwill and philanthropic intentions, even if these were ultimately misplaced and misguided.[89] Only later did he raise the privileged status which these two men enjoyed and the possibility that their actions were also motivated in part by a desire for self-preservation. The fact that they were offered and accepted special treatment and ultimately sent to 'better' camps (Cohen to Theresienstadt and Asscher to Bergen-Belsen) in exchange for their continued co-operation speaks against the purity of their motives. In mitigation, it can be pointed out that they were also offered the chance to leave the Netherlands with their families and refused.[90]

The characters of the two men also come into question. Presser provides a wealth of detail about the way they used their power to make choices, and appears to condemn them, but at the same time there are qualifications and equivocations. Like Herzberg, Presser had known David Cohen before and during the occupation, indeed they had been professional colleagues and Presser had taught in the Jewish High School where Cohen had been on the board of governors. Can this explain his inability to condemn outright the man who effectively led the Jewish Council? Certainly, Presser had no reason to favour Cohen, as his ultimate survival had come as a result of going into hiding rather than from any temporary protection afforded by the Jewish Council. Nonetheless, in spite of the many condemnatory passages in his book, Presser cannot produce an unequivocal judgement, and like Herzberg he falls back on to a series of points, some in favour and some against. De Jong is more assertive, also sensing the balance of factors but deciding that the negative aspects of the Council's actions – distributing yellow stars, assisting with the deportation orders and finally withdrawing protection from 7,000 of its own staff in the summer of 1943 – outweighed the positive organisational and welfare functions which the Council provided. Von der Dunk was more forgiving, suggesting that Asscher and Cohen's shortcomings were brutally exposed by the positions they found themselves in, and that it is difficult to judge the unique predicament of these two men when compared with that of most Jews and the entire Dutch population. The non-Jews could avoid collaboration by remaining passive and without joining the resistance, but Jews had no such choice of opting out, because of the malevolent intentions of the Germans towards them. Von der Dunk certainly argues that the co-chairmen were victims of circumstances. In some respects this does beg the question of the extent to which they sought the office the Germans asked them to fill. Could they have refused and taken the consequences, if any, while allowing others to take their place at the head of affairs? One senses from their behaviour and attitudes both before and during the occupation that this avoidance was beyond them, and that once installed as leaders they had no choice but to follow the path they had chosen.

Michman summarises the debate by pointing out that the old charges against the Jewish Council and its leadership, that alternative policies would have saved more Jews in the Netherlands, have now disappeared.[91] Moreover, the exposure of collaboration by other sections of the Dutch population has served to refocus the debate, as has a more rational ranking for the factors which led to the German 'success' in the Netherlands. This, rightly, gives prominence to the power and administrative organisation of the Germans and their ability to harness Dutch institutions and organisations to carry out their plans. While of vital importance to the history of the Jews in the Netherlands, the Jewish Council, its leadership and its actions were only of secondary importance in the execution of the 'Final Solution'. Michman argues that comparisons with other Jewish Councils may find Asscher and Cohen wanting 'in questions of political sagacity, preservation of Jewish honour and even in placing the good of the community above personal interest', but that it should always be remembered that it was their persecutors who forced the decisions upon them.[92]

Any realistic assessment of Asscher's and Cohen's conduct has to take account of their supposed knowledge about what the deportations really meant. The longer the deportations went on, the more rumours filtered back. Yet even in the later part of 1942, there was evidence that not all was well. The reported deaths of those sent to Mauthausen *could* be explained by the fact that this was a known concentration camp,[93] but the lack of communication with all those deported in the early months did raise doubts. German statements about technical difficulties and rumours about large quantities of post being held up in Berlin could be interpreted in many ways. The first death notice, of a single, unnamed Jew (b.1905) in Auschwitz was received by the Council on 18 September. The following week 52 cards and 43 letters arrived from Birkenau outlining the work and conditions in the camp, but the meeting rapidly realised that most or all of them had been written by third parties and only signed by the (supposed) senders as all the communications were in German.[94] Similar batches were received towards the end of the year from Monowitz, Theresienstadt and again from Birkenau. Again, all were in German and only a few had been actually written by the senders. Some were unsigned. The Council drew conclusions from the descriptions given of the camps, of work and conditions, but did no more than note the fact that there had been no communications at all from children, women with children or old people.[95]

With knowledge of what was really happening in these camps, the explanations are simple. But it remains difficult to understand what the Council really made of this trickle of strange and unrepresentative communications. Certainly, they had had evidence of German duplicity, as in the case of one of the early Mauthausen deportees whose family had received notice of his death from tuberculosis on 5 April, but a card signed in his own hand saying he was in good health dated 6 April.[96] The Council raised this with the Sipo as a possible bureaucratic error and continued to interpret the limited information they received in the best possible light. Other death notices were regarded with more suspicion and uneasiness, as when two very fit young men were certified as having died in Buchenwald from sudden heart failure.[97] Later notices which came via the Sipo did not give a cause of death. Clearly the Germans had learned a lesson.[98]

The view that the Jewish Council engaged in some type of class war against the mass of the Jewish proletariat has persisted in some elements of the historiography. Insofar as it is possible to ascertain the truth of the matter, the reality is more complex. Certainly, the leaders of the Jewish Council in Amsterdam did try to save themselves and their fellow workers and families. The distribution of exemptions did favour the higher-class districts at the expense of working-class neighbourhoods. Thus the higher- and middle-class districts, containing 38.8 per cent of the Jewish population, had 62.9 per cent of the exemptions.[99] However, Houwink ten Cate has argued that Jewish Council policies were developed with a different purpose. Many of those employed by the Council when its activities were expanded and the deportations began came from the 16–40-year-old age group. This was because it was precisely these people whom the Germans wished to deport. At this time, the Council leadership assumed that the Germans had no intention of removing the entire Jewish community, and thus Asscher and Cohen moved to protect those in greatest danger – and also those who formed the future generation for the community as a whole. Having awarded protection to this group and age category, they were suddenly faced with German demands which steadily increased the age range for deportees to the point where no one was automatically excluded. Unable to change the holders of exemptions, or even to maintain the validity of all those issued, the Council had effectively (but perhaps unknowingly) created the circumstances in which the older and youngest generations were deported almost in their entirety.[100]

The charge of class warfare has slightly more credibility in The Hague. Mortality figures for Jews there were marginally higher than for the rest of the country and this has been explained in three ways. Firstly, that policies against the Jews in The Hague were administered directly from the offices of IVB4 in the city and were the direct responsibility of *SS-Sturmscharführer* Fischer who saw it as his personal task to expedite the deportation of the Jews. He carried out most of the day-to-day work simply because his boss, the indolent Willi Zöpf, was 'much happier playing the piano than running his office'.[101] Having an efficient bureaucrat in charge could make some difference to the process. Moreover, the city's population registry seems to have provided a complete list of Jews by May 1942, although it proved to be less than accurate when the deportations began in the summer. The second element which is supposed to have made it harder for the Jews was the Germans' insistence on clearing the coastal districts for security reasons. This allowed them to re-house a substantial number of Jews who were then readily identifiable for transport later. The third element was simply that the Sipo and the bureaucracy in The Hague had to be seen to be efficient in the city where their superiors were based.[102]

While all these factors could be seen as differences from Amsterdam and the rest of the country, the statistics for deportations do not support the view that proportionately more Jews were deported from The Hague than from other parts of the country, the relevant figures being 77 per cent and 76 per cent respectively. However, the fact that the Jewish Council in the city seems to have collaborated more closely with the Germans even than its counterpart in Amsterdam does seem to have made some difference to the class structure of those deported. Thus by April 1943, 75 per cent of the lower classes had gone, 59 per cent of the middle classes, but only 43 per cent of the upper echelon.[103] There is evidence that this was deliberate. Fischer noted that, 'Whoever had money or contacts at the Council, was protected as long as possible .... I noticed many times that, if at all possible, the prosperous Jews were saved.'[104] This policy of 'selection' may well have been coupled with the fact that the poorer Jews in the city were more concentrated and therefore easier to apprehend. Conversely, the richer Jews living in the suburbs were more difficult to find in large numbers and their arrests would be more visible. Furthermore, being left until last gave them a greater opportunity to use their other advantage, namely wealth and contacts to try and ensure survival through going underground. The method of call-up also differed from Amsterdam. In The Hague there was no reporting to a *Zentralstelle* office, but merely a written notification to be ready for transport which would be followed up by a visit from the police to take the victims away. It does seem that in the case of The Hague, the local Jewish Council was more directly involved, even to the point of selecting those to be deported and the areas to be raided. In these circumstances, coupled with the apparent efficiency of the German administration and the apparent willing co-operation of the Dutch police, one might have expected a higher number of deportees. The reason why this was not the case may also be due to the policies of the Jewish Council. By protecting the richer Jews, they gave them the chance to use their situation to try and escape or avoid deportation. It is also the case that the city had a larger number of foreign Jews than elsewhere, who were given temporary protection by the Germans' own indecision on their status. Their exclusion also helped to keep the percentage of deportees at around the national average.

What all this tells us is that it is very difficult to reach unqualified conclusions about the role of the Jewish Councils in the Netherlands. If Council representatives' actions in The Hague appear to compare unfavourably even with those in Amsterdam, it should not be forgotten that other representatives, for example in Enschede, took a far less compliant line and did actually conspire to help people go underground. Clearly the actions of the Council did assist the Germans in certain important respects. The evidence from the Germans themselves suggests that they would have found it difficult, if not impossible, to carry out the deportations on the scale achieved without that assistance. However, this should not be used to imply that the Council leadership knew the end result of their actions. In the early months of the deportation, they seem to have assumed that the German intent was to remove a section of the Jewish community and their main task was to try and negotiate the retention of as much of Dutch Jewry as was possible. With hindsight, this was a mistake, as was any attempt to take the word of the German functionaries at face value. It could be argued that the Council leaders should have learned more quickly from their mistakes, but this begs the question of what they could then have done. Resigned *en masse* and gone underground? This would have been against every principle they understood. Warn everyone of their worst fears and tell them to escape if they could? This form of chaos was also alien, and all the time that the threat of Mauthausen – which was equated with punishment and certain death – existed, then this option was also likely to be rejected. The leadership were tied into serving the community, following through on the policies they had set out, and trying to protect themselves, probably in more or less equal measure. Undoubtedly they made mistakes and miscalculations, and their behaviour was far from perfect. However, the real tragedy was that so many of their decisions held the power of life or death over Dutch Jewry.

6

Survival: exemptions and exclusions

The empirical evidence from Jews who survived the occupation in the Netherlands suggests that there were two possible ways of avoiding deportation. One was to go into hiding when or before one was called up by the German authorities. The second was to exploit the German bureaucratic system, by either claiming or acquiring some status which provided the holder with protection in the short or long term. The most widespread example of this latter process was the granting of exemptions to Jewish Council employees and workers deemed essential for the German war effort. By and large, this was a case of people being in the right job at the right moment to receive some temporary protection, but it was also possible for individuals to seek safety by acquiring foreign nationality or by 'buying' protection from the authorities or third parties.

The whole question of exempting some people from summary deportation was inherent in the German 'system' for dealing with the Jews in the Netherlands. If sectors of the economy important to the Germans were not to be affected, and the effectiveness of the 'Jewish bureaucracy' of the Jewish Council was not to be compromised, then the selection process had to be given some rationality. Neither the call-up of male Jews for labour service inside the Netherlands in the spring and summer of 1942, nor the initial call-ups for work in Germany after 5 July 1942, were particularly selective. As a result, the German authorities had begun to operate a series of exemptions as the labour drafts were stepped up in May. Those legally married to a non-Jew, skilled workers employed under the orders of the *Wehrmacht* and ragpickers with permits were all excluded and it remained possible to obtain other dispensations.[1] In this way, the Jewish Council became involved in applying for exemptions and thus became the intermediary between individual Jews and the German authorities. Additionally, the one way for those of conscription age to avoid labour service was to demonstrate that they were unfit. The selection boards initially used Jewish doctors who proved to be too well disposed towards the draftees. Many Jews were able to fake complaints, produce false samples or letters from specialists certifying that they had this or that disease or illness. As it became more difficult to meet the quotas, and the Jewish doctors refused to continue their work, the Germans eventually replaced them with more 'reliable' practitioners. This led to a complete reversal in the way conscripts were treated. Whereas before, almost any case would have a reasonable chance of getting an exemption, now everyone – including the geniunely ill – was passed fit for work.[2] This, and the hostage-taking after the first call-ups for work in Germany, indicate that the Germans were already abandoning the idea of a structured and orderly removal of the Jews from the Netherlands in favour of pre-emptive arbitrary actions. Yet they obviously knew from the beginning that such actions only served to undermine still further the operation of the very structures and criteria they were trying to use.

There was clearly a contradiction here and one which the Germans eventually addressed by providing exemptions from labour service 'until further notice' for specific groups. This was done with a special *stempel* (stamp) in the person's identity card. In summary, the Germans gave exemptions to Jews in three categories. First of all, an exemption might be granted if there was some good administrative reason for keeping people in the Netherlands, for example the Jewish Council staff, or foreign Jews whose treatment was of concern to the *Auswärtiges Amt* (German Foreign Office). A second reason for exemption was if the Germans were unsure of an individual's status as a Jew. In this way, the Portuguese (Sephardi) Jews were given stamps while their antecedents were investigated. Similarly those in mixed marriages or baptised into the Christian faith were also protected with a stamp. Finally, Jews were given exemptions if they were useful to the German war economy. In this way, some types of skilled workers gained exemption from deportation. As we now know, the possession of such a stamp did not provide any long-term safety, but at the time the provision of officially sanctioned exemptions had colossal appeal for a society whose citizens had been imbued with a respect for the workings of government and the bureaucracy. People set great store by the stamps because they wanted to believe in a way out of their predicament. As a result, a *stempel* became the most sought-after prize for a Jewish family in the Netherlands once they became available in the autumn of 1942. The question to be posed here is how the system of stamps and exemptions, and the ways in which the Germans treated their recipients, ultimately contributed to the survival of Jews in the Netherlands. To answer this, it seems appropriate to take each general category in turn, firstly the Jews exempted for administrative reasons, secondly those about whom the Germans were unsure, and finally those retained for economic reasons.

Jewish Council exemptions

The story of the Jewish Council exemption stamps has been outlined in the previous chapter. Whatever the holders of these stamps may have believed, they had not been given any lasting protection, as events in the summer of 1943 demonstrated. After the Jewish Council itself was wound up on 29 July 1943 and its leadership conveyed to Westerbork, only a few scattered remnants of its bureaucracy remained. Apart from the skeleton *Expositur* staff, the contact-department which dealt with communications between Westerbork and the rest of the Netherlands, there were only the offices concerned with the Portuguese Jews, and one or two provincial representatives of the Jewish Council whom the Sipo seem to have forgotten. Other Jews who were able to stay included around 50 men who worked for the Puls removal firm clearing the houses of those taken to Westerbork in the final raids, the custodians of several Jewish cemeteries (apparently forgotten by the Germans), and two Jewish bicycle-makers who worked for the Sipo.[3] They, like many of the others listed above, went into hiding as the Germans finally put an end to even these few exceptions on 19 September 1944. By this stage, it was clear that the writing was on the wall for the German occupation: the Allied armies had advanced to the Rhine and were poised to make the breakthrough which would liberate the rest of the Netherlands and effectively end the war.

Whatever protection the Jewish Council gave via the issue of stamps or other exemptions did not survive its own demise. Where individual Jews connected with the Council's work were able to continue to live in the Netherlands, it was because of the specific function they fulfilled and not through the possession of a specifically numbered stamp. In some respects, the Jewish Council stamps were the most unreliable of all the exemptions granted by the Germans as they were based on the administrative usefulness of a Jewish bureaucracy. As the Jewish population of the Netherlands was removed, so the need for the bureaucracy also decreased, to the point where the whole edifice collapsed, leaving only a few unconnected and marginal parts of the structure intact. The unseemly scramble to obtain a stamp, and then a specifically numbered stamp, did nothing to heighten the reputation of the Jewish Council or its leaders and merely served to reinforce the feelings of anger felt by contemporaries excluded from this apparent means of survival. The leadership's defence – that they were trying to protect the 'core' of Dutch Jewry – rings even more hollow when viewed from the post-war period. The second line of defence – that the structured nature of the deportations and the 'notice' given to those conscripted for 'labour service' allowed many to go into hiding – also smacks of a *post facto* justification, especially when the Council continued to urge those called up to report for transportation, lest other measures were taken. Survival in hiding depended on a whole series of factors, but perhaps the only pertinent one here is that the Council's ability to keep some people inside the Netherlands until the summer of 1943 gave them longer to prepare to go into hiding and a shorter time to survive underground before the occupation came to an end.

'Calmeyer Jews'

The German reliance on a racial definition of a Jew, as embodied in the supplementary legislation of the Nuremberg Laws (and for the Netherlands in decree VO 6/1941), did allow for escape from the terms of the decree by bureaucratic (and therefore legal) means. The decree dictated that all those with 'one Jewish grandparent by race' were required to register as Jews, although race was actually defined in terms of membership of a Jewish religious community. Any doubtful cases had to be referred to the *Reichskommissar* for final decision. In the first instance, nearly all the Jews in the Netherlands had registered under the requirements of the decree, but as the implications of this became clearer, so the number of people attempting to alter their status increased. The *Reichskommissariat* was rapidly inundated with petitions which were passed to the *Generalkommissariat* for Administration and Justice, and ultimately to the *Referat Innere Verwaltung* whose chief, Dr Hans Calmeyer, was to have the final say in these matters. His office was effectively responsible for dealing with claims that one or more of the supposedly Jewish grandparents or parents was not really Jewish at all, thus entitling the individual to different status from the one originally conferred. For the lucky ones whose claims were upheld, this allowed them to be 'downgraded' from full-Jews to half-Jews, from half-Jews to quarter-Jews, and from quarter-Jews to 'aryans'. As such, they were given an 'exemption from labour service' stamp with a 30,000 number, and inclusion on the so-called Calmeyer list.[4] The importance of this 'downgrading' and inclusion on an exempt list soon became apparent as German legislation was increasingly applied only to full-Jews. The petitioners used a whole range of professionals and specialists to help with appropriate documentation. Information and certificates were inserted into state and other archives. Doctors provided blood test results to substantiate claims that parentage had been illegitimate (and thus not wholly Jewish), and the Red Cross certified blood transfusions which had never taken place. Letters were falsified, using old paper and archaic handwriting, in order to validate claims to Christian forebears, and German baptismal records were widely used for the same purpose.

Calmeyer was universally regarded as 'highly intelligent, extremely conscientious and totally incorruptible',[5] but it was his attitude to his work which was to prove the crucial factor in saving a small number of Dutch Jews from the full rigour of Nazi persecution. He was neither a Nazi, committed to the party's racial theories, nor an avowed anti-Nazi. In many cases his office did not enquire too closely into the provenance or validity of documents presented in support of individual cases. Certainly, there were some employed in his office who were sympathetic to the Jews who would try to warn those whose applications were unsuccessful, or who would be helpful when the mood took them. Dubious baptismal certificates, divorce papers and letters disputing parentage were often accepted with minimal scrutiny. However, Calmeyer went further than suspending his disbelief on cases presented to him. He would often look for loopholes in order to make the case for the appellant and went to enormous lengths to verify documentation which supported certain claims, for example where 'Jewish' grandparents had supposedly attended Christian churches. By the middle of July 1941, his office had already dealt with in excess of 1,300 applications, and the numbers were to increase as the German pressure mounted.

The stories of what Calmeyer's *Verwaltung* was able to achieve have been well documented elsewhere. His decisions were said to be unpredictable, although Herzberg suggests that he was sometimes guided by what he could justify to the SD.[6] The pressures on Calmeyer's office became even more acute as the deportations began in the summer of 1942. By this stage, the decisions were tantamount to the difference between life and death. The office was inundated with pleas and requests, most of them transparently bogus, and there was clearly little that Calmeyer could do with these. Moreover, Seyss-Inquart had set December 1942 as a final date for decisions, after which cases could only be referred by the German authorities. As a result, the work of his office was gradually wound down.

As with others who had some measure of control over the fate of the Jews in the Netherlands, Calmeyer's conduct has come under close scrutiny. Inevitably, the charge has been made that he could have done more to save (a larger number of) Jews from falling victim to Nazi policies. This view rests on the premise that his power to save through 'downgrading' was untrammelled by outside considerations, but this was clearly not the case. In part, Calmeyer was only able to operate at all by virtue of having the 'easy-going' Friedrich Wimmer as his superior. Moreover, he could not possibly accept every case put to him. This would have aroused immediate suspicions that he was favouring the Jews and would doubtless have led to his removal and replacement by someone more ideologically reliable. A further complication was that any 'Jews' who were subsequently found to be non-Jews were entitled to reclaim their property from Lippmann-Rosenthal & Co. This reversal of policy for certain individuals led to raised eyebrows in a number of quarters and inevitably led to questions being asked about the accuracy of the decisions taken. Calmeyer's actions were also carefully watched by those who were virulently antisemitic, including various officials from the SS and SD. Even in 1941, he was faced with constant opposition and obstruction to his work by the specially appointed *Judenreferat* of the *Befehlshaber der Sicherheitspolizei und des SD*, a post occupied by a fanatical member of the *Nederlandse-SS*, Cornelis Ludovicus (Ludo) ten Cate, who carried out his own investigations into people's racial origins.[7] While ten Cate could not countermand Calmeyer's decisions, he could and did make things far more difficult, especially after July 1942 when the deportations began.[8] Calmeyer's freedom of action was further limited by the fact that some of his colleagues and office staff within his own department were similarly committed to carrying out the ideological imperatives of the occupying power. During 1942 and 1943, his judgement and competence were questioned on a number of occasions. In July 1942 *Referat IVB4* wanted the number on the Calmeyer list reduced to 600 names and by August 1944 its head, *SS-Sturmbannführer* Zöpf, had sanctioned a committee of three to review the decisions already made. As it was, nothing came of this decision,[9] but it suggests that Calmeyer was working at the very margins of what was possible.

In summary, it appears that Calmeyer had a position and was given a set of circumstances which allowed him to assist some sections of the Jewish population to escape the Nazi measures. Herzberg estimates that 95 per cent of the cases he approved were falsified, and that he was probably instrumental in saving 2,000 people through his actions.[10] De Jong is more precise. By January 1944, Calmeyer is said to have certified 2,026 half-Jews and 873 quarter-Jews – a total of 2,899 people – thus removing them from immediate danger. At the same time, his investigations also 'discovered' a further 500 full-Jews who were thereby rendered liable for deportation.[11] Here was a case where someone within the bureaucracy operated, in part at least, against the wishes of his superiors. His conduct is not easily categorised: neither entirely heroic, as he undoubtedly refused at least 25 per cent of the appeals made and was happy to continue his work in making decisions with life and death significance; nor entirely worthy of condemnation, as his help for some Jews testifies. To rationalise his motivation, various commentators have tried to portray him as one who delighted in being contrary for its own sake, rather than acting out of any commitment to helping the victims of Nazi persecution.[12]

As for the applicants to the Calmeyer list, the sources give little indication of who they were, or of their personal circumstances. Some appealed in person while others used lawyers as intermediaries. The costs of providing false papers and documents would not have been insignificant, which suggests that only those with some finance, or alternatively with a genuine case, could really hope to benefit. Even then, money was no guarantee of success. Calmeyer seems to have been able to grant exemptions more readily when parentage was difficult to establish because records were difficult to verify or could be more easily falsified. In this way, applications from Jews with German origins, or those from Curaçao and Suriname, were more likely to succeed merely because it was almost impossible to disprove what the applicants claimed by referring back to the official records. In the case of the Dutch colonial records, he operated in collusion with civil servants at the Interior Ministry, advising them of the appropriate guidance to give to Jews in this situation.

Another, and in many ways more distinct, group also came within the purview of Calmeyer's office, namely the Portuguese or Sephardi Jews. The census of October 1941 had enumerated 4,303 people as belonging to this group, nearly all as full-Jews. In their case, an attempt was made to save all of them as a group by trying to persuade the German authorities that thay had nothing in common with the Ashkenazim save their adherence to the Jewish religion – and thus no racial connection whatsoever. The argument was that the Jewish element in the Sephardi community in 1600 had already been heavily diluted. In the autumn of 1941, a prominent Dutch lawyer was engaged to compile the case and Calmeyer was approached to see if they could be considered as a group. This Calmeyer refused to do, insisting that each case be treated on its merits. As a result, in the following two years his office was inundated with petitions and requests from most of the Sephardi community. In the meantime, he had requested a ruling on the Portuguese Jews from the *Reichssippenamt* in Berlin.[13] Certainly, he did not believe that they could all be excluded from being Jews, after all, they all followed the Jewish faith and this remained an important criterion for the Germans. By the 13 October 1942, 1,015 applications had been processed, of which *c*.400 had been considered worthy of some form of protection.[14] This seems to have been on the basis of how purely Portuguese they were. The problem for many families was that they had intermarried in previous generations with Ashkenazi (Eastern) Jews, making them ineligible for this new special status. An initial list of *c*.1,000 people of wholly or overwhelmingly Portuguese-Jewish origins was ultimately reduced to a core of 362 people. In the event, Calmeyer was unable to protect even this small group. Although 368 people were given an exemption stamp in late 1942, this proved no hindrance to 78 of their number being deported by the end of June 1943.[15]

The threats to this group came thick and fast in the spring and summer of 1943. First they were to be sent to Vught, then to Westerbork in order that some final decision could be made on their status. In June a new criterion was adopted whereby anyone with seven or eight Portuguese great-grandparents was given a new exemption stamp numbered 10,000. This reduced the number protected in this way to a mere 201. In August a reply was received from the *Reichssippenamt* confirming that all were to be treated as Jews, which made the final decision on their fate more or less a foregone conclusion. On 1 February 1944 the remaining Portuguese Jews still at liberty in the Netherlands were rounded up and transported to Westerbork. Of the 180 names on the Amsterdam list, only 108 were found, suggesting that the other 72 had either gone underground or died.[16]

The final inspection of the 22 families consisting of 273 individuals took place on 20 February when *SS-Sturmbannführer* Willi Zöpf and Herbert Aust, and camp commander *SS-Obersturmbannführer* Albert Gemmeker had no hesitation in designating them all as Jews for immediate transport. On 25 February 308 Portuguese Jews were deported to Theresienstadt, to be followed in April by the remainder. While the choice of destination may have something to do with keeping these people available for some form of exchange scheme,[17] the sources recall that all of them were ultimately sent to Auschwitz where they were among the last to be gassed.[18]

In spite of the efforts of the community and the involvement of Calmeyer, it proved impossible to save any of the Portuguese Jewish community through having them 'downgraded' or reclassified. Nevertheless, the defence against Nazi racial policies was ingenious, if ultimately flawed. While even Calmeyer would not accept that there was no connection between Sephardi and Ashkenazi Jewry, he was prepared to contemplate the idea that Portuguese Jews might have little or no Jewish 'blood'. Thus he attempted to save those of pure Portuguese ancestry who were 'untainted' by contact with Jews from Eastern Europe. Exemptions handed out on this basis – to obviously observant members of the Jewish community – must have looked very strange and been particularly galling to anti-semitic elements within the German leadership. In the event, the ruling to treat them all as Jews came from the bosses in Berlin and brooked no further prevarication or procrastination. Unlike those on the Calmeyer list, the protection afforded to the Sephardim by Calmeyer's research was only temporary. What remains unquantifiable is whether the delay in deciding on their ultimate status allowed more Portuguese Jews to go into hiding – and also shortened the time they needed to stay underground – or whether the minority who were protected in the short term put their trust in a bureaucratic escape which ultimately proved to be an illusion.

'Mixed marriages'

Perhaps the best demonstration of German indecision on the 'Jewish question' came in relation to Jews in the Netherlands who were partners in mixed marriages. It might be thought that these people would have been some of the first targets for German legislation, but in fact they were left more or less alone until March 1942. In that month, the Germans became aware that the number of marriages being contracted between Jews and non-Jews in the The Hague was increasing rapidly. At the end of the month, *Generalkommissar* Wimmer ordered the Dutch administration to inform the Sipo when banns for such a marriage were published in future.[19] In the meantime, the authorities in Amsterdam had already taken action, imprisoning 30 Jews who intended to marry non-Jews.[20] At this point, marriages of this nature were perfectly legal, but the Germans rapidly produced an edict to prevent Jews from contracting any form of marriage, 'mixed' or otherwise. Wielek reports that the instant implementation of this legislation meant that some Jewish wedding parties were turned away at town hall steps, unaware that they were doing anything illegal.[21]

Having stemmed any further possibility of 'race defilement', the Germans attempted to ascertain just how many mixed marriages already existed in the Netherlands. On 10 August 1942 J.L. Lentz, the meticulously efficient head of the Census Office, informed Rauter that there were 12,498 Jewish men and 7,388 Jewish women in mixed marriages, making a total of 19,886 or 27.5 per cent of all married Jews. A month later, Calmeyer was able to produce figures to show that there were 6,008 marriages with children and a further 928 childless Jewish women in mixed marriages. The implication was that there were over 10,000 childless marriages where the male was the Jewish partner. This was recognised as an arithmetical error but even his revised figure of 6,000 was thought by an anonymous commentator to be way too high.[22] A German document dated 15 June 1944 gave a total of 8,610 Jews married to non-Jews which, allowing for deportations, deaths and real or spurious divorces, seems to make more sense of Calmeyer's statistics.[23] Even armed with these figures, the Germans seem to have been reluctant to take further definitive action. At the time when exemption stamps were given out, Jewish partners in mixed marriages were allowed to register them as such with the Population Registry and in return received an exemption in the 100,000 category from the *Zentralstelle*. Some 5,000 Jews were protected in this way.[24] In December 1942, when it was decreed that all Jews be moved to Amsterdam, both Jewish and non-Jewish partners in mixed marriages were included together with any children, subsequently non-Jewish partners were exempted, then the children were also allowed to return home. In January 1943 a more considered list of restrictions was published, giving full details of the types of marriages forbidden and the ones still permitted. If this made it appear that there was some consistency in German policy, nothing could be further from the truth. Wielek described it as a 'labyrinthine winding path', and even Presser states that on this issue the Germans 'never knew what they were doing'.[25]

Certainly the staff of the *Zentralstelle* were in favour of a hard line against Jews in mixed marriages, as was *Generalkommissar* Rauter, but they had to contend with protests from Protestant churches and Germans living in the Netherlands, together with the authority of Seyss-Inquart. Attempts were made to persuade partners in mixed marriages to divorce, although this seems to have met with little success. However, this pressure could be used to advantage. There was at least one case where a Jewish husband had gone underground and was being assisted by his non-Jewish wife. She carried a set of divorce papers in her handbag. These had no legal validity but were enough to convince the Germans that the marriage had been annulled. Thus she was able to continue helping her husband unhindered. Other ideas included the removal of all Jews in mixed marriages from Amsterdam to make it truly free of Jews, but nothing came of this particular scheme. In the summer of 1943, Zöpf and his colleagues decreed that a special class of stamp (108,000) would be given to Jews in childless mixed marriages.[26] Far more sinister were the discussions about the sterilisation of all Jews married to 'aryans' which took place in the spring of 1943. This was always intended to be voluntary but perceived as an alternative to deportation. The Jewish Council protested strongly on hearing of the scheme on 20 May, but ultimately established a Medical Liaison Bureau to deal with applications for sterilisation and to have contact with the medical branch of the German security service under *SS-Sturmbannführer* Dr E.W.P. Mayer.

Mayer's role here is interesting. While he was responsible for the sterilisation programme from mid-1943 onwards, it seems clear that he was prepared to accept letters from Dutch doctors certifying that a specific individual was already sterile. It has been estimated that anything up to 2,400 people were saved in this way without the need for surgery. Moreover, his staff at the sterilisation unit, based at the *Joodsche Invalide* Hospital and later at the Portuguese Jewish Hospital, was made up of some 80 Jewish nursing and administrative personnel from there and from the Central Jewish Hospital. All of them were protected until mid-March 1944 when 70 of them were transported to Westerbork. By this stage, Mayer was under investigation for being too lenient towards the Jews. Three months later, the rest of the staff at the Portuguese Jewish Hospital were also designated for transport to Westerbork as the sterilisation programme had ceased. By this stage, most had already gone underground, and the remaining nine were given the task of inventarising the contents of the *Nederlandse Israëlitisch* Hospital for the Germans.[27]

Those who volunteered for sterilisation were given a red 'J' on their identity cards and were exempt from wearing the yellow star. Men were operated on by a Dutch Jewish surgeon who managed three or four dozen operations each week. German figures for June 1944 suggest that 1,146 men had been exempted, mainly after sterilisation, and 1,416 women – giving a total of 2,562. Wielek gives a total of 3,000 exempted in this way, of whom he estimates 600 were saved by actually having sterilisations carried out.[28] Nevertheless, he points out that this group was only a minority and the majority preferred to keep wearing the star and take their chances with deportation rather than be sterilised. In the short term this was not unreasonable. Jews in mixed marriages were called up for labour service early in 1944 and employed on various building projects in the Netherlands (there was no question of sending these Jews to work in Germany). At the end of March, the Germans once again took action, this time rounding up 300 Jews who were either in mixed marriages where the non-Jewish partner had died, or Jewish men whose wives lived abroad, or Jews who had been exempted from wearing the star but had failed to register with the Sipo. All were taken to Westerbork but then released in the following months. Even at this late stage, it seems that the German authorities were unsure what to do with these people.

Attempts by some of the more radical elements within the German administration to find a solution to the question of Jews in mixed marriages were often abandoned or countermanded from above. Thus in May 1943 when Aus der Fünten gave 103 Jews in Westerbork who were married to non-Jews half an hour to decide whether to be sterilised or deported, the project was countermanded by Zöpf who heard about it only through a complaint from one of the non-Jewish wives. The Germans also found it difficult to find Dutch and/or Jewish surgeons to begin the sterilisation of women, and when the Germans attempted to persuade five Jewish doctors in Westerbork to undertake the task they were met with refusal by one of them, and her principled stand led to the policy being abandoned.

Because of German indecision and confusion on the issue, it appears that Jews in mixed marriages did have a better chance of survival in the Netherlands, especially if they were sterilised, certified barren or deemed too old to procreate children. The pattern of their survival is much the same as other groups about whom the Germans had doubts. A large number of them were kept in the Netherlands rather than deported, although as exemption stamps ceased to be valid, some were undoubtedly sent eastwards. Moreover, even attempts to 'solve' the problem of mixed marriages through a sterilisation programme seem to have been only half-hearted and many Jews in mixed marriages who had not been exempted from wearing the star also survived the war. This points to a sense of indecision and even to conflicts within the German hierarchy in the Netherlands. Men such as Rauter and Aus der Fünten seem to have been the ones forcing the pace, but even a convinced antisemite such as Zöpf could be found rescinding demands for sterilisation. This may help to explain how the question of mixed marriages remained unresolved, but not why the German administration was so wary. Certainly Seyss-Inquart was aware of the wider political implications. The existence of Jews married to non-Jews meant that knowledge of any action against them could not be restricted to the Jewish community. Protests could be expected, and there was also the question of children from such marriages. They were, by definition, '*Mischlinge*', but did therefore have certain rights. Perhaps in this case, Seyss-Inquart was happier to let these Jews stay put rather than risk the protests from non-Jewish groups. Certainly, he was conscious of the storm of protest from the main Dutch churches which the sterilisation measures in May 1943 had evoked.

Later in the occupation, a stranger form of protection for these people may have arisen. All the sources speak of the huge increase in (often contradictory) legislation which the Germans issued in the latter part of 1943 and throughout 1944. The weight and scope of these directives seemed to be in inverse ratio to the number of Jews still in the country. A clue to the reason for this may lie in the Germans' own fears about the future. If those involved in the 'Jewish question' in the Netherlands could ever claim that the country was completely free of Jews, then there was no further need for their presence there, and they ran the risk of being transferred. By 1944, this was likely to mean active service and potentially the Eastern Front. Thus it became in the Germans' own best interests to make it appear that they were still busy and this in turn may have helped to save some of the few Jews left in the country in the last 18 months of the occupation.

Precise details of the total number of Jewish survivors from mixed marriages are hard to ascertain, but the best estimate is that there were between 8,000 and 9,000, primarily women with children and childless women. Most of the men did ultimately fall victims to the Germans. While mixed marriages had formerly been confined to the 'refined, well-to-do, irreligious circles', by 1940 this was no longer the case and they were by that time a middle-class phenomenon, with the accent on the lower middle class. Moreover, most of these marriages were of recent date, ensuring that the majority were from the younger end of the married generations.[29] Whatever the reasons for their survival, they represented the largest single group of Dutch Jews saved within the German system.

Baptised Jews

One group who may also have benefited from German indecision was the baptised Jews. The German authorities had first encountered the problem of baptised Jews in relation to the exclusion of Jews from the air-raid protection service in June 1940. At that stage, they were not prepared to make distinctions – Jews, whether baptised or not, had to be dismissed. In the following two years, Seyss-Inquart and other leading German officials received a number of protests from the Dutch churches about the treatment of the Jews.[30] After the protest on 11 July 1942 about the first deportations signed by all the major church leaders, *Generalkommissar* Schmidt informed them that 'Christian Jews' baptised before 1 January 1941 would be exempted from labour service and the work-camps. As the church leaders were to discover, this did not help those who were merely believers or associated with Christian churches, nor did it mean that all the German authorities were prepared to take the same line. Requests to the *Zentralstelle* to release arrested Jews who had been baptised at the end of 1940 produced the response from Aus der Fünten that baptisms after the

Germans' arrival had no value.[31] In the following week, the main
Protestant church *Hervormde Kerk* suggested that the protest of 11 July be
read from the pulpit on Sunday 26 July. The Roman Catholic and Calvinist
(*Gereformeerde*) church leaderships agreed to do likewise, but in the meantime Schmidt had advised against the document being read and told the
churches that they would have to take the consequences of its promulga-
tion. An attempt was made to tell churchmen throughout the country to
set aside the text, but because of the short notice the *Gereformeerde*
churches saw no way to stop their pastors from reading the proclamation
and the Roman Catholic bishops decided that it should be read anyway.
Perhaps because of the positive support given to the action, it was the
Catholic Jews who bore the brunt of German displeasure. On the night of
1–2 August, most of the Roman Catholic Jews were arrested, taken to the
Schouwburg, transported to Westerbork and a few days later deported
eastwards. After the war *Generalkommissar* Harster confirmed that Seyss-
Inquart had ordered the action in revenge for the attitude of the Dutch
Roman Catholic bishops who had spoken out not only against the deportation of Catholic Jews, but against all deportations.[32] There were approximately 690 Catholic Jews in the Netherlands,[33] of whom 300 were foreign
Jews held in camps. Of the others, some were partners in mixed marriages
who were subsequently released on the grounds of their privileged status.
A total of 92 were recorded as having been deported to Auschwitz, including the noted philosopher Edith Stein and her sister from the Carmelite
nunnery at Echt (Limburg).[34]

No action was taken against the baptised *Gereformeerden*, presumably
because the numbers were so small, or against Jews of the *Hervormde Kerk*.
The latter seem to have escaped German reprisals, either because the
Germans were prepared to accept the church's abrogation of responsibility
for the document or because at this stage the administration was not prepared to confront the most powerful Dutch Protestant church head-on. In
the following months, the *Hervormde Kerk* continued to try and obtain
exemptions for all Jews in its congregations. This was to include those
whose parents were church members, those who were being instructed for
confirmation, those who regularly attended church services, those already
baptised and those who had made confession of their Christian faith.
Although the German authorities continually tried to reduce the number of
Jews who qualified for exemptions, 1,156 stamps in the series 20,000–
30,000 had been issued by 2 December 1942. This had risen to 1,575 by
March 1943 but, like the Catholic Jews, many of the Protestant Jews were
actually protected by virtue of their marriage to non-Jews. Needless to say,
there were some who came to be in this category by acquiring false baptismal certificates.[35] These seem to have been easier to obtain from the
Hervormde than from the *Gereformeerde* churches, although there were
objections to 'quick baptisms' within both congregations.[36] At this stage,

the Germans had no intention of deporting the Protestant Jews, but by June 1943 *Reichskommissar* Seyss-Inquart was planning their removal to Westerbork where they were to be kept in separate barracks. The autumn brought the first moves to deport them, but this did not finally take place until 4 September 1944 when 500 Protestant Jews were shipped to Theresienstadt. Of these, only 150 apparently survived to form part of an exchange via Switzerland, and a few others were liberated by the Russians on 8 May 1945.[37]

The Protestant churches have always claimed a good deal of credit for having 'saved' a large proportion of 'their' Jews, yet as Presser points out, they did no more than those who attempted (and failed) to protect the Portuguese Jews. What seems more likely is that for political reasons the Germans *were* more careful in their dealings with the Protestant churches. How else can one explain the time-lapse between the initial decision to deport the Protestant Jews and its execution? The negotiations between the churches and Rauter were long-winded and seem to have been based on the Germans' moral obligation to uphold Seyss-Inquart's undertaking not to deport these people. Certainly the Germans' behaviour was at odds with their treatment of almost every other category of Jews in the Netherlands.

Foreign Jews

The limited protection afforded to the Calmeyer list, Portuguese Jews, Christian Jews and partners in mixed marriages came as a result of German indecision, internal organisational conflicts or inability to interpret their racial theories at central or local levels. However, there were also circumstances in which certain Jews were deliberately protected by the authorities for more pragmatic reasons. 'Foreign' Jews were a source of some confusion to the Germans, as they had been in the Reich prior to 1939, their status having been largely determined by the foreign policy requirements of the state, often much to the disgust of radical antisemites who saw no reason to treat foreign Jews differently. In the occupied Netherlands, some care was taken to differentiate between the Jews who held some claim to foreign nationality. Jews who were citizens of territories annexed by the Reich or occupied by its forces received no special protection and were treated exactly as their Dutch counterparts. The fate of those who were nationals of 'allied' states depended entirely on whether their governments were prepared to take an interest in their well-being. In the case of Croatia, Slovakia and Romania no such interest was forthcoming, although a few Romanian Jews were sent home at the end of 1943. Denmark, Finland and Italy did take advantage of the opportunity to reclaim their citizens, a total of 26 people in all; and the Hungarian government took back 78 of its

Jewish citizens in the summer of 1943, but not before more than 150 had already been sent to the gas chambers.[38]

Jewish citizens of neutral states were treated with slightly more circumspection, and Swedish, Swiss, Spanish, Portuguese, Liberian, Argentinian and even Turkish nationals were allowed to return home during 1943. Rescue rested in part on these neutral states being prepared to take an interest in their nationals, and also the Germans' unwillingness to create diplomatic problems for the sake of such a small number of people. Citizens of enemy powers were protected in a different way. The Germans were unwilling to mistreat them for fear that reprisals would be taken against German civilians in (for example) British, American or Latin American hands. This type of reciprocity failed to protect at least one group of Jews with British nationality who had been prioritised for transport to Auschwitz by *Referat IVB4* in The Hague at the end of 1942.[39] However, at the beginning of 1943, 81 people in this category were taken to civilian internment camps in Germany although around 100 remained behind. Only in the case of Russian Jews was there some official differentiation. Russian Jews who came from areas occupied by the Germans were automatically deported, but those from areas inside the Soviet Union were retained, at least until their precise status had been settled.[40]

The fact that the Germans were cautious in their treatment of foreign Jews created another possible escape route. It soon became apparent that consuls of many South American republics in Europe were prepared to issue papers in exchange for an appropriate payment. This availability of foreign nationality was given an extra cachet in early 1943 when several enemy South American states expressed themselves willing to consider the possibility of exchanges of their citizens for Germans in their hands. In this way, the Paraguayan, Honduran and El Salvadorean consuls in Switzerland and their Ecuadorian counterpart in Stockholm were able to trade in passports, usually without the knowledge of their respective governments. Passports could cost up to $500 and were presumably only available to those people with access to funds of this magnitude inside Switzerland or Sweden. Initially, the consuls sent the papers through the post to recipients in the Netherlands, but the German censors became aware of the trade and informed the RSHA in Berlin. The Sipo then began to intercept the passports and instruct Harster in the Netherlands that the intended recipients should be deported immediately, if this had not already occurred. Enquiries by the Swiss postal service about the non-receipt of registered mail were met with the excuse that they must have been destroyed by Allied bombing. As it became clear that the post was no longer secure, other ways were found to smuggle papers and passports into the Netherlands from Switzerland and Sweden, using businessmen and others who had reason and permission to cross the border unmolested. Thus while it is estimated that the Germans intercepted papers for around 500

Jews, by November 1943 there were about 300 Jews with valid passports from one or other of the four South American states. In addition, there was a brisk trade in forged documents produced inside the Netherlands and some Jews had whole collections of passports, making their exact status difficult to verify. Though Eichmann attempted to get the RSHA to verify all these passports, the task was abandoned in May 1944. By having these papers, some individuals were able to prolong their stay in the Netherlands, the Germans being unwilling to take action against them. Others were taken to Germany, presumably on the basis that they might still be used for exchanges. They apparently ended up at the 'exchange-camp' at Bergen-Belsen where many of them died before the liberation.[41]

The acquisition of new or replacement documents was by no means orderly or risk-free for those Jews able to take advantage of the system. Bureaucratic processes often meant that applicants would be deprived of papers for long periods. If they were arrested and transported during that time, there was often little they could do to persuade the Germans of their special status. Negotiating and organising documents from Westerbork was far more difficult than undertaking the task from home, and the longer they were in the transit camp, the more likely it was that they would be transported to the East before their documents arrived. The German attitude to these cases was reinforced by Eichmann in response to a request for a ruling on Jews applying for Swedish or Portuguese nationality via family members in those countries: 'Insofar as it is known that Jews are trying to obtain a new nationality, no account need be taken of this and the people concerned should, on the contrary, be prioritised for transport to the East.'[42]

Papers, or to be more precise certificates, played an important part in another attempt to save Jews from the Netherlands. A plan was formulated by the Dutch government to obtain 500 Palestine immigration certificates for Jewish children in the summer of 1943. The scheme was put to the *Auswärtiges Amt*, but it delayed its reply for eight months and then insisted that the children be admitted to England. This was accepted by the British but they refused to treat the scheme as an exchange and the plan foundered. Other attempts to obtain Palestine certificates for Jews in the Netherlands were also beset with problems, not least the fact that the Jewish Agency concentrated its rescue attempts on the countries of Eastern Europe. One scheme which did bear some fruit was based on the Germans' desire in 1942 to exchange a few 'Palestinian' women in the Netherlands for Germans held in Palestine. It was discovered that if the Swiss consul communicated names of people applying for Palestine certificates to German and British authorities, they were left alone by the Germans. A limited scheme involving people (primarily Zionists) with family members already in Palestine was soon extended to include those who might have been eligible for a certificate under pre-war circumstances. Ultimately the

Jewish Agency was persuaded to co-operate with the scheme and did begin to issue some certificates. However, bureaucratic delays meant that many of those registered were weeded out for deportation during 1943 before their documentation arrived, as the Germans became increasingly wary about the number of exempt Jews still in the Netherlands. By the end of 1943, some 1,297 Jews were actually in possession of *bona fide* certificates and earmarked for exchanges. In January 1944 they were transferred to the exchange-camp at Bergen-Belsen, from where 221 were ultimately transported via Turkey to Palestine in July 1944. Of the remainder, only a very few survived in the camp.[43]

The 'Barneveld group'

Another means of survival, albeit in a very different way, came from the agreement between Secretary-General of the Interior Ministry Frederiks and *Generalkommissar* Fritz Schmidt to exempt a certain number of prominent Jews from labour service and therefore from deportation. An initial list of five names was expanded through the influence of Secretary-General of Education Professor van Dam until it encompassed several hundred people who were housed in a castle and nearby villa in the vicinity of Barneveld. Arriving just before Christmas 1942, the number of 'Barneveld Jews' had reached 640 people by August 1943. Their apparently privileged treatment and the fact that many did manage to survive the war has inevitably raised the issue of the elites looking after their own and ignoring the plight of the remainder. Presser makes the point that while the group was mainly composed of people from the higher strata of society, there were also representatives of 'a host of other trades and professions'.[44] People did not pay to get on to these lists but were chosen by Fredericks or van Dam as being useful (*verdienstelijke*) Dutch Jewish citizens. More recent scholarship has suggested that many useful Dutch Jews did not get on the list while many useless individuals did. Furthermore, the people involved were overwhelmingly from the upper middle classes with just one or two people from above and below this group.[45] Presser also reiterates the claim made by Frederiks and repeated by Herzberg that Schmidt supported the plan merely because *Generalkommissar* Rauter opposed it.[46] In other words it was a product of the competition and rivalry between two Nazi satraps. Presser finds this explanation unconvincing, not least because Schmidt was known to be just as antisemitic as Rauter. De Jong implies that the Germans never had any intention of keeping their promise of allowing these people to remain in the Netherlands permanently, and that permission for this scheme was only given to maintain relations with the leading Dutch civil servants in the country.[47] It certainly seems improbable that the Germans were sufficiently worried about international opinion to give special status to a few Jewish notables in the Netherlands.

The group, which was by no means socially or politically homogenous, organised a whole range of social and educational activities.⁴⁸ There were well-reported tensions between the various elements in these isolated communities and countless discussions on what the future held. Although their movements were restricted, there were opportunities for escape, and some inmates undoubtedly considered this. However, the false sense of security engendered by the surroundings and the circumstances, together with the possibility of reprisals on those who remained, seem to have prevented defections. During the spring and summer of 1943, their existence became an increasing annoyance to Zöpf and Fraulein Slottke at *Referat IVB4* in The Hague who queried their status and *Generalkommissar* Rauter who wanted them all to be sent to Theresienstadt. In the meantime, their apparent protector, Schmidt, died in France leaving them at the mercy of their detractors. While there was no immediate change to their status and further guarantees were given on their safety, on 29 September (the same day that the Jewish Council in Amsterdam was dissolved) the Germans arrived and gave the whole group 30 minutes to prepare for transport to Westerbork. In the confusion, 25 people did take the opportunity to escape, assisted possibly by the attitude of the German commander who left the perimeter fence unguarded. At Westerbork, the group retained their separate status in the camp with segregated accommodation, even though their luxury lifestyle had been exchanged for the squalid conditions experienced by their less fortunate compatriots. At this stage, the promise to keep the group in the Netherlands had not been broken, but the authorities in Berlin were aware of their existence and intended to send them to the newly established camp for 'notables' at Bergen-Belsen. A few of the Barneveld Jews even volunteered for an early transport there in January 1944, on the basis that they might be exchanged for German prisoners-of-war and sent to Palestine. In the event, the remaining 638 members of this group were transported to Theresienstadt on 4 September 1944 at a time when it appeared that the Allied armies were about to overrun the whole of the Low Countries.⁴⁹

The ultimate fate of this group was markedly different from most of the rest of Dutch Jewry. A few died at Theresienstadt or on the journey there, but of the rest, a few reached Switzerland in early 1945 and the remainder were liberated by the Russians. Their high rate of survival is not easily attributable to a single factor, but a combination of elements seems to have made some contribution. The efforts of Frederiks and van Dam in the initial stages were of course crucial. Not only were they kept in the Netherlands for much longer than most other Jews, but also in markedly better conditions until September of 1943. This may have increased their resilience for what was to come, although conversely it must also have increased the shock value of the conditions experienced in Westerbork and later in Theresienstadt. While it is unlikely that either Schmidt or the other leaders of the German administration saw any great merit in preserving this group, their survival may well have hinged on a change of policy by Himmler. As it became increasingly apparent that the war was being lost, the decision to create a special camp for 'notables' allowed them to remain in the Netherlands while the policy was finalised. In this way, their fate was decided by decisions taken in Berlin. Had this been left to Rauter and Zöpf, they would undoubtedly have been sent eastwards much earlier and with disastrous effect.

What remains is the indisputable fact that these people survived because of their class and their contacts. The Dutch civil servants were in a position to make selections and chose, primarily, those from their own or parallel social circles. Given the small numbers of Jews in these circles, their ratio of survivors to victims is wholly disproportionate when compared with Jews from other classes. They may have lost their jobs and been removed entirely from their normal environment. They may have been driven from their houses and robbed of all their assets. They may have lost members of their families in the deportations, but they themselves were still better off than nearly all their co-religionists.[50] To demonstrate how much the role of class in the survival of Dutch Jewry was resented in the post-war era one has only to reiterate Presser's quote from the *Joodse Wachter* some 10 years after the event. Here was a group who were protected 'for no better reason than that they were members of the middle class intelligentsia. The class distinction this measure introduced belongs to the most horrible pages of the history of Dutch Jewry during the Occupation.'[51] This may be extreme, but it has been pointed out that there were no real criteria for becoming one of the chosen few and *verdienstelijkheid* (usefulness) was never defined. Barnevelders who survived cannot be censured for seeking protection in this way, but it remains the case that they were an unrepresentative group when compared with Dutch Jewry as a whole.

Other lists

While the Frederiks and van Dam lists did have practical results and long-term consequences, other categories suggested by Dutch civil servants were never adopted. At the end of 1942, Secretaries-General Six (Colonies) and Rietveld (Defence) attempted to obtain exemption from deportation for the few hundred Jews who had been in the armed forces in the Indies or in May 1940, and had been wounded or served with distinction. This idea fell at the first hurdle when it failed to gain the support of the German military commander Christiansen.[52] Other schemes to preserve some members of the Dutch Jewish community did, however, interest the Germans, not least those which involved money or assets held outside the country. While the

Germans were always keen to lay their hands on foreign currency, any suggestion that Jews might buy their way to freedom ran against the ideological objectives of the regime and smacked of corruption. For that reason alone, intermediaries had to be used to distance the occupation regime from the proposed transactions. In this way, two further exemption lists were created on a semi-official basis. One was organised by E.A.P. Puttkammer, an assistant bank manager who had supported applications for emigration permits to the Foreign Currency Control Bureau as early as 1941. Later on, applications of this nature ensured the applicant against deportation while Puttkammer tried to negotiate the purchase of exemptions or exit visas against valuables held abroad. In exchange for his help, Puttkammer only asked that the applicants make a modest donation to the German Red Cross. The other list organiser was not so philanthropic, and demanded the payment of fl.1,000 for his help. J.J. Weismann was a member of the NSNAP and a convicted bank robber. Like Puttkammer, he registered applications for Jews wishing to negotiate exemptions and exit papers against assets held abroad. The list collapsed in February 1943 when all those registered were arrested and deported.

No one from the list was given an exit permit but Weismann boasted after the war that he had made fl.125,000 from the list and there is evidence to show that he was also given 10 per cent of the deported Jews' remaining assets.[53] However, Puttkammer was no more successful. His list also collapsed in February 1943, although he did attempt to compile a second list which kept some Jews in the Netherlands for a further period. In the meantime, the RSHA raised the tariff to 'at least' fl.100,000 per person, and then only for older Jews.[54] Like Calmeyer, both men's conduct was closely scrutinised after the war, and while it became clear that Weismann had merely been profiteering at the expense of his victims, many survivors attested to the help which Puttkammer had afforded them.[55] Sundry other lists also existed, for example the list compiled by the German delegate to the Netherlands Bank, Dr Albert Bühler, of Jews who played an important role in economic life and had considerable international contacts, and the Bondy list of people who were supposedly exempt from deportation through the agency of a Sipo chief in The Hague. Some are better known than others, but undoubtedly the greatest controversy surrounds the lists involving Friedrich Weinreb.

The Weinreb controversy

While the instigators of many other lists were investigated after the war, the so-called Weinreb affair[56] served to create a division between those who felt he had been a hero of the resistance and those who regarded him as an out-and-out collaborator. At the end of the war, he was sentenced to three-and-a-half and then six years in prison for his conduct. In spite of this, he retained some supporters, most notably Jacob Presser, who made it clear that he thought Weinreb had been made a scapegoat. Finding nothing wrong with Weinreb's behaviour during the occupation, Presser asserted that the shortcomings of the non-Jews in the Netherlands required them to discover sufficient Jewish traitors to explain the catastophe. The debate was further fuelled by the publication of Weinreb's own memoirs in three volumes, *Collaboratie en Verzet 1940–45* in 1969.[57] The debate had rapidly moved outside the academic sphere and had become a matter of intense public interest. So much so, that the government commissioned the RIOD to reinvestigate the whole issue and to address the question of whether Weinreb's conduct should be viewed in any other light than the one taken by the courts in 1948.[58] To understand the confusion caused by the Weinreb affair, one must first look at what he claimed to have done, and what he was accused of doing. Only when armed with this information can the findings of the RIOD commission be placed in context.

Friedrich Weinreb was an orthodox Jew, originally from Austria-Hungary but a naturalised Dutch citizen. He had come to the Netherlands at the age of six and had ultimately become an economist working at the *Nederlands Economisch Instituut* (Netherlands Economic Institute) where he produced a number of publications, including a thesis on the development of the building industry. He worked more or less legally at the Institute until November 1941 and illegally until July 1942. As a leader of the East European Jewish community in Scheveningen, he was asked for advice by fellow Jews who had been called up for labour service in February 1942. Through enquiries via the local employment exchange, Weinreb discovered that exemption could be obtained for anyone attempting to emigrate. All that was then required was a typewriter to produce an appropriate letter. The technique worked and by the time the deportations began in June, he had managed to help around 30 people. The deportations increased the pressure on Weinreb to continue his rescue activities, and he was flattered by the idea of fulfilling such a role. To increase the 'weight' of his exemptions, he had letterheads printed bearing the title of a fictitious *Wehrmacht* officer *General-Leutnant* Herbert Joachim von Schumann, under whose authority Weinreb was supposed to be organising Jewish emigrations to unoccupied France. In total, there were some 800 people who were being 'protected' by this non-existent officer. In the initial stages, Weinreb claimed he had not received any money for his services, but eventually those wishing to register were asked for a fee. Crucially, the Weinreb list was accepted by the SD in The Hague and by the German authorities in Westerbork, which meant that none of the Jews registered was actually deported to the East.

In September 1942 he was arrested by the SD, after a young Jewess on his list had confessed that he had advised her to go underground while waiting for her emigration. At that stage, he claimed that he had been working on behalf of a mysterious German called von Rath and a Dutch accomplice named Six, and managed to convince the SD that he had been the innocent dupe in their scheme to extract assets from Jews. As a result, he was released in order to renew contact with these mysterious men, not least because the SD wanted more information on this supposed *Wehrmacht* attempt to undermine their control in the Netherlands. He then had to report daily in order to provide information, but obviously could not produce the invented von Rath or Six. An attempt to have a man impersonate Six failed and led to Weinreb's second arrest on 19 January 1943. On this occasion, he was much more harshly treated by the Germans and badly beaten. In May he was transferred to Westerbork as a punishment case and spent the following few weeks in the hospital. In July the Germans apparently persuaded him to work for them in contacting and then betraying Jews who had gone underground. He responded by proposing to establish a second 'list' which would be used to catch these people, but which would need to be given some credibility by including some Jews already in Westerbork who were apparently protected by inclusion. He was allowed to return to The Hague and to set up an office with official forms, stamps and letterheads. Even his wife and five surviving children were allowed to join him. The second Weinreb list did therefore serve to protect a number of Jews already in Westerbork for a limited period, although they were required to pay (sometimes substantial) sums of money for the privilege. Most of the money seems to have ended up in the hands of the SD. In addition, Weinreb did register some people who had gone underground, but using only their old addresses. Thus, when the second list finally collapsed on 3 February 1944, no one in hiding was betrayed, but those in Westerbork who were not protected by some other form of exemption were immediately deported to Auschwitz. Sensing that the game was up, Weinreb and his family went underground on 7 February, a day before they would have been arrested, and survived the war.

In the end, no one was saved directly by either of the Weinreb lists. Both ultimately collapsed when the Germans ran short of numbers for the transports to the East. However, it could be argued that inclusion on these lists, like all the others, and the temporary exemptions it conveyed, did provide people with some measure of protection and a better chance of survival – even if this was not apparent at the time. Certainly, there were Jews who emerged from hiding at the end of the war who attributed their survival in part to inclusion on one of the two Weinreb lists. However, there were also charges levied against Weinreb which served to put a rather different gloss on his behaviour, implying that he had betrayed people in the pursuit of monetary gain and in an (ultimately successful) attempt to save himself and his family from deportation. The indictment was, firstly, that he had defrauded a large number of Jews and others by making false claims that the possibility existed for them to emigrate abroad with the co-operation of the German authorities, and had charged 100 guilders or more for people to register with the scheme. Secondly, he was accused of having worked for the SD after his first arrest and set up the scheme to catch Jews already underground and to obtain money from those still in Westerbork. Thirdly, it was alleged that he had acted as a stoolpigeon while under arrest in the gaol at Scheveningen between January and May and July and September 1943, talking and listening to other inmates and then passing on the information to the Germans. In addition, he was also accused of a series of other betrayals.

The RIOD report, while confirming and corroborating much of what the courts and indeed Weinreb's own memoirs had claimed, did alter some aspects and interpretations of the story.[59] To begin with, the idea that Weinreb had begun his work to help people who came to him for advice was entirely spurious. The whole scheme had been designed to make money from the outset. It was estimated that he had acquired at least fl.375,000 from the first list. While some of this had been spent on his office and the staff he employed, the rest was used to defray his household expenses, pay the costs of keeping some of his relatives underground and supplied with false papers, and in the purchase of books. The report concluded that the first list had been little more than a 'swindle on a grand scale'.[60] The report also had strong indications that Weinreb's contacts with the SD in early 1943 might have been instrumental in the arrest of a number of Jews in hiding and their helpers in Amsterdam. While it is cautious on a number of other charges, the report's authors were convinced that Weinreb had told the SD about a woman in the Reinkenstraat who had 25 Jews hiding in her flat. All were arrested and ultimately deported to Sobibor. Most damning of all were the charges relating to his period in Scheveningen gaol. Here the authors were also convinced that Weinreb had co-operated with the SD in betraying other inmates in exchange for better food and conditions. Clearly, if one accepts the findings of the RIOD as conclusive, then the Weinreb story does need some modification. His role was in no way philanthropic, except in relation to his own family, and was concerned initially with material gain and later with self-preservation. His claim that the fraud involved in the first list was organised to benefit the Jews involved and not to swindle them does not stand close examination, and the charges of betrayal are more or less unanswerable.

Ultimately neither Presser's defence of Weinreb nor those of his other proponents stood up to close scrutiny. The idea that he was being used as a scapegoat to explain the failure of the Dutch people to protect their Jewish neighbours may have served to attack the traditional, orthodox and rather smug depiction of the Dutch heroically resisting the German occupation, but could not excuse or hide the crimes he had committed. Perhaps more importantly, this attack on the widely held view served to reopen the debate on the whole question of why so many Jews from the Netherlands had fallen victim to the Holocaust, and helped to stimulate new lines of enquiry. The RIOD report also highlighted a crucial problem of interpretation. In trying to determine Weinreb's individual actions as either positive or negative, the authors inevitably came up with a balance. On the one hand, Weinreb was certainly guilty of the crimes for which he had been sentenced, and also for some which had never come to trial. On the other hand, whether by accident or design, his actions had served to assist a number of Jews to escape the hands of the Germans and to survive the occupation period. As Schöffer asks, is it possible for a judiciary or historians to make hard and fast judgements on the basis of a balance, even when reduced to impersonal percentages of victims and survivors?[61]

Economic exemptions

The Germans also found pragmatic reasons to protect small numbers of Jews in the Netherlands, either because of their particular status, reputation, relationship to Nazism or individuals within the party's hierarchy, or economic usefulness. In March 1942 a specific category of people called the 'blue-knights' was created by Calmeyer's office. The name referred to the symbol placed on the individual's registration card at the *Zentralstelle* which exempted them from wearing a yellow star and gave them a certain but unspecified degree of freedom. At least 45 people were designated in this way. They including 13 ex-members of the NSB, five married to non-Jews who had sons fighting at the front, three art experts working for *Reichsmarschall* Goering, three musicians from the Conservatoire Orchestra, and a German Olympic champion of 1896. While the precise fate of all these people is unknown, at least three were allowed to emigrate (the violinist Flesch, his wife and an art dealer) and some others did survive the war.[62]

Usefulness to the German war economy also became a means to avoid deportation. In September 1942 Seyss-Inquart had decreed that all skilled Jewish workers were to be given exemptions. In this, he was backed by the military authorities who were keen to maximise the labour potential of all the workers in the Netherlands. The military cited the case of Germany where economically useful Jews were the last to be deported and certainly took precedence over those who were useless but who 'were exempted from deportation and kept in special camps, for instance in Barneveld'.[63] In opposition to this policy were *Generalkommissar* Rauter and the staff of *Referat IVB4* in the The Hague, together with their superiors in Berlin. By 3 November 1942, there were 6,716 exemptions in this category who had stamps numbered between 60,000 and 80,000 in their identity cards. Rauter consistently tried to have the numbers reduced. To reinforce his case, he claimed (not without some evidence) that Jews working for the armaments industry were part of a sabotage organisation. With Himmler's backing, he was able to place pressure on the *Rüstungsinspektion* and on 2 December it produced a list containing 1,737 names of workers who could be 'released for immediate transportation'. Further monthly lists were promised, but in March 1943 *Fräulein* Slottke noted that there were still 1,842 Jews in the armaments industry, 792 of whom were working directly for the *Wehrmacht*. In addition there were 600 in the clothing industry and a further 574 in the diamond industry. Further pressure resulted in more cuts and the remaining munitions workers being sent to work in Vught. Finally, all the exemptions were revoked at the end of May. By this stage, Zöpf was desperate to find sufficient numbers of Jews to make up his monthly quota for deportation.[64] In some respects, the fate of these skilled workers was tied up with the conflict between the economic and the ideological imperatives of the German occupation administration. In this instance, it became a battle between the power of the *Wehrmacht* and the *Rüstungsinspektion* on the one hand and the SS, represented by Rauter and *Referat IVB4*, on the other. What is clear from the outcome of the discussions on these people is that the SS had the upper hand in the Netherlands. The fact that the country was under civilian rather than military control gave the SS leadership and its representatives much more leverage in the various power struggles that took place, and led to the ideological aims of the regime taking precedence over economic necessity.

The only partial exception to this rule was in the diamond industry. As one of the world's leading centres for diamonds, Amsterdam had a large number of merchants and around 3,400 workers, although many had not worked for some time owing to the depressed state of the market. The sector was recognised as important by the Germans, but the complication for them was that 80 per cent of the merchants and 2,100 (62 per cent) of the workers were Jewish.[65] Even the SS conceded that the industry was important to the German war effort, but the position of the industry in the Netherlands was complicated by the number of authorities who claimed some control over its operation. In 1940 the *Reichskommissariat* had no specialist department to deal with the industry but used external consultants such as *Kriegsverwaltungsrat* (War Administration Councillor) Tidemann Lemberg in Antwerp, and after 1941 Arthur Bozenhardt, the owner of a diamond wholesale firm in Hamburg. Inside the German administration, the industry was dealt with by Carl Hanemann, *Referent der Gruppe 'Sonstige Industrie'* (Advisor for the Department for Special Industries). In Berlin, questions relating to the industry were dealt with by the Reich Economics Ministry until 1942, when Goering took an interest as Reich Plenipotentiary for the Four Year Plan. In addition, it should be recalled that Abraham Asscher as leader of the Jewish Council was also one of the leading diamond merchants in Amsterdam, thus linking his position with that of the industry as a whole.

Because of Germany's chronic shortage of diamonds, both cut and industrial, the industry in the Netherlands was at first protected from the aryanisation decrees VO189/1940 of 22 October 1940 and VO48/1941 of 12 March 1941. Moreover, there were no direct controls placed on diamond firms and they were allowed to function more or less normally.[66] There seemed to be an agreement by all the German authorities, including the RSHA, *Referat IVB4* and the *Zentralstelle*, that the Jews in this sector should be left alone. Only when the first indiscriminate *razzias* and deportations began in July 1942 were some diamond cutters arrested. Bozenhardt immediately pressed for a series of exemptions for both merchants and workers. As a result, two lists were drawn up, one of 300 merchants by the State Diamond Office and one of 500 diamond workers by a representative of the former *Algemene Nederlandse Diamantbewerkers Bond* (Dutch General Diamond Workers' Union).[67] While this measure served to give temporary respite to those in work, it could do nothing to assist the skilled but unemployed in the industry. These exemptions, with their special stamps, held good until January 1943 when the Sipo insisted that the number be cut from 800 to 400. When the State Diamond Bureau refused to co-operate, Hanemann and Bozenhardt carried out the task themselves.[68] On 6 June 1943 Goering ordered the Bozenhardt Company to buy up all the remaining diamond stocks in the Netherlands. This more or less legal trading meant that the remaining 'diamond-Jews' would have to stay in Amsterdam. The Germans nevertheless remained worried that some merchants would not sell all their stocks and thus began a third list whereby diamond merchants could buy exemptions for their relatives by 'paying' 50 carats of industrial diamonds per person. Some firms were able to find these from existing stocks but others tried to buy on the open market and the price shot up from fl.3 to fl.300 per carat. In this way, an exemption which might normally have cost fl.150 rose in price to something like fl.15,000. Once all the demand had been met, the Germans cynically withdrew the exemptions and some 200 people were immediately transported to Westerbork.[69] In September nearly all those involved, like so many others who had been exempted, were rounded up and sent to Westerbork or Vught. Hanemann did attempt to save a few of the leading merchants by suggesting that they might make a gift to the Reich. Stones valued at fl.600,000 were produced by 20 firms and Hanemann travelled to Berlin to try and obtain their release, but without success.[70] After this, only 40 workers and merchants (150 people including the families) were left in Amsterdam working first in a makeshift factory in the Jewish Invalid Hospital and later at Asscher's diamond works where they remained until May 1944.[71]

Hanemann and Bozenhardt were still able to afford some protection to the 'diamond-Jews' taken to Westerbork in September 1943. As a result, they were kept there until the Germans decided to move their diamond-cutting operations to Bergen-Belsen. From May until September, the dia-

mond workers were given certain privileges within the camp, but they had
little to do and were ultimately divided. The men were sent to
Sachsenhausen as skilled workers and the women to Beendorf. The operation was overseen by another Jewish diamond merchant Henri Soep, and
he and Abraham Asscher were the only two to remain with their families in
Bergen-Belsen until its liberation by Allied forces. Presser ascribes this to
Asscher's previous service as president of the Jewish Council and Soep's
adoptive Paraguayan nationality.[72]

While the Germans had 600 non-Jewish diamond workers still working
in Amsterdam, Berlin realised that in order to keep the core of the industry
intact, some of the merchants and skilled Jewish diamond cutters would
also have to be kept in the Netherlands. At the end of 1942, it appears that
Himmler, at whose instigation the deportations were carried out, tried to
set up a diamond industry in Vught, with the ultimate intention of training
disabled SS men for the work.[73] At considerable trouble and expense,
machinery was transported there from abandoned workshops in Amsterdam
and by September 1943 a few score diamond cutters and their families
had been transferred. Nothing came of Himmler's training scheme and
eventually some of the skilled workers were accidentally deported to
Auschwitz and killed rather than to Bergen-Belsen where the whole project
was transferred in May 1944.[74]

In the short term, it appears that the crucial importance of diamonds to
the German war economy did serve to protect those in the industry. The
treatment afforded to merchants, employed cutters and polishers alike
undoubtedly made them a privileged and protected group at a time when
others had no protection. Even in the final year of the war, and in a concentration camp inside Germany, they continued to enjoy a special status
until the whole edifice of the Third Reich began to crumble. By this stage,
the importance of diamonds to the German war economy had receded and
the protection which their special skills and status afforded was no longer
of any great value, either to the cutters or the merchants, but it had
allowed some of them and their families to remain exempt from deportation longer than most, and then to be transferred to a concentration camp
rather than be summarily executed in the last months of the war.
Nevertheless, in general terms it is clear that the ideological imperatives of
the SS ultimately triumphed over economic considerations, even when all
the parties concerned, including Himmler and the RSHA, could see the
advantages of keeping the diamond industry intact.

Another small group of Dutch Jews were also protected from the initial
ghettoisation and deportation programmes not so much by their economic
importance as by their employment with Philips, the large Dutch electrical
firm based in Eindhoven. The role of the Philips concern during the
Second World War has been the subject of much subsequent controversy
and debate. On the one hand, the company had been considered essential

to the German war effort and had been designated a *Luftwaffebetrieb* (German Air Force plant) under the control of a German *Verwalter* (administrator). In this way, it had received fl.200 million worth of orders from the Germans and had also used labour from concentration camps. However, the company, or at least some of its servants, had supplied the resistance with radio equipment, acted as a conduit for information between the Netherlands and England and, as mentioned above, tried to protect the most vulnerable members of its own workforce.[75] In addition, at least one leading member of the company's management had helped to smuggle false papers for Jews into the country from Switzerland.[76]

While the debate on the conduct of Philips during the war will doubtless continue, its protection of Jewish employees is worthy of more detailed consideration. At the end of 1941, the Jewish employees were designated as part of the *Speciale Opdrachten Bureau* (Special Commissions Office) in order to protect them and their families. An attempt to evacuate legally the hundred or so employees and their families to Spain or Portugal misfired and in August 1943 the Germans insisted that they be transferred to the *Judendurchgangslager* (Jews' transit camp) Vught.[77] The camp contained many non-Jewish prisoners of various sorts as well as all the Jews who had been cleared from the southern and eastern provinces of the country in April 1943. Conditions here were bad, but made worse by the attitudes of the German camp command and guards. Child mortality was especially high, testifying to the insanitary conditions and deliberate neglect which the inmates were forced to suffer. Even here, the company was able to offer some degree of protection. At the beginning of 1943, Philips had been offered the chance to use labour in this concentration camp. Although unwilling at first, Frits Philips consulted other directors and the resistance, and was persuaded that such a collaboration could be beneficial. As a result, the *Philips Speciale Werkplaats Vught* was set up inside the camp in mid-1943, with its employees designated as a separate Philips-*Kommando*. The special, if not privileged, status afforded to workers in the *Kommando* allowed the organisers to employ some Jews already in the camp, who were most in need of protection from deportation, as well as the Jewish employees brought from Eindhoven in August. Most of the Jews in the camp were transported to Auschwitz on 15 November 1943,[78] but the radio assembly work done by the *Kommando* was considered sufficiently important to allow them to stay. Only on 2 June 1944 were the Philips workers and their families, numbering 496 in all, deported to Auschwitz.[79] Yet even here, the company was able to protect at least some of them. The whole group were registered and given camp numbers, and on 10 and 23 June all but 50 were transferred to a *Telefunken* plant at Reichenbach. Those who remained behind were older women and mothers with children, all of whom later perished. Of those sent to work at Reichenbach, 160 were reported to have survived, including nine children.[80]

There is no simple explanation of why this particular group were allowed to stay in the Netherlands for so long, or why they were used as labour after their transport to Auschwitz. Unlike other concentration/transit camps in the Netherlands such as Westerbork and Amersfoort which were under Sipo command, Vught was controlled by the *SS-Wirtschaftsverwaltungshauptamt* (WVHA) in Berlin. As a result, economic function may have been given a higher priority than in other camps. Yet this can be only part of the answer. Vught had been used to accommodate other specialist craftsmen, such as the supposedly 'exempted' 453 workers brought to the camp from Amsterdam in January 1943, but there is no evidence that their skills were ever put to good use. Certainly, there were other industries in the camp, most notably the Escotex (clothing and fur) and Menist (rag-sorting) concerns. Both Jews and non-Jews were employed in these *Kommando*, as they were in the heavy labour groups which operated both inside and outside the camp. For the Jews in the camp, working in one of these other groups provided little protection and the transport on 15 November 1943 took the last of the Jewish Escotex workers from the camp.

The only conclusion can be that a combination of the particular skills of the Philips workers and the influence and importance accorded to the company's activities by the Germans helped to delay their deportation and then keep the majority of them out of the gas chambers. How that influence was exerted is another matter. It seems unlikely that the WVHA in Berlin would have regarded the work done by Philips in Vught as crucially important. It is far more likely that the Philips group was protected by the camp command. As was customary in such cases, Philips paid the camp command for the labour provided by the inmates. Given the well-documented corruption of the camp commandants,[81] it is just conceivable that they were unwilling to lose such a useful source of revenue. This implies that they were in a position to benefit personally from payments made by the Dutch companies, but the same would apply even if the money was only used to offset the running costs of the camp.

In conclusion, two points deserve emphasis. Firstly, the substance of the charge that Philips exploited concentration camp labour to fulfil contracts for the *Wehrmacht* is true but needs to be seen in the light of the estimates which suggest that the productivity of workers in the *Speciale Werkplaats* was only 40 per cent of normal and that the company probably lost around fl.1 million on the project.[82] Secondly, this brief account may suggest that the Jews held at Vught were somehow better off than those in Westerbork. Nothing could be further from the truth. While at first some people did benefit from food parcels and other help, as the war turned against the Germans so conditions gradually deteriorated. Ultimately, large numbers of people, and especially children, died in the camp, and others were so weakened as to make their death a foregone conclusion. Neither rank nor privileged status was any real protection from the 'brutal, primitive, violent and depraved' behaviour of the guards.[83] A contemporary description of the deportation of the 'privileged' Philips group in June 1944 should suffice as an example.

> The Jews were driven like beasts, and had to stand for hours in the scantiest of clothes. Many of them were sick or infirm. ... some of them were pulling up tufts of grass [to eat], only to have them snatched out of their hands. They were treated brutally.[84]

While some other Jews may have been protected or sheltered from the Germans by their employers, the Philips example is probably as close as the Netherlands came to having its own Oskar Schindler.

|7|

Survival in hiding

The numbers involved and the problem of sources

The vagaries of the Nazi system for the deportation and extermination of Jews from the Netherlands created some loopholes which allowed a small number of Jews to remain at large during the occupation period. Apart from those in mixed marriages, this form of survival was usually a matter of luck rather than judgement and often depended on circumstances and events outside the Netherlands. The majority of those who lived through the war did so by going into hiding. The Dutch developed a specific term for these people, *onderduikers* (literally 'people who go underwater' or 'divers').[1] Estimates vary for the precise number of Jews who escaped from the Germans in this way. Herzberg suggests that 4,000 children and around 8,000 adults owed their survival to going underground; Berkley puts the number who went underground at 25,000 with about 10,000 of them being caught by the Germans before the liberation. Presser, while agreeing with the latter figure, thinks that perhaps 20,000 made the attempt to hide.[2] More recent studies have suggested figures of 24,000–25,000 in hiding and 16,000–17,000 surviving, of whom around 4,000 were children.[3] Estimates of this type remain problematic, based as they are either on deducting the number of those deported from the 1941 census of the Jewish community, or on the number of surviving Jews identified by Dutch authorities at the end of the war. Moreover, the whole question of *onderduikers* and their helpers is further complicated by the fact that it was not only Jews who went into hiding. Increasing German demands for factory and other labour to work in the Reich provoked escalating levels of resistance from the Dutch population as a whole after 1942. During 1944, when the Germans were raiding Dutch cities and rounding up all able-bodied men for labour service, irrespective of their function in the Netherlands, it has been estimated that 300,000 people had also become *onderduikers* of one sort or another.[4] In other words, in the latter stages of the occupation, the Jews were a very small minority of those actually in hiding in the Netherlands and were far outweighed by non-Jews trying to avoid conscription for labour service.

To examine how Jews went underground, and then survived in the Netherlands, four main questions need to be addressed. In the first instance, some attention has to be given to the reasons why, when and where Jews decided to go underground. In looking at this, the inevitable comparison has to be made between the minority who chose this course of action and the majority who did not, or could not, follow suit. Secondly, there is the whole question of everyday life underground. What did this mean in practice and how was it organised? How did those in hiding deal with their changed circumstances and the new pressures and tensions this created? Thirdly, there is the extensively examined issue of the motivation and nature of those who gave help to Jews underground. As in every occupied European country, this has been a central feature of research on the persecution of the Jews. Help was essential for survival underground, but how was it organised? There are cases of individual rescue and of organisations who tried to save many hundreds. Did the rescuers come from identifiable groups in Dutch society or were there representatives from all classes and *zuilen*? Implicit in this investigation is a comparison with other Western European states. That same comparison is also inherent when examining the final element in the story, the factors which worked against Jews surviving underground in the Netherlands. Here, attention has to be focused on the general dangers experienced by those in hiding and the specific circumstances which made survival underground in the Netherlands so difficult.

In the most general terms, there were three different ways in which Jews were able to go underground. The term itself is misleading as it suggests going into hiding, but hiding could take a number of different forms. For example, there were a few Jews who managed to avoid registration by the Dutch authorities *as Jews* and were then legally able to remain at large as 'non-Jews' throughout the occupation. The numbers who managed the bureaucratic sleight-of-hand were extremely small and were probably confined to non-Dutch Jews who managed to obtain papers and identity cards at the very beginning of the German occupation which did not mark them out either as refugees or as Jews.[5] A second form of hiding conforms more to the stereotypical view, of going underground in cellars, attics, barns or other places where detection by the Nazis might be avoided. This naturally involved outside assistance to provide food, clothing and the other essentials needed to sustain life. In this regard, those in hiding became almost entirely dependent on third parties. The final form of underground life involved going into hiding before or when individuals were threatened with arrest and deportation by moving to new districts and/or using false papers to pass themselves off as non-Jews. This allowed the individual to live openly, albeit often with forged papers and ration cards, rather than permanently underground. This type of categorisation may make such choices appear clear-cut and straightforward, but in reality this was anything but the case.

The literature on this element of the persecution in the Netherlands has tended to create a rather uneven picture of life underground. There are a number of reasons for this. For example, the first-hand accounts of life and survival underground tend to come from those who did survive. There are, of course, exceptions where letters and diaries of those subsequently deported have been preserved, but most of the memoirs relate to success rather than failure. As a result, the experiences of Jews who went underground but who were subsequently discovered and deported are not part of the narrative, except through the medium of third parties.[6] All the major secondary sources give some space to the discussion of Jews who went underground, but these discussions are seldom of great length. Presser probably has the most comprehensive survey, drawing not only on the literature published up to 1965, but also on the material at the *Rijksinstituut voor Oorlogsdocumentatie* and on his own experience of being in hiding. However, he readily admits that the sources are incomplete: a few accounts from so many people, stories from those who survived rather than those who were deported.[7] While many more publications have appeared since 1965, this conclusion still holds good. Similarly, memoirs of those who helped Jews in hiding are scarce. While there are some notable books by individuals on their activities,[8] details of organisations assisting Jews and their day-to-day activities can only be pieced together. The RIOD has one diary of a noted rescuer for the months between July 1943 and October 1944, as well as the records from the *Landelijke Organisatie* (LO), a national rescue organisation, but most of these accounts have little to say about the years 1941–42 when Jews first went into hiding.[9]

Since the war, more attention has been given to analysing the role and motivation of those people who aided or abetted Jews hiding in occupied Europe. Personal testimonies have been collected from both survivors and their helpers. While of enormous value in their own right, these sources also have certain limitations and may present a rather unbalanced picture of the help given to Jews by the non-Jewish population at large. To understand this, one has to look at the motives behind the research. One major source used by many scholars has been the archives of the Yad Vashem, which contains details and studies of people nominated for the title 'righteous gentile'. The primary aim of this organisation is to identify and reward those who contributed to the saving of Jewish lives during the Holocaust period. Inevitably, the reports contain mainly or exclusively the 'good' side of Jewish rescue and say little of the negative elements.[10] While this bias is an inevitable part of the work, it again has to be remembered that personal testimonies collected after the war are again from those who survived. Thus most of the Jews who perished, and in many cases those who helped them, are unrepresented in the sources on which post-war accounts are based.

A further restriction comes from the time when the evidence was collected. Many of the historical, sociological and psychological studies of Jews in hiding and their helpers conducted their interviews in the late 1970s and early 1980s, some 30 or 40 years after the event. Inevitably, time and distance from the events of the occupation played a part in colouring the memories, as did the fact that many other people who had been involved in the rescue of Jews had died before their stories could be recorded. These surveys have also tended to concentrate on the positive aspects of Jewish rescue. One of the most important and wide-ranging studies, conducted by Samuel and Pearl Oliner, is specifically aimed at identifying altruism as a factor in motivating rescuers.[11] A Dutch example is a sociological study of Jewish children and their non-Jewish 'foster-parents' who hid them in the Netherlands during the war. In this latter case, the authors recognise that finding children and their hosts willing to talk about their experiences more than 40 years after the event limits the sample and also produces a picture of an 'elite' group which is unrepresentative of the experiences of Jewish children or their wartime foster-parents as a whole.[12] Historians have also tackled the issue of rescue, both in national and comparative terms.[13] Recent publications have shed new light on the nature of rescue in the Netherlands, but some of the older works on the subject need to be treated with caution. The apparent collective shame felt by post-war European states and many of their Christian churches for having done too little to save the Jews in their midst from the occupying Germans has led to a concentration on what *was* achieved by churches and secular authorities which again provides a rather unbalanced view of the overall picture in any particular country or region.[14] While not unimportant, the roles played by the churches and bureaucratic institutions in saving Jews may well have been overestimated in the literature to date, as a result of this *post facto* attempt at rehabilitation. Sources on the factors which militated against Jewish survival in the Netherlands are less problematic but nevertheless also fragmentary. Accounts written by surviving rescuers and bystanders often give detailed information on how and why Jews underground were caught. Moreover, German archives captured at the end of the war also provide important insights into the Nazis' single-minded pursuit of their Jewish victims throughout the occupation period.[15] While the culpability of the Dutch authorities in hunting down Jews in hiding has been examined mainly in relation to population registration, work on the activities of the German and Dutch police in tracking down those underground is starting to shed new light on their role.[16]

The decision to go underground

Given the statistic that only around one in seven of the Jews in the Netherlands after 1940 even attempted to go into hiding, one is forced to ask why this should have been the case. The sources and memoirs do provide at least some of the answers. First of all, the relatively mild nature of German rule in 1940 coupled with a gradual introduction of restrictive legislation militated against a sudden 'breaking point' where Jews felt that they would be better off in hiding. While Social Democrat and Communist Jews may have been an exception to this, it was not really until the introduction of compulsory labour service that going underground was considered as an option. Even then, the arguments against such a step were formidable. There was no hope in the medium term, or even the long term, that the Germans might be driven out of the Netherlands, and the increasing levels of legislative restriction and conscription gave the lie to the possibility that the Germans might eventually allow the Jews to remain in the country unmolested. All this meant planning for an indeterminate period in hiding, yet for most people this was almost an impossibility. Without work or income, the individual would be forced to rely on realisable assets, yet how long would these last? Indeed, how could one plan for the future of the occupation? Going underground made reliance on third parties inevitable, both in an active and a passive sense. Potential *onderduikers* had to depend on others to provide them with food, shelter and many other essentials of everyday life. How did one find such people who could be trusted in this way? Could such services be bought or did it depend on finding the right person? At a passive level, people living underground were also at the mercy of those who were aware of them being in hiding but who chose not to betray them to the authorities.

Innumerable practical considerations stood in the way of the potential *onderduiker*. The idea of living in hiding was alien in itself, and few, even of those who did take the plunge, really knew what they were letting themselves in for. A much quoted example is of a woman who had gone into hiding in the draughty attic of a farmhouse with her husband in September of 1942. As winter drew nearer, she wrote in her diary, 'This is the thirty-eighth day of our hiding; I so hope there won't be thirty-eight more.' In fact, she and her husband spent a further 933 days in the attic until the liberation.[17] A more important consideration was finding someone willing to take the risks involved in providing help. When the round-ups began, where did the Jews in Amsterdam look for help? Clearly, contacts within the Jewish community were of little use and one had to look outside for that most prized of possessions, an 'address' where one could hide.[18] Social or business contacts played some part in this. It has been suggested that knowing the fugitive and/or the family personally was a major factor in persuading Netherlanders to help Jews to hide.[19] Some Jews actually received offers of help,[20] while others were prepared to knock on doors, more or less at random, in the hope of finding someone who would help them rather than betray them. It may well be that more Jews did decide to go underground than the figures suggest, but failed to find anyone willing to take them in. Even allowing for this possibility, it is still true that the majority did not even make the attempt. Perhaps they regarded the problems as too great, or were too wedded to their homes and possessions to consider leaving.[21] One survivor who had planned to go underground with his business partner later recorded that the partner's wife was too sentimentally attached to her personal belongings and furniture, and refused to leave the family home.[22] This was a case where the parties involved had access to funds and a potentially secure hiding place. However, without money, valid papers or ration cards there was little chance of long-term survival, and the idea of living illegally remained alien to most. Age, infirmity or illness also played a role. For example, young people would often choose to go with their ageing parents to Westerbork rather than leave them to travel alone. Others would volunteer for Westerbork in order that they might regain contact with relatives already arrested. The strength of family ties was clearly important in preventing many Jews from considering life in hiding and Caransa recounts a case where personal illness acted as a bar to going underground. A couple whose house was raided nevertheless managed to escape. Later they were able to continue living at their old address, but when the wife was offered a more secure hiding place, the husband refused to go underground with her on the grounds that his asthma would make him too much of a liability for any host.[23] He was finally arrested and deported after the raid on south and east Amsterdam on 20 June 1943.

Even if these factors played no part in the decision-making process, there were plenty of others. How could small children, who were bound to make noise, be accommodated in hiding places where it was essential to keep quiet – at least for certain times in the day? How could older children be kept entertained for weeks and months, or educated? Again, these specific issues were often sufficient to deter some families from trying to hide. Similarly, orthodox and observant Jews found it difficult to conceive of continuing their observances underground. While there are examples of highly religious and observant Jews surviving the occupation in hiding, the special problems this created undoubtedly acted as a deterrent for many. One final factor was also important, namely the deference to authority felt by the majority of Jews in the Netherlands. This took many forms but militated against actions which were contrary to the laws of the land or the pronouncements of the Jewish leadership. A German Jew who survived the occupation in the Netherlands referred to one of his Dutch Jewish hosts as typical of so many who believed the falsehoods of the SD and the Jewish Council and 'typical of the vast majority of Dutch Jews who did not want to do anything illegal'.[24] One middle-aged German Jewess may have spoken for many thousands when she said, 'I have done nothing wrong, I have no need to hide.'[25] The dictum of the Jewish Council that because not everyone could go into hiding, no one should, may have carried weight with some. More likely, the thought of putting oneself outside the law was too much for most people to contemplate, with the concomitant risk that arrest would lead to treatment as a *strafgeval* (punishment case) and deportation to the much-feared Mauthausen camp.[26] Certainly there were many who continued to believe that deportation offered a better chance of survival than going underground.[27] Nonetheless, there were certain groups and individuals who made a conscious decision not to go into hiding. For example, some leaders of the Dutch Zionist Federation refused to go underground, adopting the maxim that 'wherever the people of Israel are, then that is where their leaders should be'.[28] The Chief Rabbi of Rotterdam, A.B.N. Davids, made a similar decision when he was offered a place to hide.[29]

As can be seen, there is no simple answer to the question of why so few Jews actually went into hiding. One or more of the factors listed above may have been sufficient to forestall action on the part of a given individual or family. Perhaps many who intended to go underground were arrested before they had the chance. Certainly, Presser believed that the impetus for going underground and the timing of the decision were part of a complex equation. 'There had to be a growing consciousness of the increasing danger and of the unavoidable choice. At some point, one had to make the decision between continuing to wait and not waiting any longer.'[30] But the number of Jews who did reach this conclusion may still bear no relationship to the numbers who actually went into hiding. Realising that it was time to go underground and finding someone willing to act as a host were two entirely different things.

This point of decision for Jews in the Netherlands varied from one individual or family to another. The first Jewish *onderduikers* came from the men called up for labour service inside the Netherlands, or those who were wanted by the police for political reasons or infringements of the innumerable laws applicable to Jews. The penalties for non-compliance were severe and deliberately well-publicised. Many were incarcerated in Amersfoort prison or shipped to Mauthausen. The two raids of February and June 1941 which led to the transport of two groups of Jews to Mauthausen and the news of their rapid deaths, if supposedly from 'natural' causes, left few in any doubt what this form of punishment meant. Jews in the provinces also became targets for the Germans as hostages and scapegoats for acts of 'sabotage' against the authorities.[31] For some individuals, their period underground may have begun as early as January 1941 when, by refusing to register as Jews, they effectively put themselves outside the law. Being underground at this stage usually meant living with false papers rather than actually being in hiding. After July 1942, this small group was joined by thousands of others called up for 'labour service' in the East. For Jews registered in Amsterdam, the point of decision usually came when their call-up papers arrived on the doorstep.[32] It then became a case of whether to report to the assembly point or not. Failure to report would give a short breathing space, but the address of the individuals was on file and would undoubtedly be the target of a police raid within days, or sometimes within hours. The fact that the numbers reporting fell so far short of German expectations meant that indiscriminate police raids on Jewish neighbourhoods were soon commonplace.

While most of these stories relate to quickly taken or even instant decisions, there were examples of individuals and families making advance preparations for going underground. Otto Frank had clearly thought out where to hide his family, and was in a position to adapt part of his workplace for the purpose and make the necessary structural alterations. Only a relatively few other potential *onderduikers* had this type of opportunity, and most relied on their hosts and helpers to provide the necessary hiding places. Yet some families did make elaborate preparations. One man hired an empty room in a storage building overlooking the Singel in Amsterdam and proceeded to provision it with food saved from the rations. The family made several trips to the room bringing more food and clothing each time. Ironically, the family never used the hiding place it had so carefully prepared and eventually went underground elsewhere. This example probably remains untypical because the father was already in contact with the resistance who were able to provide false papers and other hiding places for him and his family.[33] However, there were other examples of advance preparations. Two well-off couples from Amsterdam prepared a rented holiday cottage in Blaricum (Noord-Holland) and dug out a cellar under the building to act as an emergency hiding place.[34]

As the German measures became more severe with raids on individual neighbourhoods and the beginning of the deportations in the high summer of 1942, so the sense of uncertainty and danger became ever greater. Nevertheless, while deportation was presumed to mean a miserable existence in Eastern Europe, a German decree of 9 August 1942 reiterated that Jews who were found in hiding would be deported to Mauthausen. The reputation of this camp continued to be sufficient to delay or deter many.[35] Presser speaks of the 'inner resistance' that Jews had to overcome before going into hiding. 'They lacked energy, contacts, money, played down the dangers of deportation and exaggerated those of going underground; they were frightened, terribly frightened, they wanted to remain with their families, they did not want to depend on others or endanger them.'[36] Others spoke of a desire 'not to know'.[37] This, coupled with an abiding desire to remain within the law, probably played the major part in reducing the numbers of Jews who attempted to go underground. Fears for the safety of those who might help them were also voiced at the time, and subsequently, but this was almost certainly a subsidiary consideration for the majority.[38] Yet even for people with an 'address' to go to, there were still many advantages in remaining 'above ground' for as long as possible. For those who had plans to go underground, the arrival of call-up papers, the arrest of close family members and the thought that 'our turn cannot be far away' all played a role in determining that the time to make what arrangements they could or to disappear had arrived. Some had continued to cherish the hope that this step might not become necessary, but the real tragedy remained that the vast majority of Jews in Amsterdam had neither the money nor an 'address' to allow them to go underground.[39] Similar patterns of behaviour emerged in the provincial towns and cities, although the German desire to concentrate all the Jews in Amsterdam did provide the opportunity for some individuals to disappear *en route*. German attempts to round up entire communities also produced very variable results. In Tiel (Brabant), the Jewish community was given advance warning of German plans to arrest them. As a result, while three families had reported for transport to Westerbork, only one old woman (who had refused to go underground) was arrested and a further 67 were rescued, at least in the short term. Contrast this with the Jews in Coevorden (Drenthe) who were also warned of a raid planned for 2 October 1942 but only a few families took notice and 91 were arrested and taken to Westerbork.[40]

It does seem that people who received some temporary protection through exemption stamps issued by the Jewish Council, or by the Germans directly, had a better chance to go underground provided they did not believe that the stamps themselves were the key to long-term survival. Having time to think, plan and prepare while being protected from immediate deportation could be a distinct advantage. Moreover, the longer one could stay 'legal', the shorter the period underground was likely to be. Even towards the end of 1942, the war situation was looking more optimistic. The Allies had landed in Algeria and Morocco and this gave some hope for an attack on the Atlantic Wall the following summer.[41] If this proved to be wildly optimistic, the German defeat at Stalingrad had provided some fresh hope and by the autumn of 1943, just as the last Jews were being taken from Amsterdam, the Italian surrender added to the evidence that the Germans were slowly losing the war and gave some encouragement to those who were still able to go underground as the final exemptions were rescinded. In any case, the choices remained stark, either to go underground or report for deportation to the East. There were many examples of people who enjoyed the protection of a stamp, and then went underground when it no longer served to protect them. For example, a young Jewess who worked as a nurse at the *Joodse Invalide* until September 1943 was able to escape with the assistance of a non-Jewish porter through contact with a help organisation which hid her in a *pastorie* (manse) in

Nieuw-Beerta (Groningen).[42] Other people with Jewish Council exemptions were also able to escape in this way, but perhaps the most unusual story concerns the secretary of the Jewish community in Utrecht. He had been protected with an exemption until April 1943 when all the Jews in Utrecht had to leave except the chairman and deputy chairman of the community who were left to represent the Jewish Council and remained nominally responsible for the Jews in mixed marriages.[43] Only one other, rather obscure exemption was allowed, namely the custodian of the Jewish cemetery. This task had been in the hands of a non-Jewish man for years but, as he was in no danger of being deported, the secretary was given his job and received a special identity card. There he remained until October 1944, when he was arrested as part of the labour programme and shipped to a work-camp in Gelderland. There the authorities did not know what to make of him. As a Jew he could not work for the Germans, but his papers also precluded him from deportation. As a result, he was kept separately in the camp until the liberation.[44] His explanation for this strange turn of events was that the *Zentralstelle* had probably forgotten all about him.[45]

Hiding places and life underground

The classic account we have of Jews in Amsterdam going underground comes from members of the Frank family, but in many respects their story and experiences are untypical of *onderduikers* in the Netherlands. For example, they were refugees rather than part of the indigenous Dutch Jewish community. Moreover, Otto Frank's business partnership gave him access to non-Jewish help in a way which was impossible for many Dutch Jews whose social and economic intercourse was limited to members of their own community. Finally, the Frank story would suggest that Jewish *onderduikers* found a place to hide and then stayed there permanently, yet nothing could be further from the truth. Although having only one hiding place was not unique, for the vast majority of those underground, remaining in safety usually involved moving around. At the end of the occupation, some survivors could recount 10, 20, or even more places they had hidden for periods of time.[46] A survey of children hidden underground revealed an average number of 4.5 addresses with the highest being 37.[47] The important point to note is that going underground took many different forms and encompassed such a range of experiences that it is difficult to identify factors common even to a minority of cases. Every account of Jews who went into hiding contains some aspects which appear to be unique.

Given that most Jews in the Netherlands were town or city dwellers, it is hardly surprising to find that initial hiding places were usually in urban areas. It was inevitably easier to arrange to go underground in neighbourhoods and districts that one knew and where reliable friends could be found to help. *Onderduikers* would often be no more than a few streets away from their former homes, although it paid to move away from neighbourhoods which were considered to be 'Jewish'. This applied especially in Amsterdam where the Jews had traditionally been concentrated in the central, southern and eastern districts. Thus finding an address in the north or west of the city was likely to be an advantage as it was less likely to be raided. Nevertheless, many *onderduikers* did stay much closer to home, often in the Jewish quarter itself. Some hid in the premises of non-Jewish neighbours, others used the flats and houses of people who had already been deported, and there were even instances of individuals breaking into their own dwellings after they had been raided and sealed, and hiding there, often for months at a time.[48]

The hiding places varied enormously. Dwelling houses, upstairs rooms in cafés, even buildings used or lived in by the Germans sometimes contained hiding places. False walls and ceilings would conceal cupboards, rooms and even suites of rooms from the casual observer. Attics were also used, with areas partitioned off or accessed by hidden staircases. In the older houses which were such a feature of Amsterdam, it was often difficult for the outsider to work out where the rooms of one building ended and the next began. This assumed that those in hiding were permanently hidden away, but this was not always the case. Some hosts would allow their guests to spend time in the body of the house, at mealtimes, or at certain safe hours of the day or night. The fact that there were people staying at a particular address might not cause much comment, as they could be explained to neighbours as relatives or evacuees, but no such ruse could be used with the authorities. If discovered, the fugitives' papers would almost invariably give them away immediately. Thus even these house-guests needed a place to hide if there was an unexpected knock at the door. In this event, concealed trap-doors, coal cellars and even gaps between floorboards were used as temporary refuges.

As conditions in Amsterdam worsened and German raids escalated, so more people underground attempted to move out of the city to surrounding towns and villages. Here, it was a similar story, with Jews being hidden in all manner of places, sometimes under the very noses of the Germans or the NSB. Amsterdam Jews also found their way to other, more distant parts of the country. The rural north-eastern provinces of Friesland, Groningen and Drenthe became preferred destinations, being considered much safer than the urban areas. While the movement of people eastwards was partly by choice, it also depended to a large extent on the organisational links set up by those involved in helping Jews underground. In these rural areas, hiding places ranged from bunkers dug into the ground in unpopulated areas of heathland, turf shelters and 'converted' chicken-houses through barns and outhouses to accommodation inside farmhouses. While the location of one's hiding place was seldom a matter of much choice, each of them had both advantages and disadvantages. Living in a farmhouse with a host family had all the advantages of relative comfort, but little time to react if the location was raided. Living in outhouses or in the countryside might give more time to escape, but meant an almost entire absence of amenities which either had to be acquired by the fugitives themselves by moving around in the open, or brought in by helpers. Usually, people spent only a few nights living this way, either because they were in transit, or because their existing hiding place had become temporarily dangerous and they were waiting to move back or move on.[49] However, one or two families and groups did have permanent hiding places of this nature. For 18 months, a large number of *onderduikers* hiding in scrubland near Soeren (Gelderland) avoided persistent attempts by the Dutch SS to find them, but 80 were ultimately captured. Similarly, a number of fugitives living in wooden shacks just outside Winterswijk avoided detection for some months but were eventually located and caught.[50] Perhaps another 50 found sanctuary in government-owned forest north of Vierhouten (Veluwe). They were hidden in a camp alongside other *onderduikers* and army deserters with the knowledge of local tradesmen and even the local police. The camp was only discovered by chance when four *Waffen-SS* men came upon it while hunting wild pig. The inmates fled in all directions and many escaped, but a company of men from the *Landstorm Nederland* later raided the camp and found six Jews in the vicinity whom they summarily murdered.[51] More successful was a Jewish family of four which spent 17 months living in a hut on the Friesland/Drenthe border. The hut was so small that one could only stand up in the middle, but they remained there until the end of 1944, aided by an orthodox Calvinist pastor.[52]

Living in rural farmhouses was also a very varied experience and depended on the area, the nature of the hosts and the 'organisation' of underground life. In the eastern provinces such as Friesland, Groningen, Drenthe and Limburg, some fugitives lived openly with their hosts, being explained away to the neighbours as distant relatives or friends who had been evacuated. The stress on 'distant' was often an important factor in localities where broad Amsterdam and Rotterdam accents were immediately recognisable as 'foreign'.[53] Living openly meant either having very good (false) papers or a high degree of foolhardiness. People who 'looked' Jewish could not possibly go out openly without arousing suspicions, but others who were less obvious could and did travel around. Some younger Jews worked openly as farm hands or peat cutters in rural areas of the north-east. After 1943, their cover was improved by the sheer numbers of non-Jews who joined them in an attempt to escape the labour draft. This brought increased help and the chance to 'hide' to a larger number of fugitives, but also increased the possibility of raids by the Germans. Other *onderduikers* were only allowed out at night by their hosts, to breathe some fresh air and to stretch their legs. For the rest of the time, they had to remain either inside the house, or permanently in their designated hiding places. This largely depended on the circumstances in the household and/or the fears and insecurities of the hosts.

Similar situations occurred in the cities, and even in Amsterdam. Some *onderduikers* were cooped up for days and weeks at a time, with no access to washing facilities, or any means of stretching their legs. Others could only use the toilet at certain times of the day, or when there was no one to hear them. The restrictions may have been essential for their security, but it is easy to see how they would rapidly become unbearable. Being in hiding almost invariably meant hours of enforced idleness. Both adults and children found it hard to take this day after day, with no end in sight, although it was undoubtedly true that some people were better psychologically predisposed to deal with the pressures than others. The lucky ones could sometimes leave their hiding places, undertake chores for their hosts, or find things to do in order to pass the time. For those permanently consigned to an attic or room, daily life was little more than torment. There are accounts of Jews succumbing to depression and even suicide as a result of their prolonged incarceration.[54] One child of ten, left in a room on his own for six months, lost the power of speech.[55] One of the greatest problems for the *onderduiker* was trying to maintain a sense of stability in an alien environment with an uncertain future. Many survivors recount the hours they spent thinking of their families and their own dependent position. The feeling of helplessness that this engendered should not be underestimated. Sometimes *onderduikers* were able to send letters to their friends and relations via one or more third parties, sometimes they had opportunities to listen to the radio, and even the BBC. For the most part, however, they were hemmed in by the restrictive nature of their circumstances.[56] Given these circumstances, it is perhaps easier to understand why some people were prepared to take what appeared to be unnecessary risks in order to maintain contact with the outside world.

However difficult it was to find an 'address', this was only the beginning for Jews who tried to go underground. Their objective and material circumstances played a major role in determining the success of their enterprise. Having an apparently safe place to hide and trustworthy and amenable hosts and/or helpers were essential prerequisites, but from the beginning, having access to funds was just as important. Even if the hosts did not at first demand or request money for their guests' upkeep (and there were altruists who did behave in this way), circumstances and increasing German restrictions conspired to make it essential for long-term survival. As food became more expensive and difficult to acquire, so the costs of keeping someone hidden also increased. An identity card also became essential, even if the *onderduiker* did not need to travel, as after mid-1943 the issue of ration cards was linked to the possession of identity cards. While this German measure to root out *onderduikers* was undermined by the thefts and forgeries expedited by the LO,[57] there were many cases where it proved difficult for hosts to feed their guests and there were instances where hosts demanded that fugitives had valid identity cards and ration books before they would shelter them. The only alternative would be to try and find the food on the black market, but this again was an increasingly expensive option, even in the countryside. In the towns and cities it was always difficult, and in the last months of the occupation, during the so-called hunger-winter in the north, just about impossible.

After an 'address', an *onderduiker's* most prized possession was an identity card. While these had been compulsory since the autumn of 1940, it was only in January 1942 that the Germans began to use them as a regular means of controlling the population. In that month, regular checks were instigated: on street corners and stations, on trains and in theatres.[58] At the same time, all Jews had to have the letter 'J' stamped on their papers, making it impossible for them pass through checks unnoticed. By the end of 1943, the LO had become specialists in acquiring blank identity cards and forging appropriate stamps. Moreover, they occasionally managed to arrange the destruction or 'adjustment' of local and national population registers so that even extensive checks would not discover the fraud. In the middle of 1942, however, no such expertise was available to Jews in hiding. With all forms of travel and transport forbidden to Jews after June 1942, the only way to move from one place to another was to remove the star from one's clothing and try and acquire a false set of documents. Most of these identity cards were 'borrowed' or bought from their real owners, usually for a financial consideration. In most cases, they could not be altered and the new owner had to learn all sorts of personal details about the man or woman he or she was supposed to be. This might have been reasonable had it happened only once, but Presser recalls that he had seven different identities while underground, 'each more implausible than the last'.[59] Nor were these papers particularly convincing as they usually bore the photograph of the original owner. No one would have been deceived by these for long, unless they wished to be so deceived.

Although a major problem for Jews hiding underground, a genuine set of identity papers could also be the key to survival. Luck has often been cited as the key to staying out of German hands, but one story which combines luck with nerve, ingenuity and a knowledge of the system may help to illustrate how all these factors could combine. A Jewish couple had given refuge to a 14-year-old cousin who had to live underground as he was not eligible for an identity card until he was 15. In order to help, the wife approached a complete stranger who worked at the council offices at Oosterbeek (Gelderland) and asked for a false identity card. The risk seems to have been enormous, but in this case it paid off with the official providing not only a card for the cousin but also two for the 'parents'. Later on, the same contact was used to 'legalise' five other children, but the procedure was dangerous for all concerned because although it allowed individuals to be registered locally, it could not overcome the problem of trying to duplicate the procedure with the Central Population Registry. Moreover, these identity cards were only useful where controls were less rigorous (on the street or on stations) and the holders did not 'look' Jewish. During house-searches, where the police and SD could link individuals to addresses and scrutinise papers more carefully, forgeries were almost bound to be discovered.

To ensure greater security, a far more elaborate scheme was concocted which involved the family repatriating itself (a legitimate reason for registration). The names of a couple who had emigrated to the United States in 1935 were selected, and copies of their birth certificates were obtained. All this information was then sent to the authorities with a note to the effect that their original papers had been lost in the bombing of Strasbourg. This acquisition of legitimate papers allowed the family to move to a new district but brought with it new problems. The sons were likely to be called up for labour service, but the family's ingenuity again came to the rescue. The eldest son wrote to textile firms in south Germany and received replies offering him jobs which he could use if called up or arrested. A similar method was used to protect the second son using job offers from Dutch firms.[60]

This example of enterprise may well be unique and certainly does not do justice to the general experience of Jews in hiding. Most, if not all, of them had to travel at some time or another, to risk passing German controls on trams and trains. It is difficult to conceive of the risks taken by individuals travelling alone from one place to another, using forbidden forms of transport and carrying dubious identity papers. Yet this is what happened. Thousands of journeys were made by *onderduikers* from one 'address' to another, from one part of the country to another. More unbelievable is the fact that Jews often travelled without a known destination, going from one place to the next in the hope of finding someone to take them in. There are many accounts of such journeys. Some were crowned with success, others undoubtedly led to failure and arrest. It is impossible to say exactly how many *onderduikers* were caught on trains or *en route* for a new address, but the numbers were undoubtedly substantial.

8

Self-help, rescuers and bystanders

The Jews and their neighbours

The role of the non-Jewish populations in German-occupied Europe, as bystanders or as rescuers, has inevitably received scholarly, journalistic and political attention in the last 50 years. The state of Israel's honouring of 'righteous gentiles' has been one way in which the work of those who helped save Jews from the Germans has been highlighted. In the process of coming to terms with the behaviour of its citizens and events during the occupation period, early biographical, organisational and national historiographies all tended to stress the activities of the few who did help to rescue Jews, rather than the majority who were indifferent or downright hostile to their Jewish countrymen and women. More recently, more attention has been focused on the bystanders in an attempt to explain why active rescuers were in such a minority in both Eastern and Western occupied Europe.

The problem of interpretation is especially marked in the case of the Netherlands where it is often said that the Jewish population 'was well integrated and anti-Semitism ... relatively unimportant'.[1] This apparently favourable situation is then contrasted with the level of mortality among Dutch Jews and the relatively small number of identifiable rescuers. While this general characterisation contains a degree of truth, it should be subject to some important qualifications, given the way in which Dutch society was constructed. The vertical integration of religious and political groups in the country, although by no means complete or entirely exclusive, means that 'integration' in this context takes on a different aspect. The Jewish community was able to exist as one group within Dutch society, but functioning in parallel with other groups rather than necessarily having a great deal of contact with them. Thus levels of interaction between Jews and non-Jews were probably much less evident than the term integration would imply, although the process of social integration was undoubtedly much stronger in certain areas such as the working-class districts of Amsterdam-East and in small provincial towns. Even if antisemitism was never strong in the Netherlands, there remained a distance between the various political and religious groups (*zuilen*) in Dutch society which was to have an important effect when the Germans attempted to isolate the Jews from the rest of the population. The very nature of the society militated against the majority having had much contact with Jews, thus making a relationship between non-Jews and Jews in the latter's hour of need that much more difficult to establish or sustain. For this reason, the apparent contrast between integration and the lack of help given to Jews is not quite so marked as some scholars have made out. When the Jews in the Netherlands needed help there were still social and cultural barriers which had to be broken down.

Apart from characterising the nature of rescue in the Dutch context, this chapter is focused on a series of related questions. These can be summarised as trying to explain the small numbers of Dutch men and women who were active in helping to save Jews, examining in detail the motivations behind those who did help, assessing whether there were some victims more likely to receive help and to be successful in hiding than others, and then finally attempting some comparison between rescue attempts in the Netherlands and neighbouring Western European states.

The motives of the rescuers

The question of who helped the Jews in the Netherlands poses a number of problems. All the sources are agreed that it was very difficult for Jews to find hiding places – far more difficult than for non-Jews. People were either afraid of the severe punishments decreed by the Germans for helping Jews, or viewed Jews as alien, authors of their own misfortune or deserving of their fate. For this reason, the Jews remained substantially a group apart, even when many thousands of non-Jews also sought to go underground during and after 1943. In spite of this general impression, there were a minority in the Netherlands willing to help. This help took many different forms and came from all sections of Dutch society, although there is good reason to suppose that some people were more likely to help than others. For example, a popular maxim during the occupation was that 'the poor offer you shelter, the rich someone else's address'.[2]

At least one attempt has been made to try and categorise the motivations behind those people who did help in the rescue of Jews using the Netherlands as a case study.[3] In a short paper, Lawrence Baron has highlighted the different ways in which individuals might have become involved. He begins with situational helpers: those who had the reasons and the resources to help when asked. He concludes that their assistance was conditioned both by the nature of German rule, which became more onerous over time, and by having a positive disposition towards Jews through previous contacts. His second general category includes those who were motivated primarily by 'bonds of affection, friendship or loyalty' to a specific person or family whom they helped to rescue.[4] The third category encompasses those people who were motivated primarily by empathy with the plight of the Jews, and who 'saw parallels between it and their own experiences of persecution or sense of social marginality'.[5] A fourth, and rather different, categorisation involved distinction between those motivated primarily by moral considerations and those whose responses were conditioned by emotions. In this latter category, there was likely to be a preponderance of women. The final category includes all those whose primary motivation was either ideological or based on strong religious convictions.

While this typology may act as a useful starting point, it requires some qualification. Firstly, it is important to realise that Baron's work, although based on an (oral) historical record, was directed primarily towards understanding the motivation behind rescue for the sociological study of the 'altruistic personality' project. Secondly, as Baron readily admits, any such typology may tend to mask the complex relationship between different levels and types of motivation to be found in a single individual. Finally, his study is based on interviews carried out many years after the event among rescuers who survived the war. Thus, for perfectly valid methodological reasons the study cannot take into account the written (and sometimes contemporary) testimonies which can be found in a number of archives.[6]

The earliest, and perhaps most common forms of rescue in the Netherlands come under Baron's second category, namely those who helped through loyalty or affection for the person concerned. Involvement in rescue work began in many different ways. People with Jewish relatives, work-colleagues or even tenants were often the first to participate, looking to protect people they knew personally. In some cases the offer of help would come unprompted. Non-Jewish families would offer to take in Jewish friends. Others people were almost automatically drawn in because their wives and husbands were themselves Jewish.[7] Some personal contact with Jews, or with the mechanics of the persecution was often the spur to action. The experiences of Marion Pritchard-van Binsbergen provide a specific example of Baron's first category. She recounts being moved by the brutal treatment of Jewish children by the Germans clearing an Amsterdam children's home in 1942. From that moment, 'I decided that if there was anything I could do to thwart such atrocities, I would do it.'[8] The description of her involvement does give some indication of how wide-ranging the help for *onderduikers* had to be.

> We located hiding places, helped people move there, provided food, clothing and ration cards, and sometimes moral support and relief for the host families. We registered newborn babies as gentiles ... and provided medical care when possible.[9]

Later on, she was herself asked to take in a Jewish family, a man and his three children. This was achieved by renting part of a large house owned by a friend of her family some 20 miles from Amsterdam. All of them managed to survive there until the end of the occupation, although not without having to kill an inquisitive Dutch policeman. What this story does demonstrate clearly is the almost infinite variety of tasks required to help Jews underground and the way individuals could be drawn deeper into the realms of rescue work. In that respect, Marion Pritchard's story is typical of many rescuers. Her original motivation was personal, but she became part of an Amsterdam student group devoted to helping Jewish *onderduikers* and gradually became involved in all aspects of the work, including hiding Jews herself. Others came to the work through having helped political fugitives in the early part of the occupation. Primarily from the Left, they had been the first to develop the necessary skills for hiding people successfully. For the most part, these were individuals who volunteered to help or made a deliberate decision to participate. As they became more involved and the size of their particular task grew, so they began asking others to help, primarily in finding suitable hiding places. Relatives, trusted friends and fellow members of religious congregations were usually the first port of call. Ultimately, there were links forged between those who rescued Jews from Amsterdam and people who could arrange hiding places in the provincial towns and countryside. Some rescuers became integrated into networks through being asked to undertake specific tasks as a result of their particular expertise, knowledge or employment. For example, government officials were approached to help with stamps or papers, trusted policemen could be asked for information or to act as cover for illicit travel, forgers, printers and photographers could all be involved in the provision of false identity and ration cards. Apart from drawing more people into rescue work, provision of these specialist services also served to create links between different groups.

This still does not give a positive answer to the question of who the rescuers were. A comparison between Poland and the Netherlands has suggested that Polish rescuers were far more socially marginal than their Dutch counterparts,[10] but this seems to be contradicted by both the sources and the available evidence for the Netherlands. De Jong notes that it was the Communists and Socialists who were the first to offer help to the Jews,[11] but a contemporary account is perhaps the most telling. Arnold Douwes (the leader of a rescue organisation in Drenthe) recorded that 'those who are the most active in the resistance, those who achieve the most and who give most help to *onderduikers* are found primarily among the extreme right-wing and left-wing elements of the population, that is to say, the anti-revolutionaries [Calvinists] and the communists'.[12] In his own area (southern Drenthe) 'people who hide fugitives or help in one way or another [were] nearly all *Gereformeerden* [orthodox Calvinists]'.[13] Certainly, there is evidence that the strict Calvinists were overrepresented among those who helped rescue Jews. Numbering only 8 per cent of the population, they were probably responsible for helping 25 per cent of the Jews who went underground,[14] and the reports about help organisations are littered with the names of Calvinist pastors who led or helped with networks in various parts of the country.[15] However, this statistic may need some qualification. Many Jews in hiding were moved, or moved themselves, to the north-eastern provinces where it was widely regarded as being somewhat safer from the Germans. In these areas, the orthodox Calvinists were a larger per-centage of the community, albeit still a minority.

This qualification apart, it remains the case that the *Gereformeerden* almost certainly did play a disproportionate role in the rescue of Jews in the Netherlands. This is perhaps even more remarkable given the supposed persistence of antisemitism and the view of Jews as Christ-killers, both in orthodox Calvinist and Catholic circles. How did this come about? One explanation is that one or two highly motivated individuals in the ortho-dox Calvinist community began the work and then slowly began to enlist (or rope in) friends, like-minded individuals and other members of their community. Religious belief and membership of a congregation may have been the first stage to being recruited. While there were a number of pas-tors involved in the work of saving Jews,[16] it would be wrong to suggest that any of the church organisations themselves played a central role. A similar pattern seems to have existed in Roman Catholic communities (especially in the southern provinces of Brabant and Limburg) where moti-vated individuals, including some priests, came to extend their work through friends and members of their religious congregations. While the church hierarchy was not involved directly in helping Jews,[17] there were instances of church premises, for example in Utrecht, and church contacts being used to further the work. Another example of the detachment of church organisation from the help given to Jews comes from a group of pastors in the vicinity of Leeuwarden. Their meeting which discussed the 'Jewish question' went no further than resolving that 'when a Jew knocks on your door, open it and do your best to save the fugitive and your own household', but members of the group were actively engaged in finding addresses for Jews brought from other parts of the country. This involved personal approaches to people who were thought trustworthy, or more obtusely via sermons devoted to giving shelter to the homeless and waiting for offers of help to be made from members of the congregation.[18]

The religious or humanitarian altruism which motivated many rescuers in the Netherlands has been well documented. There are many instances of individuals taking enormous risks to help people whom they barely knew for no reward save that they were carrying out their moral duty. Certainly rescuers whose religious faith dominated their lives could be placed in this category, but other explanations have been put forward to explain even their actions. Herzberg has argued – though this is difficult to prove or disprove – that the help given to Jews later in the occupation was to compensate for earlier antisemitism.[19] Equally weighty is the charge that help from devout Christians was based on their desire to save souls. At both pastoral and secular levels, there were examples of attempts made to convert those in hiding. One of the founders of the LO, *ds.* Slomp, claimed that it was a perfect opportunity to convert the Jews.[20] During the occupation he noted that many had come gladly into the fold and 'in the last few years more Jews had been baptised than in decades before the war'. This may well have been true, but the overall numbers appear unimpressive. De Jong observes that of the estimated 3,500 Jews who were hidden in Calvinist households, only 126 were members of the *Gereformeerde Kerk* a few years after the war.[21] Slomp may have been wishful-thinking, or assuming that church-going would lead to baptism and permanent conversion, whereas in many cases this was almost certainly a cosmetic or short-term expedient. *Onderduikers* staying with Christian families would often attend church on a Sunday morning in order to allay any unnecessary suspicion. Children were almost invariably taken as they would not be left in the family home alone. If much of this church-going had no lasting effects, it could still make a difference to the relationship between those in hiding and their hosts. A Jewish couple lodged with a Friesian farmer had to be moved after 14 days because he insisted that if they did not want to become Christians, they would have to live with his animals.[22] A survivor who wrote of his experiences as a child in hiding summed up the tensions between hosts and their guests.

> Today auntie asked me if I wanted to become a Calvinist [*Gereformeerde*]. I won't do it, I won't let myself be baptised. Of course I'm glad that uncle and auntie have saved me, but that doesn't mean that I have to pray to the Christian God. Auntie doesn't understand it. She is afraid that I won't go to heaven if I don't become a Calvinist.[23]

In the post-war period, the wartime conversions to Christianity have undergone a good deal of scrutiny, with authors such as Houwaart claiming that the much-publicised conversions of people such as Anneke Beekman and Johanna-Ruth Dobschiner could not really be genuine, and were examples of Jews trying to hide their 'Jewish-selves'. His argument was that the enormous psychological and emotional pressures placed on *onderduikers* in Christian surroundings, where admission to a Christian church could be equated with physical survival, inevitably militated against genuine commitment based on faith. He recalled the fallacious nature of his own wartime baptism into the Roman church as being based entirely on fear, and his later move to a Protestant church as involving the constant denial of his Jewish-self. Whether Houwaart's own experiences should be taken as a judgement on all such wartime-Christians is another matter.

Being baptised could certainly be seen as a temporary defence, a pragmatic response to a particular situation, but there were doubtless examples of genuine conversions. In the case of Beekman, her youth may militate against the idea that she was capable of making an informed choice, but Dobschiner's decision to be baptised took place after the war, indicating that her espousal of Christianity was born of genuine faith rather than short-term expediency or psychological pressures from her hosts.[24]

Rescue networks grew around religious, political, student, pacifist and artists' groups in Amsterdam and elsewhere,[25] yet there were also individual examples unconnected with any particular group. Motivations for helping clearly varied a great deal, from the purely altruistic to the downright mercenary. Not all who were approached to help were prepared to do so without some reward, while those who hid people in their houses had some justification in asking for funds to offset the cost of their upkeep. Food had to be bought and rationing might mean that recourse might have to be made to the black market. Nevertheless, network organisers usually had a clear idea of what was reasonable and what was excessive. There were cases where help organisations paid up rather than lose the hiding place, even when the monetary demands were deemed excessive, but this did not take account of the private arrangements made between Jews and individual hosts. Here again, the responses seem to have varied from apparent altruism at one end of the scale to outright profiteering at the other. There are documented examples on the one hand of hosts consistently refusing to accept any payment, and on the other hand of huge sums changing hands. Presser records cases where individuals were charged fl.200 per week and up to fl.1000 per month. Hosts would sometimes evict their lodgers if they no longer had the money to pay, or insist that arrears were paid off after the war was over.[26] While the profiteering may have been reprehensible given the circumstances, it is important to note that there was an even more sinister motivation behind a small number of so-called rescuers. There are documented cases of people agreeing to hide Jews and then deliberately betraying them to the Nazis in exchange for monetary reward.[27]

Rescue activities

To try and encompass all the rescuers, their organisations and their activities across the entire country in one chapter would be an impossibility. Many rescuers and helpers suffered the same fate as their guests and their stories have never been documented.[28] Others, and those they helped, have lived to give an insight, through written and oral evidence, of how Jews were rescued. Here, a series of case studies and examples will have to suffice, to show the nature and extent of the help given by individuals and organisations in the Netherlands.

Self-help and escape abroad

In Amsterdam, there were a whole series of apparently independent groups as well as an unknown number of individuals acting as rescuers, helpers or assistants. The Jews themselves were by no means always the supine victims of persecution, and they had a number of networks engaged in rescue activity. A few Dutch and German refugee Jews survived in hiding outside the Netherlands during the occupation. The largest and most important group in this category came from the Zionist Palestine Pioneers. These young men and women were being trained, mainly in agriculture, for future settlement in Palestine, but their route had effectively been closed by the German occupation. The round-up of 400 trainees from the Wieringermeer training farm by the Germans in the summer of 1941 (assisted by addresses and information handed over by the Jewish Council) had convinced many in the movement that it was essential to avoid deportation.[29] In August 1942, soon after the first deportations had begun, warning came from a friend within the Jewish Council that a German raid was imminent. Prompted by this, two youth leaders from the Pioneers group based in Loosdrecht, Joachim (Schuschu) Simon, a German refugee, and Menachim Pinkhof, together with a non-Jewish friend, Johan Gerard (Joop) Westerweel, the head of a Montessori school in Rotterdam, planned an escape line to take the whole Loosdrecht group to Switzerland, to be followed ultimately by other Pioneer groups. This was organised in conjunction with the *He-Halutz* in Geneva, but an initial group of ten was captured.[30] Simon then took two groups to France before being arrested on his return. Knowing too much about the organisation, he committed suicide in the prison at Breda rather than betray his colleagues. Westerweel continued the work, using Jewish and non-Jewish help. In total, he managed to help between 150 and 200 young Jews, 70 of them Pioneers. Most were given shelter in France, but around 80 were taken to the Pyrenees and crossed into Spain.[31] Westerweel also helped to find underground addresses for the Pioneers who could not leave the country.[32] His wife had been arrested in December 1943 and ultimately he too was caught, at the Belgian border in March 1944. His mistake was unwittingly to use the identity papers of one of his couriers who had been arrested, a man wanted for a series of crimes, including the murder of a German.[33] Five months later, Westerweel was shot in the concentration camp at Vught.[34] Nevertheless, his work and that of his co-workers helped to save a number of the Pioneers, both in the Netherlands and abroad. It is clear that Simon, Westerweel and the rest of the group were motivated by the view that it was still possible to resist and that for them, action was the only acceptable option.[35]

The 'Nanno' resistance group was in some ways a successor to the Westerweel group. Its leader, Kurt Reilinger, took over the contact with

French Zionists and arranged the transfer of able-bodied people with inadequate papers to France. One group of 20 were ostensibly sent to work on the Atlantic Wall in the Pas-de-Calais region. To expedite this, the authorities issued them with appropriate permits which then allowed them to travel freely and, after a short period of time, leave to take up employment with the Todt Organisation in Paris.[36] The 'Nanno' group also continued the escort of people to the Spanish border and even the arrests of Reilinger in Paris in April 1944 and the French Zionist leader Jacques Roitman a month later did not prevent the work continuing until the liberation of Paris in August.[37] At least one refugee Jew found work on the Rhine barges, travelling to and from Germany.[38] Another German Jew who had been active in the resistance used forged papers to volunteer for work in Germany when it became impossible to continue living in the Netherlands. He was employed, ostensibly as a Dutch labourer, at a metal foundry near Bielefeld but had to avoid other Dutch workers for fear that his German accent would give him away. Hiding under the noses of his persecutors took nerve, but he seems to have compounded the risk by continuing to travel across the border, on one occasion to check the security of his papers with his contacts in the Dutch labour exchange. One of these border crossings led to his arrest, but as a political prisoner rather than as a Jew. Although deported to Auschwitz, he was able to survive the war.[39] Whether any other Jews hid themselves among Dutch workers in Germany is impossible to say, although one or two people who took refuge in the border areas of Limburg apparently found lodgings on the 'wrong' side of the frontier.[40]

There was also the *Oosteinde* group. This was based around a large house at *Oosteinde* 16 which had been established as a club for German Jewish refugees before the occupation. As such, it acted as a meeting place, but also as an unofficial centre for helping refugees come to the Netherlands and assisting those interned by the Dutch government. In 1941 the house was incorporated into the structure of the Jewish Council, but from July 1942 until early 1944 a group of activists used the premises and an adjacent shop in *de Galerij* as a base for the distribution of illegal newspapers, the storage of material for forging documents and even as a place to hide when the leaders could no longer live in the open. The whole group numbered no more than two or three dozen, but their work rapidly expanded to help those who needed to go into hiding, and even some who had already been taken by the Germans. One of their contacts was with Jacques van der Kar, a Jewish Council worker in the *Schouwburg*. Through him, they were able to help Jews to escape from the *Schouwburg*, via *de Galerij* to suitable hiding places in the city.[41] Through some of their former colleagues, contact was established with a group inside Westerbork. Through various contacts, they were able to rescue around 20 people from the camp.[42] Ultimately, the rescuers were also forced underground as the

Oosteinde became too dangerous and the *razzias* more frequent. In assessing the success of this group one can point to their origins as refugees in the Netherlands and the left-wing sympathies which many of them shared. All these factors seem to have made them better prepared for both illegal activity, and for helping themselves and others avoid deportation.[43]

In addition to these mainly Jewish groups, there were also non-Jewish networks which helped people escape to safe havens. Perhaps the most notable of these was 'Dutch-Paris', an organisation created by Jean Weidner, a Seventh-Day Adventist who had been born in the Netherlands, but had spent much of his childhood at the Adventist seminary at Collonges, near the Swiss-French border. Living in Lyon in 1940, he became involved in Christian relief work for refugees and took a special interest in the Dutch internees held by the Vichy regime. Through this work he built up contacts with influential French church leaders and the Vichy bureaucracy. When the deportations began and the numbers of refugees in the unoccupied zone increased, he reasoned that they would not be safe indefinitely and formulated the idea of an escape route to Switzerland. One of his main problems was to circumvent the travel restrictions in the border regions. To expedite this, he set up a branch of his textile business in Annecy to be run by his wife. Before her marriage, she had been a secretary in the French consulate at Geneva and thus had a permanent visa for the Swiss-French border. In this way, Weidner was able to bring refugees to Annecy and then conduct them over the border, using his local knowledge of the area acquired as a boy.[44]

In October 1942 Weidner was contacted by 'Benno' Nijkerk, a Dutch businessman living in Brussels, who was anxious to find ways of helping Dutch and Belgian Jews being assisted by the so-called Bolle-group to escape from Belgium.[45] Nijkerk wanted to use Weidner's Swiss route but also suggested Spain as a destination. At the end of December, Weidner made contact with the director of the *Office Néerlandais* (formerly the Dutch consulate) at Toulouse, and a French doctor who was prepared to organise a route.[46] Apart from the dangers of travelling, the organisation also found it hard to find addresses and hiding places for those in transit. Although about as secure from infiltration as it could be, the network did suffer one major disaster, when a courier was captured in Paris with a list of addresses. As a result around 150 members of the organisation were arrested and at least 40 died in captivity. The principals, however, survived and continued the work until the liberation, although Weidner was twice arrested and once severely beaten by the members of the *Milice*. In total, the group saved around 1,000 people, of whom 600 were Dutch, 100 pilots, 200 French and the rest Belgians and others.[47] Again, it seems that the success of 'Dutch-Paris' was primarily due to the commitment of one man and his immediate family, together with their collective particular skills and circumstances which allowed the network to function.

Organised rescue networks

By far the largest organisation involved in hiding Jews was the so-called
Landelijke Organisatie voor Hulp aan Onderduikers (LO). This was created
to help all those who needed to go underground, whether as a result of
resistance activity, avoiding forced labour in Germany, or on grounds of
racial persecution, and to facilitate the systematic placement of *onderduikers* in appropriate hiding places. At the height of its activities, it was probably helping hundreds of thousands of people with hiding places, ration
cards, identity papers and money. The great tragedy for the Jews was that
its organisation came too late to help most of them and began only in
December 1942. The LO was the brainchild of a *Gereformeerde* pastor, *ds.*
Slomp, from Heemse (Overijssel). He was already a target of the Nazis,
having spoken out against them early in the occupation. As a result, he was
forced to go underground in May 1942. There he met *mevr.* Kuipers-
Rietberg, leader of the Union of *Gereformeerde* Women's Associations, and
in late 1942 they began to organise hiding places for *onderduikers*. From
small beginnings, they were able to extend the work into other provinces,
relying initially on friends and acquaintances, and then using contacts in
the banned Christian Furniture Makers' Union. Slomp encouraged the creation of regional and provincial committees to oversee the work of hiding
people on the run from the Germans. As the numbers of young Dutch people threatened with deportation increased, so the activities of the LO
expanded, but this all took time. The LO did not really become a major
force until the autumn of 1943, by which time it was too late to help the
majority of Jews. Moreover, in spite of *ds.* Slomp's desire to integrate the
help networks for Jewish *onderduikers*, this was never systematically carried out.[48] Although the plight of the Jews had been a motivating force
behind the establishment of the organisation, their assistance was thought
to present special problems which a mass organisation could not handle. As
a result, Jewish *onderduikers* continued to be referred to specialist groups.[49]
Whether this differentiation was based on objective conditions or a form of
latent 'biblical' antisemitism among the initiators, functionaries and those
who provided the hiding places, it is difficult to determine.[50] Certainly a
case could be made for both interpretations. In practice, the division of
labour was far from complete and many Jews in hiding did benefit from
the work of the LO, either directly or indirectly. Nevertheless, the fact that
they were perceived as posing particular problems meant that their welfare
often fell outside the mainstream work of the organisation. One further
point to note, not least because of its bearing on the question of who
helped the Jews in the Netherlands, is the construction of the LO. Its formation and initial networks were the work of *Gereformeerden*, devout
Calvinists who brought family, friends and members of their congregations
into the system. The organisation was expanded using the same religious

ties to groups in other parts of the Netherlands, but later came to include
both *Hervormde* (Dutch Reformed) and Roman Catholics as well. If a
Christian obligation to help those in need may have been the initial motivation, as the occupation continued, so a wider constituency of people
became involved, motivated more by patriotism than religious or humanitarian considerations.[51]

By 1944, the LO had 14,000 members and disbursed colossal amounts
to keep the work going. The whole operation was underwritten by a
national support fund, the *Nationaal Steunfonds* (NSF), which was underwritten in turn by the government-in-exile in London and was paying out
around fl.2 million each week to the LO in the autumn of 1944.[52]
Ultimately it became a huge cartel of national, regional and local groups
providing not only hiding places, but also the essential false identity and
ration cards together with money which allowed so many people to survive
underground.[53] There were also sections of the LO which engaged in direct
action, the so-called *Landelijke Knokploegen* (LKP) or 'action groups'
which specialised in sabotaging population registers or raiding government
offices to acquire identity and ration cards. By 1944, the LO and its various component parts even superseded local authorities in some areas on
matters of food supply during the hunger-winter of 1944–45.[54] The extension of LO activities from finding hiding places to securing false identity
and ration cards and money indicates the complexity of providing effective
help for *onderduikers*. Its existence and success in the latter years of the
war nevertheless points to one of the great tragedies as far as the Jewish
community was concerned, namely that it came too late to provide a viable
escape route for the vast majority threatened with deportation from the
summer of 1942 onwards. For most Jews, going underground was an *ad
hoc* affair, unsupported by a central organisation which could be relied
upon to provide for one's basic upkeep and welfare.

In 1943 the LO in Amsterdam created or inherited a whole series of networks in and around the city. Given the traditional and later enforced concentration of the Jews in the metropolis, it is hardly surprising to record
that many hundreds and perhaps thousands of organised and private hiding places existed during the course of the occupation. Hiding inside the
Jewish quarter became increasingly difficult as the raids increased in frequency and rigour. As a result, people sought refuge in other districts.
Amsterdam-Noord was popular, especially the Blauwe Zand area, mainly
because it was separated from the rest of the city by water and attracted
less attention from the authorities.[55] Other districts and areas also had their
share of Jewish *onderduikers*. Individual networks did not know of the
extent or even existence of other organisations in their districts. LO
branches in the east, west and even the central district of Amsterdam all
reported playing host to greater or lesser numbers of Jews among the
labour-service deserters and students they helped. One story of an activist

in Amsterdam will have to suffice to show how people were drawn into the work of saving Jews, and how their involvement grew over time.

J. Hamerling's involvement began in the summer of 1941 when he was asked for help in going underground by a Jewish colleague. Having a friend working in the rationing bureaucracy allowed him to help and thus he took the first steps in illegal activity. In the summer of 1942, he and his wife played host to their first *onderduiker*, a woman who stayed for a few months. She was subsequently moved on, but Hamerling continued to provide her with ration cards and acted as conduit for money provided by her father's colleagues. Because his house was small, it was used as a transit station rather than a permanent hiding place. The friend in the rationing bureaucracy was part of a network which also eventually gave him some help. Among other places, he managed to find addresses in *Amsterdam-Noord*, but noted that prices varied between fl.25 and fl.35 per person per week and were thus only for those who were well-off. Hamerling seems to have run his own network but did have some contact with the LO. As his work snowballed, he made contact with LO district leaders in *Amsterdam-Centrum* and *Amsterdam-Noord* who provided further help with identity cards and the like, and also took all his non-Jewish *onderduikers* off his hands. In May 1943 he and his wife took in a ten-month-old Jewish child, but as it became more dangerous the wife and child moved to relatives in North Holland. In the end, Hamerling estimated that he had helped around a hundred Jews underground. Only a minority had actually stayed in his house, but he had organised their hiding places, identity and ration cards. From small beginnings he had created a substantial organisation which had helped a considerable number of people, many of whom did not even know his name. When asked why he had acted this way his reply was that he was merely thankful that his actions had saved people from the enemy's clutches.[56]

One of the most successful networks for helping Jews to escape from their persecutors was developed inside the German machinery for arrest, registration and deportation. In the first weeks of the deportations, many of those called up had to report to the offices of the *Zentralstelle* on the Adama van Scheltemaplein. This soon proved to be impractical and the work was moved to the *Schouwburg*. Here, guarded by the *Waffen-SS*, Jews were registered, their assets logged and their names placed on transport lists. This work was carried out by members of the Jewish Council's *Expositur* section and by four representatives of the Lippmann-Rosenthal Bank. The building became a veritable fortress, although de Jong points out that many who were held there had little inclination to escape, and would have had no idea what to do if they had been allowed back on the street.[57] In any given week, there could be as many as 400 Jews held in the *Schouwburg*, waiting for transport to Westerbork, and it was this delay which allowed some Jews to be saved. The scheme was masterminded by

Walter Süskind, a German Jewish refugee who worked for the *Expositur* in the *Schouwburg*, compiling the lists and indexes of those to be deported. His position allowed him to 'lose' index and registration cards, thus making it possible for the individuals concerned to be spirited away from the *Schouwburg* by help organisations. Süskind himself had help from other members of the *Expositur* staff but was also in contact with an Amsterdam student group, and another similar but separate organisation based around former students of the *Vossius Gymnasium* (Vossius High School) was in contact with the so-called *Utrechtse Kindercomité* (Utrecht Childrens Committee) which was active in hiding Jewish children all over the country. In this way, people could not only escape from the *Schouwburg* but were also locked into a network which would find them places to hide.

Helping children and adults to escape from the Germans was one thing, finding them somewhere to hide was something else. Although many people did find safety inside Amsterdam, the concentration of German activity there made it seem more dangerous and there were compelling reasons for trying to find sanctuary in another part of the country. This introduces perhaps the most important feature of Jewish rescue in the Netherlands, namely the co-operation between organisations in Amsterdam and the north-eastern provinces, and the role of clergymen in bringing them together. A nonconformist pastor living in Amsterdam, who had been begun his illegal activity by providing shelter for a German Jewess and her daughter, became a link between the city and the north-east. Through his family and through other clergymen he obtained contacts in Friesland, Groningen and Drenthe and then travelled there to try and find addresses where people could hide. This was organised by local clergymen who found suitable hosts, primarily from among the farming community, and then passed the information on. In this way, prisoners-of-war, students and Jews were removed from Amsterdam to the north-east.[58] This appears to have been another network organised by the *Gereformeerde Kerk*, helping all sorts of people on the run from the Germans. It is perhaps important to note here an important advantage which clergymen possessed, namely a reason for travelling, meeting with colleagues and visiting people at all hours of the day and night. This made them ideal for travelling to find addresses and also for conducting fugitives to those addresses. In this way, the clergy played a pivotal role in organising and expediting contacts between different areas even before the LO had come into existence.

There can be little doubt that the existence of rescue networks in the north-eastern provinces of Friesland, Groningen and Drenthe played a crucial role in saving Jews in the Netherlands. These areas were well off the beaten track and contained large tracts of low-lying farmland, sparsely populated heath and expanses of open water. Apart from Groningen and Leeuwarden there were no large towns and the majority of the population were involved in agriculture of some description. Overwhelmingly a

Protestant area, all three provinces had strong *Gereformeerde Kerken*. During the course of the occupation, these areas played host to many thousands of *onderduikers* of whom only a minority were Jews.

As has already been noted, the organisation of hiding places in these areas was partly, but not exclusively, in the hands of the local clergy. Undoubtedly they had a greater degree of moral leverage over the congregation than anyone else, but it is impossible to know exactly how far their persuasion went, either individually or collectively. Practical rescue work in the provinces often began with people being brought by train. This was usually expedited in the evening or early mornings if it was still dark. If this was impossible, times in the day were chosen when the trains would be full. Almost invariably, Jews would be disguised in some way or other.[59] Sometimes accompanied, sometimes alone, they were collected from the nearest railway station. Help organisations soon became sophisticated enough to send advance warning from Amsterdam to the provinces of who to expect. Arnold Douwes described a code system from A to I which indicated the nature of the person arriving, where A was an old woman and I a young man. Furthermore they were also classified according to their 'Jewishness' where 'I' denoted a typical Jew, 'II' someone fairly typical and 'III' someone untypical.[60] Other organisations had different systems. A network in Joure (Friesland) was run by a man with a laundry. Thus when he had places to offer, he would telegraph to Amsterdam either 'I can take a large wash' meaning he had room only for adults, or 'ordinary wash' meaning he had places for children as well.[61] Another group in Blokzijl (Overijssel) used a scale where the extremes were black rabbits (typical Jews who could not travel openly) and white rabbits who did not look Jewish at all.[62] Such a system allowed the receivers to arrange any further travel and also to earmark places for the new arrivals to stay. This makes the whole process seem very straightforward, yet it was seldom so. Finding places for the *onderduikers* to stay was the largest problem for the organisers, but their techniques also shed light on how the work came to include more and more people. Douwes gives a succinct example.

> Finding places for the varied Jewish fugitives was always an issue. First always 'temporary' places. People found it hard to say no if you said that the 'customer' would have to sleep in the open if they did not take him in. Of course, the result was an argument, but for the most part it turned out better than expected.[63]

Undoubtedly, many hosts had to be persuaded to provide hiding places, even if they had agreed to the idea in principle. In addition to the risks involved, giving up space in one's house for an indeterminate period was not to be undertaken lightly. Men and women like Douwes would sometimes organise a hiding place only for the hosts to get cold feet at the last minute. Others would object when the guest did not turn out to be as

expected. Even an initial acceptance was no guarantee of a permanent placing. Locations could easily become dangerous if the Germans began to
organise raids in the area. Hosts could be warned that too many people
knew they were sheltering Jews and neighbours could turn out to be unreliable. None of this took account of possible friction between hosts and
guests. Their culture and backgrounds were often light years apart, and it
was hardly surprising that some arrangements failed to stand the test of
time. Sometimes the problems were serious, and the helpers had to find
new hiding places, often at extremely short notice if the host had put his or
her guests out on the street. On other occasions, a visit to smooth over the
problem might be enough. Thus an LO worker in Joure (Friesland)
reported that a professor with 'a palace of a house' was sheltering a rabbi,
but his two unmarried daughters wanted someone else to take him so that
they could have their room back. In this case, the hosts were persuaded to
keep the rabbi, where he stayed until the end of the war,[64] but such inter-
ventions were not always successful. An LO worker in Utrecht brought two
Jews from Wassenaar. One, a woman, had been placed with some very
simple people in Lexmond (Utrecht), but she was very *chic*, changed her
clothes at least twice a day, and objected to the fact that her hosts had no
inside toilet. Neither she nor her hosts wanted to continue the arrange-
ment and she had to be fetched and moved on.[65] Other middle-class Jews
had similar experiences with working-class Dutch hosts. One young man
who hid with a Communist household had to sleep on straw mattresses
with the family of eight. There was no money to replace the straw and two
of the children were persistent bedwetters. He had to move on, not
because of the conditions or because the premises became unsafe, but simply because the marriage broke up, and with it the family.[66] All those
involved in practical rescue work of this nature made mention of the
inevitable frictions which occurred between hosts and guests. The insanitary practices and petty restrictions imposed by hosts or the outrageous
behaviour of guests could make life intolerable for the other parties concerned, and in extreme cases threaten their security and that of the other
people involved. An *onderduiker* who arrived at his 'address' with a huge
van full of furniture which included a full-size piano could be joked about
afterwards, but at the time represented a real threat to the people who had
agreed to take him in.[67] However amusing the story, this remained a matter
of life and death, for guests and potentially for their hosts as well. Yet even
the most passive and even-tempered hosts and guests could not maintain a
totally harmonious relationship under such fraught circumstances. Help
organisations therefore had to spend a good deal of their time *re*-locating
those in hiding. This may have been due to individual crises, but also
served to reduce friction between hosts and guests. As Douwes made clear,
people assumed that when new addresses were needed for *onderduikers*,
this was so that they could be rotated, whereas in fact, the numbers

involved were constantly increasing as people were moved to other districts and newcomers brought in from the cities.[68] It was also the case that addresses became unsafe for a whole variety of reasons. Dangers from police raids or betrayal, or from friction between guests and hosts were major contributory factors, but other circumstances also intervened. Apart from the break-up of host families or changes in their circumstances, survivors report all manner of other reasons why they had to move. Changes in neighbours for example, or the flight underground of a non-Jewish member of the household which would make the address liable to a raid by the police. One *onderduiker* recorded the fact that she had to move on from an address in Arnhem because the police were likely to make house-to-house searches after the murder of a child.[69]

The north-eastern provinces of Friesland, Groningen and Drenthe did harbour a large number of Jews, yet even here, the distribution of Jewish *onderduikers* was extremely varied. Heerenveen (Friesland) and its surrounding area may have had as many as 1,200 people in hiding in the autumn of 1942. Nearby Steenwijk had a similar number, of whom at least 40 were Jews. The report noted the constant need to find more hiding places and the persuasion used on local farmers to provide appropriate refuges. Further south, in Ommen (Overijssel), there were as many as 300 Jews, mainly sheltered by farmers. There was reportedly no shortage of demand for such people, although the conditions of their upkeep varied. Some were accommodated without charge, while others worked for their board and lodging. Only in one extreme case was a working *onderduiker* required to pay an additional fl.40 per week.[70] In contrast, the locality around Hoogkerk (Groningen) had only two Jewish families. One was rapidly rounded up and deported, while the other was very anti-Christian and neither wanted nor needed any financial help.[71]

The fact that there were more opportunities to hide in the north-east, and more people willing to accommodate Jews, probably encouraged the concentration of Jewish *onderduikers* in those districts. While the conditions endured by those in hiding were not always ideal, there seem to have been people willing to take them in. The role of orthodox Calvinism as a catalyst for action should not be understated. Some people were prepared to help on the basis of religious or moral duty. Even if they had previously regarded Jews with suspicion, the obligation to help the *Oude Volk* (Hebrew people) remained strong. This view was summed up by a rescue worker in Hoogeveen in the following terms: 'if you didn't have an *onderduiker* in your house, you weren't a proper peasant farmer' (*Als je geen onderduiker had, was je geen goede boer*). What he implied was that if one wasn't sheltering an *onderduiker* one could not be considered as a genuine member of the community.[72] Another account from a survivor who lived with a strict Calvinist working-class family in Arnhem noted an apparent conflict in their behaviour because they 'do not buy from the local grocer because he is too left wing, but do accept *onderduikers* from him as part of their joint struggle against the enemy'.[73]

However, even in the provinces, just like Amsterdam, there were people who would only hide Jews if they were given help, or money, or some other material benefit. For some would-be rescuers, help really was essential. Without ration cards or a supply of food for *onderduikers*, it could become impossible to feed them. This type of demand was an expected part of the work. More materialistic were the demands for money. What was the money for – board and lodging, recompense for the inconvenience or reward for the risks being taken? Certainly the north-eastern provinces were not immune from this type of profiteering, although one gets the impression that it was less prevalent and on a smaller scale than other parts of the country. One further motivation related primarily to babies and children. Minors were invariably seen as innocent victims of the persecution and they were easier to place than adults. The LO in *Amsterdam-Centrum* was told by an LO representative from Sneek (Friesland) that they should send as many Jewish children as they could manage to find.[74] Certainly, members of the Amsterdam LO had nothing but praise for the Friesians, describing them as stalwart and their achievements as 'extraordinary'.

This concentration on the north-east should not hide the fact that there were rescue networks and Jews underground in almost every part of the country.[75] Nonetheless, if it was difficult to find places for adult Jews in the north-east, it was almost impossible elsewhere. A report from t'Gooi (Utrecht) summed it up. 'No one who didn't live in the Netherlands during the period can realise how difficult it was to find addresses for people – when the SS and Gestapo power was so great – whereby most people refused to take Jewish *onderduikers* into their homes.' The report goes on to describe how many people had to be moved almost as soon as they had been placed and that the dangers of betrayal were always very great.[76] One of the most telling accounts of the differences encountered in finding places for adult Jews as opposed to children came from an LO worker in the same area. Recalling a meeting in an Arnhem convalescent home between representatives of various groups he noted:

> Everything was finished when one [of those present] said, 'I still have a number of Jewish babies', what should we do with them? It was a sort of Jews-market, on all sides, here two, here five, in the end there weren't enough to go round. It was certainly wonderful that the whole problem was solved so completely. But no-one would have an [adult] Jew. For adults you said, it is an *onderduiker* with black hair. Just what he looked like, you knew nothing else. In this way, they were trapped [into acceptance], as even at the end they absolutely refused to take Jews.[77]

Even late in the occupation, addresses were hard to come by. A rescuer looking for a home for a Jewish couple tried ten households who refused to help before an eleventh took them in.[78] However, the apparent ease with which Jewish babies and young children could be found foster-parents needs some qualification. One rescuer has pointed out that those who did not 'look' Jewish were easy enough to place, but if they were, for example, circumcised young boys who did 'look' Jewish, then it was far more difficult.[79]

As in the northern provinces, there were differences between one area and another, between one village and another. In Schagen (*Noord-Holland*) it was reported that people willing to help *onderduikers* were hard to find, but that the attitude of church-goers (both Roman Catholic and Protestant) contrasted favourably with that of the liberal majority of the population.[80] In Hengelo (Overijssel) they had little to do with Jews, but a few miles away in Enschede there was a major network helping Jews, run by a Calvinist pastor *ds*. Leen Overduin. This group helped up to a thousand Jews in some way or other. Although its centre of operations was Enschede, the network had contacts in both Friesland and Limburg, and accepted Jewish *onderduikers* from all parts of the country. Overduin was arrested more than once, and served nine months in Utrecht gaol, but survived to continue his work until the war's end.[81] In Ede (Gelderland) there were reportedly 300–400 Jews in hiding, mainly from Amsterdam. Some had been placed by rescue organisations while others were private arrangements where the LO helped only with food and ration cards. There were a number of people whose houses acted as stepping-off points for going underground. These 'transit houses' allowed people to stay for a few days before being moved on to other 'transit houses', usually in the north-east. Around 40 Jews had passed through the house of Sara Walbeehm, a nurse in Den Haag, on their way underground, and a further 30 were arrested there when the house was raided in March 1943. In Haarlem, the family ten Boom helped at least 80 Jews to go underground.[82] They began their work through contact with the plight of Jewish neighbours. The pattern of individual families helping large numbers of people is perhaps epitomised by the *Gereformeerde* Bogaard family in Nieuw-Vennep (a village in north Holland midway between Amsterdam and Leiden on the Haarlemmermeerpolder).

Unlike many people who helped in the rescue work, the Bogaards had decided to work against the occupiers from the beginning. They seem to have disobeyed every possible German ordinance and saw it as natural to help God's people when the time came. One of the sons knew an Amsterdam Jewish family, and went to fetch them in July 1942. Soon he was collecting other members of the family and coming into contact with others who wanted to hide at Nieuw-Vennep. The Bogaard farm thus became the centre of an entire network of people coming from the cities and then being placed with other nearby helpers. Among others, the Bogaards gave refuge to many of the children from a Jewish children's nursing home in Laren. While some of these *onderduikers* were found hiding places elsewhere, a large number stayed on the three farms owned by the family. They were raided five times. On four occasions, the Germans found some of the Jews hidden there, eleven the first time, three the next. On the third occasion, they found no one, yet there were around 100 on the the three farms at that time. The last two raids also discovered some of the *onderduikers*. A raid in October 1943 resulted in one of the Jews shooting a policeman which led to a detachment of *Ordnungspolizei* arriving to search the area. Some 34 people were taken away and Johannes Bogaard Snr. was arrested for the second time. After a spell in Vught, he was released, but insisted on complaining to the SD in Amsterdam that the police had taken his harmonium. As a result, he was arrested again and ultimately died in Sachsenhausen at 79 years old. The fifth raid in December 1943 caught still more *onderduikers* and led to the arrest of other members of the family. Even after Johannes Jnr. had been forced into hiding himself, he continued to look after the Jews he had placed with other hosts. The sheer commitment and persistence of this one family in the face of constant threat and personal tragedy (three members of the family died as a result of imprisonment or mistreatment by the Germans) can only be a cause for wonder. To be raided so often, to be imprisoned and yet to continue the work when so many others would have given up almost beggars belief. Their collective belief was that God had called them to do this work and that as good Dutch people they could do nothing else.[83]

It has been estimated that the Bogaard family helped around 200 Jews to go underground, but their attitude was in stark contrast to that of many of their neighbours. Johannes Jnr. recalled after the war that:

> it was impossible to find places for everyone. I still remember clearly visiting a farmer with a really large house (a man, his wife and one small child) and asking, it was only for a few days, to place a child there and the answer was:'Not for a million, Bogaard, will I risk my family', and what he said was held by so many, but as a result *we* took far too many people.[84]

The impression from this account, and from many others who helped to hide Jews during the occupation, is of a relatively small number of people who were directly involved and helped a disproportionately high number of fugitives. For the most celebrated cases this was true, but there were many examples of individual acts of rescue, where guests and hosts were known to each other, or were brought together by an organisation and then stayed together until the end of the war. In addition, for every person actively involved in hiding Jews there were others engaged in providing false identity cards and ration cards, acting as conductors or intermediaries, or helping to solve the inevitable problems which occurred for those underground. Individual doctors and hospitals are often mentioned for having helped to treat or even to hide Jews who were or became ill during their period underground. For example, Santpoort Provincial Hospital hid

200 fugitives until the autumn of 1944, and the Valerius Clinic and Juliana Hospital in Amsterdam were also heavily involved in helping and hiding Jews.[85] Similarly, undertakers had to be called upon when an *onderduiker* died in hiding. Insofar as was practical, such people were given a respectable burial, although not with the appropriate religious rites. In Amsterdam, it was still possible to bury people officially in the Jewish cemetery at Muiderberg with help from local bureaucrats who did not ask questions. However, many were not so fortunate. The anatomy theatre at Amsterdam University was used to 'hide' some corpses and others had to be buried in unmarked graves or consigned to the nearest canal.[86]

Apart from those who helped with such practical matters when asked, there were also legions of others who knew what was happening but did nothing to give the *onderduikers* or their hosts away; neighbours who intimated that they knew that there were Jews in the house and made suggestions to improve security; friends who came up to 'conductors' on railway stations, pointed to the accompanying children and said, 'they're not all yours, are they?' Many thousands, perhaps hundreds of thousands, were in on the secret, even if they did nothing practical to help. The secrecy of the whole undertaking served to complicate the issue, both during the occupation and afterwards. People never admitted to harbouring Jews, even to members of their family. Presser recounts the tale of a mother who did not tell her visiting daughter that she was sheltering a Jewess, unaware that the daughter was also sheltering Jews.[87] It was in everyone's interest that as few people as possible knew where Jews were hidden, even if the putative confidantes were doing exactly the same thing. No one knew when a hiding place might be discovered and the guests and host arrested and questioned. Knowledge became dangerous. Secrecy could occasionally lead to misunderstandings and misconstructions. While most refusals to help were on the basis that the hosts were unwilling to risk themselves or their families, there were occasions when those approached could not help because they already had people hiding in their house, but would not vouchsafe the information to others. Even the networks helping Jews operated independently of one another, thus one group would not know the hiding places, or even the personnel of another group. Moreover, later in the occupation the Jews were only a small minority of those underground and had to compete for hiding places with other non-Jewish fugitives.

Saving children

The rescue of Jewish children has elicited a good deal of recent scholarly interest, not least because of the post-war debates on their guardianship and the studies of their relationships with wartime foster-parents and psychological readjustment in the post-war era.[88] As the sources make clear, it was easier to hide children as they could be placed with non-Jewish 'foster-families', and there was a special sympathy for them which did not extend to their elders. The occupation gave rise to four major networks devoted more or less exclusively to the rescue of children, namely the *Amsterdam Studentengroep* (Amsterdam Student Group), the *Utrechtse Kindercomité*, the so-called *Naamloze Vennootschap* (Limited Liability Company) and the *Trouwgroep* (Loyal Group), each of which had separate origins. The first three were founded in the aftermath of the first deportations in July 1942, while the *Trouwgroep* began its activities in the early months of 1943.[89] Their activities are worth considering in detail, not only as acts of rescue in their own right, but also for the light they shed on the organisation and development of all such groups.

The *Utrechtse Kindercomité* owed its origins to the efforts of a Utrecht student, Ad Groenendijk, and Cor Bastiaanse, a woman whose husband was being held as a hostage by the Germans. On hearing of the first call-ups for deportation, Bastiaanse was able to persuade some mothers who had been told to report to the *Zentralstelle* to hand their children into her charge. She collected them from Amsterdam and then distributed them to addresses around Utrecht. Groenendijk also placed children with the mother of a fellow student, Jan Meulenbelt, whose work in contacting friends to find suitable addresses gave rise to the *Amsterdamse Studentengroep*.[90] The involvement of the (traditionally apolitical) students in resistance work of this nature seems to have been caused primarily by German interference in the universities through the exclusion of students and the removal of non-aryan staff.[91] The students gradually increased the size of their placement network but were probably fortunate that their work had begun so early, when Jewish children were not liable to be called up and there were few parents willing to give up their children to strangers.[92] Later they were able to make indirect contact with parents via a paediatrician, Ph. Fiedeldij Dop, who had a large number of Jewish patients and inherited many more from two Jewish paediatricians, thus greatly enlarging his practice.[93] In this way, the working practices of the group became more structured, but there remained problems. The work had begun during the summer vacation, but many of the students involved no longer had so much time on their hands and both groups lost some of their members but gained others who already had some practical experience, such as Hetty Voûte who had contact with the Westerweel group and had been finding homes for Jewish children in the vicinity of Noordwijk.[94]

The work also required funds, and this was expedited by using students' contacts to raise money. They were aided by one of their number who had close contacts with the Catholic Archbishop of Utrecht, who persuaded his bishops to help fund the work through the Archdiocese's special needs fund. Problems also arose when the numbers of children began to exceed the places available. Initial attempts to find hiding places in Friesland through (Dutch Reformed) *dominees* and (Orthodox Calvinist) *pastoors* failed as the stories told by the students about the raids and deportations were not believed. Only later was this to change. Attempts were also made to 'aryanise' children by having them 'found' by their prospective foster-parents and then registered as foundlings. This lasted only until the Germans noted the huge increases in the numbers involved and decreed that henceforward all foundlings were to be treated as Jewish. Another method, used by Marion Pritchard–van Binsbergen, among others, was for women to register the children as born to them out of wedlock. She apparently managed this feat three times, on one occasion with a break of only five months.[95] The extension of the work required a more complex administration to keep track of the children and to maintain their welfare, and an ever-increasing number of foster-parents and addresses. By April 1943, they had found places for around 250 children.

This was in part solved by a chance meeting of one of the students with a cousin at the house of his uncle. She was a curate at the (Liberal) Dutch Reformed Church in Sneek (Friesland) and agreed to help, partly because she had been asked, but 'naturally primarily on humanitarian grounds. As someone who was religious, I regarded it as my duty and our calling to become involved. Simply to help where you could help.'[96]

This gave the network access to a whole new community of some 5,000 souls, full of potential 'addresses', and to a group of people prepared to help with the work itself. This was further expanded when the baptist minister in Leeuwarden and a further network of like-minded families in west Friesland became involved. The pattern of expansion of this group was based on two elements, personal (student) friends and religious affiliations which served to bring in more helpers while providing only a minimal threat to the operation as a whole. Moreover, as the network grew and more towns were used as hiding places, the Utrecht centre was able to let these satellite operations function on their own. The *Amsterdamse Studentengroep* developed its own links with Friesland and networks based in Arnhem and The Hague were made independent.[97]

The *Naamloze Vennootschap* (NV) came about when a *Gereformeede* pastor in Amsterdam-South, Constant Sikkel, was asked to help two children from an Austrian (Jewish) *Gereformeerde* family who had been among the first to be called up for deportation in July 1942. After a sermon which referred to the problem in suitably obtuse terms, he enlisted the help of two brothers, Jaap and Gerhard Musch, to find hiding places for these two – and subsequently for many more. Gerard and a friend, Dick Groenewegen van Wijk, decided to work 'underground' full time, while Jaap moved to Heerlen (Limburg), where he enlisted the help of another *Gereformeerde* pastor, Gerard Pontier. This gave him access to another congregation, and to specific families with contacts.[98] The *Gereformeeden* in Zuid-Limburg were a small minority in an overwhelmingly Catholic milieu. Pontier's congregation numbered only 496, spread over the whole mining district. Many were fiercely anti-German, which gave further motivation, if one were needed, for their helping Jews. Pontier himself exemplified the mentality. On his reasons for going to Heerlen, his daughter explained:

> my father had a sort of pioneer spirit. One of his dreams was to be a missionary in the Dutch East Indies, but for various family reasons nothing came of this. Then he was given this post in Zuid-Limburg, which he grabbed with both hands.[99]

Although dealing with only small numbers of children in its early months of existence, the NV had no access to large funds or ration cards to support its work, and it became apparent that this would be a major problem if the numbers involved were to expand. This was never solved and the organisation relied on the resistance in Amsterdam to provide whatever money and cards it could. Later, it also received bread, clothing and a little money from a local bakers' co-operative. The three leaders of the organisation spent their time finding new addresses, making monthly visits to those in hiding to provide ration cards and other essentials, and making journeys to and from Amsterdam to escort children to their new foster-homes. By April 1943, the children numbered around 80. From the detailed history of this group, it appears that it suffered from marginality in its own locality – a few hundred Calvinists in an overwhelmingly Catholic community. Thus, it was never able to find enough addresses and had a limited catchment. At the same time, that very marginality had helped to give the organisation its purpose, strength and security. People helped because they saw the Jews as a fellow minority and could therefore empathise with their plight. The NV was also clearly limited by its lack of funds and struggled to support those whom it had taken under its wing. The need to move the children around when danger threatened or the foster-parents became anxious meant that new homes were constantly having to be found. In this way, Catholic households were also brought into the network and children could find themselves being moved from one denomination to another – both equally observant – and engaging in Bible study with one, and saying the rosary with another. The organisation is credited with ultimately helping around 250 children, not one of whom fell into the hands of the Germans, although many of the organisation's leaders were arrested and killed, or died in camps before the end of the occupation.[100]

The final group engaged in saving children was based around the illegal newspaper *Trouw*, but began its work much later, in April 1943.[101] It was led by two women. The first was Hester van Lennep, who had helped hide a small number of Jewish children before that date, using her contacts

within the Jewish community to find the children and then family and
friends to find them hiding places. In April she came into contact with
Gesina van der Molen, the editor of *Trouw*, who had broken from her
Gereformeerde roots in Groningen to be the first woman to obtain a doc-
torate from the *Vrije Universiteit* (Free University) in Amsterdam.
However, the newspaper consistently espoused Christian (*Gereformeerde*)
values and this became the basis for the recruitment of foster-homes.[102]

Although the risks were still very great, transporting and hiding children
was somewhat easier than doing the same for adults. Provided they were
under six years of age, they did not require papers to travel, nor did they
have to wear the Jewish star on their clothes. Students often acted as couriers, making many separate journeys from Amsterdam to Limburg or the
north-east, and then handing them over to contacts. One courier recalled
that she had read the entire *Forsyte Saga* on such train journeys.[103] It was
not unusual for any family to have children to stay. They could be passed
off as nieces, nephews or just as evacuees. Babies were even easier, especially if the foster-family also contrived to move house. This allowed the
change of address and the the birth to be registered at the same time, and
in a new neighbourhood which would effectively mask the 'sudden'
appearance of a child. Finding children to save was a different matter as
initially it relied on parents being willing to give up their offspring, often
to strangers, to prevent their being deported. As more and more Jews were
called up for transport to the East, so the various networks were asked to
hide more children, but their main source during 1943 became the crèche
of the *Schouwburg*.

Credit for the idea of removing children from the *Schouwburg* has to go
to Walter Süskind. He realised that, as the babies and smaller children
were kept in a crèche across the road from the main buildings, there were
greater opportunities to effect their removal. The crèche was less well
guarded and this made 'disappearance' that much easier. His main problem
was finding some contact with a non-Jewish organisation which could find
safe hiding places. In January 1943 he met Joop Woortman, the leader of
the NV's Amsterdam operation. Babies were smuggled out in empty milk-
churns, boxes or potato sacks.[104] Later, when nurses were allowed to take
babies outside, they went for walks but returned carrying large dolls. Older
children were sometimes taken all the way to the Central Station, or were
whisked away on a tram by their minders from the street outside the
crèche. Even more daring was the action of two members of the *Utrechtse
Kindercomité*, who, when three of their charges were discovered in Utrecht
and conveyed to the *Schouwburg*, dressed in SS uniforms and went to the
crèche to demand their return.[105]

At least three separate organisations were involved in removing children
from the *Schouwburg*, the NV together with the two student groups, but
several others also took charge of children saved in this way, for example

the Westerweel group and the Bogaard family.[106] In principle, the parents always had to give their permission for children to be smuggled out. The only exceptions were for children who had been caught in hiding and whose parents were therefore not to be found. All needed the help of Süskind and his colleagues to remove the evidence from the card indexes to prevent the discrepancies from becoming apparent, and it has been estimated that around 600 babies and children were 'kidnapped' in this way.[107] While the help organisations involved in this work were undoubtedly very effective, they also received help from a most unlikely quarter. A survivor of the *Schouwburg* commented on the paradoxical behaviour of the German functionaries employed there. She noted that they often played with the babies in the crèche and brought them presents, even though they knew that these children would soon be transported.[108] Nonetheless, apparently unknown to this woman, one of the *Waffen-SS* guards at the *Schouwburg* was reputedly helping to expedite the escape of several hundred of these children.

SS-Unterscharführer Alfons Zündler had been posted to Amsterdam as a guard after being wounded in 1941 and discharged from active service. His involvement in the escapes from the *Schouwburg* was given only one line in de Jong, and little more in Presser.[109] Certainly there is evidence that he turned a blind eye to the activities of the resistance groups removing people from the *Schouwburg* and its crèche, allowing individuals to leave the building and even on one occasion lending his SS uniform to an escapee. For Zündler, his guard duties meant keeping track of the numbers of Jews held. He estimated that he helped rescue one person per day, perhaps 400 during his year-long service at the *Schouwburg*. No selection process was involved and by his own admission he operated as circumstances permitted. If his colleagues were drunk or absent, an opportunity might arise to allow an individual escape to take place. He also claims that he acted as he did simply because he 'felt sorry' for the Jews. Late in 1943, his activities were discovered[110] and he was imprisoned at Scheveningen, tried for *Judenbegünstigung* (favouring Jews) by an SS court martial in The Hague and sentenced to death. The sentence was later commuted to ten years in Dachau, but it had been widely assumed that he had died there and it was only in the 1980s that he was discovered living in Munich. Further research by journalists and historians prompted Yad Vashem to consider him for the award of a medal as a 'righteous gentile'.

Not surprisingly perhaps, the idea of giving such an award to a former SS man provoked a storm of controversy. While the publicity attached to the case produced 23 people who felt they owed their lives to Zündler,[111] there were others who claimed that he had saved people in exchange for sexual or material favours. Moreover, they pointed out that his employment was not confined to the *Schouwburg*. He was used by the German authorities to round up Jews from addresses in the Netherlands, but even in this work he may have helped to save some of those arrested. In one case, he was involved with the Dutch police in the arrest of a family just outside Amsterdam. When the raid took place, the father of the family was absent and when he returned Zündler contrived to drive him away, removing his coat with a star on it in the process. The rest of the family were taken to the *Schouwburg*, but here again Zündler was able to help by preventing their registration and smuggling them out of a back door.[112] Perhaps there is no other explanation for his behaviour than that he did feel sorry for the Jews and opportunities for help did sometimes arise. As for his membership of the SS, this too is slightly misleading. He was born Alfons Cislowski and brought up in Danzig, changing his name to make it appear more Germanic. Drafted into the city militia in 1939, he found it transformed into an SS police division. Thus he did not join the SS of his own accord, but had no opportunity to leave while the war continued. More recent research, however, paints Zündler in a less favourable light and re-examines the original charges against him. From this it would appear that the reticence about making the award was almost certainly justified.[113]

After June 1943, it became more difficult to use the 'normal' methods to spirit children away, but when the *directrice* of the crèche, Henriëtte Pimentel, obtained permission to use part of the garden of the adjacent Reformed Church teacher training college, new opportunities arose. The director of the school, Johan van Hulst, was already well-disposed towards the idea of helping the Jewish children but it was the arrival of Gesina van der Molen as the external assessor for his students' final examinations which brought the *Trouw* group into the work of rescue. From then on, children could be taken out through the training college and well away from the crèche without arousing too much suspicion. Fears remained about the security of the work under the noses of the 84 students at the college but it continued to operate successfully until the crèche closed on 29 September 1943.[114] Flim estimates that the rescue organisations save about 600 of the 5,000–6,000 children who passed through the crèche during its exisistence, or between 10 and 12 per cent. He also notes that this disguises the fact that in the period when child-smuggling was at its height, from May to September 1943, they may have saved up to 20 per cent of the children.[115] In part this may be accounted for by parents being more willing to see their children taken into hiding, or them not being there to be consulted. However, he also recalls a more chilling note from one of the crèche-workers, namely that these children were saved by the other children acting as a smokescreen. It would have been immediately apparent if all the children disappeared – thus only a lucky minority could be saved without drawing attention to the work.

In conclusion, a number of points need to be stressed. The non-Jewish rescuers in the Netherlands did play an important role in protecting many of those who survived. The examples quoted above tend to highlight the unusual or the prominent examples of help provided during the occupation. Even with hindsight and the limited information now available, it remains impossible to make any precise judgements about the numbers of people involved, their social or religious backgrounds, or their motivations.[116] However, some broad inferences remain possible. In the first instance, it is important to note that rescuers were recruited in many different ways and with varying degrees of willingness. The literature shows that people often had to be persuaded to help and to hide Jews and then continually encouraged to keep them. Moreover, a decision to help may have been given long consideration, or have been just the result of an instant decision. For every hiding place arranged by a network, another may have come about through fugitives knocking on doors at random and asking for help.

It should also be clear that rescue could involve a whole range of activities and varying levels of commitment. Those who personally sheltered Jews in their houses tend to be given the highest profile, but there were many others who helped in other ways, by acting as couriers, suppliers of false documents or funds to pay for the upkeep of those underground. While the risks inherent in this work varied with the level of involvement, it should always be remembered that rescue was a complex affair, both for the Jews in hiding and those who tried to help them. Another critical factor in the help given to Jews is the role of the clergy (of all denominations) in establishing networks or providing assistance on an individual basis. Again this cannot be quantified. At an institutional level, the churches tended to tread carefully when dealing with the German occupiers, but there were individuals and groups prepared to go much further. Clerical involvement may have been increased by Jews looking for hiding places in a strange town or village going to the *pastorie* in the knowledge that even if they were turned away, they were unlikely to be betrayed, and by local people turning to the clergy for help and advice if they were approached to help. The leading role of members of the *Gereformeede Kerk* should not be ignored. While perhaps not as marginal in the parts of the Netherlands where they provided the most help as they were in the country as a whole, their efforts undoubtedly outweighed those of the other, larger denominations. This may have been due to the fact that the areas where they were numerically strongest were also the best localities to hide, but it is more likely that the willingness of the *Gereformeerden* to help was based on seeing the plight of the Jews as mirroring their own self-image as a persecuted people.

Finally, the evidence shows that a large number of children were rescued and hidden. While this may have been due to a qualitatitive distinction made by some rescuers between the children and their parents, there were also a whole series of structural reasons why children were much easier to hide. Physically hiding babies or small children was complicated by their special needs, and by the noise they would undoubtedly make. This was one reason for splitting up families in hiding. Whatever the emotional wrench might be, it was much easier (and safer) to have children living openly with a foster-family than trying to hide them. Children under 15 did not require an identity card and could therefore be moved around more easily, and with fewer questions being asked. Moreover, there appears to have been no shortage of homes willing to take them in. This may have been motivated by altruism, a feeling that the children were innocent victims, a desire to convert, or seen as compensation for a lack of offspring. Whatever the reason, this combination of structural and specific elements might be seen as a favourable factor insofar as children were concerned. Certainly the testimony of some rescuers leaves no doubt that distinctions were made between Jewish children and their parents.

The existence of some rescue networks and individuals willing to help could be seen as a favourable element for the Jews in the Netherlands as a whole, but this should not disguise the fact that only a minority of Dutch men and women helped those in hiding, and an even smaller number were prepared to give assistance to Jews. Whether this further selectivity was determined by antisemitic sentiments or the harsher penalties handed out to those caught harbouring Jews is now impossible to determine. Excuses of all sorts were used to explain non-involvement – the house was full, there were no usable hiding places, relatives, tradespeople or neighbours were unreliable, the Germans were based nearby. All of these were commonplace and in some cases no doubt perfectly accurate. The problem in assessing this negative response arrives when it is placed alongside the behaviour of others, who were no better placed but did take some positive action all the same. Whether, in the interests of their own safety, they were sensible to have done so is another matter. Many who took risks of this sort were caught and often ended their lives in German prisons or camps. Nevertheless, the example of the righteous few remains. They were those who saw friends in need, or considered it their Christian or moral duty to help. They may have had time to consider their response to a request for assistance, but there were also people who were faced with an immediate and instant choice, whether to help or not, when a stranger came knocking at their door.

9

Persecutors, pursuers and accomplices

The German machinery for tracking down Jews who attempted to escape from the deportation process by going underground was basically similar across occupied Western Europe. Essentially it involved the German police acting under orders from the local SS commanders who in turn were responsible to their bosses, Himmler, Heydrich, Kaltenbrunner and the RSHA in Berlin. On their own, these relatively small bodies of men would have been ineffective and they relied on the co-operation of indigenous National Socialists, fascists and antisemites to provide them with information and local knowledge. Moreover, they also benefited from the networks of paid informers and gratuitous intelligence supplied to them by the civil population.[1]

Underlying this apparent similarity, there are many differences between the Netherlands and her neighbours. The most obvious one is the geography and topography of the country which undoubtedly made it difficult to find hiding places and rendered almost every community reasonably accessible. The influence of the SS in the German civil government of the Netherlands when compared with its more marginal role in the military administrations of Belgium and France has also been cited as critical for the survival of Jews in hiding. Certainly it could be argued that French Jews benefited from the existence of the Vichy regime up to November 1942 and were afforded some degree of protection from German demands. Beyond these general points, there appear to be four elements peculiar to the Netherlands which directly affected the survival of those in hiding. These are the specific position and relative importance of the personnel dealing with the persecution of the Jews within the German administration, the role of the Dutch bureaucracy in assisting German aims, primarily through the system of population registration, the deployment of the Dutch police against the Jews, and finally the use of 'specialist' Jew-hunters to track down those in hiding.

The German administration

The fact that the Netherlands was given a German civilian government rather than a military administration, as was the case in Belgium and occupied France, is often cited as one of the main contributory elements to the ease with which Nazi-sponsored policies against the Jews were carried out. Certainly, the absence of any real *Wehrmacht* control over the running of the country, aside from purely military affairs, may have allowed the civilians more freedom. But more important was the freedom this gave to the agencies operated by Himmler's SS. As has been shown in Chapter 4, the administrative and executive contradictions so apparent inside Nazi Germany were also present in German rule in the Netherlands. The existence of overlapping and contradictory competences, and of unresolved conflicts between party and state organisations, as well as between individuals, featured in almost every aspect of organisational life. The overall control which Seyss-Inquart was supposed to have did not exist in practice. Himmler, Goebbels, Ribbentrop and Hess, among others, all had their placements inside the German administration of the Netherlands and used them as a means of extending their jurisdiction and to pursue their personal and ideological aims.[2] What emerged from this was 'a struggle of all against all', a mirror image of what continued to happen in the *Altreich*.[3]

Yet even if it was difficult for contemporaries or later historians to work out the precise chains of command and organisational structures created by the German authorities, it is another matter to argue that this actively hindered the process by which the Jews were ghettoised and then deported. At the top level, the increasing dominance of Rauter and the SS was achieved in part through the accommodating attitude of Seyss-Inquart. Seeing himself more as an arbiter between warring subordinates, he was ultimately unable to match the powers of the SS and party in Berlin whose backing *Generalkommissare* Rauter and Schmidt were able to marshal to their respective causes. Moreover, his power was further undermined as a result of decisions taken by Hitler. On 12 August 1942 Bormann had issued a directive granting Himmler the sole right to negotiate with 'Germanic-*völkisch* groups'. Six months later this was extended by Hitler to include the jurisdiction over civilian administration of the occupied territories as well.[4] Realising that he was becoming answerable to Himmler as well as directly to Hitler for the running of affairs inside the Netherlands, Seyss-Inquart adopted an increasingly conciliatory stance and relied on his rank as *SS-Gruppenführer* and good relationship with the *Reichsführer-SS* to maintain his own position. In these circumstances, there were few meaningful competing jurisdictions which could seriously hamper the work of the SS or *Referat IVB4* in the Netherlands. Moreover, at lower levels, compromises were also being made. Presser notes that the office of Böhmcker and the *Zentralstelle* under Willi Lages and Ferdinand Hugo Aus der

Fünten came to a practical division of labour whereby the former dealt with administrative tasks such as provisioning and finance, while the latter concerned itself with police matters. Although this did not preclude some disagreements between the authorities which the Jewish Council and its personnel at the *Expositur* tried hard to exploit,[5] the collective German response to challenges was usually a new set of decrees to remove loopholes or anomalies in the regulations governing the Jews. Seldom, if ever, did the tactics of the *Expositur* succeed in doing anything more than delay German intentions.

The German leadership in the Netherlands was naturally not solely concerned with the 'Jewish question'. Although central to an understanding of how policies were formulated and carried out, Seyss-Inquart, Schmidt, Wimmer, Rauter and Böhmcker all had a multiplicity of other concerns to deal with. Even Rauter's subordinate, Harster, as commander of the SD, had innumerable other responsibilities. As a result, the day-to-day organisation and execution of policies towards the Jews was delegated to subordinates. This raises a further question. Was there anything unusual in the behaviour or character of the German functionaries employed to carry out these tasks in the Netherlands? Were they more assiduous or efficient than their counterparts elsewhere? Such comparisons are difficult to sustain, but commentaries on the character of these bureaucrats do suggest that they were ideally suited to the tasks allotted to them: for example, Willi Lages, the trained policeman and SD chief for Amsterdam who took over the running of the *Zentralstelle;* his assistant, Ferdinand Hugo Aus der Fünten, the former Cologne shop-assistant who gave the impression of being an unwilling participant in the organisation, but who was renowned for his cynical attitude to the whole process; and Willi Zöpf, who may have been less than efficient, but owed his preferment to his friendship with Harster and his continued status to his role as a functionary of the RSHA, and to the efficiency of his subordinates. Perhaps his closest associate deserves some further mention in this respect. *Fräulein* Slottke was employed as a police-clerk by *Referat IVB4*, but she clearly had a role within the system which was out of proportion to her lowly rank. She attended many of the meetings which decided on the direction of policy against the Jews. The only woman who had managed to carve out an executive role within the system, a description of her quoted by Presser from an inmate of Westerbork paints a chilling picture:

> She was of small stature, a brunette, with a long pointed nose and many of the camp inmates thought she was a Jewess. She insisted on seeing everyone whose case she had to review; on the whole, she was to the point and friendly, although more often than not she would give a negative decision. Sometimes she could be brought round by pleading, but I do not think that she herself said anything that was true ... While she pretended to be friendly, she was in fact a human automaton, working from early morning to late at night.[6]

The cold, bureaucratically efficient image created by this portrait may have been no more than an illusion. There is little or no evidence to suggest that the SS/SD personnel in the Netherlands were any more efficient or potentially ruthless than their counterparts elsewhere in Western Europe. The one possible explanation for German 'success' in the Netherlands relates not to their level of efficiency, but to their sheer numbers. Many scholars have pointed out that the German police presence in the Netherlands, at around 5,000, was much greater than in France where the total never exceeded 3,000.[7] However, there is one further but unquantifiable factor which should at least be mentioned. Seyss-Inquart and three of his four *Generalkommissare* (Rauter, Fischböck and Wimmer) originated from Austria and it has been argued that this so-called 'Austrian connection' served not only to facilitate the persecution of the Jews inside the Netherlands, but also to maintain smooth relations with other prominent members of the RSHA Berlin such as Kaltenbrunner and Eichmann. It should be pointed out that this relationship was not unique to the Netherlands and Austrians also figured prominently in the machinery elsewhere, most notably *SS-Hauptsturmführer* Aloïs Brunner in France.[8]

The dominant role of the SS in the Netherlands has often been cited as a fundamental difference when comparisons are made with German rule in other occupied Western European countries. Certainly, Seyss-Inquart's accommodating attitude made an important contribution to that dominance, but the question remains as to whether the SS were comparatively more efficient in their activities as a result of their personnel, or whether this was due to the advantageous circumstances they encountered. The prominence of the SS, its functionaries, departments and specifically *Referat IVB4* in the Netherlands, does seem in stark contrast to the situation in Belgium and France. In Belgium the 'caution' of the military served to delay rather than halt the wishes of the SS. The anti-Jewish measures were in the hands of the Jewish section of the Brussels Sipo and SD headquarters. The German police were nominally under the control of the military administration but ultimately answerable to the RSHA in Berlin. The Jewish section occupied only 'a lowly place in the command hierarchy' and 'possessed only limited personnel', numbering no more than 20 men.[9] Its first two leaders, an *Untersturmführer* and captain, were both tried and sentenced by a Police and SS Court for appropriating Jewish property. In spite of this inauspicious leadership, with limited help from the military police (*Feldgendarmerie*) and currency police (*Devisenschutzkommando*), together with more plentiful support from the Flemish SS and Guard units, these men engineered the deportation of over 25,000 Jewish men, women and children. Moreover, after the main deportations had ended in October 1942, they also managed to capture around 8,000 Jews in hiding. This 'success' was achieved in spite of the military leadership which, with one exception in each case, refused to allow the use of Belgian police for deportations, and also forbade their use in mass raids to capture those in hiding.[10]

Like the representatives of the RSHA in Belgium, their counterparts in occupied France were also nominally subordinate to the military command in France (*Militärbefehlshaber in Frankreich*). However, the organisational pattern was more like the Netherlands with a number of agencies competing for a share of the 'Jewish question' in France and being led by high-ranking officials, notably *Judenreferent SS-Hauptsturmführer* Theodor Dannecker as head of *Referat IVB4* and Dr Werner Best as chief of the *Verwaltungsstab*.[11] However, it is clear that those charged with taking measures against the Jews had to work within the wider framework of sustaining the policy of collaboration with the Vichy regime. As Adler so clearly outlines it:

> Accordingly the German authorities sought at all times to have Vichy carry out the anti-Jewish measures ... The *Judenreferenten*, though determined to maintain from 1942 onward the momentum of deportations, never obtained ... the level of priority they sought.[12]

In the summer of 1943 the increasing desperation of the RSHA and its *Judenrefenten* in their pursuit of the Jews in France led them to abandon any co-operation with the French and bring in their own specialists to head teams of German police and French collaborators. This represented a change in political priorities and created a new and potent threat for the Jews still living in France, but success was limited, both by the absence of French bureaucratic help in identifying and locating targets, and by the the fact that the potential victims had had time to arrange methods of evasion and escape. Some Jews found alternative addresses, but many others stayed in their legally declared residences until a few weeks before the liberation.[13]

The high profile of those charged with policy against the Jews in the Netherlands and their relationship to the sources of power and influence, together with their own internal power-struggles for competence, undoubtedly assisted and may well have accelerated the process of isolation and deportation. This access to influence through having a direct channel to Seyss-Inquart or the ability to call on directives from Berlin was a major advantage in finding resources for the campaign against the Jews or circumventing potential political problems. Even if the SS bureaucrats were no more efficient than their counterparts in Belgium or France, their circumstances were such that even the incompetent could be successful – or at least rely on the efforts of efficient subordinates like *Fräulein* Slottke, whose influence in the system belied her lowly rank.

The Dutch bureaucracy

Hirschfeld's detailed examination of Dutch state institutions and their collaboration with the Germans during the occupation highlights a number of factors which have some bearing on the persecution of the Jews. Perhaps the most notable is the behaviour of the civil service generally. Overall, it appears that all sections of the Dutch bureaucracy adopted an accommodating attitude to the Germans. This was not a result of massive changes in the personnel. Although the Germans did appoint an increasing number of NSB members and other Germanophiles to senior posts like secretaries-general and mayors, neither their numbers nor their ideological influence on the administration were extensive.[14] Far more telling were the traditional attitudes of the Dutch civil service, who were wedded to the principles of administrative and public order above all other considerations. These values transcended any assessment of whose interests a continued adherence to this philosophy served. The Dutch government-in-exile noted the inability of the civil service to adapt to the changed circumstances.

> They [the civil servants] had spent their whole lives accustomed to obey, they were always – and rightly – so proud of the impeccable execution of their tasks and conscientious fulfilment of their duties, that they brought the same conscientiousness and the same fulfilment of duty to the scrupulous organisation of the plunder of our country, to the advantage of the enemy.[15]

Certainly, there is no evidence that the Germans found much fault with the attitudes of the Dutch bureaucrats – at least not until the later stages of the occupation. It appears that the accommodating attitude of the secretaries-general and leading civil servants set the tone for all their subordinates. If one accepts the view that resignation was not a viable response for civil servants unhappy about certain German ordinances, the position taken by their superiors removed any possible sympathy from a higher authority.

Comparisons of the civil services under occupation in the Netherlands, Belgium and France are too beset with national particularities to allow more than general conclusions. Unlike the Netherlands, the Belgian administration could still call on the crown and issues of competence and sovereignty to counteract German demands, and this, coupled (perhaps) with a more accommodating attitude by the German military administration, set limits to the degree of their co-operation. In France, the continued existence of the Vichy regime and the unoccupied zone gave the French some considerable leverage against German demands, a leverage which continued to have some effect even after the Germans took over control of the whole country.

While the majority of Dutch civil servants could have little or no real effect on the ability of the German occupiers to achieve their administrative or ideological aims, one specific aspect of the Dutch bureaucracy looms large in the history of the Holocaust in the Netherlands and requires further detailed analysis. This was the system of population registration which formed an integral part of the Dutch state machinery. Innocent

enough in peacetime, this system became an 'unfavourable factor' peculiar
to the Netherlands in its comprehensiveness. Neither Belgium nor France
had such a complete registration. Moreover, the Dutch system was long-
established with its own specialist bureaucracy. Where the Germans
attempted to have lists made up, for example the Tulard list for the Jews of
Paris,[16] anyone suspecting the motives for the registration could try and
evade enumeration. The Jews in the Netherlands, habitually registered
alongside the rest of the Dutch population, would have had no such
qualms in the 1930s. Only in the case of 'foreign' Jews was there some
degree of parity with Belgium and France. Police registers of resident foreigners were used by the Germans in all three countries. While far from
complete or accurate, they often provided a good deal of detailed information. Thus in Belgium, where over 90 per cent of the Jews did not hold
Belgian nationality, and in France, where their numbers were also substantial, these particular police records had a greater impact than in the
Netherlands where the number of foreign Jews was proportionally smaller.

There is no question that the population registers in the Netherlands
assisted the German occupiers in a number of important respects. For
example, their use as the basis for the introduction of increasingly sophisticated personal identity cards provided a major headache for all those
underground and/or working illegally. However, it is the role they played
in the persecution of the Jews which concerns us here. As has already been
shown, the registers were used to compile and to check lists for arrests and
deportation. In addition, their existence often convinced Jews that there
was little point in trying to evade later censuses on the grounds that the
authorities already had the information to hand. Moreover, this particular
issue also demonstrates how a specific individual in the right (or wrong)
place could become an 'unfavourable factor' almost in his own right. The
man in question was Jacob Lentz, who had risen from humble beginnings
to become the head of the *Rijksinspectie van de Bevolkingsregisters* (State
Inspectorate of Population Registers). In 1936 he had instituted rules to
standardise the population registers and their compilation throughout the
country. For this he was decorated by the crown. However, his ambition
was to create a complete registration system which would include identity
cards. The idea of such a card was discussed by the government in 1939,
but mainly in relation to the possibility of war and the need for an effective
rationing system. The resulting *distributiestamkaart* (ration card) did not
begin to fulfil Lentz's wishes. It did not carry a photograph, and a government commission report in March 1940 noted that the introduction of a
compulsory identity card, with the implication that every citizen was a
potential criminal, was contrary to Dutch tradition.[17] The arrival of the
Germans gave renewed impetus to Lentz's ambitions. In the aftermath of
the surrender, the College of Secretaries-General had accepted that some
form of identity card was advisable in order to control any social unrest. In

the interim, this involved the use of passports and appending photographs to existing *stamkaarten*. In the meantime Lentz set about creating the ideal identity card. Using watermarked paper and special inks, the document included personal details about the owner as well as his or her photograph and fingerprint. He was so successful that his new cards were deemed by the Germans as better and more secure than their own *Kennkarte*.[18]

The introduction of these cards took time and was not completed until the end of 1941.[19] Once in place, it allowed the Germans to carry out regular checks on cards in public places, thus greatly increasing the risks for people without valid papers when venturing on to public transport, or even on to the street. All the details on the identity cards were kept in a huge card index, thus making it possible to check if a card had been falsified in some way, or was being used by a third party. The use made of this register by the SD is testimony to its importance. Lentz later defended himself by saying that the same information could have been found in the normal population registers, but the depth of information, the photographs, fingerprints and signatures, as well as the ease of access, all militate against this defence. A compliment to the thoroughness of Lentz's work came from a leader of the LO who claimed that it had never been possible to create a false identity card which would have escaped detection by anything but the most cursory of checks. The fact that people could survive and travel with false papers was because most checks were superficial, or carried out rapidly by officials with no desire to ask too many questions.[20] Mainly because the resistance had no other choice, attempts continued to beat the system and produce accurate forgeries. Things became even more pressing when Jews began to be rounded up, and the 'J' stamped in their genuine identity cards would betray them immediately. One of leading members of the resistance, Gerrit-Jan van der Veen, spent two years trying to perfect a way of reproducing Lentz's card, yet had to send out imperfect versions as the need became greater.[21] His *persoonsbewijzencentrale* (centre for identity cards) produced between 60,000 and 70,000 blank cards before the printers were arrested in June 1944.

The extent of the population registration and the apparent inviolability of the identity card system were undoubtedly a factor unique to the Netherlands in relation to other German occupied territories, and provided a major hindrance for any type of illegal work. Lentz, however, also took a particular interest in the German desire to identify the Jews in the Netherlands. The Germans had decided in September 1940 that there should be a separate registration of the Jews. Their intention had been to use the existing population registers, even though Lentz had informed them that they were far from complete. He set to work compiling detailed instruction for the local authorities to carry out the registration of Jews decreed on 10 January 1941. The information gained from this registration was then transferred to the existing population registers and the cards were

marked with a special stamp. He also made a special study of Jewish sur-
names which was ultimately used to investigate people with such names
who might not have registered as Jews. Lentz did, however, make the mistake of presenting a copy of his study to *Generalkommissar* Wimmer, who
was less than impressed to find his own family name mentioned in the
list.[22] Lentz was also involved in the German scheme to introduce a new
system of ration cards which would only be issued to holders of valid identity cards and in person. Begun in the middle of 1943 and designed primarily to force *onderduikers* out into the open, the link between identity cards
and ration cards was abandoned as the resistance was increasingly successful in acquiring genuine blank identity cards and the necessary stamps to
validate them.[23] Thus by 1944 the Germans were losing the battle to control the population through Lentz's cards and indexes, but they remained a
hindrance to all illegal work until the end of the occupation.

In many respects, Lentz was the ideal servant for the Germans.
Uncommitted to National Socialism although undoubtedly pro-German[24]
(perhaps because of their supposed efficiency in all things), he immersed
himself in his work to the exclusion of everything else, including his marriage. His aim and motivation was bureaucratic perfection, apparently
without concern for the practical effects of his work. One of his officials
intimated that he had no love for the Jews, perceiving them as attempting
to undermine the smooth running of his registration system, but whether
this was the product of an ingrained antisemitism or just the perfectionist
railing at those who would upset his quest for perfection remains uncertain. If this is the only evidence for an antisemitic stance, the fact that he
did not join the NSB or any other known antisemitic group, either before
or during the occupation, suggests that he was that strange animal, the
bureaucrat who was always anxious to please his masters and for whom
perfect organisation was everything. However, Lentz cannot be seen
merely as a cypher, happy to please by carrying out the orders of others.
The arrival of the Germans gave him the chance to carry out his dream of
complete population registration without being hampered by the restraints
of democratic government. In his mind, the uses which the Germans might
make of his work were only of secondary importance. Even in 1943, he
could not understand it when someone suggested whether it might not be
better if all the population registers were destroyed. Certainly others
thought this was true. In March 1943 the resistance attempted to burn
down the population register in Amsterdam, and on 11 April they arranged
an RAF raid to bomb the headquarters of Lentz's *Rijksinspectie* at
Kleykamp, in The Hague. Neither raid was completely successful, but the
damage done was substantial.[25] Lentz became worried when he was
attacked as a scoundrel (*schurk*) in the underground press, and even more
nervous when he received death-threats through the post. The Germans
gave him a bodyguard but refused to let him resign. He was absent from

his office the day it was bombed and returned to work afterwards, but this may have been the final straw. A few weeks later, he gave up altogether, a mental wreck.[26] After the war, he was sentenced to a mere three years in gaol, yet his struggle for perfection and his unswerving dedication to this work undoubtedly contributed to the arrests and therefore the deaths of many thousands of Jews and non-Jews at the hands of the Germans. If nothing else, here was a case where the traditional Dutch civil service ethos of obedience and order had shown itself capable of implication in the most heinous crimes when all moral and legal controls were removed.

The Dutch police

The role of the Dutch police in the persecution of the Jews has come under increasing scrutiny in recent years. On arriving in the Netherlands, the Germans found the Dutch police arranged into five separate organisations and supervised by three different government ministries. This 'very jumbled spectacle', as Rauter described it, could not be allowed to continue, and he took steps to co-ordinate the *Marechaussee* (state), *Rijksveldwacht* and *Rijksrecherche* (criminal/investigative) organisations under the control of the Ministry of Justice. In March 1941 this ministry came under the control of Secretary-General Jacobus Schrieke, a loyal member of the NSB. Rauter then created a 'plenipotentiary for the reorganisation of the Dutch police', Leo Broersen, who oversaw the increasing subordination of the *Gemeentepolitie* (municipal police, traditionally controlled by the mayors and the Ministry of the Interior) to the Ministry of Justice. In effect, the Dutch police were co-ordinated and streamlined in accordance with German wishes,[27] and their structures were made to mirror those of their German counterparts. It also became apparent that the Germans wanted to have a section of the Dutch police ideologically as well as organisationally restructured. To that end, they established a re-education programme in all police stations, and when this failed, set up a specific police training establishment at Schalkhaar near Deventer.[28] In this way, the Germans were able to call on ideologically trained police units to carry out measures against the Jews rather than rely on the 'ordinary' Dutch policemen. More than half of the 'Schalkhaarders', as they were known, were deployed in Amsterdam.[29] In addition, in May 1942 Rauter also created a Voluntary Auxiliary Police, made up exclusively from Dutch SS and NSB *Weerafdeling* members. The men, who numbered around 2,000, were trained by the Germans and then deployed in their home towns under the command of the local police chiefs. Almost solely concerned with the pursuit of Jews, they rapidly gained a reputation for brutality and illegality.[30] Wound up two years later, this organisation nevertheless provided many of the most virulent and committed Jew-hunters. Spread round the country, with no moral qualms about what they were doing and possessing vital specialist knowledge about their own localities and neighbours, these units were of invaluable service to German aims.

The German desire to use the Dutch police to carry out measures against the Jews seems clear, and the way was opened with a complete overhaul of police organisation and leadership in the first 18 months of German rule. The general picture seems to have been of the police accepting German orders when it came to the Jews and very little in the way of opposition or resistance. While Presser does not attempt to counter this general picture, he does nevertheless show some sympathy for the 'ordinary' policeman. Working for an increasingly Nazified or indifferent police leadership, there were few logical choices if one was ordered to participate in actions against the Jews. Refusal to obey orders or going into hiding would have severe material and personal consequences for the individuals concerned – and for their families and dependants. There were examples of 'police resistance': in the autumn of 1941 when some officers refused to participate in capturing Jews, and again in February 1943 when six Roman Catholic officers refused to obey orders as it would contravene the instructions given in a pastoral letter the previous Sunday. These latter men were threatened with dismissal and loss of pension with the rider that any further disobedience would be regarded as sabotage and dealt with accordingly.[31] The six were subsequently pursued by the Germans and although they escaped, their wives and families were arrested.[32] The following month, local policemen in Groningen refused a Sipo order to arrest a Jewish family and 11 of them were ultimately arrested and sent to Vught.[33] These high-profile cases undoubtedly mask a much larger number of acts designed to frustrate German intentions. Policemen could and did warn potential victims of forthcoming raids or turn a blind eye to forged or invalid documents.

In summing up the role of the Dutch police in the arrest and transfer of Jews to concentration and transit camps, Hirschfeld notes that there are no simple answers. The police actions against the Jews were not all carried out by the German police or the 'Schalkhaarders', although some post-war commentaries have found it useful to lay all the blame at the door of the latter to exculpate the rest of the Dutch police. While these units may have been primarily responsible for the round-ups, the *Gemeentepolitie* were also drawn into the work. In small communities, it was often only the local police who were responsible for conveying Jews to the collection points. In this context both the local mayors and the police were complicit in the round-ups. Certainly Rauter was not prepared to countenance any disobedience from the Dutch police and was prepared to act firmly against any recalcitrants. In some places, special 'Jewish Departments' were set up within Dutch police forces, staffed by detectives whose sole purpose was to track down Jews in hiding. Others were assigned to Sipo branches in the large cities, and even to *Referat IVB4* in The Hague.[34]

The Dutch police in the provinces were far from innocent when it came to the apprehension and incarceration of the Jews. For the most part, the majority appear to have acted normally and obeyed their superiors without openly questioning the nature of their orders. In Utrecht, when the 'Schalkhaarders' and Auxiliary Police proved insufficient, detectives and traffic police were offered overtime to escort Jews to Westerbork. Some 50 policemen were known to have volunteered, and not all of them were members of the NSB. One defended his actions, clearly demonstrating the mundane motivations which sometimes led to collaboration:

> It was very worthwhile to take on those extra duties, not only because of the money, but also because on return to the station at Utrecht you were given a bag with well-filled sandwiches. All of that at a time when anything extra was very useful and when food had become scarce.[35]

While there were also examples of help given by officers to Jews in hiding, there is no means of gauging how widespread this undermining of German objectives was.

The crucial impact of Dutch police co-operation was felt in Amsterdam, where the bulk of the Jewish population was to be found. As with other municipalities, the Amsterdam police were under the control of the mayor, but in practical terms, the Chief of Police had a large measure of independence. Both were formally appointed by the crown, and the mayor, de Vlught, had held office since 1921. The crucial changes occurred in the aftermath of the February 1941 strike, when the Germans used the disorders as an excuse to remove the incumbents of both posts and replace them with more 'reliable' men. In this way, de Vlught was replaced by the Germanophile E.J. Voûte and Chief of Police Versteeg by the former colonial soldier, NSB and Dutch SS member, Sybren Tulp.[36]

Even before this change, it has been argued that the municipal leadership had been drawn into carrying out German wishes. The attitude of the secretaries-general had set the tone by apparently agreeing to set aside Dutch law in the interests of executing German wishes. As a result, the municipalities had no recourse to higher authority and were forced to concede much of their traditional autonomy. In both cases this was done in the wider interest of protecting the competence of the existing Dutch authorities over local government. Moreover, this conciliatory attitude extended as far as collaboration with the German-inspired registration of Jews in January 1941. Soon afterwards, the police were implicated in measures against the Jews. The *Gemeentepolitie* were deployed alongside the German *Ordnungspolizei* in the creation of the Jewish quarter on 12 February 1941, even though it was pointed out that this was only a measure to exclude vehicular traffic. More sinister was the use of the police after Tulp had taken over from Versteeg.

It has been argued that the majority of Amsterdam police superinten-
dents (from educated, middle-class backgrounds) and their subordinate,
working-class patrolmen were opposed to the measures against the Jews.
It appears that Tulp was anxious that the Amsterdam police should be
seen to be helping the Germans in all respects, not because he was particularly antisemitic, as there is no evidence for this in spite of his National
Socialist leanings, but as part of his strategy for helping Rauter in his
struggle for supremacy within the German administration. On 11 June
1941 Tulp used detectives to round up the 300 German Jews who were
subsequently handed over to the Sipo and deported to Mauthausen, yet
even this was done on the pretext of checking on the work of the Aliens'
Registration Office. Two weeks later, uniformed police were deployed to
enforce the closure of shops on Sundays. However, while Tulp was anxious to carry out every German order to the letter, his men were not
nearly so keen. Regulations forbidding Jews from using parks and swimming pools went unenforced and local policemen could not be compelled
to notice transgressions. Moreover, in September 1941, when Tulp did
not wait for official clearance of new restrictions but tried to have them
enforced immediately on his own authority, some of his subordinates
challenged him to produce the ordinance and he was forced to back
down. Even in early 1942, when he had tried to make his men personally
responsible for the enforcement of new laws against the Jews, many were
not rigorously applied and it was only the introduction of the compulsory
wearing of stars and Sipo supervision which made this form of disobedience
impossible.

By the beginning of September 1942, it had become clear that Jews
were not going to report for deportation when sent notifications in the
post, and the *Gemeentepolitie* were drafted in to help in the task of catching those selected. Again, there was some resistance to the work and one
inspector who refused to take part.[37] Others may well have used their position to warn those at risk or to make only perfunctory searches. The extent
of this type of disobedience is impossible to quantify, although contemporary and post-war accounts testify to its existence. In spite of objections
from his men, Tulp continued the actions and, on the night of 2 October
1942, personally led an action involving more than 200 detectives and
inspectors, and a battalion of 'Schalkhaarders', which arrested several hundred Jews in a single night. An action planned for the following day was
cancelled when Tulp was taken ill and he died less than three weeks later.
While this did not excuse the Amsterdam police from carrying out measures against the Jews, their new chief did not see the need to force the
issue in the face of continuing opposition from the ranks. In any case, by
this time, the Germans had already acquired new instruments in the form
of the 'Schalkhaarders' and the Voluntary Auxiliary Police to perform the
necessary tasks.

It would be wrong to suggest that there was a clear dividing line within the police – between the leadership anxious to please the Germans in all things and the rank and file disgusted with many German orders including those directed against the Jews. Even in the early months of Tulp's tenure, there were policemen prepared to enforce laws and ordinances to the letter and to arrest Jews whenever the opportunity arose. However, it is the figure of Tulp himself which is most important in understanding the role of the Amsterdam police. His compliant attitude and his determination to fight administrative and political battles alongside Rauter for competence and control meant that legal and moral issues were swept aside. His attitude also meant that there was no amelioration of German orders when it came to their execution, and no sympathetic superior ear for those policemen who saw the iniquity of what they were being asked to do.

As a result, the weight of evidence speaks against the Dutch police in general and the Amsterdam police in particular. One Amsterdam detective reported after the war that 90 per cent of the Amsterdam police had co-operated 'in the Jewish detentions' and that 'the cells were full of Jews day after day'.[38] He gives the impression that far from abhorring their task, the police were keen to be involved, even at the expense of normal criminal investigations. It may have been that this observation came from a later year when the Auxiliary Police were active, but far more telling is the post-war testimony of Willi Lages who commented that:

> The main support of the German forces in the police sector and beyond was the Dutch police. Without it, not 10 per cent of the German occupation tasks would have been fulfilled ... Also it would have been practically impossible to seize even 10 per cent of Dutch Jewry without them.[39]

While neither source can be regarded as entirely reliable, the impression given is that a substantial number of policemen did co-operate, even if they were not entirely happy about what they were being asked to do. Hirschfeld points to a change in police behaviour brought about by the German attempts to reintern the Dutch army and the subsequent April–May 1943 strike wave. Many policemen began to see how they were being isolated from the rest of Dutch society for carrying out increasingly unpopular German measures, and especially those which had a direct impact on people's day-to-day lives. Perhaps the realisation that the war was turning against the Germans coupled with an increasingly vindictive attitude towards the Dutch civil population in general rather than just minority groups like the Jews may have effected this apparent change of attitude. Certainly the German hierarchy commented on it and concluded that the Dutch police were at best unreliable.[40] Like the rest of the population, the police could start to think of a future world free from Nazi domination. While Rauter continued to use a 'stick and carrot' approach to keep the Dutch police in line and loyal to the occupying power, the zeal, dedication to duty and respect for authority which had been a hallmark of its personnel in earlier days had all but disappeared by 1944.[41] Increasing numbers of policemen went underground or worked with the resistance but, as with so many of the other organisations set up to oppose aspects of German rule, this sea-change came too late to save the Jews.

Comparisons with Belgium and France do highlight the very different part played by the police and its various organisations in the Netherlands from other Western European states. In the case of Belgium, the Germans had much less success in amalgamating and centralising the police. Measures against the Jews were carried out mainly by the Jewish section of the German police in Brussels. This unit numbered no more than 20 and relied on help from the Flemish SS and Rexists. Only once were Belgian police used in a raid – in Antwerp on 28 August 1942[42] – but the experiment was not repeated. Moreover, the Germans were never able to tamper with the command structures of the Belgian police or impose their placemen into critical positions, as the Belgian administration, and particularly Gérard Romsée as Secretary-General at the Ministry of the Interior, carried out a reform from within.[43] Some co-operation was forthcoming from Belgian government departments, but this stopped when the deportations began. The Jewish section was persistently short of manpower and also had to face limitations on its actions by the military command. After November 1942, it had to rely on checks and controls, denunciations and sundry other methods to catch the remaining Jews in the country. The military authorities under General Alexander von Falkenhausen forbade the use of mass raids for fear that they would provoke civil disturbance and disobedience. Only once was this restriction lifted, when Berlin ordered the capture, detention and deportation of the remaining Belgian Jews. With some misgivings, von Falkenhausen gave permission for *Aktion Iltis*, a mass raid on 3–4 September 1943 against Jews in hiding in Antwerp and Brussels. This backfired when some well-known captives were suffocated while being transported in a sealed van. The Belgian authorities threatened to withdraw all co-operation and the German military authorities then banned any further such actions.[44] The policy of trying to maintain a working relationship with the Belgian authorities and minimising the potential for civil disorder was seen as more important than the capture of Jews. In effect, these priorities did have some effect in limiting the operations of the Jew-hunters in Belgium. In spite of these restrictions, the Germans in Belgium did have their successes. Like their counterparts in the Netherlands, they were able to use street patrols, non-Jewish and Jewish informers, denunciations and 'financial incentives' to have Jews in hiding betrayed. In the 23 months from November 1942, they caught and deported around 8,000 Jews.[45]

In France, the situation was different again. While the Germans had more control in the occupied zone, they had to take account of the wider political implications in their dealings with Vichy. German success and French willingness to hand over foreign Jews for deportation owed more to a long-term French racial and national antipathy to the foreign Jewish community than to a desire to fulfil German wishes. For this reason, René Bousquet was able to instruct the French police to round up foreign Jews after May 1942. Only on 25 June 1942, when the German authorities in the person of *Judenreferent* Theodor Dannecker ordered that 40 per cent of the Jews to be deported from the occupied zone should be French, did the Vichy authorities begin to dig in their heels.[46] This was a direct attack on French sovereignty and control over the population, and also produced the spectre of French policemen arresting French (Jewish) citizens at the behest of the occupying power.[47] In this case, a clear agenda on the part of the Vichy authorities and an ability to have a negotiating position allowed them to give a clear lead to the police. The Germans were well aware that they did not have the manpower to undertake actions against the Jews on the scale required to meet the imperatives of the deportation programme decreed for France, and thus found a compromise with the French government, that joint Franco-German police actions against foreign Jews should take place across France but that French Jews should be left alone. Indeed even this compromise proved that the Vichy authorities had moved beyond what the French police and public thought acceptable. The arrests of non-French Jews carried out in July and August 1942 provoked a wave of negative reactions from all sections of French society.[48]

Inevitably, the situation changed after the German occupation of Vichy, but the opposition to actions against the Jews continued. It is difficult to estimate the extent of compliance or sabotage by individual regular French police officers against German measures against the Jews. However, their superiors continued to take a principled stand on the use of the French police against French (Jewish) citizens. In February 1943, when the deportations from France resumed, Bousquet informed the Germans that no French police would be be allowed to assist with transports containing French Jews who had infringed anti-Jewish regulations.[49] Moreover, after June 1943, when the police were asked by *Referat IVB4* to assume the initiative in the arrest of Jews, there was a widespread refusal (presumably sanctioned by the Vichy authorities) and a consequent steep decline in the numbers captured.[50] Soon afterwards, the Germans finally realised that they were never likely to get the necessary co-operation from the French police for their ideological agenda and the whole matter was placed in the hands of *SS-Hauptsturmführer* Aloïs Brunner who had arrived in Paris in June 1943 under orders from Eichmann to speed up the deportation process from France. His reign of terror, which lasted more or less until the liberation, bypassed the French police and used the limited German police force and the much more numerous collaborationist *Milice*.[51]

In comparative terms, the most notable difference between the police in the Netherlands and their counterparts in Belgium and France centres around their leadership. In the Netherlands the Germans were able to subvert the system by placing men they could trust in positions to oversee the workings of the Dutch police, whereas in both Belgium and France wider political issues prevented this from happening. Security and other considerations stopped the German authorities from placing undue pressure on the police forces to carry out measures against the Jews in the interests of maintaining their co-operation. Thus even if there was no real difference in the attitude of Dutch, Belgian or French policemen towards the Jews, the former had to contend with a leadership and Dutch administration prepared to collude with the Germans while the latter could rely on a more robust defence of national sovereignty. In both Belgium and France, the authorities went a long way to protect *their* Jewish citizens, even at the expense of foreign Jews. In the Netherlands, no such distinction was made.

The 'Jew-hunters'

Beyond the official structures of the German administration and the Dutch bureaucracy, there were also the organisations set up exclusively to deal with the 'Jewish question'. In the spring and summer of 1942, special groups were formed within the police service whose sole task was to track down Jews in hiding. Made up mainly of committed National Socialists and members of the Auxiliary Police, these groups existed in many of the main cities and were attached to the *Zentralstelle* in Amsterdam or *Referat IVB4* in The Hague. Their methods were to roam the streets to check passes of people who 'looked Jewish', and also to respond to information from the public. During the occupation, amongst the welter of information sent in by the public, the police received thousands of denunciations, most of them anonymous, identifying Jews in hiding. There were instances where sympathetic police officials could destroy the letters and/or tip off those in danger, but large numbers of Jews were undoubtedly betrayed by neighbours whose pro-German, pro-Nazi or malevolent sentiments fell into indifferent hands or were passed directly to the SD. Notwithstanding the efforts of these specialist policemen, in the spring of 1943 the officials of *Referat IVB4* estimated that there were still between 10,000 and 15,000 Jews in hiding. For the German authorities, the problem was how to track them down. Raids by the *Ordnungspolizei* on farms in the countryside had been carried out since the autumn of 1942, but without overwhelming success. Often, the farmers were warned by sympathetic local Dutch policemen and the pursuers came away empty-handed.

As the last phases of the deportations from Amsterdam began, the Germans stepped up their campaign to find Jews still in hiding. More 'Jew-hunters' were drafted in to assist. In Amsterdam, men were brought in from the staff of the *Hausraterfassung* of the *Zentralstelle*. These were mainly Dutch antisemites anxious to help the German cause in any way, and also to enrich themselves at the same time if possible. They were joined by a certain number of policemen. Organised into 'columns' (*colonne*) and taking their names from their leaders, these groups proved highly successful. Working on their own initiative, they did not confine their activities to Amsterdam, but spread out into other cities and into the countryside in search of Jews in hiding. Their work, and doubtless their enthusiasm for the task was further enhanced by a decision of the RSHA to pay a bounty for each Jew apprended. This bounty began at fl.5 but was raised steadily until the summer of 1944 when it stood at fl.40 per head. The most infamous of these groups was the Henneicke-*colonne* which was led by a former car mechanic turned black-marketeer and police informer. Reliable estimates show that this group, consisting of 35 men, managed to arrest around 3,400 people in the period between April and September 1943. Given the 'rates' then in force, this would mean that each man would have received at least fl.750 in bounty money for his work.[52] The *colonne* was disbanded by Willi Lages, the head of the SD, at the end of 1943, although Henneicke and some of the more zealous members continued their work under a different banner.

The surviving records from this group give a further insight into their work. There were frequent reports on Jews arrested at the Muiderpoort station, a major control point for those travelling to and from the city. Others related to people apprended on the street, either with forged papers, or with still valid documents which were in some way deficient. The apprehension of one person would often lead to the discovery of entire families, and of others whom they might have been sheltering. In one instance, a Jewess with an exemption was held because she had not reported to the *Zentralstelle* in accordance with a German ordinance. The report on her arrest also listed others with whom she lived, and the fact that her child had been fostered out to an 'aryan' family in Leeuwarden. Even the address of the family was given.[53] Exactly how all this damning information was acquired remains unclear, but there were few if any controls on the activities of these Jew-hunters and they were known to use all manner of barbarities in order to extract information from the Jews they caught.[54] Clearly the Germans cared little what they did provided the results were good.

Another Jewess, again with a valid exemption, was also arrested because she was sheltering another woman who did not have valid papers. A large number of the arrest reports note that when houses were searched, the ('aryan') owners were not apprehended for having sheltered Jews. This seems strange given the severe penalties in force for such 'crimes'. Excuses such as the fact that the owner 'did not know the tenants were Jews' or that he/she had a large number of dependent children were often considered sufficient. These seem rather lame given the alacrity with which the *colonne* operated, but may be explained in at least two ways. First of all, the Jew-hunters might have been satisfied that owners really did not know the identity of their tenants, but even if they were suspicious, the arrest of non-Jews would involve more paperwork and, crucially perhaps, would not bring in any extra money. Secondly, it was not impossible that the owners had themselves tipped off the police, either because they wanted to be rid of their tenants, or in exchange for a share of the bounty.[55] Certainly there are documented cases of people who succeeded in trapping Jews in this way.

In each report, all the formalities were scrupulously observed. Every Jew captured had his or her name, date of birth, nationality and profession carefully recorded. Moreover, the agents had to certify that they had not taken any gold or other valuables either from those captured or from their dwellings – a sensible precaution for the German authorities to take given the propensity of these men to steal from their victims. It meant that if they were subsequently discovered to have removed items of value, they could be summarily punished. There was at least one case where some 30 Dutch policemen had been dismissed for stealing Jewish property.[56] Invariably the reports also contained a final, chilling phrase, namely that those caught had been 'delivered up to the *Schouwburg*'.

The Jew-hunters managed to catch many people who had evaded all the other agencies. A report of August 1943 notes the apprension of a well-off Jew who had already contrived to escape from the *Schouwburg* and from Westerbork.[57] However, their activities were not confined to Amsterdam and as it became more difficult to find Jews in the city, so they began to cast their net more widely into the countryside and into other provinces. Help in locating those underground could come from informers (*Vertrauensmänner*), auxiliary policemen or the local police force. They operated as far afield as the north-eastern provinces of Drenthe, Groningen and Friesland. During raids, they often discovered people in hiding, but more often than not these were 'aryans' hiding from labour service and the men of the Henneicke-*colonne* had no interest in apprehending them.[58]

Even if some raids failed, it is undoubtedly the case that these groups of specialist Jew-hunters were very successful. The reports and diaries of these men show that arrests were being made almost every night, sometimes in concert with the *Ordnungspolizei*, sometimes alone. Moreover, their 'catches' could involve whole families or groups of *onderduikers*. One diary recorded the arrest of 24 Jews on a single night in the Weesperstraat and personal responsibility for the arrest of around 200 Jews in the space of two weeks.[59] During their relatively short period of operation through

1943, it has been estimated that they were probably responsible for the arrest (and therefore the deportation and ultimate deaths) of something like 6,000 Jews who had attempted to go underground. Of this total, two-thirds or 4,000 people were captured as a result of information received by the police.[60]

This last statistic may have to be treated with some care. Undoubtedly, most of the information came freely, either attributed or anonymously, from the public at large.[61] However, given the full nature of many reports, it would seem likely that a proportion of the Jewish *onderduikers* were caught as a result of information extracted from those apprehended by Henneicke and his colleagues. Moreover, as word spread that Jews were actually worth money, so the potential for betrayals increased. People gave information to the police in order to settle old scores with those in hiding, or with those who helped them. A few probably also made money from such transactions. Even some Jews have been identified as having helped in the betrayal of their co-religionists, albeit for very different reasons. It is clear that the Germans placed captured *onderduikers* under enormous pressure to turn traitor and to betray others they knew to be underground or to remain at large, in order to uncover help networks, their operations and Jews still in hiding. There was at least one instance of a German Jew who saw himself as German rather than Jewish and worked for the Sipo in Amsterdam. Employed in tracking down Jews after the summer of 1942, he was probably responsible for the arrest of a few dozen people, but was rewarded by the fact that neither he nor his family were deported.[62] Others who helped in this way were seldom so fortunate. Failure to deliver a continuing flow of arrests was likely to result in summary deportation. The most successful Jewish informant also presents the most complex case. Ans van Dijk had had her business shut down by the Germans and then become active in helping other Jews. She had facilitated the escape of a friend to Switzerland and by the summer of 1942 was helping to collect and distribute false identity cards. Having gone underground in early 1943, she had been betrayed and was then persuaded (under threat of being treated as a punishment case) to act as an informer. Using her reputation as an illegal worker, she set up a house ostensibly to provide papers for Jews underground. Once identified, these hapless victims could then be arrested on the street to prevent the trap being exposed. Van Dijk was also used as a spy, in similar manner to Friedrich Weinreb, by being placed in cells with captured *onderduikers* to obtain information on where they had hidden, who had helped them, and the whereabouts of others still underground. She alone was estimated to have brought about the arrest of at least a hundred Jews.[63]

There were other examples of Jews acting as traitors. Two men among a group of 40 hiding in the grounds of a castle were found to have been corresponding with the Germans. They were executed by two members of a *knokploeg* (action group) brought in for the task. Jews in hiding were also known to have threatened 'if we go, then you go as well' to their hosts. Given the circumstances, perhaps the most surprising thing is how few Jewish traitors there were. The German hold over these people was more or less complete. Clearly, national feeling, money and primarily fear all played a role in explaining the behaviour of those who did inform. Moreover, it is ironic that only a few of these traitors actually survived. Some were ultimately deported by the Germans in spite of their efforts. Ans van Dijk survived the occupation but was put on trial by the post-war Dutch authorities and condemned to death. Her treatment is compared unfavourably by de Jong with the fate of other Jew-hunters. As he points out, only four others lost their lives as a result of their activities. Henneicke was assassinated by a resistance group at the end of 1944, and another three men (including van Dijk's 'handler') were executed after the war. Nearly all the other people involved, including committed National Socialists and antisemites who had carried out their tasks willingly, received either pardons or light sentences.[64]

Of course the *colonne* were not the only Jew-hunters. The Germans used their own (Green) police and other German and Dutch SS and NSB formations to assist with the work at different times, including the Auxiliary Police and even the Jewish *Orde Dienst*. This picture was mirrored in both France and Belgium where German formations and collaborationist nationals, often members of local National Socialist, antisemitic or fascist organisations, were used. In Belgium the small Jewish section of the German police relied heavily on the manpower and expertise of the Flemish SS and the Rexists. In France, both occupied and unoccupied, the Germans had to work through the Vichy authorities prior to November 1942. Beginning with the *Police aux Questions Juives* which operated as part of the *Commissariat Général aux Questions Juives*, the numbers of Jew-hunting organisations increased after the Germans occupied the whole country. The Permilleux service in Paris, the *Milice* and more or less unofficial groups working with German police and SD operations in the provinces all contributed to the war against the Jews in the last years of the occupation.[65] Thus, however reprehensible and brutal the activities of the Jew-hunters in the Netherlands may have been, their presence was not a unique or even an unusual factor. The same type of behaviour and collaboration can be seen in other occupied countries. This in turn begs the question of whether the activities of the Jew-hunters in the Netherlands were any more effective than their counterparts elsewhere. Clearly, they did have an impact on the numbers able to survive in hiding, but this was also true of the Flemish SS and Rexists in Belgium and the *Milice* and others in France.

In the later years of the occupation, when all the remaining Jews were in hiding and information from the population registers was effectively worthless, the local knowledge possessed by these men was often of great value to the Germans, but far more valuable was the information received from the general public. This raises the vexed question of how far the public at large contributed to the arrest and deportation of the Jews by informing. There are no reliable statistics on this as a factor. Actions were often carried out 'on the basis of information received', but there is no means of assessing the sources or their quantity. Both German and Dutch authorities were the recipients of such information. Presser notes that some of these denunciations have been preserved in Calmeyer's papers. There was one antisemite anxious that the Germans should do everything possible to remove the Jews from his neighbourhood. Another reported Jews who were secretly hiding their furnishings. Others informed against their Jewish colleagues at work and one woman was desperate to stop her daughter's relationship with a Jewish man.

Yet this behaviour was not limited to the 'Jewish question'. People informed on their neighbours for all manner of reasons and on every matter under the sun. Moreover, it was not peculiar to the Netherlands. The police files in all three countries bear witness to the existence of denunciations as the source of information.[66] Josephs notes that the Vichy and German authorities received between three and five million poison-pen letters in 1940 alone.[67] It seems unlikely that the Dutch people as a whole were any more predisposed to betray their neighbours or fellow citizens than any other nationality.

10

The survival of foreign Jews

A better chance of survival?

In identifying certain factors which may have contributed to the higher levels of mortality for Jews in the Netherlands, Blom has highlighted a further paradox as far as the Netherlands is concerned, namely that the level of mortality in other Western European countries bears some relationship to the proportion of 'foreigners' in the total Jewish population.[1] Thus in Belgium where 90 per cent of the Jews were foreign nationals, the mortality rate was around 40 per cent. In France, foreigners accounted for about 50 per cent of the Jewish population and the mortality rate was around 25 per cent, with French Jews having a much better chance of avoiding deportation and death than their foreign counterparts.[2] Only in Norway and especially the Netherlands is there some evidence to suggest that this situation was reversed, with foreign Jews possibly having a better chance of survival than the 'native' population.[3] Blom notes that his source for this suggestion, Jacob Presser, provides no empirical evidence. Indeed, the relevant passage is particularly vague and says merely that 'there are reasons to assume that the German Jews came out of the war somewhat better than the Dutch'.[4] Neither Presser's footnotes nor the original manuscript held by the RIOD shed any further light on the subject,[5] yet he uses the assertion to suggest that the total of victims of the 'Final Solution' should be reduced from c.106,000 to around 90,000 in order to take account of the many foreigners who were included in the total but who may not have returned to the Netherlands at the end of the war.[6] It seems likely that Presser drew this conclusion from the earlier work of Herzberg, who makes the same claim that while it is impossible to know how many of the German Jews were deported or survived underground, there 'remains the conclusion that the Dutch Jews suffered more under the German persecution than the German [Jews]'.[7]

The evidence is no more than impressionistic but the question remains to be answered. Did the foreign (largely refugee German, Polish or stateless) Jews who were resident in the Netherlands in May 1940 really have a better chance of survival than their Dutch counterparts? If the high level of Jewish mortality can be explained by the lack of a favourable factor which existed in one form or another in other Western European countries,[8] is it possible that the non-Dutch Jews had certain factors or circumstances which favoured them, but not their Dutch counterparts? In his survey of victims and survivors, Houwink ten Cate has suggested, insofar as it is possible to ascertain, that nationality was not a factor in survival. He cites the fact that non-Dutch Jews survived in much the same proportions as Dutch Jews at around 21–23 per cent.[9] In a purely Dutch comparison, this requires no explanation, but when compared with higher levels of mortality among 'foreign' Jews in other Western European countries, there is still a question to be answered, namely why survival rates among foreign Jews were on a par with others in the Netherlands but much lower in Belgium and France. While the 'stubborn particularities' of these latter countries may hold part of the answer, it is also possible that there were specific factors which actually assisted foreign Jewish survival in the occupied Netherlands.

At first glance, the foreign Jews in the Netherlands on the eve of the occupation would seem to have had few obvious advantages over their Dutch co-religionists. According to the available statistics (see Appendix), they numbered around 22,000 'full-Jews', or about 15 per cent of the total Jewish population of the Netherlands. As such they were a a smaller minority group than the foreign Jews in either France or Belgium. Moreover, the refugees themselves were hardly a homogenous entity, and contained representatives of many divergent social groups: middle-class liberal Jews from Berlin and the cities of western Germany, orthodox and observant *Ost-juden*, and working-class left-wing activists.

Their position *vis-à-vis* Dutch society was also disadvantageous. They were widely resented by Dutch Jews as a burden on their charitable resources and as potential catalysts for increasing antisemitism inside the Netherlands. They had markedly different religious, social, linguistic and cultural traditions from their hosts, making assimilation, integration, or even qualified acceptance between the two sides difficult. Their perceived behaviour and demeanour also did nothing to endear them to their Dutch hosts. Often outspoken and apparently ungrateful, they were difficult to treat sympathetically, especially when they established businesses which operated in direct competition with existing, but economically hard-pressed Dutch (Jewish) concerns, or moved into dwellings in Amsterdam-South that most Dutch Jews could only dream of. In age terms, there was probably little difference between the refugees and the indigenous Dutch Jews. While the age profile of refugees coming into the Netherlands shows a preponderance of younger people, they were also those most likely to re-emigrate. In this way, it was often the older generation of refugees who remained behind in the Netherlands.[10]

The occupational structure of the non-Dutch refugee Jews should also be borne in mind when assessing their vulnerability in the occupied Netherlands. Those who arrived in 1933 had at least some chance of finding employment, or of setting up in business. Nevertheless, the effects of the depression militated against this, and legislation in May 1934 severely restricted the ability of foreigners (and that included refugees) to find paid employment with which to support themselves and their families.[11] Those already in employment were usually given permits, but newcomers found it almost impossible to survive. Self-employment allowed some to stay in the country, but only those who could demonstrate a clear danger of persecution in Germany were able to find direct financial help from the CJV, and then help was often only on a limited basis. The picture is one of an occupational cross-section of Jewry from Germany, a large proportion of whom were living in reduced circumstances as the realities of refugee life began to bite. In some cases, the normal economic structure of the family was reversed with male breadwinners forced into idleness by legislation against the employment of aliens, while wives and daughters were still able to bring in money by undertaking domestic employment.[12] However, it would be unwise to assume that all the refugees who came to the Netherlands were poor. Family and business contacts and the ability to move assets out of Germany or arrange for their exchange meant that a select few were able to live in some style and many others were able to give the impression of being well-off, even if their money eventually ran out. This wide disparity between the few rich and the many poor did not necessarily differentiate the refugees from their Dutch counterparts.

Taking all this into account, there is no doubt that the majority of the refugee Jews faced many disadvantages. They were regarded as an unwelcome problem by the Dutch government, which took steps to make the Netherlands an unattractive destination and imposed severe restrictions on those people who did arrive in the country legally. After November 1938, illegal entrants were sometimes sent back – if this was practical – or incarcerated in camps so that a punitive element was imposed on their continued residence in the country. As refugees, these people had no protection from their own government and effectively had to rely entirely on the international machinery of the League of Nations High Commission and the 'humanitarian norms' of the period. The Dutch government was adamant that these people should receive no special treatment. On the eve of invasion, a minority was already in government-run camps with the intention that more should join them. For the rest who were still allowed to live in the community there were other problems. Many were short of funds or were unemployed and relied on financial assistance from the CJV or other charitable institutions. Families had often been separated, either in coming to the Netherlands or as a result of men being put in camps while their wives and children were allowed to remain outside. Few refugees had been in the country long enough to put down roots or to integrate into the community and their concentration in certain districts of Amsterdam, while wholly understandable, probably contributed to their isolation from the host country and its people.

As the German armies swept into the Netherlands on 10 May, the foreign refugee Jews with fewer family, emotional or material ties to their adoptive homeland were more able to consider flight to another country of refuge, or into illegality. It is impossible to know if the non-Dutch Jews were overrepresented in the crowds of Jews and others who flocked to the North Sea ports on 13 May 1940 when it became clear that the country was about to be overrun, or whether the non-Dutch Jews took flight southwards to France more readily than their Dutch counterparts. Undoubtedly, the refugee Jews were collectively more afraid of the German invasion and what it would mean. They had far less to lose through flight than the Dutch. A young German Jew lodging with a family in Bussum panicked on 10 May, insisting that it was essential to flee immediately, to which the hostess's response was that 'one [could] not leave without a visa, and what [would be done] with the house and furniture'.[13] Many others must have reacted in much the same way, but one major practical obstacle to their mobility was the Dutch authorities' curfew on all enemy aliens. Germans, even if they were refugees, were likely to be arrested if found on the street. One refugee in Amsterdam found himself arrested and taken to a police station with a whole group of Nazis. Only through the intervention of a Dutch policeman and the fortuitous acquisition of a pass signed by the Dutch military administration was he able to flee with his family to France.[14] Yet for every one who contemplated flight, there was another refugee who was likely to stay put, especially if they had been in the Netherlands for some time and felt loyalty for their adoptive country, or had dependent relatives who could not easily be moved, either because of their age or infirmity, or because they were already housed in a refugee camp.[15]

In any assessment of the evidence as to whether Dutch or non-Dutch Jews found it easier to escape in the immediate aftermath of the invasion, one is forced back to the conclusion of a contemporary observer. Wielek made no distinction between Dutch and non-Dutch Jews in their ability to escape.[16] In other words, it was money and contacts which made all the difference, rather than nationality or origin. Thus even if the refugee Jews were more likely to have been afraid of the invasion by virtue of their experiences inside Nazi Germany, and far more willing to move on as a result of having few ties with the host country, their avenues for escape were probably more constrained by a lack of money or contacts with which to expedite such an escape.

For those refugees already in camps, the situation on 10 May must have seemed even bleaker. Apart from the inmates of Westerbork, other non-Dutch Jewish refugees were being held in various locations throughout the country. Effectively, their fate was in the hands of the Dutch authorities, but in the chaos which ensued after the invasion, there was little chance that they would be allowed to save themselves. Indeed, as has been shown earlier, some attempts were made to evacuate the camps and move the inmates to supposed safety, but with no success. In many cases, men were held in camps while their wives and children were allowed to remain at liberty. In these circumstances it was unlikely that either party would flee without the other. In sum, the position of the non-Dutch Jews would seem to have many disadvantages when compared with their Dutch counterparts.

The 'favourable factors'

Despite such disadvantages, there do appear to be at least three favourable factors, while not immediately obvious at the time, which were to have some impact on the ability of the refugee Jews to survive in the Netherlands. First of all, their experiences of persecution in Germany and exposure to a malevolent state bureaucracy had made them somewhat more wary of dealing with government officials and the police. This suspicion may well have been carried over into the country of refuge. Most of the new arrivals up to 1938 complied with Dutch law and registered with the aliens department of the police, but in the pre-war Netherlands, registering as an alien with the authorities held no particular threat except for political refugees, those who had entered illegally, and *Ost-juden*. The Dutch government could and did take action to deport or imprison left-wing émigrés who were seen as dangerous, so many members of the German Communist and Social Democratic parties (KPD and SPD) attempted to avoid any contact with the authorities. Similarly, refugees who managed to cross the border illegally after it had been closed in December 1938 had a vested interest in staying underground. In the period 1933–38, the Netherlands' government also made attempts to exclude the *Ost-juden* on the somewhat spurious grounds that their supposed rootlessless and alien culture made them unsuitable as immigrants and in any case they could return to the East rather than seek refuge in the West.[17] It is probable that these three groups of Jewish refugees in the Netherlands were less likely to have come into contact with the authorities before the war, thus making it easier for them to avoid detection once the Germans had taken over the Dutch government machinery, its population and aliens registers, and the records of the CJV.

The second factor which may have assisted the survival of German Jews in the Netherlands was their role in the bureaucracy of the Jewish Council. In the 1930s, the CJV had employed a limited number of refugee Jews to help in the running of the organisation. These people were assisted by other refugees who were not salaried, or at least not formally on the payroll. In February 1941, when the secular leaders of the Jewish communities established the Jewish Council, the natural reaction was to use the existing expertise and personnel of the CJV. As the organisation of the Council mushroomed, so more and more employees were recruited and some key positions were in the hands of former refugees. The most striking example was of Dr Edwin Sluzker, a former advocate from Vienna, who headed the *Expositur* which became responsible for the allocation of exemptions from labour service.

Given how well placed some of the non-Dutch Jews were to influence the distribution of those permits, then the advantages which the structure of the Jewish Council gave to a number of German, Austrian and stateless Jews becomes clear. Their 'circle' did not include most of Dutch Jewry, but did include many other refugees like themselves. Undoubtedly the same prejudices against individuals and groups existed within the refugee circle as they did in Dutch Jewish circles, but the position of certain refugee Jews within the Council bureaucracy allowed them to save (albeit temporarily) their families and friends. In this sense, Sluzker's role as chief of the *Expositur* was crucial. While the Dutch Jews may have believed that Sluzker and the other *Expositur* staff abused their position, this charge is difficult to substantiate. Certainly, it is likely that refugee (German) Jews received a disproportionate number of exemptions, simply because they formed the basis of the CJV bureaucracy which had gone to create the Jewish Council, and it is equally true that these exemptions did have an effect on the individual's chances of survival. Possession of an exemption did still allow the individual more time to prepare to go underground and may have been of indirect assistance in saving its holder.

A further factor to be considered is whether there was any discrimination between Dutch and non-Dutch Jews when it came to providing help. Although very difficult to measure, there is no direct evidence that aid organisations or individuals made distinctions of this type. In other words, the *onderduikers* were seen primarily as Jews rather than as Germans, and there are instances where committed anti-Germans such as the Bogaard family were nonetheless prepared to take in German Jews. The same appears to have applied to the LO where there was no apparent discrimination between Dutch and non-Dutch Jews. Both adults and children of all nationalities and backgrounds were treated alike.

The final possible favourable factor for German Jews in the Netherlands arose from the most unlikely quarter. Although the German, Polish and stateless Jews in the refugee camps of 1939, and especially in Westerbork, must have seemed the most poorly placed of any of the refugees, their situation as the first inhabitants ultimately proved to be of enormous value. When Westerbork was liberated in April 1945, the Canadian army compiled a list of the inmates and noted that many of them had been there since the beginning of the war.[18] As the details from the list indicate, a large number of the survivors were of German origin and had managed to stay in the camp while so many thousands of others had been transported in from the towns and cities of the Netherlands, and transported out to Auschwitz, Sobibor, Bergen-Belsen and Theresienstadt. Obviously the camp required an administration and a bureaucracy in order to fulfil the role of refugee camp and later a processing and transit camp, and the first inmates were in the best position to take on and retain these roles in 1940 and 1941.[19] Moreover, the Germans who took over the camp and their masters in The Hague and Berlin were thought to have a preference for dealing with Germans rather than the Dutch (even if they were Jews).

The first Dutch Jews did not arrive in Westerbork until the summer of 1942. In March changes had been made to organisation within the camp, large numbers of administrative and maintenance tasks had been allotted to the existing (German Jewish) camp population.[20] This was reinforced when the Jewish Council sent part of their staff to act as a registration department within the camp. The preponderance of German Jews within the bureaucracy of the Jewish Council meant that their hold on the administrative posts within the camp was almost complete. Philip Mechanicus, a journalist and camp inmate, gives a clear account of their position and power. Although some tasks were allotted to incoming Dutch Jews, 'they [the German Jews] held on resolutely to the key posts and more or less every one of the important jobs so that they could be in control of the whole organisation and could give priority to the interests of German Jews'.[21] This was compounded by the SS Commandant, *Obersturmführer* Erich Deppner, after his arrival on 1 July 1942. The first deportations to the East began on 15–16 July, but Deppner soon gave 2,000 of the 3,000 original camp inmates long-term resident status which effectively excluded them from consideration for deportation.[22]

Mechanicus refused to implicate all the German Jews in this collaboration, stressing that it was 'not the morally strongest among them' who had acted in this way, but concluded that:

> The German Jews have undeniably abused their position of supremacy and continue to do so. They form, as it were, an almost exclusive association for the protection of the interests of German Jews. As individuals and acting together they do their best to save all the Germans brought here from being deported and endeavour to keep them here. They have done this from the time the Dutch Jews began arriving in Westerbork. In this way they have, in point of fact, handed over the Dutch Jews to the Germans to suit their own convenience. Wherever possible, they have pushed the Germans into jobs and have kept the Germans here.[23]

In addition he highlighted the increasing tension between the nationalities, caused not so much by the positions occupied by the German Jews but by their attitudes. Speaking mainly of the subordinate staff, he noted that they 'dictate and bawl and bark and snap and shriek ... often just like the National Socialists or Prussian soldiers'.[24] The animosity of the Dutch towards the Germans was fuelled by their behaving like 'typical Boche'. Mechanicus seems to suggest that their actions were not entirely conditioned by national characteristics but came from the German Jews' relative insecurity. Although thinking of themselves as German in every respect, they had been deprived of their citizenship and had endured a great deal at the hands of the German state. This created a heightened sense of uncertainty which manifested itself in extreme and intolerant behaviour towards the Dutch Jews who were in the same peril from the Nazis but nevertheless retained their sense of nationality and belonging. This often manifested itself in the form of threats or actual denunciation to the German authorities for some real or imagined slight which would ensure immediate deportation. One example involved the famous football commentator Han Hollander who held a privileged position within the camp, but some unguarded comments by his wife about the Germans had led to their incarceration and subsequent deportation.[25]

Subsequent accounts and analyses have reinforced Mechanicus's view. Boas reiterates how the first inmates held all the important positions which gave many of them immunity from deportation and also the power of life and death over their fellow (Dutch) inmates. Apart from echoing Mechanicus, he also makes the point that three or more years of camp-life and the view that they had been abandoned, both by the Dutch government and their co-religionists, made the German Jews even more ill-disposed towards their Dutch counterparts and even more enthusiastic to exploit their new positions of power.[26] To see how this worked in practice, one need only look at three German Jews who held crucial positions in the camp bureaucracy.

By far the most important was Kurt Schlesinger. Interned with his wife by the Dutch in January 1939 after crossing the border, he was one of the camp's first residents.[27] At first, he was employed building the camp but then moved to the Jewish Council bureaucracy in the camp. Later his apparent influence over the Dutch camp commander, Schol, allowed him suggest that the inmates take some role in the running of the camp. This led to the changes in the camp structure of March 1942, and to his informal status as camp-elder being transformed into the practical leadership of the camp bureaucracy, which now included a fire brigade and the *Orde Dienst* (OD) of 20 men. When the Germans took over the camp on 1 July 1942 and renamed it as a *Polizeiliches Durchgangslager* (police transit camp), Commandant Deppner, who had no particular interest in administrative matters, was quite content to appoint Schlesinger as head of

Victims and Survivors

Dienstbereich II, the camp administration. In this way, a trend inherent in the origins of the camp as a holding area for refugees effectively determined the domination of the camp structure by German Jews. Schlesinger and his colleagues controlled the whole apparatus including, crucially, the compilation of lists of deportees for the transports to the East. By making the 'system' work efficiently, the Jewish bureaucrats preserved their 'protected' status and kept the SS out of the camp. While it was so efficiently organised, there was no need for them to interfere. Under Commandant Gemmeker, Schlesinger was promoted still further, to *Oberdienstleiter*,[28] which gave him control of the whole administration. Even when the last regular transport left Westerbork on 29 September 1943, the camp administration remained, with many of its members surviving even the later occasional clearances in 1944. In April 1945, when the camp population had been reduced to a core of around 900 people and the Allied armies were almost at the gates, Gemmeker completed the *Oberdienstleiter's* rise when he 'surrendered' the camp to Schlesinger's command by handing over his pistol.[29]

Schlesinger's position in the camp was supported by other non-Dutch Jewish subordinates. The head of the OD was a former officer in the Austrian army, Arthur Pisk. Appointed by Schol in the reforms of March 1942, he began with a small detachment of 20 men (18 German and 2 Dutch) but rapidly expanded its strength to about 200 (50 per cent Dutch, 50 per cent German) by 1943. Created primarily to keep order in the camp, they also became involved in the deportations through being in charge of loading the trains with people for the journey to the East. As has already been shown, their duties were not confined to the camp. In January 1943 100 of their number were involved in the infamous raid on the Jewish asylum *Het Apeldoornsche Bos*,[30] and some six months later they participated in raids in Amsterdam. For these reasons alone, Pisk was often described as the most hated man in the camp, but he and his men also chose to play the part. In June 1943 Mechanicus described them thus:

> drawn from the dregs of Jewish society, rough, coarse fellows without refinement, human feelings or compassion; they just live for their cigarettes and for an easy affair with women like themselves ... They are hated like the plague and people would flay many of them alive if they dared.[31]

With leather caps and uniforms similar to those of the despised Green Police, only the yellow star marked them out as different. Pisk himself also dressed every inch the German officer with 'riding breeches, boots, a whip and the requisite leather' and even sported a Hitler-moustache.[32]

Eight months later, Mechanicus had not changed his view.

> the OD men ... are the officially recognized keepers of the peace, but they understand nothing about the business of keeping order and

only get going when there is something to be scrounged or when there is a girl to run off with. They are hated because of their brutishness and because people can get no legal redress from them.[33]

The OD employed a disproportionate number of German Jews in its ranks, and in this way perhaps a hundred non-Dutch Jews protected themselves and their families. Their conduct was anything but honourable and the treatment of fellow inmates often despicable,[34] but like all the other inmates of the camp, they used whatever power and influence they could muster in order to stay in the camp rather than be deported. The narratives about the camp speak of many other people, placed in charge of various camp or productive functions, who saw the efficient execution of those tasks as their passport to protection, even if it meant browbeating and chastising those who worked under them. Moreover, some saw their newly found status as a path to enrichment by soliciting material gifts and sexual favours in exchange for temporary exemption from deportation.[35] One could point to several of the functionaries who served under Schlesinger: Todtmann, his adjutant, or Mozes, who was head of the Huts Administration. These and many others formed a type of camp aristocracy. Certainly, it appears that German Jews gained a disproportionate number of these favoured positions, but Dutch Jews who also became part of this aristocracy did not behave differently. If the key to long-term survival was to stay in the camp, then these people were in the best place to ensure this for themselves, their families and friends. Only in the early months of 1944 did things begin to change, with inmates more or less being offered the chance to volunteer for Theresienstadt rather than wait for the certainty of deportation to Auschwitz.

One member of the camp aristocracy presents more of an enigma. Dr Fritz Spanier, his wife and two daughters had been passengers on board the liner St Louis which had sailed from Hamburg in 1939 only to be turned away from Cuba and forced to return to Europe. There, its 'cargo' of refugees was divided between Britain, France, Belgium and the Netherlands. In this way, the Spaniers also became some of the earliest inmates of the camp. As one of the first arrivals with specialist medical skills, Spanier was placed in charge of the camp hospital which by 1944 had developed into a medical complex which would not have looked out of place in a modern metropolis.[36] With 1,800 beds, more than 120 doctors and over 1,000 members of staff, the medical facility was by far the largest institution inside the camp, and at the same time the most incongruous. Here, the sick and infirm were brought to be nursed back to health so that they could be loaded on to the cattle wagons for the journey to Poland.

The hospital was Spanier's private empire. Inside its walls, he was said to be all-powerful and did not even rise from his chair when Gemmeker came in. Explaining Spanier's power over the camp commandant is problematic.

Both men came originally from Düsseldorf but there is no other clue as to
the nature of the link between the two men. Nevertheless, its result was that
Spanier did wield substantial power and was, for example, able to give
orders which kept individuals off the transports and which no one would
countermand. This power could only be used sparingly, to protect his hospital staff and their dependants, and some other favoured individuals. Too
many exemptions would have doubtless brought him into conflict with the
administration much earlier. Some people, thus favoured, undoubtedly
owed him their lives.[37] Others who had enjoyed his protection but had then
offended him were almost certainly to be found on the next transport. Such
a fate befell Dr Elie Cohen, a member of the hospital staff whose wife had
unintentionally insulted a German Jew.[38]

Spanier was considered as by far the least corrupt of the aristocrats. He
helped to save a few people from the transports and was known to drop hints
to others about the Nazi's future plans. Even he was powerless to prevent the
clearance of the hospital on 9 February 1944. Mechanicus called it 'perhaps
the most abominable transport that has ever gone', containing as it did hundreds who were sick or dying as well as children from the orphanage.[39]
Spanier had apparently tried to empty the hospital by telling the doctors that
it would be in their patients' best interests if they were returned to their huts,
but to no avail. The doctors had failed to take the hint and Spanier had been
unwilling to make his warning of events to come any plainer.

Although there is evidence to suggest that members of the camp 'aristocracy' were aware of the true meaning of Auschwitz by March 1944, they
did not share the secret with the other inmates. In truth, it was not in their
interests to do so. The resultant panic would have upset the smooth running of the camp and undoubtedly threatened their security which had
been so carefully protected through all the period of programmed deportation.[40] To that extent, the 'aristocracy' protected itself right through to the
bitter end. The information collected on the camp inmates by the Canadian
army gives some indication of those who had managed to survive. Of the
918 people in the camp the list gives details of 773, including their age,
last residence in the Netherlands and place of birth. While this cannot be
considered an infallible guide to nationality, the overall totals are striking,
as shown in Table 10.1.

Table 10.1 Westerbork camp survivors, April 1945[41] (by place of birth)

Place of Birth	Male	Female	Children	Total
Netherlands	233 (56.3%)	198 (62.9%)	34 (77.3%)	465 (60.2%)
Elsewhere	181 (43.7%)	117 (37.1%)	10 (22.7%)	308 (39.8%)
Total	414 (100.0%)	315 (100.0%)	44 (100.0%)	773 (100.0%)

Superficially, this does support the view that non-Dutch Jews had been much more successful as survivors of the camp. Their numbers are substantially more than might have been expected given the proportion of foreign Jews in the Netherlands in May 1940. Known members of the 'aristocracy' such as Schlesinger, Spanier and their families are included in the lists. Nevertheless, although this may seem appealing evidence for the efficacy of the camp regime in protecting non-Dutch Jews, a note of caution has to be sounded. First and foremost, the numbers or survivors from the camp are small, even in relation to the total number of Jews from the Netherlands who did survive the Holocaust. The emptiness of a camp in April 1945 which at one time had held many thousands of people is testimony to the efficiency of the system which sent so many people to their deaths, rather than the survival skills of a few. Moreover, of more than 900 inmates at the end of the war, only 600 had been in the camp for a long period, the remainder having been arrested for living underground after the last transport had left in the autumn of 1944. Finally, around 145 people are missing from the list. It is likely that many of these were Dutch Jews who were able to make a rapid return back to their homes from the camp in the days after the liberation.

None of this can take away the fact that Westerbork was a place where some Jews did manage to survive in the Netherlands, some for the entire occupation period. What seems clear is that the organisation of the camp administration by both the Dutch and then the German authorities, favoured the first inmates. These non-Dutch Jews had a strong sense of injustice against their Dutch co-religionists whom, they felt, had abandoned and betrayed them in the pre-war years and even during the first stages of the occupation. Thus when they had accumulated positions of power in the camp and the roles were reversed, they were the ones to lord it over the less fortunate Dutch. While the behaviour of many non-Dutch Jews in authority could be seen as a settling of collective old scores, the stakes involved were high – nothing less than a matter of life and death. Even if we cannot altogether blame those involved for using the system to save themselves at the expense of others, it is clear that the same system did bring out the worst in many of those involved when all the controls on their behaviour were removed.

Perhaps the most remarkable aspect of the camp was how little SS control was required. One could point to a large number of SS organised camps with similar structures which used the inmates for almost every task, including the maintenance of order. The term 'Jewish SS' was not peculiar to Westerbork. Nonetheless, the efficiency of the camp in organising the regular transit of specified numbers of Jews to the East is remarkable. The German SS commanders seem to have been unexceptional men concerned only with having a smooth-running operation, and this is what the internal Jewish administration provided for them. The offer of exemption from deportation acted as the carrot for people like Schlesinger and Pisk to carry on their work, yet even their position would have come under threat eventually, as the numbers of other Jews who could be deported dwindled. The ultimate survival of people in the camp probably owed a great deal to the winding down of the programmatic extermination policies in the East as the Russians advanced and the supposed usefulness of the work being carried out in the camp for the German war effort.

The idea that non-Dutch Jews had were more likely to have survived the Holocaust in the Netherlands than their Dutch counterparts must remain conjecture. There are no reliable statistics, especially given the upheaval in the post-war period and the fact that many survivors chose to move on to other places in the world rather than return to their pre-war homes. Even where there are figures, as in the case of Westerbork, they have to be treated with caution, not least because of the impact which even small percentage variations may have on totals which are themselves very small. Similarly, the evidence of survivors also has to be carefully evaluated. Westerbork again provides a good example. While Mechanicus and many others have chronicled the malevolent behaviour of the German Jews in positions of power, they have also noted that Dutch Jews in similar positions did not behave any differently. The survival instinct was the same for all and it was the structures within the system which gave a select few a head start on the rest in the scramble within the camp for position which could ensure (at least temporary) safety.

|11|

The last year of occupation and the realities of liberation

The Nazi persecution of the Jews did not end with the last transport from Amsterdam in September 1943. The pursuit went on into 1944, even to the point where Dutch territory began to be liberated by advancing Allied forces. As a result, the struggle of the minority to survive underground and in the camps continued to the bitter end. Those in hiding had to remain unseen, sharing with their hosts the vicissitudes of living in a country increasingly victimised by the occupying Germans. The question needs to be asked: what new threats did this last phase of the occupation pose for those still at large and how did they overcome them? Moreover, did the fact that, unlike most of France and Belgium, the northern Dutch provinces were not liberated until April and May 1945 make a difference to their chances of survival?

In addition, it would be easy to assume that liberation brought with it an end to the story, yet this is far from the truth. All manner of problems emerged for the Jews remaining in, or returning to, the Netherlands at the end of the war in Europe. A comprehensive treatment would require another complete volume but there are some important themes which form an appropriate epilogue for this study. These can be summarised under five headings. The first two relate to the reception afforded to Jews returning to the Netherlands from the camps in Germany and Poland, and to the reaction of the Dutch population to their fellow citizens who had been underground or 'absent' for two or three years. The remaining three are more related to workings of the post-war Dutch state and society in dealing with the problems left by the murder of 75 per cent of its Jewish population. They involved the return and/or disposal of Jewish property, the fate of Jewish children left orphaned by the Holocaust, and charges if any to be made against the leaders of the Jewish Council for complicity in the deportation and deaths of their co-religionists. These issues, although technically having a legal remedy within the existing Dutch judicial system, almost inevitably created major disputes and debates during and after 1945 as the desire to adopt 'normal' solutions clashed with the perception of the Holocaust as a unique event without precedent.

The last year of occupation

It is clear that the German desire to make the Netherlands truly *judenrein* (free of Jews) continued into 1944 and even 1945. In comparison with the circumstances in neighbouring countries, there are again some specific features of the occupation of the Netherlands which militated against the survival of Jews. The most obvious is that whereas most of France and Belgium had been liberated by the autumn of 1944, a large part of the Netherlands, namely all the areas north of the big rivers, remained in German hands until the Allied advance in April 1945. This in itself gave the Germans more time to 'catch' the Jews, but there were other factors which made living underground progressively more difficult.

There is no doubt that the news of the Allied landings in Normandy and the rapid advance into France in the late summer of 1944 brought renewed hope of an early end to the occupation to the people of the Netherlands. This gained even more credence as Eisenhower's forces advanced through Belgium towards the Dutch border. Such was the level of expectation that when the BBC reported (erroneously as it turned out) on 4 September that Breda had been liberated, people assumed that the liberation of the entire country was only days away. Reinforcing this was the flight of many Germans and Dutch National Socialists eastwards to the German border. The following day became known as *dolle dinsdag* (mad Tuesday) as celebrations began, flags were displayed and children sang patriotic songs in the street.[1] Many people who had been in hiding came out, thinking that salvation was at hand. However, the euphoria was short-lived. The Allied troops did not arrive and the German occupiers regained their composure. Exactly how many Jewish *onderduikers* betrayed themselves by emerging too early is impossible to verify, but an impressionistic report from Amsterdam suggests that a few certainly fell into German hands.[2]

In the following days, the pattern for the final and most harrowing year was set for the occupied Netherlands. The failure of the Allies to establish a bridgehead across the great rivers at Nijmegen and Arnhem after 17 September effectively consigned the northern provinces to another winter under German rule. Worse still was the fact that Dutch co-operation with the Allies, including a rail strike to prevent the Germans moving troops to the battle area, led to German reprisals. Rather than restore the rail system, the Germans allowed the stoppage to continue. Afraid of reprisals, railway workers stayed away from work. They were replaced by German personnel who ran a skeletal service for the *Wehrmacht* but effectively precluded the restoration of normal passenger and freight services. This, coupled with the occupier's inability or unwillingness to guarantee food and fuel supplies for the big cities, ushered in a winter of scarcity and starvation. The *hongerwinter* (hunger-winter) of 1944–45 has been well-chronicled as one of the enduring experiences for the Dutch urban population as a whole.[3] What remains to be seen is whether the privations of this last year of the war had any specific and more damaging effects on those underground.

The *hongerwinter* was felt most keenly in the cities of western Holland. Farming districts further east had little or no trouble in feeding themselves, and were regularly visited by people from the west desperate to trade anything they had for food. It can be assumed therefore that those Jews hidden in the north-eastern provinces were seldom directly affected. Crucially, however, it was Amsterdam which bore the brunt of the shortages. How did people who were entirely dependent on those hiding them fare when everyone was engaged in finding food and fuel to support themselves through the winter? The photographs of the time tell a grim story – of men and women on hands and knees sifting through piles of clinker to find what little coal remained, or digging up the cobbled streets to remove the wooden sleepers from abandoned tramlines. Houses were gutted for fuel, furniture, doors, floorboards and even roof sections were sacrificed in the attempt to keep warm. The precise effects of these privations on the *onderduikers* will probably never be known. On the one hand, the more extensive operation of the LO in this final year of the occupation undoubtedly helped many Jews in hiding and their hosts through the provision of false papers and appropriate ration cards. The sense that help was at hand, both in the city and from the advancing Allies, also helped to raise morale. On the other hand, the lack of food and fuel in the city was acute. Cases of disease and starvation became commonplace. It seems likely that the ability of Jews to survive underground was determined more by their specific circumstances rather than by any general rules. Some *onderduikers* still had access to funds to support themselves even through the hardest times, others did not. Some hosts continued to be able to support their guests with food and fuel, others did not. Finally, some hosts and guests were 'adopted' by LO networks while others remained independent and unsupported.

Beyond the threat of the *hongerwinter* itself, there were other dangers. Although the activities of the 'Jew-hunters' seem to have petered out during 1944, the German pursuit of resistance workers and their desire for labour to work in Germany continued unabated. There were examples of Jewish *onderduikers* falling victims to such raids. One example emanates from Tilburg (Brabant) where the Germans raided the home of a prominent resistance worker on 2 August 1944 and found at least ten Jewish *onderduikers*.[4] Their capture was essentially a bonus for the German authorities. Similar chance captures were likely to have taken place when the occupiers engaged in wholesale and indiscriminatory round-ups of people under 45 for labour in Germany.[5]

In the south and south-east, liberation came in the autumn of 1944. The rapid Allied advance allowed those underground south of the rivers to emerge from hiding. Many areas experienced little fighting, but some areas of Limburg remained battlegrounds throughout the winter. Although the majority of Jews surviving in the Netherlands were further north, the beginnings of liberation brought some important steps towards reconstruction. On 5 January 1945 a Jewish Co-ordination Commission (*Joodse Coördinatie Commissie*) was set up in Eindhoven to oversee the welfare of the Jews and to rebuild Jewish life.[6] In some respects, its formation was more important than its activities. Its founders, such as Abraham de Jong, had strong Zionist convictions and this fact was to have a major impact on the JCC's relations with the post-war Dutch state and society. Nonetheless, with the collapse of the pre-war Jewish organisations and structures, together with the compromised nature of the Jewish Council and its off-shoots, this was the first organisation which linked all the various elements of Judaism in the Netherlands. Its precursor had been the short-lived Co-ordination Commission of 1940 headed by Lodewijk Visser which, unlike the Jewish Council, had refused to have any dealings with the Germans.[7] Although still finding its feet in the liberated Netherlands, the JCC became the central organisation in defending Jewish interests in the post-war period and became directly involved in the debates over Jewish orphans, Jewish assets and the culpability of the Jewish Council.

Liberation and the return home

Of the few Jews from the Netherlands who managed to survive the camps in Germany or Poland and return home, each had a different story to tell, some pleasant, others less so. A mother and daughter liberated from Theresienstadt were evacuated by air to Konstanz by the French Red Cross. After two days in hospital, they were allowed to take whatever they needed from the deserted German hotels and were then moved via Geneva and Lyon to Brussels from where they completed the journey to Amsterdam by car.[8] Others from the same camp were flown by the Americans direct to Eindhoven.[9] A survivor from Auschwitz reported a longer odyssey via Chernowitz, Odessa, Marseilles and Belgium before returning to the Netherlands.[10] Another young girl recalled walking miles westwards before being picked up and taken to a collection point at Bamberg. From there, she was shipped with other Dutch people, both Jews and non-Jews, by train to Roermond. The transportation was hardly luxurious, consisting of box-cars with liberal amounts of straw, but the returnees were given American rations for the journey. Although she described the officials as 'kind and understanding', the Dutch authorities insisted that returnees went through the proper formalities and each individual had to obtain medical, security and customs clearance before being allowed to go on his or her way. Single people were then given a guilder to facilitate their onward journey. In the case of this girl it was insufficient to pay her train fare and the balance had to be borrowed from a former school friend living in the locality.[11]

These were all Dutch citizens, but former German Jewish refugees returning to their adoptive homeland were not necessarily treated the same way. One man, liberated by the Russians, was handed over to the western powers on 15 June 1945 at Leipzig and then spent eight days on a train bound for the Netherlands. On arrival he was (presumably) screened and then placed in a camp at Vilt (south Limburg) for criminals which included former members of the NSB and SS. All his possessions were stolen and the conditions, which included three roll-calls a day and hard labour, he regarded as little better than those in Bergen-Belsen. He saw all this as sanctioned by high-ranking Dutch officers and was only freed when the Dutch press got hold of the story.[12] This man was one of 18 who had been segregated from fellow returnees and placed in this camp. Nor was this the only group to be so treated. Other non-Dutch and stateless survivors were also sent there in the summer of 1945. One young girl remembered the barbed wire round the camp, the constant shouting of the guards and the poor food.[13] This mixing of victims and former persecutors was by no means unique. The camp at Westerbork was liberated by the Canadians on 12 April 1945, and the Dutch authorities insisted that none of the inmates should leave before being screened. This task was to be carried out by three junior officers who proved incapable of processing more than 8–10 people each day (at a time when the camp still had 896 occupants), yet by 24 May the first 200 NSB internees arrived, to be followed by thousands of others until the end of June when the camp population stood at around 10,000. At this stage there were still 300 Jews held there. Their continued internment was ludicrous. An appeal on behalf of an Austrian mother and daughter, relatives of Karl Kautsky, to be allowed to live with another daughter in nearby Ommen pointed out that the two women had been *onderduikers* until captured by the SD. If they had succeeded in remaining in hiding, they would have been free to go where they pleased. As it was, the only reason for their incarceration was their arrest by the SD as Jewish *onderduikers*![14] As a result of the appeal, they were allowed to leave. Only on 23 June did the Dutch military authorities decree that all the former inmates, irrespective of nationality, could be allowed to leave. Even then, 120 stateless Jews were still in the camp on 7 July, ostensibly held for reasons of 'security'.[15]

To understand the formalism of the authorities and how these returning survivors of the Holocaust could have been treated in this apparently

callous way, one has to look in detail at the way in which the post-liberation
Dutch authorities re-established controls over their borders, planned for the
repatriation of their nationals and reasserted immigration procedures. Aware
that many Dutch men and women had been deported by the Germans,
either as Jews or for labour within the Third Reich, the Dutch government-
in-exile in London had been planning for the repatriation of its citizens displaced by the war ever since the end of 1943.[16] A Government Commissioner
for Repatriation, G.F. Ferwerda, had been appointed to oversee the task and
to head a group of repatriation officers who would work in Germany and
other countries to expedite the return of their countrymen.[17] While the commission had some early successes in France and Belgium, and managed to
place officers in several other countries, its work inside Germany at the war's
end was hampered by a lack of resources, and especially transport. While the
Dutch *Militair Gezag* (Military Government) had access to at least 90 ambu-
lances and other vehicles, Ferwerda was told that they were all needed for
the provinces most affected by the *hongerwinter*.[18] In 1943 the government
assumed that there were up to 600,000 Dutch nationals to be repatriated,
including 70,000 Jews. Even in May 1944 Ferwerda was still referring to
60,000 survivors, an amazing assumption given all the sources of information available to the Dutch by that stage in the war.[19] However, the Dutch
government's policy on repatriation was conditioned not by the numbers of
camp survivors, or even the Dutch forced labourers still in Germany, but by
the continent-wide problem of millions of displaced persons, many assumed
to be sick or diseased, who might find their way into the Netherlands unless
proper controls were enforced.

The attitudes involved here hark back to the pre-war precepts of immigration policies in most Western European countries. The attitude was
narrow and formalist. One looks in vain for some differentiation in treatment – to make a special case for those people returning from the horrors of the camps. The truth was – at least at this stage – that the Dutch
in London did not recognise that there had been a Holocaust. Moreover,
as the scale of the tragedy began to emerge, they were incapable of providing an appropriate response to the question of repatriants, and all
were therefore treated alike. However, this implies a purely structural
argument for the treatment of returning Jews, but recent research has
shown a different facet to the issue. Firstly, it is clear that the government-in-exile was told in 1944 how few Jews remained alive in Eastern
Europe. Secondly, it held rigidly to the principle that there should be no
distinction between one Dutch citizen and another. The ministers consistently refused to countenance any special help for Dutch Jews, as this
would not only break this distinction, but also provide recognition of a
specific 'Jewish question' in the Netherlands.[20] In any case, it was argued
that the end of the war would bring an end to the discrimination against
the Jews, thus presumably removing their need for special status. If spe-

cial help for Jews was required, it was the responsiblity of other Dutch Jews who had avoided deportation or the international Jewish charities.[21] It was a response which smacked at best of naïvety and at worst of anti-semitism on the part of the authorities in London. Certainly, the official attitudes expressed in 1944–45 mirror those of the pre-war period and suggest that little had changed in the workings of the Dutch bureaucratic 'mind' since 1940.

Yet even this does not explain the variability in treatment meted out to both Dutch and non-Dutch Jews. In spite of the advance planning, the Dutch preparations and execution of their post-hostilities immigration procedures left a great deal to be desired. The fears of a huge influx of foreign displaced persons from a Germany in chaos seems to have conditioned the policies pursued. A memorandum of 17 March 1945 suggested that the border controls could expect an influx of anything up to 1.5 million people.[22] The idea was that all people crossing the border would be sent from initial reception posts to reception centres in the larger border towns. They would then be given medical and security screening before being sent to internment camps, aliens' camps or repatriants' camps. In fact, relatively few people arrived before the end of the war, and the big rush took place in May and June, but on nothing like the expected scale. By July and August, many of the reception centres were being closed down. In spite of directives from central government, it appears that procedures in the reception centres also varied from one to another. All carried out the basic screening functions, but other help varied. Some were given food, some only coffee and a bowl of soup. Others remembered being given vouchers. Financial help also varied. While the girl screened in Roermond was only given one guilder, some returnees in Amsterdam were given fl.25 each.[23] Repatriants who had been greeted with celebrations in many places in France and Belgium arrived at the Dutch border to find only disappointment. There was no greeting, no recognition of their circumstances, only 'the rain and Dutch bureaucracy'. For many, the only welcome was from delousing officials with huge sprays and enormous tins of DDT.[24] Another repatriant spoke of his journey to the Netherlands by train.

> The train ran through to Maastricht. We were not allowed out but could listen to a speech filled with many clichés and many references to the Fatherland. A scratched record of the 'Wilhelmus' was played around five times [and] we were treated to a beaker of soup unsuitable for human consumption and some tins of ship's biscuits.[25]

Reception centres were often just as unwelcoming, comprising unsuitable buildings surrounded by barbed wire and with few if any comforts for the returnees. The Philips building in Eindhoven had no furniture and only huge straw mattresses. There were loudspeakers and sirens used to dictate the bureaucratic and daily life of the inmates.

There were excuses. The station at Maastricht had to handle 271 trains containing 359,576 repatriated Dutch, French and Belgian people in the space of five and a half months, necessitating resources which could not easily be provided. Most of Dutch society could not begin to imagine the experiences of those who were coming back from Germany or Poland, and this included the officials charged with their reception. It is not surprising to note that most Dutch people were more concerned about coming to terms with their own war experiences than about understanding the experiences of others. However, perhaps the most telling factor in assessing the psychological impact on the returnees is the huge chasm between their utopian expectations, built up to help them survive in the camps and then reinforced during the journey home, and the realities of the post-war Netherlands.[26] For the 5,500 returning Jews, this chasm was further enlarged by contact with renewed and even increased antisemitism. In itself, this was bad enough, but some Jews undoubtedly fared worse than others at the hands of the Dutch bureaucracy.

In theory, Dutch policy was to treat all Germans as enemy aliens and incarcerate them in internment or prisoner-of-war camps, but this did not take account of the fact that many of the 'Germans' coming back were Jews who had fled to the Netherlands as refugees before 1939 and had obtained residence qualifications. Most had been rendered stateless by the Nazi regime. The Supreme Headquarters Allied Expeditionary Force (SHAEF) had decreed that stateless people were not to be forcibly repatriated but treated as displaced persons, yet there seemed to be a continuing Dutch suspicion of stateless people which ensured that some were incarcerated in internment camps. The worst example, the camp at Vilt, seems to have been compounded by a camp leadership which was openly hostile to both Germans and to Jews. Not all stateless Jews were treated so badly, but they seem to have been the sole victims of this particular Dutch policy. The official explanation given for survivors being sent to Vilt – 'shortage of space' – was weak in the extreme. It might explain a one-off occurrence, but not the subsequent billetting of whole Jewish families to live among the NSB and SS in a labour camp. It is conceivable that this was just an example of bureaucratic bungling or incompetence, but more probably represents the re-emergence of a pre-war policy which involved making the Netherlands as unwelcoming as possible to stateless people. Saddled with the SHAEF directive which prevented the Dutch from deporting aliens, the authorities saw the only available alternative as incarceration (as had been the case after November 1938). Only when the threatened millions did not materialise was it considered safe to allow the pitiful remnants involved to be released. This collision between Allied policy and the Dutch predilection for denying stateless foreigners access to their territory may help to explain the dreadful treatment handed out to some returning non-Dutch Jews.

Jewish orphans

The question of what should happen to the Jewish children who had been fostered out as *onderduikers* during the occupation and subsequently orphaned became one of the most contentious issues of the post-war period. The debate centred on two contradictory objectives. On the one hand there was the government's desire to see that all war orphans, both Jews and non-Jews, were properly looked after and that decisions about their future be taken with their perceived interests given priority. On the other hand was the desire of the residual Jewish community to rebuild itself and lay claim to Jewish children orphaned by the war. Before the end of hostilities, some of the groups responsible for rescuing children had co-operated with the Ministry of Justice in creating legislation to meet the unusual circumstances of these children. This became an Order in Council, passed on 13 August 1945, which set up a government commission (*Commissie voor Oorlogspleegkinderen*) (OPK) whose prime consideration was to be the interest of the children concerned.[27]

Some commentators, such as Fishman, have argued that the resistance organisations were given a disproportionately large influence over the fate of these children. Their participation in the framing of the initial legisla-tion ensured that the children were legally defined as *oorlogspleegkinderen* (war foster-children) rather than *weeskinderen* (orphans). The term foster-child was usually associated with children whose family ties had been sev-ered through abandonment or neglect, yet this hardly applied to the surviving Jewish boys and girls. Furthermore, the resistance groups were also given a privileged place within the OPK. This allowed them to fulfil their own agendas while at the same time restricting Jewish participation to those who were deemed moderate.[28] The *Gereformeerde* group around chairwoman Gesina van der Molen (formerly of the *Trouw* group) was accused of imposing a one-sided view of the circumstances in which chil-dren were handed over to resistance groups, which took little or no account of the pressures on the parents. It was also accused of assuming that children 'who had had the good fortune to end up with a Christian family should not be returned to Jewish non-belief'.[29] Van der Molen put a rather different gloss on this by arguing that whatever type of family fos-tered the children, provided they were loved and well brought up, this was God's will and should not be altered unnecessarily.[30] Members of the group also voiced sentiments about the Jews having a double loyalty, being un-Dutch and not being sufficiently grateful for what had been done to save the children.[31] Those seeking to defend the work of the OPK have ques-tioned the idea that there was simply a conflict between the resistance and the post-war Jewish community by pointing out that some (assimiliationist) Jewish members of the OPK also prioritised the needs of individual chil-dren over the ideal of having them as the foundations for a new Jewish community.[32] Nonetheless, the criticism remains that the OPK with a non-Jewish majority was charged with deciding on the future guardianship and well-being of war orphans who were for the most part of Jewish origin.

The task of the OPK was in any case complicated by the extreme circumstances of the original fostering of the children. A high proportion of the Jewish war orphans had been fostered with non-Jewish families, often ones with strong Christian (Calvinist, Protestant or Roman Catholic) beliefs. They had often grown up in this environment for two years or more, completely cut off from any contact with their familial roots. Was it therefore in the children's best interests to leave them where they were, subject to the general suitability of the foster-parents, without regard for their origins or religious backgrounds? This was no more than normal handling of a social welfare problem within the terms of the Dutch legal code, but for many of the remaining Dutch Jews it failed to take account of the abnormal circumstances of the period. This view was embodied in the work of the JCC. It saw its role to reconstruct Jewish life in the Netherlands, yet one aspect of that task was, presumably, to try and reclaim all the remaining Jews in the country, and especially the all-important younger generation.

To make its case, the JCC had to argue that the circumstances were exceptional. In every legal sense, the OPK was acting in accordance with the law. There was no provision in Dutch law for the representatives of a 'community' to lay claim to orphans whose parents had been members of that 'community'. However, the debate soon drifted from purely legal to more emotive issues and even divided the members of the OPK itself. The OPK line was a straightforward one. Its task was to ensure the well-being of all the children divided from their parents by the war. By March 1946, this consisted of 680 non-Jews and 3,458 Jews. Of the Jewish children, 1,417 had been reclaimed by one or both parents, leaving a further 2,041.[33] During the occupation, these children had been fostered out to anyone prepared to risk their lives to help. At the time, little or no attention had been paid to the niceties of status, hygiene or appropriateness of the foster-parents, and this was what needed to be sorted out now that the war was over.[34] Where parents had survived after leaving their children with others, the OPK used its best offices to reunite families, but often it was the parents who had to do the searching. This was not always easy. The networks which had spirited children away from Amsterdam to the villages of the north-east did not have written records and many of their workers had been caught or had died in the interim. Where an individual child had been placed was often a question of memory rather than record. Moreover, the fact that *onderduikers*, both adult and children, had been moved around made the task even more complex. The tale of one couple who survived the occupation will have to suffice as an example.

Having given up their eight-year-old boy to a network in 1942, a Jewish couple then spent the next three years in hiding, hearing only now and then of their son's well-being. At the war's end, they set out in search of their child. They knew the codename of the woman who had helped to hide him, but she was only a courier and had no idea of where the boy had ended up. The couple then enlisted the help of a journalist from *Vrij Nederland*. Eventually they located an office clerk who had organised the reception point for the children. He knew the alias given to the child for the purposes of registration. Via a whole series of contacts as well as a few dead ends, the couple were told that the group in which their son had been placed had all been sent to a network in Sneek (Friesland) run by a local commercial traveller. Even he could not remember where the boy had been placed, but another member of the group provided the key to the mystery. The boy was found, lodged with a widow who had looked after him for the previous three years. The boy had grown up, learning about agriculture and speaking Frisian rather than Dutch! Nonetheless, he was old enough to remember his parents and the reunion was a happy one, if tinged with some sadness as the foster-mother had to give up her adoptive son of three years.[35]

Stories such as this one were probably played out in many instances where parents and children survived the war. In this case, there was no question of the boy not remembering his parents, but for smaller children this was always going to be a problem. They often had no memory of any-one other than their foster-parents and the people who arrived to claim them might as well have been strangers. While this was not an issue where the parents or family were able to claim the children, it did take on an importance for the 2,041 who were left as orphans. The OPK argued that it would not be in the children's best interest to be moved from their wartime foster-parents *just* to place them with a Jewish family.[36] Michman places this argument in a different light by pointing out that there were 'a not inconsiderable number' of children living with foster-parents who had Jewish family members willing to take on their upbringing, or whose nat-ural parents had been so strongly Jewish that it would be unthinkable for the children to be placed in a non-Jewish environment.[37] This was the crux of the matter. Should these children be automatically reclaimed by the Jewish community and be placed in families with a religious affiliation appropriate to that of their parents? Clearly members of the Jewish minor-ity on the board of the OPK thought that this should be done, but they were overruled. The majority of the OPK argued that, in Dutch law, the Jewish community had no special rights over the children,[38] and it was also unhappy about handing over all the children to a community whose repre-sentatives were supposedly dominated by the orthodox Zionists. This, it was argued, would be like handing over all Lutheran and liberal Protestant orphans to the orthodox Calvinists.[39] The arguments raged on. The split within the OPK became so serious that on 17 July 1946 the Jewish minor-ity withdrew.[40] The JCC saw the non-Jewish majority on the OPK as an insult, if not a conspiracy, given that 84 per cent of all the orphans were of Jewish origin. Moreover, it claimed that the OPK saw assimilation as the ultimate goal for these orphans and viewed Zionism as alien and 'un-Dutch'.[41] The OPK claims that only 18 of 192 cases dealt with involving Jewish children with non-Jewish foster-parents were dismissed as being unrepresentative of what would happen to the bulk of the 2,041 children involved.[42] It was noted that all the cases of children with non-Jewish foster-parents were in overtly Christian households and the OPK's detractors speculated as to the outcry if children from orthodox Calvinist backgrounds had been treated in this way. The charge was that not only were the OPK attempting to have these Jewish orphans assimilated into Dutch society, but were also keen to have them converted to Christianity. The argument put forward by some of the networks which had saved the children, that 90 per cent of the Jewish parents did not want their children to be given an orthodox upbringing, was also dismissed given that this did not represent a rejection of Judaism as a whole.[43] The Minister of Justice had to set up a separate commission to sort the dispute out.[44] It decided that children from overtly Jewish backgrounds should be placed with Jewish families unless there were educational or psychological difficulties. Moreover, in cases of dispute, the minority view would be entitled to send a separate report to the court responsible.[45] This was agreed by all sides and the minority group returned to continue their work with the OPK in February 1947. Criticism of some OPK decisions reappeared in the Jewish press, together with public protests in 1949,[46] but the organisation was shut down soon afterwards and its remaining work transferred to the Minors Protection Board of Amsterdam. During its operation, it oversaw the decisions on the guardianship of 1,363 children. Some 359 were still unresolved on is dissolution and of the remaining 1,004, 601 went to Jewish households and 403 to non-Jewish households.[47]

With the benefit of 50-year hindsight, it is possible to view the arguments more objectively. Given the basic aims of both sides, conflict over the orphans and their future was inevitable. The OPK, basing its policies on Dutch law and its interpretation of the childrens' best interests, was bound to collide with the JCC doing everything in its power to restore Jewish life in the Netherlands.[48] Both had honourable objectives and acted from the best of motives as they saw them. However, the conflict which arose served to highlight both official suspicions about the nature of post-war Dutch Zionism on the one hand, and the assimilationist and perhaps even proselytising objectives of the OPK on the other. At the root of this conflict was the unwillingness of the OPK or the Dutch government in general to make a special case of the Jews and to accept that their specific suffering warranted exceptional treatment. Their view was that post-war Dutch society should not recognise denominational differences. Resistance organisations, sometimes represented by Calvinists on the OPK, also felt they had a stake in determining the future of the children that they had helped to save and were less than enthusiastic about a (Zionist) Jewish community which used racial definitions to claim back the children. For some this smacked of a return to the phraseology of the Nazi oppressors. Conversely, the remains of Dutch Jewry found it hard to understand this rejection of their special circumstances. One construction was that the state was attempting to hide its own role in collaborating with (or at least failing to defend against) the destruction of Dutch Jewry during the occupation. In effect, the refusal to treat the Jews as a special case, and as a definable community, meant that many rights which had been available in the 1930s were actually lost in the post-war era.[49]

Nor did the conflict entirely subside when the work of placement was complete. Legitimate attempts to reclaim children were in some cases baulked by erstwhile foster-parents. The most famous case of this nature concerned a Jewish infant girl called Anneke Beekman. In early 1943, her parents had attempted to find their 2½-year-old daughter a safe hiding place as German raids increased. Through an intermediary, Anneke was placed with the five van Moorst sisters in Hilversum. Devoutly religious, the sisters kept a Roman Catholic rest home. Both parents perished at Sobibor during the summer of 1943, but some of the child's relatives survived, and they asked the JCC's guardianship organisation, *Le-Ezrath Ha-Jeled*,[50] to ensure that Anneke was raised in a Jewish home.[51] In July 1946 the OPK recommended that she be transferred to a Jewish foster-family as the van Moorsts did not constitute a 'normal' family. This advice was passed to the courts and a potential foster-family found. However, the van Moorsts clearly intended to keep the child. First the sisters hid their charge and then obtained a guardianship order from the Amsterdam District Court. This was overturned on appeal and backed up by the Supreme Court. On 3 May 1950 *Le-Ezrath Ha-Jeled* was awarded guardianship, but when detectives went to the van Moorst's house the child was no longer there. Her fate, and that of another Jewish orphan girl, Rebecca Meljado, remained a matter for the courts until a parallel case in France was reported in the Dutch press during 1953. In this case, French Jewry had used every means at its disposal to find two young Jewish boys who were being hidden by their wartime foster-parents. This publicity and a reawakening of press interest in the Beekman affair forced the Jewish organisations to consider their position. Should they continue to use the low-key methods of legal remedy to try and obtain the child (which had thus far failed to work), or should they adopt the more direct and forceful methods of their French co-religionists (which seemed to produce results)? Inevitably, the resultant debate produced all the familiar arguments – about whether the Jewish community could press its case to the limit (as any other section of Dutch society might do and with the moral imperative of Holocaust survival to assist them) without it provoking an adverse reaction in Dutch society.[52]

The continued press interest in the case and a more active response from the JCC, including letters to the Queen, cabinet and acting Roman Catholic Archbishop of Utrecht, did produce some results. While the Queen and cabinet expressed themselves happy with the measures taken, the acting Archbishop did suggest to the van Moorst sisters that they should not see it as their duty as Catholics to hang on to the child. However, it was the police who, in concert with Belgian colleagues, raided a convent in Sint Truiden (Belgium) on 13 March 1954, finding Rebecca Meljado and ascertaining that Anneke Beekman had also been kept there. This undermined the Catholic hierarchy's claim that it had no direct interest or involvement in the matter. At the very least, some members of the clergy had been involved in hiding these two girls in contravention of the law. The defence put forward by the Catholic hierarchy in the Netherlands, that the Jewish community were 'persecuting and hounding' a child whose will had been so clearly been made apparent, served only to outrage and polarise opinion still further.[53] In Protestant circles, support was split between those who wished to see the orders of the courts carried out, and those who preferred a settlement which encompassed the status quo with the Jewish organisations giving up their claim to guardianship. Although two of the van Moorst sisters were condemned (initially *in absentia*) to terms of imprisonment by Dutch courts, Anneke Beekman did not return to the Netherlands until she reached the age of majority. By that stage, there was no doubt that she would remain a Catholic and reporters' questions also made it clear that she knew little or nothing of the Jewish faith or the fate of her co-religionists during the occupation. The court proceedings and published documents demonstrated clearly that the Catholic hierarchy had played more of a role in the affair than its Archbishop was prepared to admit, but the case was ultimately laid to rest when mej. Beekman married a Frenchman in 1962.

It could be argued that the Jewish community was somewhat tardy in standing up for its rights in this case. Certainly its organisations chose not to seek a full enforcement of their legal rights until pushed by external factors. The traditional reticence of the community in making a case to Dutch society as a whole, which was so clearly visible in the 1930s, remained apparent in the 1950s. Moreover, the Zionist element which might have pushed for a higher-profile response had been weakened by the emigration of many of its leaders to Israel in the late 1940s. Yet in spite of this, the community organisations did ultimately make a stand. In 1949 Professor Kisch, a Jewish member of the OPK, made a scathing attack on the whole process, arguing that it had been too rigid in defining who was 'sufficiently Jewish' to be returned to a Jewish environment.

The Jewish community cannot help suspecting that, in the matter of the war foster children, they have been treated with less consideration than a minority had once upon a time the right to expect. This is no new experience. But the honourable Dutch tradition by which each denomination, regardless of its size, has a right to be defined within its own identifying criteria, has been lost sight of.[54]

Five years later, the community published a white book (*witboek*) in 1954 to state its case on the Beekman affair.[55] As Fishman has pointed out, 'the appearance of the Witboek did not have a decisive effect on public opinion ... Neverthless, it is a valuable historical document; its importance lies in its very existence.'[56] In essence, this was the community making a public statement in defence of its rights under the law.

By 1949, most of the Jewish war orphans had been placed by the OPK. Of the 2,041, some 1,500 were placed in Jewish foster-homes or taken to Israel. Only around 500 were left with non-Jewish families, and even some of these subsequently returned to Judaism in adult life.[57] But the numbers are not the issue here. The question of Jewish war orphans became a matter of how the Dutch state and society was going to react to the issues of recompense and compensation for its remaining Jewish citizens, and how the residual Jewish community was going to position itself in the post-war world. The cases of Anneke Beekman and Rebecca Meljado merely served to prove what a painful and complex process this was to be.

The restoration of Jewish property

During 1943, the Dutch government-in-exile, being well aware of the ways in which the Germans were plundering the Dutch economy, associated themselves with an Allied declaration which reserved the right to annul all transactions on property and business rights apparently carried out under duress. In the Dutch case, this was given legislative form by the Decree for the Restoration of Legal Transactions, usually referred to as E100. This measure effectively created a framework and an administrative machinery under the control of the Ministry of Justice to deal with the legal problems created by the occupation and the activities of the occupiers and their collaborators.[58]

Within this wider context, the restoration or restitution of Jewish property and assets was fraught with specific difficulties. These manifested themselves at a number of different levels. The experiences of Jews returning to the Netherlands from the camps in the East or from hiding inside the country were far from uniform. Attempts to reclaim dwellings and property met with widely differing responses from both neighbours and the local authorities. Some dwellings had been left empty after the departure of their owners but others had either been occupied by the Germans or sold on or let to third parties. Thus the returnee had no guarantee of being able to go 'home' immediately – or at all. The question of moveable assets was even more problematic. The Germans had contrived to remove

huge quantities of Jewish-owned property with willing assistance from the
Puls removal firm. Seeing this happen, many later deportees had attempted
to place their belongings in the hands of friends and neighbours for safe-
keeping, often at short notice, in the hope that they would return to
recover them at some future date. Reports about the response of these
guardians after the liberation were, perhaps not surprisingly, mixed. Some
were genuinely delighted to see their friends come back – returning property and possessions and engaging in all manner of kindnesses to ensure the
best possible homecoming. Others were at best indifferent or at worst hostile. There were those who returned property only grudgingly, perhaps
upset that the owners had survived to reclaim what was theirs. Cases also
came to light where people who had been given furniture, clothes or other
assets to store denied all knowledge of them, in spite of physical evidence
to the contrary.[59] In such matters, the authorities usually claimed to be
powerless, as there were seldom any written agreements between the parties, and any verbal understandings were usually unwitnessed and open to
differing interpretations. Some people had given over their property in the
hope that they might return, for others it had been a gesture of defiance
against the Germans – giving away their property to others rather than
allowing it to fall into the hands of the oppressor. Whatever the wishes of
the donors, and in spite of the cases where people did come back to claim
their property, it must be concluded that a good deal of the goods and
assets left by those deported remained unclaimed in the hands of those to
whom they had been given.

Needless to say, the question of this type of moveable property created
a good deal of bad feeling among the returnees faced with the intransigence or ill-will of those whom they had regarded as friends and neighbours. However, disputes of this type were only one aspect of the much
wider problem, namely that of all the assets owned or held by Jews before
1941 and subsequently subject to forced sales or confiscated by the
German authorities. This served to involve the post-war Dutch state in
finding solutions to some extraordinarily complex legal questions. In
essence, the problems can be grouped under three headings. The first was
to identify the legal heirs and successors to estates of those who had been
deported and murdered. In some cases, this included attempts to ascertain
whether children had been killed before or after their parents in order to
see whether they had become – albeit briefly and unknowingly – the lega-
tees of their parents as this directly affected the nature of the inheritance.
One example was of a Rotterdam Jewish family hidden by a woman for six
months in 1943. Having been betrayed, the father managed to smuggle a
letter to the woman bequeathing her an estate of around fl.60,000. After
the liberation, this was contested by a brother and sister of the man who,
with his family, had perished in Sobibor. However, the courts ruled that as
a son had survived his father for a period of around two weeks in the

camp, the father's wishes had to be respected and the relatives were entitled only to the legitimate inheritance of the son and the rest should go to the woman who had hidden them.[60] Surviving children also became an issue, especially when they were the offspring of 'mixed' couples unable to marry because of German racial laws. Could they inherit the estate of their subsequently murdered father? Similar problems arose with 'mixed' couples who had divorced in order to protect the non-Jewish partner. Could the survivor nevertheless inherit the estate? In such cases, the authorities found in favour of the children and the remaining partners but often after some considerable delay.[61]

These cases serve to highlight the essential problems faced by the state when the rule of Dutch law was restored. How could the post-war legal establishment use 'normal' criteria to regulate, legislate for, or attempt to reverse actions carried out in the extraordinary climate of the German occupation? In this first example, there was only the legal question of inheritance and whether a person was entitled to an estate. A second complication arose where the apparent wishes of Holocaust victims, either as wills, or other, more informal expressions of intent, were challenged by interested parties. Wishes expressed in letters and other forms of unofficial testament had to be examined carefully to ensure that they were both genuine and uncoerced. Herein lay the crux of the issue: could any or all of the decisions taken by Jews during the occupation and under the threat of property sequestration or deportation be regarded as free choices? Even agreements which appeared to have the force of law behind them could not necessarily be taken at face value. Some lawyers and notaries had been known to collude in fraud and thus every piece of evidence had to be carefully screened. The burden of this task fell on the *Afdeling Rechtspraak* (Department for the Administration of Justice) whose various regional chambers dealt with all the legal complications caused by the German occupation. As de Jong points out, no group in society had undergone such systematic injustice as the Jews,[62] and the *Afdeling Rechtspraak* had to expend a good deal of time and effort trying to piece together evidence from the shattered Jewish community in an attempt to see that some form of justice was done.

These first two forms of legal problem arose out of Jews who had made more or less free choices about the disposal of their assets. An entirely different and far more extensive problem was that of assets stolen or sequestered by the German authorities. In general terms they can be categorised under two headings. Firstly, there were the businesses, property and life assurance policies seized by the *Vermögensverwaltung und Rentenanstalt* (Property and Revenue Administration Organisation, VVRA). Secondly, there were the moveable assets: money, cheques, stocks, shares and securities, gold, silver, precious stones, artworks, antiques, and the deeds of ownership to vehicles, boats and horses. All of these were

accumulated by the Germans using Lippmann-Rosenthal as a front. This
was no more or less than theft, although the 'depositors', of whom there
were to be around 13,000, all had separate accounts. In fact, the Germans
took steps to realise the value of all these assets. The 'Omnia'
Treuhandgesellschaft (trust company) was reputedly responsible for the sale
of nearly 2,000 Jewish firms to new non-Jewish owners, and the liquida-
tion of a further 10,000 – presumably involving the sale of company assets
and machinery. Of the 19,000 pieces of land and property seized in this
way, 8,000 had been officially sold to non-Jews by October of 1943.
Mortgages owned by Jews were sold and life assurance policies redeemed.
It was estimated that the total realised by these sales amounted to around
fl.410 million.[63]

After the liberation, offices were set up to administer the workings of
the VVRA and Lippmann-Rosenthal in order that property and assets
seized or held by them might be returned to their surviving rightful owners. However, the task was far from simple. Many of the assets had been
liquidated and the proceeds used to fund the building and maintenance of
the concentration camps in the Netherlands and the deportation costs of
the Jews. These had been entirely lost. Other assets were held in the form
of German treasury bills which had been rendered worthless by the collapse of the Third Reich. Much of this loss was made good indirectly from
Dutch state funds, although not without some problems. Only in 1952 did
the liquidators of the VVRA and Lippmann-Rosenthal receive the final
restitution payments at which point they were able to meet 85 per cent and
90 per cent respectively of the total claims made against them.[64] More
complex still were the problems associated with businesses which had been
transferred rather than sold. How could they be returned to the rightful
owners? Moreover, if the business were handed back, how were the
wartime purchasers to be compensated (if at all) and what was to happen
to the profits from trade during the period when the original owners had
been (illegally) deprived of their rights? The question of the life assurance
policies was dealt with by insisting that the companies concerned restore
the rights of policy-holders or their heirs provided that all premiums were
paid up to date, and that the companies submit their claims to compensation
to the liquidators of Lippmann-Rosenthal. The 8,000 pieces of Jewish land
and property sold during the occupation were, by rights, to be returned
to their owners, but who was to bear the cost of this? If the property had
been bought direct from the Germans' selling agency, the *Niederländische
Grundstücksverwaltung* (Dutch Landed Property Administration), or via
another German or collaborationist Dutch organisation, then the answer
was simple, the present owner would merely be instructed to hand the
property back. However, there were many legitimate cases where the land
or property had been sold on to people unaware that they were purchasing
assets sequestered from Jews. In these cases, the principle still applied that

the original owner had the right to repossess, but it could also be agreed that the original owner be compensated by the full market value. In either case, the last buyer could claim compensation from the assets of Lippmann-Rosenthal.[65]

All of these matters had to be heard and decided upon by the *Afdeling Rechtspraak*, but what became the most difficult and contentious issue, namely restitution for the stocks, shares and securities sold by the Germans, was placed in the hands of a separate authority, the *Afdeling Effectenregistratie van de Raad voor het Rechtsherstel* (Securities Registration Department for the Council for Legal Restitution). The E100 law had stated that all illegal seizures of property had to be reversed, meaning that all shares and securities should have been been returned to their Jewish owners, unless the post-war owners could show that they had acquired them in good faith in the course of normal trading. In many cases this did appear possible as such securities had often passed through several hands since their initial appearance on the market, and the task was made simpler by a further government decree in November 1945 which accepted that stocks and securities bought at public sales or at the stock exchange were to be deemed as *bona fide* acquisitions.[66] In effect, this shifted the onus from the present owners to prove their good faith to the previous owners having to demonstrate bad faith. While an owner buying direct from one of the four stock market dealers acting for Lippmann-Rosenthal could not really claim ignorance, subsequent purchasers would have a case. The problem was how to track down the stolen securities, define what was meant by good faith and normal trading, and then arrange for appropriate restitution or compensation for the original owners. All of these tasks proved difficult. The registration produced a total of around 20 million shares and a total of 154,000 ownership claims[67] – claims which it took many years to settle. The real problems arose in trying to interfere in the normal post-war capital markets and to allocate losses to those traders deemed to have acted in bad faith by selling securities which they had known to be stolen. For the Jews trying to claim back assets, the result was often a negative one which changed their claim for restitution from the current owners to one of compensation against Lippmann-Rosenthal.

The *Afdeling Rechtspraak* continued in operation until 1967, dealing with over 13,500 cases. Its counterpart, the *Afdeling Effectenregistratie*, lasted four years longer, being finally wound up in 1971. Van Schie noted that the fundamental problem was that both sides (pre-war and post-war owners) thought they had justice on their side when it came to questions of settling ownership. He argues that the one flaw in the process was its speed. This might have been substantially remedied if the government had chosen to take over the claims of the dispossessed and thus cushion the process of restitution with public funds. However, such a remedy was probably not a practical alternative, given the demands on the post-war public purse for economic reconstruction and the attempted retrieval of an East Indian empire.[68] While it is impossible to be precise about the efficiency or effectiveness of the operation as a whole, de Jong concludes that although there were complaints, there were no gross miscarriages of justice. The post-war laws did act as a base for restitution, and once the terminology had been ironed out so that those forced to sell their assets were also compensated, and the defence of good faith removed from any transactions with Lippmann-Rosenthal or its agents, the procedures operated smoothly, if not particularly quickly. Nevertheless, some banks, insurance companies and even government departments did still have to be 'persuaded' by the courts to do the right thing. Moreover, the discrimination against German Jewish refugees from the pre-war era continued. Although they had lost their citizenship in 1941, they were still treated as enemy nationals by the post-war Dutch government.

This handling of financial matters as they affected Jews seems to contrast with the rather offhand way they were treated by the authorities in other respects. A number of explanations might be advanced for this. Was it that the whole question of restitution was dealt with more expeditiously because it affected the whole of society and not just the remaining Jewish community – even if they were the prime beneficiaries? Was it the case that the prime considerations were either the regularisation of Dutch financial markets or the reclamation of assets from the Germans – with private claims for compensation being a part of the equation? Was it just that regularising financial markets and commerce formed part of the return to the rule of Dutch law and favoured the interests of the Jews in the Netherlands whereas making a special social or political case from them tended to conflict with that same law? These may seem very functional explanations, but the conclusion seems to be that the state was happier dealing with financial rather than social questions, happier dealing with the interests of property rather than the person, more at ease dealing with the interests of the middle classes than those of the dispossessed.

'Jewish collaboration'

One final issue remains to be discussed: the treatment of Jews who were perceived to have played some role in the destruction of their co-religionists. It has already been noted that some Jews were tried and condemned by the post-war Dutch state for their part in betraying others to the Gestapo or units like the Henneicke-*Colonne*. Yet five members of the Jewish Council had also survived the war and returned to the Netherlands, including Abraham Asscher and David Cohen. The question therefore arose: should they be punished for the complicity of the Council in the deportation and ultimate destruction of so many of their fellow Jews? Certainly, there were enough returning survivors from the camps to make the case. The Council and its officials had collaborated with the Germans and this was at least worthy of censure, if not treasonable. Attaching blame to Jewish actions was nonetheless extremely problematic. Unlike the rest of Dutch society, the Jews had been under almost permanent threat from the Germans. Who was to say what was 'proper' behaviour for those placed in such a situation? Yet if any purges were to take place, some criteria needed to be established.

Two separate attempts were made to address this issue. In the highly charged atmosphere of post-war Jewish society, there was a desire that the Jewish leaders during the occupation should be brought to account. Two of the five surviving members of the Council had taken up positions in Jewish organisations, while many of its leading functionaries had also reappeared in both Jewish and non-Jewish social associations. Nevertheless, the debate became focused almost exclusively on Asscher and Cohen. They, and they alone, became the representatives of Jewish collaboration during the occupation.[69] In the early months of 1946, the Contact Commission of the JCC discussed the creation of an *Ereraad* (Jewish Court of Honour) to examine the behaviour of those who were thought culpable in having acted against Jewish interests.[70] Enthusiasm for this was limited to three groups: returned deportees, former (critical) Jewish Council employees, and students from the *Gemeente Universiteit Amsterdam* where Cohen taught ancient history. At the time, doubts were expressed about the legitimacy of this *Ereraad*, especially by those being investigated. Could the Contact Commission be regarded as fully representing the whole of Dutch Jewry? The situation was further complicated by the re-establishment of the *Nederlandse-Israëlietische Kerkgenootschap* (Dutch-Jewish Religious Community) and of a Permanent Commission which functioned as a national body. These organisations were reconstituted at almost the same moment that the *Ereraad* was being set up, and theoretically had greater authority to organise such a tribunal. Nonetheless, the plans went ahead – and with the tacit or active support of most established Jewish organisations. Finding a panel of 'impartial' court members was inevitably problematic. How could any Dutch Jews have been unaffected by the events of 1940–45, or not have come into contact with the activities of those to be investigated? Anyone who had worked for the Jewish Council or had received an exemption stamp was automatically excluded and the only people considered as appropriate participants were those who had survived underground. Asscher and Cohen could not expect to be judged by fellow surviving members of the old elite.[71] In spite of this, a group was assembled which set out criteria for procedures and areas to be investigated. Judgements were to be made on those whose behaviour was thought to have been detrimental to their fellow Jews.[72] Inevitably, Cohen and Asscher were to be its main focus, although the *Ereraad* did examine the conduct of 21 other people, including two who were investigated at their own request.

Asscher refused to recognise the authority of the *Ereraad* and had nothing to do with its proceedings. Cohen's response was more circumspect. He adopted a cautious policy, boycotting the first meetings of the tribunal, but suddenly attending on 15 December 1946 and, flanked by his lawyer, agreeing to an investigation of his conduct. His change of heart may have been primarily the result of pressures from outside. There had been a good deal of opposition to his resuming his chair at Amsterdam University, and the Minister of Education was on record as saying that he would not want Cohen's conduct to be investigated by a state tribunal but felt that this was a task for his Dutch co-religionists.[73] It does appear that Cohen's change of mind owed more to the threat to his professional position than to any change of view about the constitution or processes of the *Ereraad* itself. Hearings continued into the early months of 1947 but ground to a halt in May. Changes of tribunal personnel complicated matters, but the chairman was anxious to bring matters to a close. No further action occurred until October, when it appears that the *Ereraad* had prepared a judgement which awaited adjustment in the light of final defence pleas. However, it was at this moment that other events intervened.

Up to November 1947, it seemed that the Dutch authorities were unwilling to proceed against any former members of the Jewish Council. In March of that year, an inspector of the *Politieke Recherche Afdeling* (Political Investigation Department, PRA) made a statement in a leading Dutch newspaper that there was nothing in his files on the joint-chairmen of the Jewish Council which gave any credence to the charge that they had deliberately planned the deportation of their co-religionists.[74] The PRA had conducted several interviews with the two men, but had found no evidence that they had intentionally assisted the enemy. In effect, the officials responsible seemed content to allow the matter to rest. Thus it came as a tremendous shock to all concerned when, some eight months later, the *Procureur-Fiscaal* of the Special Court of Amsterdam, *mr.* N.J. G. Sikkel, ordered the arrest of both men on the grounds of their activities during the war. Having been involved in investigations of the wartime conduct of leading civil servants, he had occasion to demand the PRA file on the Jewish Council on 10 June 1947. At the same time, he also received further information, most notably from an interrogation of Willi Lages who claimed that 'without the Jewish Council we would not have achieved anything'.[75] However, no one has thus far produced a complete explanation for the arrests. Sikkel argued that the evidence already existed to indict the two men, yet this flew in the face of public statements made by the PRA. It was possible that new material or new complaints had made a difference, but there was nothing to suggest that there was a coherent case to be answered. An attempt on 17 October to interview the two men in turn and to have the 'blockhead' Asscher incriminate the 'sly fox' Cohen backfired when Asscher failed to appear, claiming he was delayed by business matters.[76]

Even if the frustration of this ploy was one possible reason, the arrest order still seems to have been made more or less on impulse, although Sikkel had tried to sound out opinion beforehand. He had contacted a leading Jewish jurist A. Belinfante, who had in turn passed him on to Professor Kisch of Amsterdam University as being more in tune with Jewish opinion. Kisch's response had been to say that if Sikkel had grounds for proceeding against the two men, he should not stay his hand. Certainly Kisch was aware of the continued strength of feeling against the former chairmen of the Jewish Council in certain Amsterdam Jewish circles, but he refused to testify directly against either Asscher or Cohen.[77] Whether this response encouraged Sikkel to act cannot be proved, yet clearly he was trying to assess the potential reaction to his proposed action. After the arrests on 6 November 1947, there was an 'invasion' of the RIOD offices by squads of investigators looking for material on the Jewish Council.[78] These were not the actions of a man sure of his ground.

In the event, the arrests backfired. Sikkel had no real legal grounds for holding the two, and the justifications for having taken them into custody were almost laughable – that the investigations had reached the stage where their continued liberty was detrimental. As was pointed out, if the two had wanted to skip the country, concoct stories or influence witnesses, they had already had more than two years in which to do so. The press reaction was almost unanimous in its condemnation. On 4 December the Minister of Justice had to answer in the *Tweede Kamer* for the actions of his subordinate and intimated that he knew in advance of the action being contemplated. However, he also made it clear that the two men would be released within the week.[79] This official intervention inevitably complicated the proceedings of the *Ereraad*. The lawyers involved realised that their positions might be compromised if legal action was taken against their clients. Although the two men were released on 7 December, the investigation and the threat of legal action remained. This did not prevent the *Ereraad* from publishing its judgement in the *Nieuw Israëlietisch Weekblad* on 26 December 1947. It concluded that the conduct of the two chairmen during the German occupation had been blameworthy in four cases and severely blameworthy in a fifth.[80] They were judged culpable of having formed the Jewish Council at the behest of the Germans, having published the newspaper *Het Joodsche Weekblad*, having been complicit in the introduction of the Jewish star, and having sent out the instructions for Jews to go to Westerbork. They were considered severely culpable of having co-operated with the selections for deportation. The 'sentence' of the *Ereraad* was that both men should be banned from holding any office in any Jewish organisation for the remainder of their lives.[81] As both had long since given up any such office, the verdict was in effect only a moral censure.[82]

This action did nothing to end the affair. By making its judgement public, the *Ereraad* had opened up the whole debate to public scrutiny. It was accused of ignoring the principles of the law and of natural justice in its procedures. Certainly, the later conduct of the *Ereraad* in its judgements on other people did not suggest that proper and detailed consideration was given to the collection or evaluation of evidence. The official investigation continued, taking testimony from 109 witnesses, including convicted German functionaries held in the prison at Breda. However, on 23 May 1950 the Minister of Justice decided to let the case drop, 'in the public interest', but that this should not be seen as exonerating those accused.[83] On 26 July 1951 Cohen was finally, officially informed that the case against him was being closed (Asscher had died in the interim). By this stage, both the government and the public at large had grown tired of the wartime events. No one was interested in opening old wounds. If Asscher and Cohen had been guilty of crimes (and their stated defence of their behaviour was in many instances less than convincing), any attempt to begin judicial processes against Jews when so many non-Jewish collaborators were being quietly allowed to reassimilate themselves into Dutch society had become more or less unthinkable.

The legal and quasi-legal 'remedies' taken against the chairmen of the Jewish Council were uniformly unsatisfactory. The absence of legal action against Asscher and Cohen may have dissatisfied many in Jewish circles, but no post-war government had the strength or moral authority to take such a step against the wartime representatives of a people who had suffered so much more under German occupation than any of their Dutch fellow citizens. Conversely, the lack of official proceedings also denied the men a chance to defend themselves in public. Cohen's published memoirs dealt exclusively with his work for refugee relief in the pre-war period, although he did subsequently dictate a memoir of 140 pages on the occupation period.[84] He also continued to defend his conduct in private. A letter to James G. McDonald (former League of Nations High Commissioner for Refugees) in 1953 is instructive of his view of his own conduct. The word 'duty' appears often. On the formation of the Jewish Council, 'I think I acted in the right way', and crucially on the true nature of the deportations:

> Of course we [he and Asscher] did not know which [*sic*] really was the fate of those who had been transported (I was told about it for the first time in the spring of 1945 at Theresienstadt); otherwise we should have resigned immediately.[85]

Until his death, Cohen continued to maintain that, although some mistakes had been made, he had done his duty to the community he served. Others continued to take a different view. The conflict between the supporters of Asscher and Cohen and their detractors, or more properly between Herzberg and Kisch, was reignited after Cohen's death. In 1967 Herzberg went on the offensive, claiming that Sikkel had admitted his antisemitism (born of his father's missionary work among the poor Jews of Amsterdam) in an interview.[86] Moreover, he also attacked Presser, who had been saved three times by the Jewish Council, but who now wished to speak on behalf of those who were unprotected and deported. In the following years, he and Kisch continued their acrimonious debate in the academic press as the works of de Jong and Sijes began to appear in the public domain.[87]

Post-war antisemitism

One final aspect of the post-war period is worthy of consideration here, namely the manifestations of antisemitism catalogued by nearly every writer on the subject, both Jewish and non-Jewish. Those emerging from hiding, such as Jacob Presser, or returning from the camps in the East could recount remarks made, in the street or in company, detrimental to the Jews or cite practical examples of discrimination in the first months after the liberation. This has been the subject of an extensive study by Dienke Hondius, and it is her conclusions which form the basis for what follows. Antisemitism at a mild, informal and cultural level had been apparent in Dutch society before the occupation, and may even have been growing. German regulations in the early part of the occupation merely served to reinforce the picture of the Jews as an 'apart' group, after which they were progressively removed from Dutch society altogether. Those prepared to flout German laws and help Jews were undoubtedly in the minority and for most people the victims of Nazi racial policies represented a threat to their law-abiding lifestyle. Even during the occupation, stories of *onderduikers* betraying their hosts or behaving badly were commonplace. Thus even in these extreme conditions, the victims were never perceived as entirely worthy of charity and help. In the first post-war months there seems to have been an unwillingness or inability on the part of many Dutch men and women to accept what had become of the tens of thousands of Jews deported from the Netherlands who had not returned. (This was reinforced by governmental refusal to treat them as a special case.) This non-acceptance can be explained in a number of ways. The Dutch people as a whole had come through the occupation with a series of collective experiences. These included the privations of the hunger-winter, the material losses sustained through German edicts (confiscations and forced labour), and the existence of a national resistance. These experiences became the common currency of conversation after the liberation, but their content paled into insignificance when compared with the privations of those in hiding, or the stories of those who returned from the

camps. Individual tales of confiscated bicycles had no place alongside those
of mass murder. In this way, there was resistance to accepting that the
Jewish experience of the occupation had been far worse, both because it
diminished the importance of the shared experience, and because it ques-
tioned the efficacy of the resistance in having been able to counteract
German plans.

This non-acceptance allowed the cultural antisemitism of the 1930s to
reappear and even to take more virulent forms. While there were examples
of Jews being well-treated and of people going out of their way to provide
help and assistance, it has been argued that the negative experiences far
outweighed the positive ones.[88] There were numerous examples of bureaucratic correctness, for example with insurance companies who cancelled
policies because the holders, who had gone undergound or been deported,
had not kept up the premiums. Job discrimination, statements that Jews
should be grateful to be allowed to live in the Netherlands (and should
therefore know their place), apparent envy of Jews' possessions, and use of
Nazi racial terminology were all manifest in these months. Unedifying as
these reactions undoubtedly were, they do need to be put into context, as
Hondius herself makes clear. While antisemitism did re-emerge, it was not
primarily a product of the occupation, but a continuation of something
apparent in pre-war Dutch society. Moreover, the sentiments expressed
could often be reinterpreted as primarily motivated by material envy or
general anti-foreigner resentment rather than specifically racist antisemitism. It may also have been the case that such behaviour and comments were more visible and audible in the circumstances of the
post-occupation world.

Certainly the Jews who survived and attempted to assimilate into society
had to do so as individuals.[89] There was no longer any real semblance of a
Jewish community on which to depend. Indeed, it could be argued that the
survivors were actually attempting something which Jews (as Jews) had
never been able to achieve before, namely assimilation into mainstream
Dutch society. Certainly, the Jewish communities had been integrated into
pre-war Dutch society, but individuals who had become part of the mainstream had done so mainly by denying or downplaying their Jewish origins. In the post-war era, the survivors could not remain in their own
circle, as they had done before 1940, simply because that circle no longer
existed. It is therefore possible to argue that the vertically structured nature
of Dutch society made this transition and acceptance even more difficult
than might have been the case otherwise. For the most part, the surge in
antisemitism in the Netherlands did not last for long. As the true nature of
what had happened in the East became apparent and accepted, so the voic-
ing of antisemitic sentiments became increasingly unacceptable, but the
reconstruction of even the semblance of Jewish communities in the
Netherlands was to take a great deal longer.

All three case studies given here demonstrate the post-war Dutch state's desire to treat the Jews in exactly the same way as other Dutch citizens, even where the experiences and circumstances of the Jews had undoubtedly been exceptional. The legal settlement of Jewish property and guardianship of Jewish orphans was placed in the hands of courts and organisations which dealt with both Jewish and non-Jewish matters. Given the complexity of many such cases, it was almost inevitable that their resolution would drag on for many years, although the guardianship issue perhaps highlights the extent to which the refusal of special status for 'Jewish' claims was taken. Charges of Jewish collaboration with the Germans were always likely to be a hot potato for the authorities. Few such cases came before the courts and these were clear-cut examples. The attempted legal action taken against Asscher and Cohen must primarily be seen as the work of an isolated individual within the legal establishment. All the other evidence suggests that the state had no interest in investigating the activities of the Jewish Council and its functionaries any more carefully than other government departments, civil servants, organisations and individuals (whom the authorities wished to protect). In this case, the dictum of no special case ensured (the activities of *mr.* Sikkel aside) that evaluation of the Jewish Council and its leaders was left to the residual Jewish community, journalists and historians. The works of their supporters and detractors have served to keep the whole debate on the role of the Council and on the wider issues connected with Dutch Jewish mortality during the occupation alive to the present day.

The ways in which the returning and re-emerging Jews were treated in the Netherlands does not make an edifying spectacle and demonstrates little of which the post-war Dutch state can be proud. While it is impossible to condone the actions of the Dutch state, its servants, or society as a whole, the issue has to be placed in context. The country had been under foreign domination for five years. That domination had been increasingly oppressive and had created colossal problems for post-war government. The question of the deported Jews was only one among many thousands of issues which needed resolution. Crucially, the murder of around 100,000 Jews from the Netherlands did not immediately register in the official mind (whether by accident or design). As a result, the Jews were not considered as a special case and the true story of the camps only began to emerge in the months after the final liberation – by which time the bureaucratic processes used to handle returnees had run their course. Perhaps more damaging was the delay in dealing with questions of Jewish orphans and Jewish property. These were undoubtedly complex legal matters, but again the refusal to make them a special case almost certainly delayed matters. In sum, none of this can excuse the conduct of the Dutch authorities, but it may at least go some way to explaining it.

A final judgement on the behaviour of the post-war Dutch state requires some reference to what took place in other parts of Western Europe. In Belgium and France, the circumstances were somewhat different. Earlier liberation gave more time to prepare for returnees from camps in Germany and the East. It does appear that both Paris and Brussels *were* better organised but also less concerned about the potential for mass immigration. As a result, the bureaucratic formalism of the Dutch was not repeated at the French or Belgian frontiers. This difference may owe more to the longer-term traditions of the respective states than to the objective conditions pertaining in 1944–45. In the case of Belgium, the government took positive steps to rebuild the Antwerp Jewish community in order to reconstruct the diamond industry, recalling those who had fled as refugees and permitting immigration from Eastern Europe.[90] Although all three states had to deal with individual Jewish 'traitors' and informers,[91] only the Netherlands was faced with having to judge the behaviour of a Jewish Council and its surviving leaders. Similarly, only the Netherlands had seen the wholesale destruction of its Jewish population. The survival of around 55 per cent of the Jews in Belgium and 75 per cent in France meant that there were community and former resistance organisations capable of taking on the process of reconstruction and catering for returnees and orphans. The tragedy in the Netherlands was there were so few remaining Jews to pick up the pieces and begin the process of rebuilding.[92]

|12|

Conclusion

In the first major historical works on the Holocaust, the high Jewish mortality in the Netherlands was often attributed to one or two specific factors such as the nature of Dutch society, the landscape, or the greater efficiency of the SS bureaucracy. Subsequent authors uncovered other possible explanations, which led to the demand for more comparative research to provide some form of ranking to isolate the elements of *decisive* importance in explaining this disproportionate number of victims. The work of Griffioen and Zeller represents the most recent and most comprehensive attempt to do this.[1] Their comparison of the Netherlands with Belgium has led them to discount many of the factors which have traditionally been cited as important. They argue that the Dutch Jews were not seriously disadvantaged by the lack of opportunity to flee in May 1940 as the Belgian Jews, with more time to make their escape, were also overtaken by the speed of the German advance, even though some had found their way into France. The idea that the Netherlands had few places to hide has also been undermined, not least by the numbers of non-Jews who did manage to go into hiding as *onderduikers*, even though this was later in the occupation. The third element they have dismissed – the nature of the German police apparatus and the willingness of the local police to help – is not quite so straightforward. There is a strong case for saying that the Dutch police were rendered more co-operative than their Belgian counterparts, and that the Germans' use of this local knowledge had an effect on their ability to find and arrest Jews. This may not have been decisive, but could well be seen as a contributory factor.

Their overall conclusion is undoubtedly correct, that there was no single factor, but a series of interrelated factors which were decisive. They point to the deportation 'system' which developed from the establishment of Jewish work-camps and provided the smooth-running machinery which enabled the responsible authorities to have a pool of victims ready for the transports. This became crucial when movement to Auschwitz was temporarily halted and the deportations to Sobibor were set in motion in the first half of 1943. At a time when the SS in France and Belgium were finding it practically and politically difficult to track down victims, their counterparts in the Netherlands had no such problems. Griffieon and Zeller also refer to the relationship between the victims and the circumstances: the potential opportunities for going into hiding and the time they became available. This in turn relates to the point at which Jewish and general resistance organisations came into existence, and the extent of their subsequent co-operation. Their third fundamental factor was the relationship between persecutors and victims: the extent to which the Germans continued to use the Jewish Council, and the reaction of the Jews to the measures taken against them. They contrast the behaviour of Jews in Belgium who went underground and into illegality once raids began to take place, and those in the Netherlands who refused to take up even the obvious legal possibilities for escape which the Germans appeared to be offering them.

Using the comparative approach to try and isolate the decisive factors has provided some crucial insights into the reasons behind the high levels of mortality among Jews from the Netherlands. However, in trying to differentiate the material from the immaterial, even recourse to a model which stresses the interrelationships between particular factors can exclude elements which, as Griffioen and Zeller admit, still have some importance.[2] Generalisations about the processes which led to the destruction of Dutch Jewry can mask the fact that relatively minor alterations in particular factors or circumstances could lead to disproportionate effects on the chances of survival for the Jewish population as a whole, for specific groups, or for individuals. It is therefore important to keep in mind the factors which, while perhaps not decisive, did contribute to the severity and 'efficiency' of the Holocaust in the Netherlands.

First we turn to the perpetrators, and the nature of German rule in the Netherlands. The existence of a civilian *Reichskommissar* and German administration undoubtedly provided a greater opportunity for the Nazi Party (NSDAP) and SS to function, and this was in stark contrast to Belgium and France where the military administrations served to limit their influence and effectiveness in carrying out the ideological aims of the regime in Berlin. Thus, whereas SS men like Rauter and Harster could receive their orders more or less directly from Himmler, their contemporaries elsewhere in Western Europe had to operate through the military authorities. This was reflected in the speed with which anti-Jewish measures were enacted. Although deportations from both the Netherlands and Belgium did start in the same week, it could be argued that the functionaries in the Netherlands had made their plans more thoroughly and were therefore in a better position to carry out the process of programmatic deportation than their colleagues to the south. Of equal importance here is the possibility that the very nature of the competition between individuals and organisations within the German administrative structure served to accelerate the process by which the 'system' for the isolation and deportation of the Jews was developed. If the 'system' was driven initially by internal conflicts and the wishes of German functionaries inside the Netherlands, by the summer of 1942 their leadership had been superseded by the demands being made from Berlin. After the deportations had begun, the likes of Lages, Zöpf and Aus der Fünten were no longer free to determine the pace of measures against the Jews but constantly under pressure to meet quotas dictated by Eichmann and *Referat IVB4* of the RSHA. In this context, the constant changes in legislation, closure of loopholes and rescinding of exemptions can be seen as the consequence of this pressure as well as a manifestation of their antisemitism.

The apparent smooth running of the system also raises the question of whether the Germans organising the deportations in the Netherlands were any more efficient than their counterparts in other occupied countries. The Nazi personnel allotted to this task may have been comparatively more numerous, but there is little or no evidence to suggest that they were more adept at their work. Their 'success' in constructing the machinery which sent so many Jews in the Netherlands to their deaths was more to do with the circumstances which prevailed in the Netherlands than any particular attributes which they themselves possessed.

The 'system' of persecution in the Netherlands and the attitudes of the German administration had an effect in determining which Jews were given a chance of survival. Certain people, by virtue of their status or usefulness, were protected from deportation, either temporarily, or in some cases permanently. For example, Jews in specific trades or occupations were afforded some temporary protection by the exemption stamp system if they were useful to the German war effort. This usefulness, combined with the active help of the employer, was epitomised in the survival of members of the 'Philips-*kommando*' even after they had been removed to Germany. Members of the Jewish Council bureaucracy also received exemptions. They were an integral part of the machinery for deportation, and the leaders were afforded further privileges, even after their own incarceration. Their removal to Bergen-Belsen or Theresienstadt may have been seen as a 'reward' for services rendered, but also reflected the Nazi's belief that the elite they represented could still be useful as bargaining counters as the tide of war turned against them.

The Nazi predilection for dealing with 'fellow' Germans, even if they were Jews, also provided an opportunity for long-term survival. A number of the German Jews who, as refugees, had been the first inmates of Westerbork camp and formed its bureaucracy and administration, were able to stay in place when the Germans arrived. Kurt Schlesinger and his colleagues continued their work of administering the camp and overseeing the transport of the Dutch Jews, while at the same time protecting themselves from deportation. Even after the transports had stopped, a few hundred inmates remained to be liberated by the Canadian First Army. Similar protection was afforded to Edwin Sluzker and a few of his colleagues at the *Expositur*. Not only did the German preference for dealing with other Germans protect these people, but their survival may also have been a function of the German administration's unwillingness to admit that the task was over. Could the preservation of a skeleton administration have been due to the Germans' own fear of redeployment to other tasks, or a belief that further victims would still be designated by their masters in Berlin? The only substantial group of Jews still in the Netherlands who could have been targeted were those married to non-Jews, but they were allowed to remain, although not entirely unmolested. This was very much a function of Nazi indecision over the precise status of these people, but this indecision did provide their means of survival, and the Jews in mixed marriages formed by far the largest single group of survivors.

In looking at the victims, there is also no doubt that there were a number of factors which made the Jews in the Netherlands peculiarly vulnerable. Like their fellow Dutch citizens, they were singularly unprepared for war and occupation. Like so many others, they went on believing in the talisman of neutrality and lived in the hope that the war, and therefore the Nazi menace, would pass them by. Their integration into Dutch society was well advanced, but the very nature of that society – subdivided into pillars based on religion or political ideology – meant that the Jews, with their own community organisations and structures, were still separated from the mainstream. For the most part, the organisations were either religious or welfare based and, once the occupation had begun, they proved entirely incapable of organising any form of representation or resistance to the German occupying power. This left the way open for the Germans to impose their own solution, although their precise purpose in suggesting a 'Jewish Council' is still open to some question. Was it their intention to have a representative body for all the Jews in the Netherlands? Certainly this was what ultimately emerged, but the role of the Jewish secular elite – essentially Abraham Asscher and David Cohen – in the formulation of this organisation remains to be resolved.

The role of the Jewish Council can be seen as a major contribution to the 'success' of the Germans in identifying, isolating and then deporting the Jews from the Netherlands. Its precise role is still a contentious issue, with opinions varying from the apologist to the outright condemnatory. Lacking any other viable leadership, many put their faith in the Council and its edicts. This may help to explain their passivity in the face of threatened deportation, but other elements have to be considered here. The first is the deference shown to authority. This was not by any means peculiar to the Jews, but had disastrous consequences for them when both German and Dutch bureaucracies were mobilised against them. Secondly, there was the lack of any alternative for the vast majority of Jews. Even though the system of calling up Jews created by the Jewish Council and the *Zentralstelle* produced only a limited response, most of the victims then merely waited for the police to arrive to take them away. Even if the individual was prepared to go into hiding and illegality – a major step in itself – family ties, material circumstances and the lack of contacts outside the Jewish community made this all but impossible for the majority. Having said all of this, it is clear from the evidence that many Jews did not believe the strictures of the Jewish Council even if they felt powerless to do anything to save themselves. Many also made some attempt to avoid deportation, even if for the majority these attempts were ultimately doomed to failure. Only a minority organised themselves into formal resistance groups to help those in hiding and in a few cases to take direct action against their German oppressors.

The final element relates to the circumstances within which this tragedy was played out. First and foremost, there was the compliant nature of the Dutch bureaucracy. At no time did the Dutch civil service or its leadership seek to oppose directly the wishes of the Germans. This allowed the occupying power to make full use of the police force and to install their placemen when necessary. The attitude of the leading civil servants undoubtedly set the accommodating tone for occupation, and made it doubly difficult for subordinates to defy German instructions. Some functionaries, such as Sybren Tulp of the Amsterdam Police and Jacob Lentz of the *Bevolkingsregister*, needed little encouragement to follow their own particular 'reforms' which, by virtue of their quest for efficiency, aided the purposes of the Germans. The mere existence of a comprehensive population register was also an important factor. Apart from the co-operative and collaborative behaviour of Lentz, the fact that such a system already existed made the Jews feel that there was little point in not co-operating with other forms of registration. Failure to comply would be identified from other records and lead to discovery and punishment.

A further issue is the reaction of the Dutch population to the persecution of their Jewish fellow citizens. Ostensibly, the civil population do not have a particularly good record. The responses to German actions against the Jews which led to the February strike in 1941 were not repeated. The instigators of the strike realised that further actions would be counterproductive, and the Germans organised their activities more carefully. Only in the spring of 1943 did another strike take place, but by this time the issue was a different one and in any case the protest came much too late for the vast majority of the Jews who had already been deported. At a communal and individual level, there is no doubt that the traditions of deference to authority and a collective unwillingness to take risks meant that the majority of Dutch men and women were unlikely to become willingly involved in helping Jews. This may have had a number of root causes. Hiding Jews was perceived to carry greater penalties than other forms of sheltering. Many people continued to see the Jews as alien and an apart group. The most charitable explanation is that this was probably based more in the traditions of a *verzuild* society than on outright antisemitism, but the latter cannot entirely be discounted.

The relatively slow development of resistance networks, combined with the speed with which the Germans carried out their deportation plans, was also a contributory factor. By the time that national and local organisations had been established, for example to help those underground, most of the Jews had already been transported to the death camps. However, even Jews who survived long enough to be helped by such organisations still found disadvantages. For example, there is evidence to suggest that the LO had more difficulties finding hiding places for Jews than for other *onder-duikers*. While the history of the Jews in hiding contains some immensely heroic and brave people who took enormous risks to give shelter to those in need, there were also others, even among the rescuers, whose motives were less than pure. Some saw it as a means to engineer religious conversions, others as a means of making money. Ultimately, it has to be concluded that the ability of individual Jews to survive in hiding was more a matter of chance and luck than the result of careful planning or particular favourable factors.

While the general explanations for the high Jewish mortality in the Netherlands undoubtedly rest on a complex interaction of factors, they tend to concentrate on the Jews as a homogenous mass and highlight the particular advantages of identifiable groups: Jewish Council employees, foreign Jews, Jews in mixed marriages. This is a perfectly valid form of analysis given that these groups are undoubtedly overrepresented among the survivors. However, it is important to realise that this complex interaction of factors also worked at an individual level among the mass of Dutch Jewry who were not favoured with any special advantages. The factors involved, and the relative weight they carried, would vary according to the circumstances of each individual. No two cases were entirely alike. Personal circumstances, particular decisions and priorities all played a role, as did chance events. In this context, there can only be generalisations. The danger is that in a quest for objectivity and answers, sight is lost of the tens of thousands of individual tragedies played out during the occupation as the Nazi's murderous policies were put into practice.

Appendix

Table A1 Jewish population of the Netherlands, 1930–1941

	1930 Census		1940 Census Office		1940 Jewish Council	
	No.	%	No.	%	No.	%
Full-Jews:						
Dutch	111,917	100.0	118,455	84.5	118,295	84.2
German	–	–	14,493	10.3	} 22,252	15.8
Others	–	–	7,297	5.2		
Sub-Total	111,917	100.0	140,245	100.0	140,547	100.0
Half-Jews	–	–		–	{ 14,549	
			19,561			
Quarter-Jews	–	–		–	5,719	
Total			159,806		160,815	

Source: G. Hirschfeld, 'Niederlande', in W. Benz, ed., *Dimension des Völkermords. Die Zahl der jüdischen Opfer des Nationalsozialismus* (Munich, R. Oldenbourg Verlag, 1991), p. 137; A.J. Herzberg, *Kroniek der Jodenvervolging 1940–45* (Amsterdam, Meulenhoff, 1978), pp. 66–7, 317.

Table A2 Jewish survivors of the Holocaust in the Netherlands (1945) as registered with the Jewish Co-ordination Commission

Survived underground	16,224
Residents of transit camp Westerbork in 1945	918
Returnees from camps in the East	4,532*
Total	21,674

Source: A.J. Herzberg, *Kroniek der Jodenvervolging 1940–45* (Amsterdam, Meulenhoff, 1978), p 316. *The JCC estimated that no more than 5,450 people in total had returned from the camps.

Chronology of the Persecution of the Jews in the Netherlands

In some instances, the precise date of enactment or implementation of legislation is open to doubt. In these cases, the most widely accepted dates for enactment are given, with appropriate comments about implementation.

1940

10 May	German invasion of the Netherlands.
15 May	Surrender of all Dutch forces. German occupation of the Netherlands begins.
1 July	Jews have to leave the air-raid precaution service.
2 July	Jews excluded from labour drafts to Germany.
31 July	Bans on ritual slaughter (VO 80/1940) effective from 5 August.
20 August	Special regulations on administrative matters (VO 108/1940).
28 August	College of Secretaries-General informally instructed not to appoint, elect or promote anyone of 'Jewish blood' within the civil service.
6 September	College of Secretaries-General instructed not to appoint any more Jews to the civil service.
13 September	Measures concerning the employment of Jews and others in government service (VO 137/1940).
14 September	Jews banned from markets in Amsterdam.
20 September	Measures for a survey of non-economic associations and institutions (VO 145/1940).
30 September	Circular to local authorities defining a Jew as anyone with one Jewish grandparent who had been a member of the Jewish community.
5 October	Civil servants forced to sign 'aryan attestation'.

22 October	Order for the registration of Jewish businesses at the *Wirtschaftsprüfstelle* (VO 189/1940).
27 October	Proclamation against the 'aryan attestation' read from many pulpits of the Dutch Reformed Church.
21 November	Circular sent out banning all Jews from holding public office.
December	The creation of the Jewish Co-ordination Commission.
19 December	Bans on Germans working in Jewish households (VO 231/1940).

1941

7 January	The Dutch Cinema Association bans Jews in all cinemas, publicised in daily newspapers on 12 January.
10 January	Compulsory registration of all persons 'wholly or largely of Jewish blood' (VO 6/1941).
1 February	Introduction of *numerus clausus* in education.
5 February	Doctors have to declare if they are Jewish.
8 February	WA incited fighting on the Rembrantplein, Amsterdam.
9 February	Attack on the café 'Alcazar'.
11 February	Restrictions on Jewish students (VO 27/1941) Decree of Secretary-General of Department of Education, Science and Culture implementing the above decree (VO 28/1941).
11 February	Contrary to German orders, Dutch Nazis (WA) go into the Jewish quarter of Amsterdam and are attacked by a Jewish Action Group (*knokploeg*). One Nazi, Hendrik Koot, dies of his wounds.
12 February	German authorities seal off the Jewish quarter and insist on the establishment of a Jewish Council.
13 February	Establishment of the Amsterdam *Joodsche Raad* (Jewish Council).
15 February	Further public demonstrations in Amsterdam.
19 February	German police raid on Jewish Action Group headquarters, an ice-cream parlour in the Jewish quarter of Amsterdam. Police are attacked.
22–3 February	German reprisal arrest of 425 young men from the Jewish quarter. Brutality of the raid causes further public indignation.
25 February	Protest strike in Amsterdam brings city to a halt.
26 February	Protest strike spreads beyond Amsterdam but civil servants forced back to work and strike brought to an end by German coercion and declaration of a state of emergency.

27 February	Decree for the Secretary-General of the Department of Social Affairs on Jewish blood donors.
28 February	Measures against Jewish non-commercial organisations (VO 41/1941).
12 March	Measures for the registration of Jewish businesses and the appointment of *Verwalter* (administrators) (VO 48/1941).
31 March	Creation of the *Zentralstelle für jüdische Auswanderung*.
2 April	Series of local prohibitions of Jews in Haarlem.
11 April	First issue of the *Joodsche Weekblad*.
15 April	Instruction by Commissioner-General Rauter to all Jews to hand in their radio sets on the basis of regulation of 11 February (VO 26/1941).
1 May	Ban on Jewish doctors, apothecaries and translators working for non-Jews. Jews no longer allowed to own radio sets.
1 May	Ban on Jews attending stock and commercial exchanges.
6 May	Certain streets in Amsterdam designated 'Jewish streets'.
15 May	Synagogue in The Hague destroyed by fire. 'Aryanising' of orchestras.
27 May	Decree on declaration and treatment of agricultural land in Jewish hands (VO 102/1941).
31 May	Jews banned from using swimming baths, public parks and from hiring rooms in certain resorts and coastal localities.
4 June	Freedom of movement for Jews restricted.
11 June	*Razzia* (raids) against Jews in Amsterdam.
13 June	Jews banned from public swimming baths.
mid-June	Jewish lawyers banned from working for non-Jewish clients.
26 June	Shops forbidden to open on Sundays.
1 August	Ban on Jewish estate agents from working for non-Jews.
8–11 August	Regulations on the handling of Jewish assets and property. Registration of assets with Lippmann-Rosenthal Bank.
1 September	Jewish children forced to attend separate schools (1 October in Amsterdam).
14 September	Raid (*razzia*) in Twente area (east Overijssel).
15 September	Signs 'Forbidden for Jews' appear. Jews no longer allowed to visit parks, zoos, cafés, restaurants, hotels, guest houses, theatres, cabarets, cinemas, concerts, libraries and reading rooms. (VO 138/1941). Registration of land and property owned by Jews with Lippman-Rosenthal.
16 September	Travel permits introduced.

22 September	Jews barred from all non-economic organisations and associations.
24 September	Permits made compulsory for the establishment of certain trades and professions.
25 September	Seyss-Inquart meets Hitler in Berlin.
7–8 October	Raids against Jews in the Achterhoek, Arnhen, Apeldoorn and Zwolle.
8 October	Plenary meeting between Seyss-Inquart, *Generalkommissäre*, and leading Nazi functionaries.
20 October	Further regulations on the establishment of businesses by Jews (VO 198/1941). Jewish Council sanctions the creation of a card index of Jews in the Netherlands.
22 October	Jews forced to resign from non-Jewish associations (VO 199/1941), and banned from bridge, dance and tennis clubs from 7 November.
27 October	Germans limit their recognition to Jewish Council; Jewish Co-ordination Commission forced to disband.
1 November	Jews required to resign from associations with non-Jewish members. Legislation VO 198/1941 used to rescind 1,600 business permits for Jews.
3 November	Jewish markets established in Amsterdam.
7 November	Jews banned from travelling or moving house without permission.
10 November	Final dissolution of the Jewish Co-ordination Commission.
5 December	All non-Dutch Jews ordered to register for 'voluntary emigration'.

1942

1 January	Jews not permitted to employ non-Jewish domestic servants.
9 January	Jews banned from public education.
10 January	First Jews from Amsterdam sent to work-camps.
17 January	Beginning of the concentration of Jews in Amsterdam with removal of Jewish community from Zaandam.
20 January	Wannsee Conference in Berlin outlines practical measures for the extermination of European Jews.
23 January	Jews forbidden from using motor cars. Identity cards for Jews to carry a letter 'J'.
9 February	150 stateless Jews from Utrecht moved to Amsterdam or Westerbork.

17 February	Church representatives protest to Seyss-Inquart about the treatment of the Jews.
20 March	Jews forbidden to dispose of furniture or household goods.
25 March	Ban on marriage between Jews and non-Jews. Extra-marital relations to be severely punished.
26 March	First transport of Jews from occupied Western Europe (Drancy) to Auschwitz.
27 March	Effective introduction of the Nuremberg Laws in the Netherlands.
1 April	Jews banned from marrying in Amsterdam town hall.
19 April	Protest against German policies read out in Catholic and Protestant church services.
24 April	Most Jewish butchers are closed.
3 May	Introduction of the Jewish Star for people and houses.
12 May	Jews no longer allowed to have accounts with the Postgiro.
21 May	Jews forced to hand in all their assets and possessions valued at more than fl.250 to Lippmann-Rosenthal by 30 June 1942. No longer allowed to hire safety deposit boxes (VO 58/1942).
29 May	Jews prohibited from fishing.
June	Weinreb sets up his first 'list'.
5 June	Total ban on travelling for Jews without prior permission.
11 June	Jews banned from the fish-market.
12 June	Jews no longer allowed to buy fruit and vegetables in non-Jewish shops. Bicycles and other transport has to be handed in. All forms of sport forbidden for Jews.
26 June	Jewish Council receives notification of the beginning of deportations.
30 June	Curfew on Jews from 8.00 p.m. Jews no longer allowed to ride bicycles. Jews banned from certain trades and professions. Jews banned from using public transport.
1 July	SS take over the supervision of Camp Westerbork under leadership of *Obersturmführer* Erich Deppner.
4 July	First call-up notices sent out for 'labour service in Germany'.
6 July	Jews no longer allowed to use telephones or visit non-Jews.
11 July	Churches protest against the plans for deportation of Jews.
14 July	Raid (*razzia*) in south and central Amsterdam
15 July	First trainload of Jews leaves Amsterdam. Deportations begin from Westerbork to Auschwitz.
17 July	Jews may only shop between 3.00 p.m. and 5.00 p.m., and are banned altogether from many streets in The Hague and Scheveningen.

25 July	Prime Minister Gerbrandy urges help for the Jews via a broadcast from London on Radio-Oranje.
26 July	Protest against persecution of the Jews read from all church pulpits (excepting the Dutch Reformed).
2 August	Arrest of all Catholic Jews, excluding those in mixed marriages.
6 August	Raid on Jews in south Amsterdam.
9 August	Further raid on south Amsterdam.
August	Series of raids throughout the Netherlands. All Jewish street names altered.
1 September	*Obersturmführer* Josef Hugo Dischner replaces Deppner as commandant at Westerbork.
11 September	Registration of those in 'mixed marriages'.
15 September	Jewish students excluded from education.
16 September	First issue of exemption stamps.
2–3 October	Raids against Jewish work-camps.
9 October	*Obersturmführer* Albert Gemmeker replaces Dischner as commandant at Westerbork.

1943

8 January	Weinreb's first list collapses.
16 January	First Jews arrive in Vught concentration camp.
21 January	Raid on Jewish asylum 'Het Apeldoornsche Bos'.
5 February	Jews forbidden from sending requests or letters to the German authorities. All of these to be directed via the Jewish Council.
2 March	Deportations to Sobibor begin.
27 March	Amsterdam population registry attacked and set on fire.
April	All Jews to leave the provinces and be accommodated at Vught.
23 April	Provincial Netherlands declared free of Jews.
5 May	Harster gives the orders for the final phase of Jewish deportations.
15 May	Jews in mixed marriages offered choice of deportation or sterilisation.
19 May	Church protest against sterlisation of Jews in mixed marriages.
21 May	Jewish Council instructed to select 7,000 of its 'exempt' staff for deportation.
26 May	Huge raids in Amsterdam to capture remaining Jews.
20 June	Further huge raids in south and east Amsterdam.
15 July	Rauter gives instructions for raids in the countryside.

29 September	Last major raid in Amsterdam. Jewish Council wound up.
5 October	Seyss-Inquart gives instructions for the treatment of the legally remaining Jews in the Netherlands.
December	Those in mixed marriages called up for service in work-camps.

1944

3 February	Second 'Weinreb list' collapses.
16 May	Raid against gypsies and a-socials.
5 September	*Dolle Dinsdag.* NSB leader Mussert orders the evacuation of Dutch National Socialists from the west and centre of the country to the east.
5–6 September	Two large transports of inmates from Vught concentration camp eastwards to Germany.
17 September	Operation Market Garden, the Allied airborne landings around Nijmegen and Arnhem, begins.

1945

5 May	Official liberation of the entire Netherlands.

Sources

L. de Jong, *Het Koninkrijk der Nederlanden in de Tweede Wereldoorlog* (The Hague, Staatsuitgeverij, 1969–88) IV, pp. 879–83; V, pp. 1059–65; VI, pp. 827–32; VII, pp. 1329–34, Xa, pp. 1039–44.

Joods Historisch Museum, Amsterdam, *Documenten van de Jodenvervolging in Nederland 1940–45* (Amsterdam, Athenaeum-Polak & van Gennep, 1979), *passim.*

K.P.L. Berkley, *Overzicht van het Ontstaan, De Werkzaamheden en het Streven van de Joodse Raad voor Amsterdam* (Amsterdam, n.p., 1945), pp. 97–101.

C. van Dam, *Jodenvervolging in de Stad Utrecht: De Joodse Gemeenschap in de Stad Utrecht 1930–50* (Zutphen, De Walburg Pers, 1985) pp. 145–6.

RIOD LO-LKP 251a LO-BO4 (LO-II Drenthe) chronology.

Notes

1 Introduction

1 Werner Warmbrunn, *The Dutch under German Occupation 1940–1945* (Stanford, Stanford University Press, 1963), pp. v–vi.
2 Even the widespread publication of books by those who helped the Frank family, such as Miep Gies, *Anne Frank Remembered: The Story of the Woman who Helped Hide the Frank Family* (New York, Simon and Schuster, 1987) and a recent (1995) film documentary of the same name seem to have had only a limited impact on this popular perception.
3 David Barnouw and Gerrold van der Stroom, *The Diary of Anne Frank: The Critical Edition* (London, Viking, 1989), pp. 59–77.
4 Gerhard Hirschfeld, 'Niederlande', in Wolfgang Benz, ed., *Dimension des Völkermords. Die Zahl der jüdischen Opfer des Nationalsozialismus* (Munich, R. Oldenbourg Verlag, 1991), p. 165. B.A. Sijes, 'The Position of the Jews during the German Occupation of the Netherlands: Some Observations', *Acta Historiae Neerlandicae* IX (The Hague, Nijhoff, 1976), p. 170. J.Th.M. Houwink ten Cate, 'Het Jongere Deel. Demografische en sociale kenmerken van het jodendom in Nederland tijdens de vervolging', *Ooorlogsdocumentatie '40–'45, Jaarboek van het Rijksinstituut voor Oorlogsdocumentatie* I (1989), pp. 9–66.
5 J.C.H. Blom, 'Nederland onder Duitse bezetting 10 Mei 1940–5 Mei 1945', in D.P. Blok *et al.,* eds, *Algemene Geschiedenis der Nederlanden* XV (Haarlem, Fibula-van Dishoeck, 1982), p. 406, gives the total civilian casualties at around 250,000.
6 Leon Shapiro and Boris Sapir, 'Jewish Population of the World', *American Jewish Year Book* L (1948–49), pp. 691–724. Raul Hilberg, *The Destruction of European Jews*, 3 vols (New York, Holmes and Meier, 1985), pp. 594, 608, 658, 1220.
7 H. Wielek (W. Kweksilber), *De Oorlog die Hitler Won* (Amsterdam, Amsterdam Boek- en Courantmij N.V., 1947). The book was begun in 1941 by two Jewish journalists, H. Minkenhof (*De Telegraaf*) and Hugo Heymans (*Het Volk*), but both were ultimately arrested and deported. Their notes and opening chapters were hidden and retrieved only at the end of the war when Wielek agreed to finish the task. See pp. 417–18.

8 J. Harari (J. Pick), *Die Ausrottung der Juden im besetzten Holland. Ein Tatsachenbericht* (Tel Aviv, n.p., 1944). I. Taubes, *Persecution of the Jews in Holland 1940–1944: Westerbork and Bergen-Belsen* (London, 1945). S. de Wolff, *Geschiedenis der Joden in Nederland. Laatste Bedrijf* (Amsterdam, n.p., 1946). K.P.L. Berkley, *Overzicht van het Ontstaan, de Werkzaamheden en het Streven van den Joodsche Raad voor Amsterdam* (Amsterdam, n.p., 1945).

9 E. de Wind, *Eindstation … Auschwitz* (Amsterdam, n.p., 1946). Loden Vogel, *Dagboek uit een Kamp* (The Hague, n.p., 1946). Boud van Doorn, *Vught. Dertien Maanden in het Concentratiekamp* (Laren, A.G. Schoonderbeek, 1945).

10 H.C. Touw, *Het Verzet der Hervormde Kerk* (The Hague, Boekcentrum N.V., 1946). J.J. Buskes, *Waar Stond de Kerk?* (Amsterdam, De Volkspaedagogische Bibliotheek, 1947). Th. Delleman, ed., *Opdat wij niet vergeten* (Kampen, n.p., 1949). S. Stokman, *Het Verzet van de Nederlandsche Bisschoppen tegen Nationaal-Socialisme en Duitse tyrannie* (Utrecht, Het Spectrum, 1945).

11 To his credit, Delleman makes the point that the accounts of Calvinist (*Gereformeerde*) rescue would have filled another complete book (*Opdat wij niet vergeten*, p. 173).

12 J.J. Bolhuis *et al.*, eds, *Onderdrukking en Verzet. Nederland in Oorlogstijd*, 4 vols (Arnhem, van Loghum Slaterus, 1947–55), *Kroniek der Jodenvervolging 1940–1945* (1950). Latest edition reprinted as Abel Herzberg, *Kroniek der Jodenvervolging 1940–1945* (Amsterdam, Querido, 1985).

13 This included defending Abraham Asscher, co-chairman of the Amsterdam Jewish Council when he was threatened with prosecution by the Dutch authorities in 1947. C. Kristel, 'A Sacred Duty. The Holocaust in Dutch Historiography', *Low Countries Yearbook* II (1995), p. 187.

14 The *Rijksinstituut voor Oorlogsdocumentatie* (Netherlands State Institute for War Documentation). Set up in the immediate aftermath of the liberation, the Institute was charged with the collection of information, and ultimately the production of an official history of the Netherlands in the Second World War.

15 J. Michman, 'The Controversy Surrounding the Jewish Council of Amsterdam. From its Inception to the Present Day', in Michael Marrus, *The Nazi Holocaust* (Westport/London, Greenwood, 1989), VI, pp. 832–3.

16 Jacob Presser, *Ondergang. De Vervolging en Verdelging van het Nederlandse Jodendom 1940–1945*, 2 vols (The Hague, Staatsuitgeverij, 1965).

17 Kristel, 'Sacred Duty', p. 188.

18 Henriette Boas, 'The Persecution and Destruction of Dutch Jewry 1940–1945', *Yad Vashem Studies* VI (1967), p. 361, notes the very public launch of the book and its saturation coverage by television, radio and the press.

19 Ivo Schöffer, 'Een geschiedenis van de vervolging der Joden in Nederland 1940–1945', *Tijdschrift voor Geschiedenis* LXXIX (1966), pp. 38–63, especially pp. 49–50.

20 Abridged English editions (trans. Arnold Pomerans) *Ashes in the Wind: The Destruction of Dutch Jewry* (London, Souvenir Press, 1968), *The Destruction of the Dutch Jews* (New York, 1969).

21 Schöffer, 'Een geschiedenis', pp. 49–54.

22 Boas, 'Persecution and Destruction', pp. 366–7, 372.

23 Boas, 'Persecution and Destruction', p. 370. There was also criticism that the book was too soft on the Dutch government and its officials, p. 364, and that Presser had done little 'active' research but had used the material in the RIOD and relied on people bringing him memoirs and reminiscences, pp. 371–2.

24 Kristel, 'Sacred Duty', p. 190.

25 Louis de Jong, *Het Koninkrijk der Nederlanden in de Tweede Wereldoorlog,* 13 vols (The Hague, Staatsuitgeverij/SDU, 1969–92). All page references are from the academic edition of this work.

26 See, for example, B.A. Sijes, *Studies over Jodenvervolging* (Assen, van Gorcum, 1974). A.H. Paape, *Studies over Nederland in Oorlogstijd* I (The Hague, Martinus Nijhoff, 1972).

27 A.J. van der Leeuw, 'Meer Slachtoffers dan elders in West-Europa', *Nieuw Israelitisch Weekblad,* 15 November 1985.

28 J.C.H. Blom, 'In de ban van goed en fout? Wetenschappelijke geschiedschrijving over de bezettingstijd in Nederland', in G. Abma, Y. Kuiper and J. Rypkema, eds, *Tussen Goed en Fout: Nieuwe gezichtspunten in de geschiedschrijving 1940–45* (Franeker, T. Wever, 1986). A summary of his conclusions can be found in B. Moore, 'Occupation, Collaboration and Resistance: Some Recent Publications on the Netherlands during the Second World War', *European History Quarterly* XXI (1991), pp. 109–18.

29 Gerhard Hirschfeld, *Nazi Rule and Dutch Collaboration: The Netherlands under German Occupation, 1940–1945* (Oxford/New York/Hamburg, Berg, 1988).

30 See, for example, Lucy Dawidowicz, *The War against the Jews, 1933–1945* (Harmondsworth, Penguin, 1975). Gerald Reitlinger, *The Final Solution* (London, Sphere, 1971). Martin Gilbert, *The Holocaust* (London, Collins, 1986). Michael Marrus, *Holocaust in History* (Toronto, Meckler, 1987).

31 Pim Griffioen and Ron Zeller, 'Jodenvervolging in Nederland en België tijdens de Tweede Wereldoorlog: Een Vergelijkende Analyse', *Oorlogsdocumentatie '40-'45* VIII (1997). They cite Léon Poliakov, *Bréviaire de la haine. Le IIIe Reich et les Juifs* (Paris, Calmann-Lévy Éditeurs, 1951), pp. 54–6, 64–5, 193–201. Raul Hilberg, *The Destruction of European Jews,* 3 vols (New York/London, Holmes and Meier, 1985), pp. 568–70. Robert M.W. Kempner, *Eichmann und Komplizen* (Zürich, Europa Verlag, 1961), p. 358. Lucy Dawidowicz, *The War Against the Jews,* p. 364.

32 Helen Fein, *Accounting for Genocide: National Responses and Jewish Victimisation during the Holocaust* (New York, Free Press, 1979).

33 Michael Marrus and Robert Paxton, 'The Nazis and the Jews in Occupied Western Europe 1940–1944', *Journal of Modern History* LIV (1982), pp. 687–714, see p. 713.

34 J.C.H. Blom, 'The Persecution of the Jews in the Netherlands: A Comparative Western European Perspective', *European History Quarterly* XIX (1989), pp. 333–51.

35 Blom, 'Persecution', p. 335.

36 Blom, 'Persecution' pp. 335–6. It has been argued, and Blom is the first to admit this, that Dutch Jews were marginally less well-equipped to survive in the appalling conditions of the concentration and extermination camps. This applied only to those who were not selected for immediate extermination, and in any case measured survival rates in terms of days and weeks, rather than the months and years it would take to outlast the Nazi regime.

37 E.A. Cohen, *De negentien treinen naar Sobibor* (Amsterdam, Sijthoff, 1985).

38 Blom, 'Persecution', p. 343.

39 Blom, 'Persecution', p. 347.

40 Griffioen and Zeller, 'Jodenvervolging in Nederland en België tijdens de Tweede Wereldoorlog'.

41 Dan Michman, 'De oprichting van de "Joodsche Raad voor Amsterdam" vanuit een vergelijkend perspectief, in D. Barnouw *et al.* eds, *Oorlogsdocumentatie* III (Zutphen, De Walburg Pers, 1992), pp. 75–100; 'De joodse emigratie en de Nederlandse reactie daarop', in Kathinka Dittrich and Hans Würzner, eds,

Nederland en het Duitse Exil 1933–1940 (Amsterdam, van Gennep, 1982); *Het Liberale Jodendom in Nederland 1929–1943* (Amsterdam, van Gennep, 1988). Jozeph Michman (Melkman), *Met Voorbedachten Rades Ideologie en Uitvoering van de Endlösung der Judenfrage* (Amsterdam, Meulenhoff, 1987); 'Gothische Torens op een Corinthisch Gebouw', *Tijdschrift voor Geschiedenis* LXXXIX (1976), pp. 493–517; 'Planning for the Final Solution against the Background of Developments in Holland in 1941', *Yad Vashem Studies* XVII (1986), pp. 145–80; *Dutch Jewry during the Emancipation Period (1787–1814): Gothic Turrets on a Corinthian Building* (Amsterdam, Amsterdam University Press, forthcoming).

42 See, for example, J.Th.M. Houwink ten Cate, 'De Joodse Raad voor Amsterdam 1941–1943', in W. Lindwer, ed., *Het Fatale Dilemma. De Joodsche Raad voor Amsterdam, 1941–1943* (The Hague, SDU Uitgeverij, 1995).

43 For example, see the papers presented at the conference 'Deportation Management and Resistance in (Western) Europe', 23–24 November 1992. J. Houwink ten Cate, 'The *Sicherheitspolizei* and SD in Western Europe'; P. Romein, 'Local Government in the Netherlands and the Deportation of the Jews'; B.E. ten Boom, 'The Deportation of the Jewish Community in Den Haag'; and G. van Meershoek, 'The Amsterdam Municipality, its Police Force and the Persecution of the Jews'. See also G. Meershoek, 'De Amsterdamse hoofdcommisaris en de deportatie van de joden', in N.D.J. Barnouw *et al.*, eds, *Oorlogsdocumentatie '40–'45*. Derde jaarboek van het Rijksinstitut voor Oorlogsdocumentatie (Zultphen, De Walberg Pers, 1989) III, pp. 9–44.

44 Houwink ten Cate, 'Het jongere deel', pp. 9–66.

45 H. Avni, 'Zionist Underground in Holland and France and the escape to Spain', in Y. Gutman and E. Zuroff (eds), *Rescue Attempts during the Holocaust* (Jerusalem, Yad Vashem, 1977), pp. 555–90. Jac. van de Kar, *Joodse Verzet. Terugblik op de Periode Rond de Tweede Wereldoorlog* (Amsterdam, Stadsdrukkerij, 1981). Ben Braber, *Passage naar Vrijheid. Joods Verzet in Nederland 1940–1945* (Amsterdam, Balans, 1987). Ben Braber, *Zelfs als wij zullen verliezen. Joden in Verzet en Illegaliteit 1940–1945* (Amsterdam, Balans, 1990).

46 Samuel and Pearl Oliner, *The Altrusitic Personality: Rescuers of Jews in Nazi Europe* (New York, Free Press, 1988). Lawrence Baron, 'The Dynamics of Decency: Dutch Rescuers of Jews during the Holocaust', *Frank P. Piskor Faculty Lecture* (St Lawrence University, May 1985). Mordecai Paldiel, 'The Altruism of Righteous Gentiles', in Yehuda Bauer, ed., *Remembering for the Future* (Oxford, Pergamon, 1989), pp. 517–25.

47 See Bloeme Evers-Emden, *Onderduikouders en hun Joodse 'kinderen' over de onderduikperiode* (Utrecht, Stichting ICODO, 1988) and more recently, Elma Verhey, *Om het Joodse Kind* (Amsterdam, Nijgh & van Ditmar, 1991) and *Geleende Kinderen. Ervaringen van onderduikerouders en hun joodse beschermelingen in de jaren 1942 tot 1945* (Kampen, Kok, 1994). Bert Jan Flim, *Omdat Hun Hart Sprak. Geschiedenis van de Georganiseerde Hulp aan Joodse Kinderen in Nederland, 1942–1945* (Kampen, Kok, 1996).

48 Joel S. Fishman, 'The Anneke Beekman Affair and the Dutch News Media', *Jewish Social Studies* XL/1 (1978), pp. 3–24. Joel S. Fishman, 'Jewish War Orphans in the Netherlands – The Guardianship Issue 1945–1950', *Wiener Library Bulletin* XXVII (1973–74), nos 30–31, pp. 31–36. Joel S. Fishman, 'The War-Orphan Controversy in the Netherlands: Majority-Minority Relations', in J. Michman and T. Levie, eds, *Dutch Jewish History* (Jerusalem, Tel Aviv University/Hebrew University of Jerusalem, 1984), pp. 421–32.

49 Z. Valkhoff, *Leven in een niet-bestaan. Beleving en betekenis van de joodse onderduik* (Utrecht, ICODO, 1992). A. Tjepkema and J. Walvis, *'Ondergedoken': Het Ondergrondse Leven in Nederland tijdens de Tweede Wereldoorlog* (Weesp, De Haan, 1985).

50 J. Michman, H. Beem and D. Michman (eds), *Pinkas. Geschiedenis van de joodse gemeenschap in Nederland* (Ede/Antwerp/Amsterdam, Kluwer/ Nederlands–Israëlitisch Kertgenootschap) Joods Historisch Museum, 1992). J.C.H. Blom *et al.*, eds, *Geschiedenis van de Joden in Nederland* (Amsterdam, Balans, 1995).

51 N.K.C.A. in't Veld, *De Joodse Ereraad* (The Hague, SDU, 1989). J. Houwink ten Cate, 'De Justitie en de Joodsche Raad', in E. Jonker and M. van Rossem, eds, *Geschiedenis en Cultuur. Achttien Opstellen* (The Hague, SDU, 1990), pp. 149–68.

52 A.J. van Schie, 'Restitution of Economic Rights after 1945', in Michman and Levie, eds, *Dutch Jewish History*, pp. 401–20.

53 Dienke Hondius, *Terugkeer: Antisemitisme in Nederland rond de bevrijding* (The Hague, SDU, 1990).

54 Philip Mechanicus, *In Depôt. Dagboek uit Westerbork* (Amsterdam, Polak & van Gennep, 1964); *Waiting for Death* (London, Calder and Boyars, 1968).

55 Perhaps the best known of these is David Koker, *Dagboek Geschreven in Vught* (Amsterdam, G.A. van Oorschot, 1977).

56 Only a very few of the more recent ones can be mentioned here. From the survivors, Sophie en Joop Citroen, *Duet Pathétique. Belevenissen van een joods gezin in oorlogstijd* (Utrecht/Antwerp, Veen, 1988). Hanna and Walter Kohner, *Hanna and Walter – A Love Story* (New York, Random House, 1984; *Hanna en Walter. Een liefdesgeschiedenis* (Amsterdam, H.J.W. Becht, 1985)). From the helpers, Corrie ten Boom, *The Hiding Place* (Washington, DC, Chosen Books, 1971); *De Schuilplaats* (Hoornaar, Gideon, 1972).

57 Volker Jacob and Annet van der Voort, *Anne Frank war nicht allein: Lebensgeschichten deutscher Juden in den Niederlanden* (Berlin/Bonn, Dietz, 1988). See also André Stein, *Quiet Heroes: True Stories of the Rescue of Jews by Christians in Nazi-Occupied Holland* (New York, New York University Press, 1988).

58 See, for example, Ab Caransa, *Verzamelen op het Transvaalplein: ter Nagedachtenis van het Joodse Proletariaat van Amsterdam* (Baarn, Bosch en Keuning, 1984). S. Leydesdorff, *Wij Hebben als Mens Geleefd: Het Joodse Proletariaat van Amsterdam 1900–40* (Amsterdam, Meulenhoff, 1987).

59 Friedrich Weinreb, *Collaboratie en Verzet. Een poging tot ontmythologisering*, 3 vols (Amsterdam, Meulenhoff, 1969). D. Houwaart, *Weinreb: Een Witboek* (Amsterdam, Meulenhoff, 1975). D. Gilthay Veth and A.D. van der Leeuw, *Rapport door RIOD inzake activiteiten van drs. F. Weinreb gedurende 1940–45*, 2 vols (The Hague, Staatsuitgeverij, 1976).

60 While a few professional journalists have made important individual contributions, for example A. van Ommeren and A. Scherphuis, 'De Creche, 1942–43' *Vrij Nederland* 18 (January 1986), some of the monographs have tended towards the emotional or the extreme rather than the objective. See, for example, Hans Knoop, *De Joodsche Raad: Het Drama van Abraham Asscher en David Cohen* (Amsterdam, Elsevier, 1983).

61 See, for example, Isaiah Trunk, *Judenrat. The Jewish Councils in Eastern Europe under Nazi Occupation* (New York, Macmillan, 1972). Raul Hilberg, 'The Judenrat: "Conscious or Unconscious Tool"', in Marrus, ed., *Nazi Holocaust* VI, pp. 162–4. Yehuda Bauer, 'The *Judenräte* – Some Conclusions', in Marrus, ed., *Nazi Holocaust* VI, pp. 165–77. Yisrael Gutman, 'The Concept of Labor in Judenrat Policy', in Marrus, ed., *Nazi Holocaust* VI, pp. 521–50.

Dov Levin, 'The Fighting Leadership of the Judenräte in the Small Communities of Poland', in Marrus, ed., *Nazi Holocaust* VII, pp. 73–89. Aharon Weiss, 'Jewish Leadership in Occupied Poland – Postures and Attitudes', in Marrus, ed., *Nazi Holocaust* VI, pp. 440–70.
62 Houwink ten Cate, 'Jongere Deel', p. 16.
63 Houwink ten Cate, 'Jongere Deel', p. 16.

2 The Jews and the Netherlands before 1940

1 H. Daalder, 'Dutch Jews in a Segmented Society', *Acta Historiae Neerlandicae* X (1977), p. 177.
2 For example, H. Boas, 'The Persecution and Destruction of Dutch Jewry 1940–1945', *Yad Vashem Studies* VI (1967), p. 359 argues that the integration was apparent rather than real.
3 Daalder, 'Dutch Jews', p. 178.
4 I. Schöffer, 'Nederland en de joden in de jaren dertig in historisch perspectief', in K. Dittrich and H. Würzner, eds, *Nederland en het Duitse Exil* (Amsterdam, van Gennep, 1982), p. 80.
5 Daalder, 'Dutch Jews', p. 178.
6 J. Michman, 'Gothische Torens op een Corinthisch Gebouw', *Tijdschrift voor Geschiedenis* LXXXIX (1976), pp. 493–517.
7 Schöffer, 'Nederland en de joden', p. 85.
8 R. G. Fuks-Mansfeld, 'Moeizame Aanpassing (1814–1870)', in J.C.H. Blom *et al.*, eds, *Geschiedenis van de Joden in Nederland* (Amsterdam, Balans, 1995), p. 238.
9 Daalder, 'Dutch jews', p. 185. Schöffer, 'Nederland en de joden', pp. 85–6.
10 Daalder, 'Dutch Jews', pp. 182–3.
11 S. Kleerekoper, 'Het joodse proletariaat in het Amsterdam van de 19e eeuw', *Studia Rosenthaliana* Ii (1967), pp. 97–108, Iii, pp. 71–84. The two were not necessarily seen as mutually exclusive. See Selma Leydesdorff, 'In Search of the Picture: Jewish Proletarians in Amsterdam Between the Two World Wars', in J. Michman and T. Levie, eds, *Dutch Jewish History: Proceedings of the Symposium on the History of the Jews in The Netherlands* (Jerusalem, Hebrew University Institute for Research on Dutch Jewry, 1984), pp. 315–33, especially p. 322.
12 E. H. Kossmann, *The Low Countries 1780–1940* (Oxford, Clarendon, 1978), pp. 348, 351–2. Daalder, 'Dutch Jews', p. 176.
13 J.C.H. Blom, *De Muiterij op de Zeven Provinciën. Reacties en Gevolgen in Nederland,* 2nd edn (Utrecht, HES, 1983), pp. 352–3. H. Daalder, 'The Netherlands: Opposition in a Segmented Society', in R. A. Dahl, ed., *Political Oppositions in Western Democracies* (New Haven, Yale University Press, 1966), pp. 188–236.
14 J.C.H. Blom and J.J. Cahen, 'Joodse Nederlanders, Nederlandse Joden en Joden in Nederland', in Blom *et al.*, eds, *Geschiedenis van de Joden,* pp. 273, 289. Jaap Meijer, *Hoge Hoeden, Lage Standaarden: De Nederlandse Joden tussen 1933 en 1940* (Amsterdam, Het Wereldvenster, 1968), p. 151.
15 J. Michman, H. Beem and D. Michman, eds, *Pinkas. Geschiedenis van de joodse gemeenschap in Nederland* (Ede/Antwerp/Amsterdam, Kluwer/Netherlands–Israël-itisch Kerkgenootschap/Joods Historisch Museum, 1992), pp. 128, 130–1.
16 Michman, *Pinkas,* p. 130. Blom and Cahen, 'Joodse Nederlanders', p. 266 point out that the two trends are not synonymous as non-religious Zionists

were strongly anti-assimilationist, but at the same time rejected the religious in favour of the secular.

17 Michman *et al.*, *Pinkas*, p. 596.
18 Michman *et al.*, *Pinkas*, p. 128.
19 Meijer, *Hoge Hoeden*, p. 10. Blom and Cahen, 'Joodse Nederlanders', p. 254. Both cite E. Boekman, *Demografie van de Joden in Nederland* (Amsterdam, Hertzberger, 1936).
20 Blom and Cahen, 'Joodse Nederlanders', p. 257.
21 Blom and Cahen, 'Joodse Nederlanders', p. 260.
22 A more detailed but similar table derived from the 1930 census can be found in Blom and Cahen, 'Joodse Nederlanders', p. 262 which cites data from J. P. Kruit, 'Het jodendom in de Nederlandse samenleving', in H. J. Pos, ed., *Antisemitisme en jodendom* (Arnhem, 1939), p. 212.
23 Blom and Cahen, 'Joodse Nederlanders', pp. 263–4.
24 D. Cohen *et al.*, 'Activities of the Dutch Jewish Refugees Commission', Annual Report of the *Comité voor Joodsche Vluchtelingen* (Amsterdam, 1937).
25 Jan Beishuizen and Evert Werkman, *De Magere Jaren. Nederland in de Crisistijd*, 3rd edn (Alphen a/d Rijn, Sijthoff, 1980), p. 97.
26 This process is described in more detail by Leydesdorff, 'Jewish Proletarians', pp. 323–7.
27 Leydesdorff, 'Jewish Proletarians', pp. 330–3.
28 Blom and Cahen, 'Joodse Nederlanders', p. 260.
29 Blom and Cahen, 'Joodse Nederlanders', p. 274.
30 Bob Moore, *Refugees from Nazi Germany in the Netherlands, 1933–40* (Dordrecht, Nijhoff, 1986), p. 28. See also Bob Moore, 'Refugees from Nazi Germany in the Netherlands: The Political Problem and Government Response, 1933–1940', unpublished Ph.D. thesis (Manchester University, 1983), p. 94. L.R. de Jong, *Het Koninkrijk der Nederlanden in de Tweede Wereldoorlog*, 14 vols (The Hague, Staatsuitgeverij, 1969–92), I, p. 512–13. Blom and Cahen, 'Joodse Nederlanders', pp. 298–9.
31 RIOD Collectie 181b (CJV), File 1, Letter David Cohen to Henri Eitje, 25 January 1935.
32 This limited description does no justice to Asscher. He had been the *de facto* secular leader of the Jewish communities since 1932, but his work within Judaism had been almost overshadowed by his economic role as a leader of the Amsterdam Chamber of Commerce and his political career as representative of the Liberal Party in the provincial estates of north Holland from 1917. Michman *et al.*, *Pinkas*, p. 138.
33 Blom and Cahen, 'Joodse Nederlanders', p. 298. Moore, *Refugees*, p. 28 n. 55.
34 Blom and Cahen, 'Joodse Nederlanders', pp. 284–7.
35 Moore, *Refugees*, pp. 52.
36 Bob Moore, 'Jewish Refugee Entrepreneurs and the Dutch Economy in the 1930s', *Immigrants and Minorities* IX (1990), pp. 46–63. Moore, *Refugees*, pp. 75, 77.
37 Dan Michman, 'De Joodse emigratie en de Nederlands reactie daartop tussen 1933 en 1940', in Dittrich and Würzner, eds, *Nederland en het Duitse Exil*, pp. 105–6.
38 Moore, 'Refugees from Nazi Germany', II, p. 417.
39 RIOD Collectie 181b (CJV). File 4 Letter W.K.S. van Haastert, to CJV, 9 September 1937. Moore, 'Refugees from Nazi Germany', II, p. 416.
40 G. Hirschfeld, 'Niederlande', in W. Benz (ed.), *Dimension des Völkermords. Die Zahl der jüdischen Opfer des Nationalsozialismus* (Munich, R. Oldenbourg Verlag, 1991), p. 138.

41 D. Cohen, *Zwervend en Dolend* (Haarlem, Bohn, 1955), pp. 25–6.
42 Meijer, *Hoge Hoeden,* p. 151.
43 A.J. Herzberg, *Kroniek der Jodenvervolging 1940–45* (Amsterdam, Querido, 1985), p. 18. De Jong, *Het Koninkrijk* I, p. 510–11.
44 For a more extreme view of this relationship, see Meijer, *Hoge Hoeden,* p. 151.
45 Michman, 'De joodse emigratie', p. 94. Moore, *Refugees,* pp. 81, 106. Michman *et al.*, *Pinkas,* p. 154 gives totals of 34,000 and 15,174 but this latter statistic is based on the German census of January 1941 and takes no account of the small number who were not registered and those who left the country during 1940.
46 Moore, *Refugees,* pp. 22, 24–5. The CJV figures suggest that 29 per cent of the refugees coming to the Netherlands in 1933–35 were *Ost-Juden* and were either Polish or stateless.
47 Moore, *Refugees,* p. 186.
48 Moore, 'Jewish Refugee Entrepreneurs', pp. 51–2.
49 Moore, *Refugees,* pp. 32–52.
50 Michman *et al.*, *Pinkas,* p. 155.
51 Michman, 'De Joodse emigratie', p. 107.
52 Moore, *Refugees,* pp. 88–90. These camps were the *Heijplaat* Quarantine Station in Rotterdam and the Lloyd Hotel Quarantine Station in Amsterdam. The Catholic and Protestant refugees were Germans with Jewish backgrounds who had been baptised but who had nevertheless fallen foul of the racially based definitions used by the Nazis.
53 The camps were at Hoek van Holland, Reuver, Hellevoetsluis and Nunspeet. Re-emigration and the 'legalisation' of some inmates after six months allowed the closure of Reuver and Hellevoetsluis in September 1939 and Hoek van Holland in March 1940, but 85 inmates were still resident there in May 1940 – presumably because they had nowhere else to go. Moore, *Refugees,* p. 97.
54 Moore, *Refugees,* pp. 91–2. At least one site was discounted because of its proximity to the royal palace at Soest.
55 B. J. G. de Graaff, '"Strijdig met de tradities van ons volk". Het Nederlandse beleid ten aanzien van vluchtelingen in de jaren dertig', *Jaarboek van Buitenlandse Zaken* (The Hague, 1988), pp. 169–84, especially pp. 173–4, 184. Moore, *Refugees,* p. 183.
56 Moore, *Refugees,* p. 98.
57 Moore, *Refugees,* p. 184.
58 De Jong, *Het Koninkrijk* I, pp. 492–3, 512–13.
59 Harry Paape, '… Originally from Frankfurt-am-Main', in D. Barnouw and G. van der Stroom, eds, *The Diary of Anne Frank: The Critical Edition* (London, Viking, 1989), pp. 2–9. Victor Kugler became a naturalised Dutch citizen in 1938.
60 The Dutch census of 1930 gives 111,917 Jews in a total population of 7,935,565 people (1.41 per cent). R. Hilberg, *The Destruction of European Jews,* 3 vols (New York, Holmes and Meier, 1985), p. 362. F. Caestecker, *Ongewenste Gasten. Joodse vluchtelingen en migranten in de dertiger jaren* (Brussels, VUB, 1993), p. 113, estimates the Jewish population in 1930 at 50,000 (out of a population of 8.1 million) or 0.62 per cent. R. Poznanski, 'La résistance juive en France', *Revue d'Histoire de la Deuxième Guerre Mondiale* CXXXVII (1985), pp. 3–32. The Jewish population in France in 1940 was around 260,000 or 0.7 per cent of the French population as a whole. Jacques Adler, *The Jews of Paris and the Final Solution: Communal Response and Internal Conflicts, 1940–1944* (New York/Oxford, Oxford University Press, 1989), pp. 7–8. Jeremy Josephs, *Swastika over Paris. The Fate of the French Jews* (London, Bloomsbury, 1989), p. 12.

61 Caestecker, *Ongewenste Gasten*, pp. 112–13. M. Steinberg, *L'Etoile et Le Fusil*, 3 vols (Brussels, Vie Ouvrière, 1983–86), *Vol. I La question Juive 1940–42*, pp. 36, 98–9, note. 34. Caestecker notes that these figures do not take account of the 'not unimportant' number of Jews who fled the country on the eve of war in 1940.

62 Y. Cohen, 'French Jewry's Dilemma on the Orientation of its Leadership. From Polemics to Conciliation: 1942–44', *Yad Vashem Studies* XIV (1981), pp. 167–204, see p. 168.

63 Steinberg, *La Question Juive*, pp. 77–8, notes that the German census of 1940 gave 51.42 per cent of Jews in Belgium living in Brussels and 40.42 per cent in Antwerp, but that these figures reflect the method of enumeration and give no real indication of residence.

64 Jacques Gulwirth, 'Antwerp Jewry Today', *Jewish Journal of Sociology* X (1968), pp. 121–37. He cites W. Bok, 'Considérations sur les estimations quantitatives de la population juive en Belgique', in Centre National des Hautes Études Juives, Bruxelles and Institute of Contemporary Jewry of the Hebrew University, Jerusalem, *La vie juive dans l'Europe contemporaine* (Brussels, 1965), p. 102. Bok suggests that there were 55,000 Jews in Antwerp out of a total population of 85,000 on the eve of war.

65 Steinberg, *La Question Juive*, pp. 71, 76.

66 Adler, *Jews of Paris*, p. 5, cites a figure of 45,000 Jews from the Netherlands and Belgium who chose to stay in France after the armistice in June 1940. Even allowing for the fact that many of these people were German and Austrian refugees, and that some did return home during 1940, the total still represents a massive 22 per cent of all the Jews in those two countries. B. Sijes, 'The Position of the Jews during the Occupation of the Netherlands: Some Observations', *Acta Historie Neerlandicae* IX (The Hague, Martinus Nijhoff, 1976), p. 170, suggests that only 3,000 Jews managed to escape abroad from the Netherlands. This must also cast some doubt on the total of 45,000.

67 Adler, *Jews of Paris*, pp. 18–20.

68 Adler, *Jews of Paris*, p. 5. Caestecker, *Ongewenste Gasten*, pp. 113–30.

69 Herbert A. Strauss, 'Jewish Emigration from Germany. Nazi Policies and Jewish Responses (II)', *Leo Baeck Institute Yearbook* XXVI (1981), p. 345.

70 Strauss, 'Jewish Emigration', pp. 353–4.

71 H. J. B. Stegeman and J. P. Vorsteveld, *Het Joodse Werkdorp in de Wieringermeer, 1934–1941* (Zutphen, De Walburg Pers, 1983), p. 26. In the Netherlands, there had been a training farm run by the *Hechalutz* movement in Deventer since 1918, and the CJV established its own agricultural training facility on the Wieringermeerpolder in 1934, primarily to train refugees for re-emigration.

72 Caestecker, *Ongewenste Gasten*, p. 112.

73 Steinberg, *La Question Juive*, p. 72.

74 Steinberg, *La Question Juive*, pp. 74–5.

75 Adler, *Jews of Paris*, p. 6. Timothy P. Maga, 'Closing the Door: The French Government and Refugee Policy, 1933–1939', *French Historical Studies* XII (1982), pp. 424–42. M. Marrus and R. Paxton, *Vichy France and the Jews* (New York, Basic Books, 1982), pp. 23–72. Vicki Caron, 'Prelude to Vichy: France and the Jewish refugees in the Era of Appeasement', *Journal of Contemporary History* XX (1985), pp. 157–76.

76 Caron, 'Prelude to Vichy', p. 158.

77 Caron, 'Prelude to Vichy', p. 160.

78 J.C.H. Blom, 'The Persecution of the Jews in the Netherlands: A Comparative Western European Perspective', *European History Quarterly* XIX (1989), pp. 341, 349.

79 Adler, *Jews of Paris*, p. 54. Caestecker, *Ongewenste Gasten*, pp. 31–2. Moore, *Refugees*, pp. 27–31.

3 Invasion and occupation: the first months

1 L.R. de Jong, *Het Koninkrijk der Nederlanden in de Tweede Wereldoorlog*, 14 vols (The Hague, Staatsuitgeverij, 1969–92), IV, pp. 744–5.
2 J.C.H. Blom, *Crisis, Bezetting en Herstel: Tien Studies over Nederland 1930–1950* (The Hague, Universitair Pers Rotterdam, 1989), p. 61. See also H.W. von der Dunk, 'The Shock of 1940', *Journal of Contemporary History* II (1967), pp. 169–82.
3 De Jong, *Het Koninkrijk* III, pp. 105–10, 480–6.
4 A.J. Herzberg, *Kroniek der Jodenvervolging 1940–45* (Amsterdam, Querido, 1985), p. 16.
5 Herzberg, *Kroniek*, p. 17.
6 H. Fein, *Accounting for Genocide: National Responses and Jewish Victimization during the Holocaust* (New York, Free Press, 1979), p. 264, cites Cohen, *De afgrond. Een egodocument* (Amsterdam/Brussels/Paris, Mantreau, 1971), p. 18, who noted the behaviour of his father and father-in-law in Groningen in the years and months leading up to the invasion.
7 Interview with *Mevr.* A. Hoek-Wallach, 16 September 1987. She had come to the Netherlands as a German Jewish refugee in 1933 and had lived in Enschede since then. Transcript Wiener Library (WL), London.
8 V. Jakob and A. van der Voort, *Anne Frank war nicht allein* (Bonn, Dietz, 1988) (Herman Z.), pp. 115–16.
9 De Jong, *Het Koninkrijk* III, pp. 101–5.
10 De Jong, *Het Koninkrijk* III, pp. 437–8.
11 G.L. Durlacher, *Strepen aan de Hemel: Oorlogsherinnering* (Vianen, ECI, 1986), pp. 30–1, recalls that he was unable to escape from Rotterdam in May 1940 because all the bridges were closed.
12 L. de Jong, *The Netherlands and Nazi Germany* (Cambridge, Mass., Harvard University Press, 1990), pp. 3–4. C. van Dam, *Jodenvervolging in de Stad Utrecht: De Joodse Gemeenschap in de Stad Utrecht 1930–50* (Zutphen, De Walberg Pers, 1985), p. 45.
13 H. Wielek, *De Oorlog die Hitler Won* (Amsterdam, Amsterdam Boek- en Courantmij N.V., 1947), p. 11. J. Presser, *Ondergang. De Vervolging en Verdelging van het Nederlandse Jodendom 1940–45* (The Hague, Staatsuitgeverij, 1965), I, p. 12.
14 De Jong, *Het Koninkrijk* III, p. 444. Presser, *Ondergang* I, pp. 11–12.
15 Presser, *Ondergang* I, pp. 12–13, argues that the most charitable explanation for this was of contradictory orders being followed by the authorities. Thus although the government had provided shipping to allow some of its citizens to escape, the military authorities prevented the people from reaching the ports. He refuses to accept the idea that there was deliberate obstruction on the part of the Dutch authorities and their functionaries.
16 De Jong, *Het Koninkrijk* III, pp. 443–4.
17 It was originally intended that the 5,600-ton *Bodegraven* would be scuttled and used to block access to the port of Ijmuiden. At some point there must have been a change of heart by the authorities to use her as a boat for refugees and allow her to sail for England.
18 Wielek, *De Oorlog*, p. 12.
19 De Jong, *Het Koninkrijk* III, p. 444. Jakob and van der Voort, *Anne Frank* (Renate van H.), pp. 224–5.
20 Presser, *Ondergang* I, p. 13.

21 PRO AIR9/130 Vice Admiral, Dover to Admiralty, X5372, 13 May 1940, C-in-
    C Nore to Admiralty D.N.I., X6063, 15 May 1940. WO106/1733 Report,
    Capt. Keeble to O/C Kent Fortress (R.E.), 15 May 1940. Bob Moore, 'British
    Economic Warfare and Relations with the Neutral Netherlands during the
    "Phoney War", September 1939–May 1940', *War and Society* XIII (1995), pp.
    81–2.
22 Presser, *Ondergang* I, p. 13.
23 Presser, *Ondergang* I, p. 12. De Jong, *Het Koninkrijk* III, pp. 411–12. Fein,
    Genocide, pp. 264–5, refers to Gertrude van Tijn (unfootnoted) as saying that
    although these children had been given an authorised passage by the govern-
    ment, they were obstructed by officials because they did not have all the neces-
    sary documentation. This seems to misrepresent the case, as these busloads of
    children did escape, and understates the role of Geertruida (Truus) Wijsmuller-
    Meijer in persuading and cajoling *local* officials and military commanders to
    approve transit for her charges. She herself blamed a lack of available transport
    for her inability to evacuate more people. Presser, *Ondergang* I, p. 12. For a
    different account of events, given by one of the children, see M. Gilbert, *The
    Holocaust. The Jewish Tragedy* (London, Collins, 1986), p. 120, J. Michman,
    H. Beem and D. Michman, eds, *Pinkas. Geschiedenis van de joodse gemeen-
    schap in Nederland* (Ede/Antwerp/Amsterdam, Kluwer/Nederlands–Israëlitisch
    Kerkgenootschap/Joods Historisch Museum, 1992), p. 171 gives the ship on
    which they escaped as *De Brederode*.
24 De Jong, *Het Koninkrijk* III, pp. 438–9.
25 Presser, *Ondergang* I, p. 13.
26 Presser, *Ondergang* I, p. 13.
27 For an account of one German Jewish family which did escape to France and
    ultimately survive the war, see Jakob and van der Voort, *Anne Frank*, pp.
    67–75.
28 M.R. Marrus, *The Unwanted: European Refugees in the Twentieth Century*
    (Oxford, Oxford University Press, 1985), p. 258.
29 Wielek, *De Oorlog*, p. 12.
30 Van Dam, *Utrecht*, p. 46.
31 See Wielek, *De Oorlog*, p. 12, where he debates the (very similar) reasons for
    going or staying.
32 S. Citroen, *Duet Pathétique: Belevenissen van een Joods Gezin in Oorlogstijd
    1940–45* (Utrecht, Veen, 1988), p. 20.
33 Herzberg, *Kroniek*, p. 11.
34 Citroen, *Duet Pathétique*, p. 34.
35 Herzberg, *Kroniek*, pp. 12–13.
36 Herzberg, *Kroniek*, p. 13.
37 Herzberg, *Kroniek*, p. 19.
38 Michman *et al.*, *Pinkas*, p. 171.
39 Fein, *Genocide*, p. 264.
40 Van Dam, *Utrecht*, p. 45.
41 W. Warmbrunn, *The Dutch under German Occupation 1940–45* (Stanford,
    Stanford University Press, 1963), p. 166.
42 Presser, *Ondergang* I, p. 15. Fein, *Genocide*, p. 264. See also RIOD Collection
    61 *Archief van het Generalkommissariat zur besonderen Verwendung* Box 73,
    'Stimmungsberichte' KR538 June 1940.
43 Warmbrunn, *German Occupation*, p. 166.
44 Jakob and van der Voort, *Anne Frank*, p. 109.
45 De Jong, *Het Koninkrijk* III, p. 105.

46 It seems that the evacuation was so rapid that even the camp commander was unaware that his charges had left until he arrived in the morning of 10 May to find they had already departed.

47 ARA 2. 04. 55 *Archief Afdeling Armwezen* File 592. Weyburg to *Ministerie van Binnenlandse Zaken*, 25 May 1940. Syswerda to *Ministerie van Binnenlandse Zaken*, 8 June 1940.

48 De Jong, *Het Koninkrijk* III, p. 105.

49 De Jong, *Het Koninkrijk* III, p. 105.

50 T. Wijsmuller-Meijer, *Geen Tijd voor Tranen* (Amsterdam, n.p., 1961), p. 165. De Jong, *Het Koninkrijk* IV, pp. 753–4.

51 PRO ADM202/401 Report on Operations carried out by Mitchell Force at Hook of Holland (Operation Harpoon) 11–15 May.

52 De Jong, *Het Koninkrijk* III, pp. 488–9. WL Eyewitness Accounts PIIId/539.

53 De Jong, *Het Koninkrijk* III, p. 487.

54 De Jong, *Het Koninkrijk* IV, p. 754. Some 84 Protestant and 137 Catholic Jews were taken from the camps at Sluis to Westerbork in mid-July 1940.

55 Blom, *Crisis*, p. 61.

56 Presser, *Ondergang* I, pp. 15–16. An edited version of this same quote can be found in the English edition, *Ashes in the Wind*, p. 10. See also Fein, *Genocide*, p. 265 who cites Cohen, *De afgrond*, p. 26.

57 H. J. Neuman, *Arthur Seyss-Inquart: Het Leven van een Duits onderkoning in Nederland* (Utrecht, Ambo, 1967), pp. 133–4.

58 Presser, *Ondergang* I, p. 16.

59 Neuman, *Seyss-Inquart*, pp. 131–2.

60 Presser, *Ondergang* I, p. 19.

61 G. Hirschfeld, *Nazi Rule and Dutch Collaboration: The Netherlands under German Occupation, 1940–1945* (Oxford/New York/Hamburg, Berg, 1988), pp. 213–14. For more details, see Gerhard Hirschfeld, 'Der "freiwillige" Arbeitseinsatz niederländischer Fremdarbeiter während des Zweiten Werltkrieges als Krisenstrategie einer nichtnationalsozialistischen Vervaltung', in H. Mommsen and W. Schulze, eds, *Vom Elend der Handarbeit. Probleme historischer Unterschichtenforschung* (Stuttgart, Klett-Cotta, 1981), pp. 497–513.

62 Presser, *Ondergang* I, p. 21.

63 Wielek, *De Ooorlog*, p. 13. Presser, *Ondergang* I, p. 22.

64 VO 80/1940, 31 July 1940. Presser, *Ondergang* I, pp. 23–4.

65 Presser, *Ondergang* I, pp. 32–3.

66 De Jong, *Het Koninkrijk* IV, pp. 769–80.

67 Presser, *Ondergang* I, p. 49.

68 Blom, *Crisis*, p. 144.

69 De Jong, *Het Koninkrijk* IV, p. 782.

70 Hirschfeld, *Nazi Rule*, p. 135. The Secretary-General for Defence, C. Ringeling, resigned in June 1940 and his colleague the Secretary-General for Social Affairs, A. L. Scholten, in August of the same year.

71 Michman *et al.*, *Pinkas*, p. 172.

72 De Jong, *Het Koninkrijk* IV, pp. 785–6. Presser, *Ondergang* I, p. 45.

73 De Jong, *Het Koninkrijk* IV, pp. 788–803.

74 Joseph Michman, 'The Controversial Stand of the Joodse Raad in the Netherlands: Lodewijk E. Visser's Struggle', *Yad Vashem Studies* X (1974), p. 13.

75 Presser, *Ondergang* I, p. 42. De Jong, *Het Koninkrijk* IV, pp. 821–2.

76 De Jong, *Het Koninkrijk* IV, pp. 755–6.

77 Wielek, *De Ooorlog*, p. 22. Presser, *Ondergang* I, pp. 74–5.

78 De Jong, *Het Koninkrijk* IV, pp. 752–3.

79 Presser, *Ondergang* I, p. 70.
80 Herzberg, *Kroniek*, p. 69. Presser, *Ondergang* I, pp. 76–7.
81 De Jong, *Het Koninkrijk* IV, pp. 748–9. De Jong suggests that this last outrage was probably the work of the NSNAP in Haarlem, but in spite of German assurances that the perpetrators would be punished, they were never found.
82 RIOD 15/28–29 HSSpF *Meldungen aus den Niederlanden* No. 18, 22 October 1940, p. 57.
83 Ian Kershaw, *The Nazi Dictatorship: Problems and Perspectives of Interpretation*, 3rd edn (London, Arnold, 1993), p. 99. For a more detailed study of the development of SS power in the Netherlands, see N.K.C.A. in 't Veld, *De SS en Nederland* (Amsterdam, Sijthoff, 1987).
84 J. Adler, *The Jews of Paris and the Final Solution: Communal Response and Internal Conflicts 1940–1944* (New York/Oxford, Oxford University Press, 1989), pp. 16–17. G. Reitlinger, *The Final Solution* (London, Sphere, 1971), pp. 327–8. M.R. Marrus and R.O. Paxton, *Vichy France and the Jews* (New York, Basic Books, 1982), pp. 3–7. Serge Klarsfeld, *Vichy-Auschwitz. Le Rôle de Vichy dans la Solution Finale de la Question Juive en France. 1942* (Paris, Fayard, 1983), p. 14.
85 De Jong, *Het Koninkrijk* IV, p. 749.
86 Joseph Michman, 'Planning for the Final Solution against the Background of Developments in Holland in 1941', *Yad Vashem Studies* XVII (1986), pp. 145-52.

4 Isolation

1 L.R. de Jong, *Het Koninkrijk der Nederlanden in de Tweede Wereldoorlog*, 14 vols (The Hague, Staatsuitgeverij, 1969–92), IV, pp. 871–4.
2 De Jong, *Het Koninkrijk* IV, pp. 873–4. The illegal newspapers called on the population to boycott the cinemas as a result of this. De Jong suggests that the appeal had little success as many people had already decided not to pay to watch German propaganda.
3 J. Michman, 'Planning for the Final Solution against the Background of Developments in Holland in 1941', *Yad Vashem Studies* XVII (1986), p. 146, makes the point that these laws were always very carefully drafted by the lawyer, Dr Kurt Rabl, and that VO 6/1941 went through nine drafts before reaching its final form.
4 De Jong, *Het Koninkrijk* IV, p. 875, note 2, suggests that Presser subsequently received information on one such case and the RIOD a further three. To this can be added at least three other cases investigated by the Amsterdam police during 1941.
5 J.C.H. Blom, 'The Persecution of the Jews in the Netherlands: A Comparative Western European Perspective', *European History Quarterly* XIX (1989), p. 348. J.C.H. Blom et al., eds, *Geschiedenis van de Joden in Nederland* (Amsterdam, Balans, 1995), p. 320.
6 A.Z. Herzberg, *Kroniek der Jodenvervolging 1940–45* (Amsterdam, Querido, 1985), pp. 64–5. J. Presser, *Ondergang. De Vervolging en Verdelging van het Nederlandse Jodendom 1940–45* (The Hague, Staatsuitgeverij, 1965), I, pp. 62–3.
7 J. Michman, H. Beem and D. Michman, *Pinkas. Geschiedenis van de joodse gemeenschap in Nederland* (Ede/Antwerp/Amsterdam, Kluwer/Nederlands–Israëlitisch Kerkgenootschap/Joods Historisch Museum, 1992) p. 173.
8 Herzberg, *Kroniek*, pp. 64–5.

9 WL Eyewitness Accounts P/III/d No. 626; P/III/d No. 833.

10 De Jong, *Het Koninkrijk* IV, p. 875, notes that Jews of Russian and Polish origin could claim that their archives were inaccessible, thus preventing a detailed examination of their 'racial' origin.

11 De Jong, *Het Koninkrijk* IV, p. 877, notes that the Dutch SS were specifically excluded from this action, and those who transgressed were immediately dismissed.

12 Böhmcker, a former mayor of Lübeck, was also the representative of the German Foreign Office in the Netherlands. W. Warmbrunn, *The Dutch under German Occupation 1940–45* (Stanford, Stanford University Press, 1963), p. 62. G. Hirschfeld, *Nazi Rule and Dutch Collaboration: The Netherlands under German Occupation, 1940–1945* (Oxford/New York/Hamburg, Berg, 1988), pp. 175. De Jong, *Het Koninkrijk* IV, p. 879. W. Lindwer, ed., *Het fatale dilemma* (The Hague, SDU Uitgeverij, 1995), p. 17.

13 Warmbrunn, *German Occupation*, p. 106. De Jong, *Het Koninkrijk* IV, pp. 879–80. B. A. Sijes, *De Februari-staking: 25–26 Februari 1941* (Amsterdam, Meulenhoff, n. d.), pp. 90–1.

14 Sijes, *Februari-staking*, p. 100.

15 Sijes, *Februari-staking*, pp. 100–12. Warmbrunn, *German Occupation*, p. 107, cites RIOD, *Nederland in Oorlogstijd 1940–45*, V, p. 4, Rauter to Himmler, 20 February 1941, that 'a Jew had bitten through Koot's jugular vein and sucked out his blood'. De Jong, *Het Koninkrijk* IV, p. 881, notes that Böhmcker had reported to Seyss-Inquart that a Jew had attacked Koot's face 'like a wild animal'. Neither account was borne out by the post-mortem.

16 De Jong, *Het Koninkrijk* IV, pp. 882–4.

17 Warmbrunn, *German Occupation*, p. 107, cites Befehlshaber der Sicherheitspolizei und des SD, *Meldungen aus den Niederlanden* No. 33 (18 February 1941), p. 78.

18 J.Th.M. Houwink ten Cate, 'Heydrich's Security Police and the Amsterdam Jewish Council (February 1941–October 1942)', *Dutch Jewish History* III (Jerusalem, 1993), pp. 381–93, see p. 383. He notes that Rauter assumed that Seyss-Inquart had been consulted on this measure.

19 Herzberg, *Kroniek*, p. 106.

20 These were from the Dutch-Jewish (Ashkenazi) community, the chief rabbi, L. H. Sarlouis, and its chairman, Abraham Asscher, and from the Portuguese-Jewish (Sephardi) community, the chief rabbi, D. Francès, and its deputy-secretary.

21 Blom *et al.*, eds, *Geschiedenis*, pp. 320–1. De Jong, *Het Koninkrijk* IV, pp. 884–5. H. Knoop, *De Joodse Raad: Het Drama van Abraham Asscher en David Cohen* (Amsterdam, Elsevier, 1983), pp. 81–2.

22 Knoop, *Joodse Raad*, p. 82, quotes Asscher as saying that 'one could not allow the Jews to be represented by the baker and the butcher'. This analysis remains problematic. The precise form of this new body may not have been as predetermined as some authors make out. It is possible that Böhmcker in his meeting with the Jewish leaders had nothing more in mind than a sort of neighbourhood committee for the 'Jewish quarter' itself. This interpretation would give a much larger role to Abraham Asscher in having broadened the scope of this putative organisation into something much more extensive. In this light, the fact that the organisation was initially called De Commissie van Vertegenwoordiging voor de Amsterdamse Joden (Representative Commission for Amsterdam Jews) was simply because Böhmcker had no particular desire to designate it as anything other than a local body. While Knoop cannot be ignored, he cites evidence from 'a few documents' to support his conclusions,

but annoyingly provides no footnotes or direct citations as to what these documents are or where they are to be found.

23 J. Michman, 'The Controversial Stand of the Joodse Raad in the Netherlands: Lodewijk E. Visser's Struggle', *Yad Vashem Studies* X (1974), p. 14.

24 Michman, 'Controversial Stand', pp. 18–19.

25 Michman, 'Controversial Stand', pp. 48–9.

26 Michman, 'Controversial Stand', p. 16. De Jong, *Het Koninkrijk* IV, p. 885.

27 Knoop, *Joodse Raad*, pp. 87–9.

28 M. Kopuit, 'Herinneringen Prof. Dr. David Cohen', *Nieuw Israëlitisch Weekblad* (May 1982), p. 5.

29 De Jong, *Het Koninkrijk* IV, p. 885.

30 De Jong, *Het Koninkrijk* IV, pp. 888–9.

31 Herzberg, *Kroniek*, pp. 117–18. De Jong, *Het Koninkrijk* IV, pp. 889–90. Michman *et al.*, *Pinkas*, p. 177.

32 Ladislas de Hoyos, *Klaus Barbie: The Untold Story* (London, W.H. Allen, 1985), p. 19. Ben Braber, 'De Activiteiten van Barbie in Nederland in de jaren 1940–1945' (Doctoraalscriptie, University of Amsterdam, 1984), pp. 23–32.

33 Presser, *Ondergang* I, pp. 86–9. Herzberg, *Kroniek*, pp. 119-25.

34 It is important to differentiate between the 'illegal CPN' and its pre-war counterpart, the Communistische Partij Nederland (CPN). The illegal CPN was an elite group of party members who were actively engaged in subversive and sabotage activities. De Jong, *Het Koninkrijk* IV, p. 904. Sijes, *Februari-staking*, pp. 34–69.

35 Warmbrunn, *German Occupation*, pp. 106–11. De Jong, *Het Koninkrijk* IV, pp. 876–96, 913–34.

36 Michman, 'Planning', pp. 146–7.

37 Michman, 'Planning', p. 147.

38 Hirschfeld, *Nazi Rule*, p. 46, cites letter from Himmler to Seyss-Inquart, 7 January 1941, from *SS en Nederland* vol. 1 no. 54, p. 532.

39 Houwink ten Cate, 'Heydrich's Security Police', pp. 383–4.

40 Michman, 'Planning', p. 150–1.

41 De Jong, *Het Koninkrijk* V, pp. 1010–12. Michman, 'Planning', p. 150. B. Sijes, *Studies over Jodenvervolging* (Assen, van Gorcum, 1974), p. 67.

42 Michman, 'Planning', p. 162.

43 Sijes, *Studies*, p. 68.

44 De Jong, *Het Koninkrijk* V, pp. 996–7.

45 De Jong, *Het Koninkrijk* V, pp. 1011–12.

46 Michman, 'Planning', p. 152. De Jong, *Het Koninkrijk* V, pp. 1012–14.

47 De Jong, *Het Koninkrijk* V, pp. 1019–20.

48 Houwink ten Cate, 'Heydrich's Security Police', pp. 385–6.

49 Michman, 'Planning', p. 166. De Jong, *Het Koninkrijk* V, pp. 1024–5. Herzberg, *Kroniek*, pp. 105-7, 111.

50 For recent discussions see, for example, Christopher Browning, *The Path to Genocide: Essays on Launching the Final Solution* (Cambridge, Cambridge University Press, 1993), *passim*, and Philippe Burrin, *Hitler and the Jews: The Genesis of the Holocaust* (London, Edward Arnold, 1994), pp. 93–131.

51 De Jong, *Het Koninkrijk* V, pp. 1024–5.

52 De Jong, *Het Koninkrijk* V, pp. 1026–7.

53 Michman, 'Planning', p. 168.

54 Michman, 'Planning', p. 170–1. De Jong, *Het Koninkrijk* V, pp. 1030–1.

55 Sijes, *Studies*, p. 71.

56 De Jong, *Het Koninkrijk* V, pp. 1018–19.

57 Sijes, *Studies*, p. 88–9.

58 Sijes, *Studies*, p. 89–90.
59 De Jong, *Het Koninkrijk* V, pp. 1018–19.
60 Michman, 'Planning', p. 171.
61 Houwink ten Cate, 'Heydrich's Security Police', p. 388.
62 Presser, *Ondergang* I, p. 98.
63 De Jong, *Het Koninkrijk* V, p. 522.
64 Herzberg, *Kroniek*, pp. 238–40. Presser, *Ondergang* I, pp. 104–8. This system of having one newspaper exclusively for the Jews had earlier been instituted in Vienna where the *Zionistische Rundschau* performed the same function.
65 RIOD JR 6c, Böhmcker to Joodse Raad, 22 March 1941.
66 De Jong, *Het Koninkrijk* V, p. 522. Presser, *Ondergang* I, pp. 108–10.
67 Presser, *Ondergang* I, p. 106. Herzberg, *Kroniek*, p. 232.
68 De Jong, *Het Koninkrijk* IV, p. 931, refers to his appointment as *Regeringscommisaris* (State Commissioner) in March 1941. Presser, *Ondergang* I, pp. 104–5.
69 De Jong, *Het Koninkrijk* V, pp. 545–7.
70 H.B.J. Stegeman and J.P. Vorsteveld, *Het Joodse Werkdorp in de Wieringermeer 1934–1941* (Zutphen, De Walberg Pers, 1983), p. 122. De Jong, *Het Koninkrijk* V, pp. 549–50. De Hoyos, *Klaus Barbie*, pp. 21–2.
71 Stegeman and Vorsteveld, *Joodse Werkdorp*, p. 123. De Jong, *Het Koninkrijk* V, pp. 549–50. Lindwer, *Fatale Dilemma*, p. 19.
72 RIOD JR 5c, Cohen and Asscher to Blumenthal (Sipo), 7 May 1941.
73 De Jong, *Het Koninkrijk* V, pp. 550–1. Herzberg, *Kroniek*, p. 132.
74 Stegeman and Vorsteveld, *Joodse Werkdorp*, pp. 124–5. De Jong, *Het Koninkrijk* V, pp. 552–3.
75 Stegeman and Vorsteveld, *Joodse Werkdorp*, p. 122.
76 Stegeman and Vorsteveld, *Joodse Werkdorp*, pp. 125–6.
77 Herzberg, *Kroniek*, pp. 125–9, 131.
78 Herzberg, *Kroniek*, pp. 91–2.
79 Herberg, *Kroniek*, pp. 73–4. De Jong, *Het Koninkrijk* V, pp. 553–8.
80 Herzberg, *Kroniek*, pp. 74–5.
81 Herzberg, *Kroniek*, pp. 95–7.
82 RIOD JR 1c, Minutes, 17 September 1941.
83 De Jong, *Het Koninkrijk* V, pp. 558–62.
84 Houwink ten Cate, 'Heydrich's Security Police', p. 387.
85 Herzberg, *Kroniek*, p. 132.
86 De Jong, *Het Koninkrijk* V, pp. 1048–9.
87 Presser, *Ondergang* I, p. 173. M. Gilbert, *The Holocaust. The Jewish Tragedy* (London, Collins, 1986), p. 213, records similar reactions from Jews in Germany when the deportations began.
88 De Jong, *Het Koninkrijk* V, pp. 1048–51. All the other non-Dutch Jews (around 8,000 people) had been ordered to register for emigration in November 1941.
89 De Jong, *Het Koninkrijk* V, p. 1051, note 1, records that in May 1942 Aus der Fünten had asked Gertrud van Tijn for a list of those who had not registered and she had refused on the grounds that she had sworn never to reveal the address of any other Jews to the SS after the episode of the June *razzia*. In spite of expecting the worst, she was not punished.
90 Hirschfeld, *Nazi Rule*, pp. 213–14. G. Hirschfeld, 'Der "freiwillige" Arbeiteinsatz niederländischer Fremdarbeiter während des Zweiten Werltkrieges als Krisenstrategie einer nichtnationalsozialistischen Vervaltung', in H. Mommsen and W. Schulze, eds, *Vom Elend der Handarbeit. Probleme historischer Unterschichtenforschung* (Stuttgart, Klett-Cotta, 1981), pp. 500ff.
91 Hirschfeld, *Nazi Rule*, p. 220.

92 De Jong, *Het Koninkrijk* V, pp. 1021–2.
93 De Jong, *Het Koninkrijk* V, pp. 1052–3.
94 RIOD JR 1c, Minutes, 7 January 1942. De Jong, *Het Koninkrijk* V, p. 1053. Presser, *Ondergang* I, pp. 183–4.
95 Presser, *Ondergang* I, pp. 187–8.
96 RIOD JR 1c, Minutes, 12 January 1942.
97 Herzberg, *Kroniek*, p. 80. De Jong, *Het Koninkrijk* V, p. 1055.
98 RIOD JR 1c, Minutes, 3 March 1942.
99 De Jong, *Het Koninkrijk* V, p. 1055. Presser, *Ondergang* I, pp. 190–1.
100 RIOD JR 1c, Minutes, 3 March 1942. De Jong, *Het Koninkrijk* V, pp. 1055–6, cites the minutes of the *Joodse Raad*, 5 March 1942.
101 Herzberg, *Kroniek*, pp. 79–80. Presser, *Ondergang* I, pp. 200–1.
102 Herzberg, *Kroniek*, p. 79. De Jong, *Het Koninkrijk* V, pp. 1058–9.
103 De Jong, *Het Koninkrijk* V, pp. 1059–60.
104 Presser, *Ondergang* I, pp. 198–9.
105 De Jong, *Het Koninkrijk* V, p. 1056.
106 RIOD JR 1d, Record of a meeting between Cohen, Asscher and Rodegro, 23 March 1942.
107 De Jong, *Het Koninkrijk* V, p. 1062–3.
108 Herzberg, *Kroniek*, p. 81.
109 De Jong, *Het Koninkrijk* V, p. 1064.
110 RIOD JR 46d. Report on the removal of Jews from Zaandam and Hilversum, 9 February 1942.
111 See, for example, RIOD, JR 1b, Circular to the Jews in Zeeland, 19 March 1942.
112 De Jong, *Het Koninkrijk* V, pp. 1066–7.
113 Herzberg, *Kroniek*, p. 64. The 'J' stood for *Jood* and the 'B' for *bastaard*. The latter term was soon replaced by 'G' for *gemengd* (mixed). C. van Dam, *Jodenvervolging in de Stad Utrecht: De Joodse Gemeenschap in de Stat Utrecht 1930–50* (Zutphen, De Walburg Pers, 1985), p. 72.
114 RIOD JR 1c, Minutes, 26 March 1942.
115 Herzberg, *Kroniek*, p. 82.
116 De Jong, *Het Koninkrijk* V, p. 1069.
117 Herzberg, *Kroniek*, p. 82.
118 De Jong, *Het Koninkrijk* V, p. 1076, notes that in the whole province of Friesland, only one café owner refused to put up the sign.
119 Presser, *Ondergang* I, pp. 218–23. De Jong, *Het Koninkrijk* V, pp. 1085–6.
120 M. J. Adriani Engels and G. H. Wallagh, *Nacht over Nederland* (Amsterdam, Ons Vrije Nederland, 1946), p. 15. Bob Moore, 'The Netherlands', in J. Noakes, ed., *The Civilian in War: The Home Front in Europe, Japan and the USA in World War II* (Exeter, Exeter University Press, 1992), pp. 138–9. Herzberg, *Kroniek*, pp. 88–9.

5 Deportation and extermination

1 B. Sijes, *Studies over Jodenvervolging* (Assen, van Gorcum, 1974), p. 122. Gerald Fleming, *Hitler and the Final Solution* (Oxford, Oxford University Press, 1986), pp. 112–13. N. Lindwer, ed., *Het Fatale Dilemma* (The Hague, SDU Uitgeverij, 1995), p. 23.
2 J. Adler, *The Jews of Paris and the Final Solution: Communal Response and Internal Conflicts, 1940–1944* (New York/Oxford, Oxford University Press,

1989), pp. 41–4. Christopher Browning, *The Final Solution and the German Foreign Office* (New York, Holmes and Meier, 1978), p. 100.

3 J.C.H. Blom, 'The Persecution of the Jews in the Netherlands: A Comparative Western European Perspective', *European History Quarterly* XIX (1989), p. 337.

4 J. Presser, *Ondergang. De Vervolging en Verdelging van het Nederlandse Jodendom 1940–45* (The Hague, Staatsuitgeverij, 1965), I, p. 247.

5 RIOD JR 1d, Note of meeting between Asscher and Cohen (JR) and Aus der Fünten and Wörlein (*Zentralstelle*), 30 June 1942.

6 L.R. de Jong, *Het Koninkrijk der Nederlanden in de Tweede Wereldoorlog,* 14 vols (The Hague, Staatsuitgeverij, 1969–92), VI, p. 4.

7 A.J. Herzberg, *Kroniek der Jodenvervolging 1940–45* (Amsterdam, Querido, 1985), p. 140. Sijes, *Studies*, p. 122, cites the letter from the Auswärtiges Amt to the RSHA on 29 July 1942 which had no objection to the deportation of Western European Jews to Auschwitz as long as the stateless (and that included the German and Austrian) Jews were sent first.

8 De Jong, *Het Koninkrijk* VI, p. 6.

9 RIOD JR 1b, Circular to all staff, 15 July 1942. H. Wielek, *De Oorlog die Hitler Won* (Amsterdam, Amsterdam Boek- en Courantmij N.V., 1947), p. 148. Presser, *Ondergang* I, p. 257. R. Hilberg, *The Destruction of European Jews,* 3 vols (New York, Holmes and Meier, 1985), p. 585. Herzberg, *Kroniek*, p. 141. The latter gives the figure of those arrested as 750.

10 RIOD JR 1c, Minutes, 14 July 1942. Presser, *Ondergang* I, p. 257. A copy of the circular can be found in RIOD JR 5d, dated 14 July 1942.

11 Presser, *Ondergang* I, pp. 262–3. Joods Historisch Museum, *Documenten van de Jodenvervolging in Nederland, 1940–1945* (Amsterdam, Athenaeum-Polak and Van Gennep, 1979), p. 115, cites figures provided by the RIOD in 1964 where the three trains from Westerbork to Auschwitz conveyed a total of 2,030 individuals.

12 Presser, *Ondergang* I, p. 250. De Jong, *Het Koninkrijk* VI, pp. 25–6.

13 De Jong, *Het Koninkrijk* VI, pp. 25–6. Presser, *Ondergang* I, p. 285. The term 'Jewish Theatre' had been coined in the autumn of 1941 when all theatres were segregated and the '*Hollandse* Theatre' was used exclusively by the Jews.

14 De Jong, *Het Koninkrijk* VI, pp. 27–8. Presser, *Ondergang* I, pp. 268–73.

15 De Jong, *Het Koninkrijk* VI, p. 28.

16 Presser, *Ondergang* I, p. 270, cites Cohen, *Herinneringen*, p. 73.

17 Presser, *Ondergang* I, p. 278. RIOD JR 1c, Minutes, 3 September 1942.

18 RIOD JR 1c, Minutes, 3 September 1942, record a transport of old people from Haarlem, 'one of the most miserable occurrences'.

19 RIOD JR 1c, Minutes, 1 October 1942.

20 Lindwer, *Fatale Dilemma*, p. 29.

21 Presser, *Ondergang* I, p. 291, cites Gertrude van Tijn-Cohn, *Bijdrage tot de Geschiedenis der Joden in Nederland van 10 Mei 1940 tot Juni 1944* (unpublished), p. 48.

22 Presser, *Ondergang* I, pp. 291–2.

23 Presser, *Ondergang* I, p. 296.

24 Presser, *Ondergang* I, pp. 280–2. V. Jakob and A. van der Voort, *Anne Frank war nicht allein* (Bonn, Dietz, 1988), pp. 225–6.

25 Presser, *Ondergang* I, pp. 282–3.

26 De Jong, *Het Koninkrijk* VI, pp. 238–9. Presser, *Ondergang* I, pp. 300–1. Lindwer, *Fatale Dilemma*, p. 28.

27 In this context, 'foreign' meant Jews from countries other than the Netherlands, Germany and Austria.

28 RIOD JR 1c, Minutes, 20 October 1942.
29 Presser, *Ondergang* I, p. 302.
30 Presser, *Ondergang* I, pp. 304–5.
31 Presser, *Ondergang* I, p. 302. De Jong, *Het Koninkrijk* VI, pp. 240–1.
32 De Jong, *Het Koninkrijk* VI, pp. 235–6.
33 RIOD JR 11a, Note, 24 August 1942.
34 De Jong, *Het Koninkrijk* VI, p. 254.
35 RIOD JR 11b. Note, 2 December 1942, records a transport of 825 people who were mainly the employees and their families of the Hollandia-Kattenburg factory.
36 De Jong, *Het Koninkrijk* VI, pp. 285–7. Presser, *Ondergang* I, pp. 307–8.
37 Blom, 'Persecution', pp. 338–9. M. Steinberg, *L'Etoile et le Fusil,* 3 vols (Brussels, Vie Ouvrière, 1983–86), *Vol. II Les Cent Jours de la Déportation* (1984), p. 235.
38 RIOD JR 1c, Minutes, 17 December 1942, note that 47,000 Jews had been sent to Westerbork of whom 38,600 had been sent to Germany. RIOD JR 7b, Letter from Asscher and Cohen to Böhmcker, 23 December, reports 8,000 Jews in Westerbork and 40,000 sent as labour to Germany.
39 This had not precluded some earlier raids on rest homes. See RIOD JR 11b, Note, 8 November 1942.
40 De Jong, *Het Koninkrijk* VI, pp. 319–20. Presser, *Ondergang* I, p. 323. The hospital had around 1,100 patients and a nearby institute a further 94 invalid or educationally subnormal children.
41 RIOD JR 1b, Circular to all staff, 22 January 1943. Also File 1c, Minutes, 25 January 1943, notes endless reports about the behaviour of the *Ordedienst.* Presser, *Ondergang* I, pp. 324–33. De Jong, *Het Koninkrijk* VI, pp. 319–26. Sijes, *Studies*, pp. 119–20. M. Gilbert, *The Holocaust. The Jewish Tragedy* (London, Collins, 1986), pp. 525–9.
42 Sijes, *Studies*, pp. 119–20.
43 De Jong, *Het Koninkrijk* VI, pp. 326–7. Presser, *Ondergang* I, pp. 341–3.
44 De Jong, *Het Koninkrijk* VI, pp. 333–4, 371–2.
45 Hilberg, *Destruction*, p. 590. De Jong, *Het Koninkrijk* VI, pp. 333–4.
46 RIOD JR 1c, Minutes 25 February 1942. De Jong, *Het Koninkrijk* VI, pp. 332–3.
47 Hilberg, *Destruction*, p. 586–7, cites a communication from Rauter to Himmler of 10 September 1942 that all the remaining Jews would be placed in these two camps, which would have a combined capacity of 40,000.
48 The only exception was a transport of 196 specially selected people sent to Theresienstadt on 27 April 1943.
49 E.A. Cohen, *De Negentien Trienen naar Sobibor* (Amsterdam, Sijthoff, 1985), p. 22.
50 Blom, 'Persecution', p. 339. A transport from Paris on 4 March was also apparently diverted away from Auschwitz to Chelm, from where most of its deportees were transferred to Sobibor. Gilbert, *Holocaust*, pp. 546–7.
51 Blom, 'Persecution', pp. 339–41. P. Griffioen and R. Zeller, 'Jodenvervolging in Nederland en België tijdens de Tweede Wereldoorlog: Een Vergelijkende Analyse', *Oorlogsdocumentatie* VIII (1997), n.p., note that from the end of November 1942 to March 1943, the *Reichsbahn* did not provide any trains for deportations from Belgium.
52 Cohen, *De Negentien Trienen naar Sobibor*, p. 22.
53 Ph. Mechanicus, *Waiting for Death*, trans. I.R. Gibbons (London, Calder and Boyars, 1968), p. 40. Hilberg, *Destruction*, p. 591.
54 Joods Historisch Museum, 'Documenten', pp. 118–19.

55 RIOD JR 1c, Minutes, 25 March 1943 and 8 April 1943. JR 6b, Letter Cohen to *Zentralstelle*, 2 April 1943, tries to have 600 taken from Vught to Westerbork recalled.
56 RIOD JR 6b, Cohen to *Zentralstelle*, 11 April 1943.
57 RIOD JR 1c, Minutes, 22 May 1943. Wielek, *De Oorlog*, pp. 208-9. Presser, *Ondergang* I, pp. 370–1. Hilberg, *Destruction*, p. 592.
58 RIOD JR 1a, Note on cutbacks in administration, Summer 1943.
59 RIOD JR 1b (circulaires) provides an example of the call-up papers sent out to individuals, complete with the usual threats about non-compliance.
60 Wielek, *De Oorlog*, p. 210. Presser, *Ondergang* I, p. 373.
61 Presser, *Ondergang* I, pp. 381–2.
62 RIOD JR 1a, Memorandum of 23–24 July 1943.
63 RIOD JR 6b, Letter Cohen to Lages, 30 July 1943.
64 Hilberg, *Destruction*, p. 594. Presser, *Ondergang* I, pp. 381–2, 386–7. Wielek, *De Oorlog*, p. 262.
65 Wielek, *De Oorlog*, pp. 254–5.
66 Hilberg, *Destruction*, pp. 593–4. Presser, *Ondergang* I, pp. 382–7.
67 Cohen, *De Negentien Trienen naar Sobibor*, p. 22.
68 A special section of the *Zentralstelle* created to carry out this task.
69 The Lippmann-Rosenthal Bank had been a Jewish-owned concern, but was taken over and converted by the Germans into an agency for the collection and distribution of Jewish assets.
70 De Jong, *Het Koninkrijk* VI, pp. 335–6.
71 De Jong, *Het Koninkrijk* VI, pp. 337–8.
72 Wielek, *De Oorlog*, p. 257.
73 Some of those involved ultimately found new employment in hunting down Jews in hiding for bounties given by the German authorities.
74 De Jong, *Het Koninkrijk* VI, p. 338.
75 Presser, *Ondergang* I, pp. 458ff.
76 RIOD JR 1d, Note of a meeting between Aus der Fünten, Cohen, Asscher and Sluzker, 27 September 1942.
77 See, for example, RIOD JR 6a, Letter from Cohen to Sluzker, 16 April 1943, asking him to help someone with an exemption who had been arrested.
78 Presser, *Ondergang* I, pp. 467–8.
79 Presser, *Ondergang* I, pp. 471–2.
80 J. Michman, 'The Controversy Surrounding the Jewish Council of Amsterdam. From its Inception to the Present Day', in M. Marrus, *The Nazi Holocaust* (Westport/London, Greenwood, 1989), VI, pp. 821–43.
81 Michman, 'Jewish Council', p. 822, cites Mechanicus, *Waiting for Death*, p. 167.
82 Mechanicus, *Waiting for Death*, p. 167.
83 Michman, 'Jewish Council', p. 824.
84 Michman, 'Jewish Council' p. 826, cites a memorandum by Meijer de Vries of 12 October 1941, which claims the the joint presidents were the only men to negotiate with the Germans. This hierarchy was justified on the grounds that there had to be consistent line presented. A copy of the memorandum can be found in RIOD JR 1a.
85 Wielek, *De Oorlog*, p. 255.
86 Michman, 'Jewish Council', p. 833.
87 Michman, 'Jewish Council', p. 834.
88 Herzberg, *Kroniek*, pp. 190–1.
89 Michman, 'Jewish Council', p. 836, makes the point that Herzberg had been more critical of Jewish Councils before he had defended them after the war.

90 Michman, 'Jewish Council', pp. 837–8.
91 This has not prevented further emotive critiques of Asscher and Cohen, most notably H. Knoop, *De Joodsche Raad: Het Drama van Abraham Asscher en David Cohen* (Amsterdam, Elsevier, 1983).
92 Michman, 'Jewish Council', pp. 842–3.
93 RIOD JR 1c, Minutes, 16 October 1941, noted the growing list of deaths.
94 RIOD JR 1c, Minutes, 18 September 1942; JR 11a, Note regarding communications for Birkenau, 29 September 1942.
95 RIOD JR 11d, Internal Information Bulletins, 6, 12, 15 December 1942, 26 January 1943, 19 March 1943, all signed by Dr G. Fränkel.
96 RIOD JR 5c, JR to Sipo, 15 April 1941.
97 RIOD JR 5c, Cohen and Asscher to Blumenthal (Sipo), 7 May 1941.
98 RIOD JR 5d, Circular, 14 September 1942, lists further deaths in Mauthausen.
99 J.Th.M. Houwink ten Cate, 'Het Jongere Deel. Demografische en sociale kenmerken van het jodendom in Nederland tijdens de vervolging', *Oorlogsdocumentatie '40–'45 Jaarboet van het Rijksinstituut voor Oorlogsdocumentatie* I (1989), pp. 29–30.
100 Houwink ten Cate, 'Het Jongere Deel', pp. 38–9.
101 Bart van der Boom, *Den Haag in de Tweede Wereldoorlog* (The Hague, SeaPress, 1995), p. 155.
102 B.E. ten Boom, 'The Deportation of the Jewish Community in Den Haag' (Unpublished conference paper: 'Deportation Management and Resistance in (Western) Europe', RIOD, 23–24 November 1992), n.p.
103 Van der Boom, *Den Haag*, pp. 169–71.
104 Van der Boom, 'The Deportation', n.p.

6 Survival: exemptions and exclusions

1 J. Presser, *Ondergang. De Vervolging en Verdelging van het Nederlandse Jodendom 1940–45* (The Hague, Staatsuitgeverij, 1965), I, pp. 194–6.
2 Presser, *Ondergang* I, pp. 197–9.
3 H. Wielek, *De Oorlog die Hitler Won* (Amsterdam, Amsterdam Boek- en Courantmij N.V., 1947), pp. 256–7. Presser, *Ondergang* II, pp. 231–2. B. van der Boom, *Den Haag in de Tweede Wereldoorlog* (The Hague, SeaPress, 1995), p. 167.
4 A.J. Herzberg, *Kroniek der Jodenvervolging 1940–45* (Amsterdam, Meulenhoff, 1978), p. 180. L.R. de Jong, *Het Koninkrijk der Nederlanden in de Tweede Wereldoorlog*, 14 vols (The Hague, Staatsuitgeverij, 1969–92), V, pp. 536–7. Presser, *Ondergang* II, pp. 51–3.
5 Presser, *Ondergang* II, p. 54.
6 Herzberg, *Kroniek*, p. 182.
7 De Jong, *Het Koninkrijk* VI, pp. 306–7. Ten Cate's *Centrale Dienst voor Sibbekunde* compiled meticulous dossiers from baptismal records, the Jewish registers of 1811, the records of the *burgerlijke stand*, from old notarial records and from East Indian and especially West Indian newspapers. The fact that ten Cate had this information acted as a substantial brake on Calmeyer's freedom of action.
8 De Jong, *Het Koninkrijk* V, pp. 540–3.
9 Presser, *Ondergang* II, p. 60. Herzberg, *Kroniek*, p. 183.
10 Herzberg, *Kroniek*, p. 184.
11 De Jong, *Het Koninkrijk* VI, pp. 309–10.

12 Herzberg, *Kroniek*, p. 184.
13 De Jong, *Het Koninkrijk* V, pp. 1093–4.
14 Presser, *Ondergang* II, p. 79.
15 De Jong, *Het Koninkrijk* VI, p. 307.
16 Presser, *Ondergang* II, pp. 81–2, notes 108 Portuguese Jews from Amsterdam and 13 plus three children from Rotterdam, Leiden and Katwijk. De Jong, *Het Koninkrijk* VII, pp. 405–7.
17 De Jong, *Het Koninkrijk* VII, pp. 406–7, notes that in 1943 the Portuguese government had given some thought to saving these people but communications with the *Auswärtiges Amt* proved fruitless.
18 Presser, *Ondergang* II, p. 83. De Jong, *Het Koninkrijk* VII, p. 407. Herzberg, *Kroniek*, pp. 186–7.
19 Wielek, *De Oorlog*, p. 299, dates this measure from January 1943, but his document appears to be a modified version of an order by Schrieke (Secretary-General at the Ministry of Justice) of 8 April 1942, modified on 5 May 1942 and 8 January 1943.
20 Presser, *Ondergang* I, pp. 212–14. In spite of intervention by the Jewish Council, only two were released and the other 28 were sent to Amersfoort as punishment cases for 'special treatment'. The men involved were ultimately sent to Mauthausen and the women to a prison in Cleve. Wielek, *De Oorlog*, pp. 297–8.
21 Wielek, *De Oorlog*, p. 297.
22 Presser, *Ondergang* II, p. 89.
23 Presser, *Ondergang* I, p. 366. It may be that Lentz's figures included quarter- and half-Jews as well as full-Jews which may help to explain the discrepancy between the two sets of figures.
24 Wielek, *De Oorlog*, p. 300.
25 Wielek, *De Oorlog*, p. 300. In J. Presser, *Ashes in the Wind* (London, Souvenir Press, 1968), p. 315, this is translated as 'the devious labyrinth' and seems to suggest that there was a German 'line' on this issue, but then states that they never knew what they were doing. The Dutch version, *Ondergang* II, p. 90, indicates only that people did not know what the Germans intended as there were so many contradictory or countermanded statements.
26 Presser, *Ondergang* II, p. 91.
27 Wielek, *De Oorlog*, pp. 315–17.
28 Presser, *Ondergang* I, p. 366. Wielek, *De Oorlog*, p. 317.
29 J.Th.M. Houwink ten Cate, 'Het Jongere Deel. Demografische en sociale kenmerken van het jodendom in Nederland tijdens de vervolging' *Ooorlogsdocumentatie '40–'45, Jaarboek van het Rijksinstituut voor Oorlogsdocumentatie I* (1989), p. 20.
30 Wielek, *De Oorlog*, pp. 213–15.
31 Wielek, *De Oorlog*, p. 217.
32 Robert M. W. Kempner, *Twee uit Honderdduizend: Anne Frank en Edith Stein* (Bilthoven, H. Nelissen, 1969), pp. 99–100.
33 Kempner, *Twee*, p. 93, gives a precise figure of 694.
34 Kempner, *Twee*, p. 93.
35 Presser, *Ondergang* II, p. 85.
36 Th. Delleman, ed., *Opdat wij niet vergeten* (Kampen, n.p., 1949), pp. 175–6.
37 Presser, *Ondergang* II, pp. 86–7. Kempner, *Twee*, p. 155.
38 De Jong, *Het Koninkrijk* VII, p. 407. The women and children were sent to Ravensbrück and the men to Buchenwald.
39 De Jong, *Het Koninkrijk* VI, p. 276, note 1, records that many Jews claiming British nationality were deported in this way and that a list submitted by the

British authorities via the Swiss contained the names of 138 people who had been deported.

40 De Jong, *Het Koninkrijk* VI, pp. 274–6.
41 De Jong, *Het Koninkrijk* VI, pp. 276–7; VII, pp. 407–9. Presser, *Ondergang* I, pp. 423–30.
42 De Jong, *Het Koninkrijk* VI, p. 276, note 1, quotes a letter from Eichmann to Zöpf in June 1943.
43 De Jong, *Het Koninkrijk* VII, pp. 407–8; VI, p. 278. Presser, *Ondergang* II, pp. 43–9.
44 Presser, *Ondergang* I, pp. 441–2.
45 Boris de Munnick, 'Uitverkoren in uitzondering? Het Verhaal van de Barneveldgroep, 1942–1943', *Skript Historisch Tijdschrift* XII (1990), p. 68.
46 De Munnick, 'Uitverkoren', pp. 67–8.
47 De Jong, *Het Koninkrijk* VI, pp. 287–8.
48 De Munnick, 'Uitverkoren', p. 71.
49 Presser, *Ondergang* I, pp. 439–47. De Jong, *Het Koninkrijk* VI, pp. 285–90. Herzberg, *Kroniek*, pp. 172–5.
50 De Munnick, 'Uitverkoren', p. 75.
51 *Joodse Wachter*, 19 February 1954, cited in Presser, *Ondergang* I, p. 447.
52 De Jong, *Het Koninkrijk* VI, p. 286. Presser, *Ondergang* II, pp. 100–1.
53 De Jong, *Het Koninkrijk* VI, pp. 279–80.
54 De Jong, *Het Koninkrijk* VI, pp. 280–1. De Jong also records the activities of a Swiss, Walter Büchi, who organised exits to Swizerland in exchange for money, diamonds and Persian carpets. He was almost certainly in league with the Sipo and the few Jews who made the journey were arrested at Cologne station and most ended their lives at Auschwitz.
55 Presser, *Ondergang* II, p. 100.
56 The details for this section are taken from Herzberg, *Kroniek*, pp. 233–7, 339–47. Presser, *Ondergang* II, pp. 101–10. Given the importance which Presser attaches to the interpretation of Weinreb's activities, it is somewhat surprising that this section was omitted from the English translation. De Jong, *Het Koninkrijk* VII, pp. 446–60.
57 Friedrich Weinreb, *Collaboratie en Verzet. Een poging tot ontmythologisering*, 3 vols (Amsterdam, Meulenhoff, 1969). See also, Dick Houwaart, *Weinreb: Een Witboek* (Amsterdam, Meulenhoff, 1975).
58 Herzberg, *Kroniek*, pp. 339–42.
59 D. Gilthay Veth and A.D. van der Leeuw, *Rapport door RIOD inzake Activiteiten van drs. F. Weinreb gedurende 1940–45*, 2 vols (The Hague, Staatsuitgeverij, 1976). This is not to say that the report itself did not go uncriticised. In an important article Schöffer argued that it fell into the same trap as many other RIOD publications by being too moralistic and by being too judgemental with its conclusions (both for and against) and leaving little room for the reader's own judgement. Ivo Schöffer, 'Weinreb, een affair van lange duur', *Tijdschrift voor Geschiedenis* XCV (1982), pp. 196–224, esp. pp. 210–11.
60 Herzberg, *Kroniek*, p. 344, cites the RIOD report, Gilthay Veth and van der Leeuw, *Rapport*, p. 586.
61 Schöffer, 'Weinreb', p. 215.
62 Presser, *Ondergang* II, pp. 83–4.
63 Quote from the Armaments Inspectorate (*Rüstungsinspektion Niederlande*) in spring 1943, cited in Presser, *Ondergang* II, p. 94.
64 Presser, *Ondergang* II, pp. 94–9.

65 Presser, *Ondergang* II, p. 223. He notes that by 1941 there were only about 1,000 'active' workers in the industry of whom around 60 per cent were Jewish.

66 De Jong, *Het Koninkrijk* VI, p. 298.

67 Presser, *Ondergang* II, p. 224. A.J. van der Leeuw, 'Die Aktion Bozenhardt & Co', in A.H. Paape, ed., *Studies over Nederland in Oorlogstijd* (The Hague, Martinus Nijhoff, 1972), I, p. 262. De Jong, *Het Koninkrijk* VI, p. 299 gives a figure of 800 workers, which is strange as he claims this section of his work is based on van der Leeuw.

68 Van der Leeuw, 'Bozenhardt', pp. 257–77, esp. pp. 260, 262. The Dutch administration of the industry took place through the *Rijksbureau voor Diamant* (State Diamond Bureau) which was part of the *Departement voor Handel, Nijverheid en Scheepvaart* (Department for Commerce, Industry and Shipping).

69 De Jong, *Het Koninkrijk* VI, p. 299.

70 De Jong, *Het Koninkrijk* VII, pp. 308–9. Presser, *Ondergang* II, pp. 225–6.

71 De Jong, *Het Koninkrijk* VII, pp. 314–15.

72 Presser, *Ondergang* II, pp. 226–7.

73 De Jong, *Het Koninkrijk* VI, pp. 297–8. Presser, *Ondergang* II, p. 226.

74 De Jong, *Het Koninkrijk* VII, pp. 314–15. Presser, *Ondergang* II, pp. 226–7.

75 De Jong, *Het Koninkrijk* VII, pp. 92–3.

76 De Jong, *Het Koninkrijk* VII, pp. 916–17, notes the work of W.E.A. de Graaff in smuggling South American passports from Switzerland for Jews in Belgium and the Netherlands.

77 V. Jakob and A. van der Voort, *Anne Frank war nicht allein* (Bonn, Dietz, 1988) (Gert R.), pp. 134–5. Officially a concentration camp, *Konzentrationslager Herzogenbusch* included a *Schutzhaftlager* (protective custody camp) for non-Jews and (political) prisoners as well as the transit camp for Jews.

78 Herzberg, *Kroniek*, p. 158.

79 Herzberg, *Kroniek*, p. 277. De Jong, *Het Koninkrijk* VIII, pp. 670–1. Presser, *Ondergang* II, pp. 403–4. The group consisted of 90 men, 389 women and 17 children. For a detailed description of one family's stay in Vught as part of the Philips-*Kommando*, see David Koker, *Dagboek Geschreven in Vught* (Amsterdam, G.A. van Oorschot, 1977).

80 One of those who survived was Joop Citroen, whose story is told in S. Citroen, *Duet Pathétique: Belevenissen van een Joods Gezin in Oorlogstijd 1940–45* (Utrecht, Veen, 1988). De Jong, *Het Koninkrijk* VIII, p. 672, lists the proportion of survivors as *c.*40 males and *c.*160 females.

81 Presser, *Ondergang* II, p. 390.

82 De Jong, *Het Koninkrijk* VIII, pp. 670–1.

83 Presser, *Ondergang* II, pp. 402–4.

84 Presser, *Ondergang* II, pp. 403, cites the description of the transport by Professor Cleveringa (then an inmate of the camp).

7 Survival in hiding

1 W. Warmbrunn, *The Dutch under German Occupation 1940–45* (Stanford, Stanford University Press, 1963), p. 187. S. and P.M. Oliner, *The Altruistic Personality: Rescuers of Jews in Nazi Europe* (New York, Free Press, 1988), p. 37. J. Presser, *Ondergang. De Vervolging en Verdelging van het Nederlandse Jodendom 1940–45* (The Hague, Staatsuitgeverij, 1965), II, pp. 241–83 does not need to explain the term to a Dutch audience and his translator Pomerans

avoids its use altogether, *Ashes in the Wind* (London, Souvenir Press, 1968), pp. 381–405. The term *fietsers* or cyclists was also used.

2 A.J. Herzberg, *Kroniek der Jodenvervolging 1940–45* (Amsterdam, Querido, 1985), pp. 316–18. Presser, *Ondergang* II, p. 245. K.P.L. Berkley, *Overzicht van het Outstaan, De Werkzaamheden en het Streven van den Joodsche Raad voor Amsterdam* (Amsterdam, n.p., 1945), p. 94.

3 J.Th.M. Houwink ten Cate, 'Het Jongere Deel. Demografische en sociale kenmerken van het jodendom in Nederland tijdens de vervolging', *Oorlogsdocumentatie '40–'45, Jaarboek van het Rijksinstituut voor Oorlogsdocumentatie* I (1989), p. 17 and L.R. de Jong, *Het Koninkrijk der Nederlanden in de Tweede Wereldoorlog*, 14 vols (The Hague, Staatsuitgeverij, 1969–92), VI, pp. 359–60 and VII, p. 453 suggest 25,000 while G. Hirschfeld, 'Niederlande', in W. Benz, *Dimension des Völkermords. Die Zähl der jüdischen Opfer des Nationalsozialismus* (Munich, R. Oldenbourg Verlag, 1991), p. 156 derives a figure of 20,000 but accepts that it is impossible to be precise.

4 The most famous of these raids took place in Rotterdam on 10 November 1944 when 50,000 men were taken away. See B. A. Sijes, *De Razzia van Rotterdam* (Amsterdam, Sijthoff, 1984) reprint of 1951 edition. Warmbrunn, *The Dutch under German Occupation*, p. 188.

5 Interview with *mevr.* Annie Hoek-Wallach. Text and tapes held by Wiener Library, London.

6 The most important exceptions to this being, of course, the diaries kept by Anne Frank, *Het Achterhuis* and Philip Mechanicus, *Waiting for Death* (London, Calder and Boyars, 1968).

7 Presser, *Ondergang* II, pp. 241–2.

8 See, for example, M. Gies, *Anne Frank Remembered: The Story of the Woman who Helped Hide the Frank Family* (New York, Simon and Schuster, 1987). Corrie ten Boom, *De Schuilplaats* (Hoornaar, Gideon, 1992). Frank Visser, *De Pensionhoudster en de Onderduiker* (Baarn, Bosch & Keuning, 1980).

9 J. Zwaan, 'Het protestants-christelijk verzet, de LO-LKP', in R.F. Roegholt and J. Zwaan, eds, *Het Verzet 1940–45* (Weesp, Unieboek, 1985), pp. 43–73. RIOD Files LO-LKP 251a, LO-BP1, LO-BP2, LO-BO3/BO4.

10 Mordecai Paldiel, 'The Rescue of Jewish Children in Poland and the Netherlands', in Alice L. Eckardt, ed., *Burning Memory: Times of Testing and Reckoning* (Oxford/New York, Pergamon, 1993), p. 138. See also Mordecai Paldiel, *The Path of the Righteous. Gentile Rescuers of the Jews during the Holocaust* (Hobokcn, NJ, Ktav, 1993).

11 Oliner and Oliner, *The Altruistic Personality*. This study also used the Yad Vashem archives to identify and locate suitable persons for interview.

12 B. Evers-Emden, *Onderduikouders en hun Joodse 'kinderen' over de onderduikperiode* (Utrecht, Stichting ICODO, 1988), p. 50.

13 Louis de Jong, 'Help to People in Hiding', *Delta* VII (1965), pp. 39–79. Henry L. Mason, 'Testing Human Bonds within Nations: Jews in the Occupied Netherlands', *Political Science Quarterly* XCIX (1984), pp. 315–43. Helen Fein, *Accounting for Genocide: National Responses and Jewish Victimization during the Holocaust* (New York, Free Press, 1979). Lawrence Baron, 'The Dynamics of Decency: Dutch Rescuers of Jews during the Holocaust', *Frank P. Piskor Faculty Lecture*, St Lawrence University, May 1985. Paldiel, 'The Rescue of Jewish Children' and Lawrence Baron, 'The Dutch Dimension of Jewish Rescue', both in Eckhardt, *Burning Memory*, pp. 119–39 and 153–65 respectively. Leni Yahil, 'Methods of Persecution: A Comparison of the Final Solution in Holland and Denmark', *Scripta Hierosolymitana* XIII (1972), pp. 279–300. Other material on the Netherlands can be found in Philip Friedman, *Their*

Brother's Keepers. The Christian Heroes and Heroines who Helped the Oppressed Escape the Nazi Terror (New York, Crown, 1957) and Eva Fogelman, *Conscience and Courage. Rescuers of the Jews during the Holocaust* (London, Victor Gollancz, 1995).

14 See, for example, J.M. Snoek, *De Nederlandse Kerken en de joden. De protesten bij Seyss-Inquart. Hulp aan joodse onderduikers. De motieven voor hulpverlening* (Kampen, Kok, 1990) and its review by D. Barnouw, 'Vijftig jaar na de inval', *Bijdragen en Mededelingen betreffende de geschiedenis der Nederlanden* CVII (1992), pp. 287–95.

15 See, for example, RIOD Collection 181a HSSpF/111 and US National Archives, RG242 (Captured German Archives) T175 (RfSS-CdP) Rolls 670 and 671.

16 RIOD, HSSpF167/263H Gruppe Henneicke. G. van Meershoek, 'De Amsterdamse Hoodcommissaris en de deportatie van de joden', *Oorlogsdocumentatie '40-'45: Derde Jaarboek van het Rijksinstituut voor Oorlogsdocumentatie*, pp. 9–44. J.J. Kelder, *De Schalkhaarders: Nederlandse Politiemannen naar Nationaal-socialistische snit* (Utrecht/Antwerp, Veen, 1990).

17 De Jong, 'Help to People in Hiding', p. 51. Presser, *Ondergang* II, p. 266.

18 Presser, *Ondergang* II, p. 251.

19 Baron, 'The Dutch Dimension', pp. 157–8.

20 Presser, *Ondergang* II, pp. 245–6.

21 Presser, *Ondergang* II, p. 248.

22 W. Emanuel, *Underground in Holland* (Amsterdam, mimeogr. RIOD, 1979), p. 16.

23 A. Caransa, *Verzamelen op het Transvaalplein: ter Nagedachtenis van het Joodse Proletariaat van Amsterdam* (Baarn, Bosch & Keuning, 1984), p. 69.

24 WL-PIIId/197.

25 V. Jakob and A. van der Voort, *Anne Frank war nicht allein* (Bonn, Dietz, 1988) (Carlotta M.), p. 149.

26 Emanuel, *Underground*, p. 12.

27 L.R. de Jong, *The Netherlands and Nazi Germany* (Cambridge, Mass., Harvard University Press, 1990), p. 41. Eva Fogelman, *Conscience and Courage, Rescuers of Jews during the Holocaust* (London, Victor Gollancz, 1995), pp. 51–2.

28 C. Rittner and S. Myers, *The Courage to Care: Rescuers of Jews during the Holocaust* (New York, New York University Press, 1986), p. 34 (Max Rothschild) notes similar sentiments on the part of some Palestine Pioneers. Caransa, *Verzamelen*, pp. 48–9.

29 De Jong, *Het Koninkrijk* VI, pp. 339–40.

30 Presser, *Ondergang* II, p. 245.

31 Herzberg, *Kroniek*, pp. 131–2.

32 See, for example, Jakob and van der Voort, *Anne Frank* (Hans B.), p. 126. D. Barnouw and G. van der Stroom, eds, *The Diary of Anne Frank: The Critical Edition* (London, Viking, 1989), p. 211.

33 Eva Schloss, *Herinneringen van een Joods Meisje* (Amsterdam, Sua, 1989), pp. 30–3.

34 Emanuel, *Underground*, pp. 8–9.

35 De Jong, *Het Koninkrijk* VI, pp. 339–40.

36 Presser, *Ondergang* II, pp. 391–2.

37 Ben Braber, 'De activiteiten van Barbie in Nederland in de jaren 1940–1945' (Doctoraalscriptie, University of Amsterdam, 1984), p. 34.

38 De Jong, *Het Koninkrijk* VI, pp. 339–40.

39 J. van der Kar, *Joodse Verzet. Terugblik op de Periode Rond de Tweede Wereldoorlog* (Amsterdam, Stadsdrukkerij, 1981), p. 49.

40 RIOD Collection 251a (LO-LKP), LO-BP1, LO/II Betuwe; LO-BO3/BO4, LO/II Drenthe. De Jong, *Het Koninkrijk* VI, pp. 356–7 gives further examples.

41 The counter-argument to this was that the BBC sounded too optimistic. By predicting the almost immediate collapse of the German regime, they encouraged people to hang on rather than to go underground. Rittner and Myers, *Courage to Care*, p. 35.

42 WL-PIIIg/918, Johanna-Ruth Dobschiner, *Te Mogen Leven: Een Nederlandse Jodin vertelt haar geschiedenis* (Franeker, T. Wever, 1974), pp. 113–128. The story of another Jewess who survived above ground for some time at the *Joodse Invalide* and *Nederlands-Israëlitisch Ziekenhuis* is in Leesha Rose, *The Tulips are Red* (New York, A.S. Barnes, 1981), R. Ruth Linden, *Making Stories, Making Selves: Feminist Reflections on the Holocaust* (Columbus, Ohio, Ohio State University Press, 1993).

43 C. van Dam, *Jodenvervolging in de Stad Utrecht: De Joodse Gemeenschap in de Stad Utrecht 1930–50* (Zutphen, De Walburg Pers, 1985), pp. 118–19. The deputy chairman was arrested in 1944 and died in Poland, but the chairman survived legally until the liberation.

44 Van Dam, *Jodenvervolging*, pp. 118–19.

45 A.J. van der Leeuw, 'Utrecht in de Oorlogsjaren', in J. van Miert, ed., *Een gewone stad in een bijzondere tijd: Utrecht 1940–1945* (Utrecht, Het Spectrum, 1995), p. 39.

46 De Jong, 'Help to People in Hiding', p. 51. Presser, *Ondergang* II, p. 251, notes one Jewish couple who had 26 different 'addresses'.

47 Bert Jan Flim, *Omdat Hun Hart Sprak. Geschiedenis van de Georganiseerde Hulp aan Joodse Kinderen in Nederland, 1942–1945* (Kampen, Kok, 1996), p. 398. Bloeme Evers-Emden and Bert Jan Flim, *Ondergedoken Geweest* (Amsterdam, 1995), p. 50.

48 Caransa, *Verzamelen*, p. 69.

49 RIOD LO-LKP 251a LO-BO4, *Dagboek* Arnold Douwes, 10 March 1943, p. 16.

50 De Jong, *Het Koninkrijk* VI, pp. 342–4.

51 De Jong, *Het Koninkrijk* VII, pp. 477–81.

52 Presser, *Ondergang* II, pp. 394–5.

53 RIOD LO-LKP 251a LO-BO4 (Zwolle).

54 Presser, *Ondergang* II, p. 267 quotes H. Musaph, *Doodsdrift, castratie-complexen en depressie* (1948).

55 Presser, *Ondergang* II, p. 280.

56 De Jong, *Het Koninkrijk* VII, pp. 474–6.

57 Warmbrunn, *German Occupation*, pp. 52–3.

58 Warmbrunn, *German Occupation*, p. 52, cites VO197/1940.

59 Presser, *Ondergang* II, p. 246.

60 WL-PIIId/833.

8 Self-help, rescuers and bystanders

1 See, for example, H.L. Mason, 'Testing Human Bonds within Nations: Jews in the Occupied Netherlands', *Political Science Quarterly* XCIX (1984), p. 315.

2 J. Presser, *Ondergang. De Vervolging en Verdelging van het Nederlandse Jodendom 1940–45* (The Hague, Staatsuitgeverij, 1965), II, p. 255.

3 L. Baron, 'The Dynamics of Decency: Dutch Rescuers of Jews during the Holocaust', *Frank P. Piskor Faculty Lecture*, St Lawrence University, May 1985).

4 Baron, 'Dynamics', p. 6.
5 Baron, 'Dynamics', p. 8.
6 A more recent study, E. Fogelman, *Conscience and Courage. Rescuers of Jews during the Holocaust* (London, Victor Gollancz, 1995), pp. 161ff, identifies a different set of motives for rescue including those swayed by morality, Judeophiles, concerned professionals, network rescuers and child rescuers.
7 Frank Visser, *De Pensionhoudster en de Onderduiker* (Baarn, Bosch & Keuning, 1980). RIOD LO-LKP BO/BP2 (Haarlem), LO/BP2 (LO II-I Amsterdam, Interviews with T. van Leeuwen and J.W.J. Hamerling).
8 C. Rittner and S. Myers, *The Courage to Care: Rescuers of Jews during the Holocaust* (New York, New York University Press, 1986), p. 29.
9 Rittner and Myers, *Courage to Care*, p. 29.
10 L. Baron, 'The Dutch Dimension of Jewish Rescue', in Alice L. Eckhardt, ed., *Burning Memory: Times of Testing and Reckoning* (Oxford/New York, Pergamon, 1993), pp. 162–3.
11 L.R. de Jong, *Het Koninkrijk der Nederlanden in de Tweede Wereldoorlog*, 14 vols (The Hague, Staatsuitgeverij, 1969–92), VI, p. 343.
12 RIOD LO-LKP 251a LO-BO4, *Dagboek* Arnold Douwes, 3 November 1943, p. 55.
13 RIOD LO-LKP 251a LO-BO4, *Dagboek* Arnold Douwes, 3 November 1943, p. 55. De Jong, *Het Koninkrijk* VII, p. 467.
14 De Jong, *Het Koninkrijk* VI, p. 347.
15 Th. Delleman, ed., *Opdat wij niet vergeten* (Kampen, n.p., 1949), p. 173. See also, J.M. Snoek, *De Nederlandse Kerken en de joden 1940–1945* (Kampen, Kok, 1990), pp. 143–73.
16 See, for example, RIOD LO-LKP 251a LO-BO3 (Emmererfscheidenveen) which notes the work of *Gereformeerde* Pastoor de Graaf.
17 S. Stokman, *Het Verzet van de Nederlandsche Bisschoppen tegen Nationaal-Socialisme en Tyrannie* (Utrecht, Het Spectrum, 1945), pp. 114–17.
18 Andre Stein, *Quiet Heroes. True Stories of the Rescue of Jews by Christians in Nazi-occupied Holland* (New York, New York University Press, 1988), pp. 57, 70.
19 De Jong, *Het Koninkrijk* VII, pp. 462–3.
20 RIOD LO-LKP LO/BP2 (Amsterdam, interview with ds. Feenstra) who regarded saving Jews as a task given by God which also gave the opportunity to proselytise them.
21 De Jong, *Het Koninkrijk* VII, p. 462.
22 RIOD DocII/364a (Joodse Onderduikers) Letter: Tusveld.
23 H. Wolf, *De Gespijkerde God* (Nijmegen, SUN, 1995), p. 79.
24 Dick Houwaart, *Verduisterde Bevrijding* (The Hague, Omniboek, 1982), pp. 19–20. Snoek, *De Nederlandse Kerken*, pp. 159–60. J-R. Dobschiner, *Te Mogen Leven: Een Nederlandse Jodin vertelt haar geschiedenis* (Franeker, T. Wever, 1974), pp. 214–21.
25 De Jong, *Het Koninkrijk* VII, p. 464, notes this from Presser but argues that there were many other groups not connected with either students or the artistic community.
26 Presser, *Ondergang* II, p. 258.
27 See, for example, Koos Groen, *Als slachtoffers daders worden. De zaak van de joodse verraadster Ans van Dijk* (Baarn, Ambo, 1994).
28 De Jong, *Het Koninkrijk* VII, pp. 461–2.
29 H. Avni, 'Zionist Underground in Holland and France and the Escape to Spain', in Y. Gutman and E. Zuroff, eds, *Rescue Attempts during the Holocaust* (Jerusalem, Yad Vashem, 1977), pp. 555–90. De Jong, *Het Koninkrijk* VI, pp.

354–5. Not all the Palestine Pioneers felt this way. De Jong notes that some of the orthodox Jews felt that they could continue their training as pioneers after deportation.
30 Avni, 'Zionist Underground', p. 558.
31 Avni, 'Zionist Underground', pp. 584–5.
32 Figures differ here. De Jong, *Het Koninkrijk* VI, p. 356, gives a total of around 250 of the remaining 530, while A.J. Herzberg, *Kroniek der Jodenvervolging 1940–45* (Amsterdam, Querido, 1985), p. 229, suggests that 323 went underground. Both authors agree that around 80 were captured by the Germans. The overall survival of Pioneers in hiding or returned from the camps is comparatively very high at 44 per cent.
33 W. Westerweel, *Verzet zonder geweld. Ter herkenning van Joop Westerweel* (n.p., n.d.), mimeogr. RIOD, pp. 71–2.
34 Herzberg, *Kroniek*, p. 230. De Jong, *Het Koninkrijk* VI, p. 356.
35 B. Braber, *Zelfs als wij zullen verliezen. Joden in Verzet en Illegaliteit 1940–1945* (Amsterdam, Balans, 1990), pp. 85–7.
36 Avni, 'Zionist Underground', p. 567. WL-PIIId/229, WL-PIIId/230.
37 Avni, 'Zionist Underground', p. 570.
38 WL-PIIId/197.
39 WL-PIIIh/139/Auschwitz.
40 WL-PIId/785.
41 B. Braber, *Passage near Vrijheit. Joods Verzet in Nederland 1940–1945* (Amsterdam, Balans, 1987), pp. 23–34, 37–8.
42 Braber, *Passage*, pp. 40–1.
43 The grouping was often referred to as the *Oosteinde* or van Dien group. Braber, *Zelfs*, pp. 88–94.
44 De Jong, *Het Koninkrijk* VII, pp. 927–8.
45 De Jong, *Het Koninkrijk* IX, p. 587.
46 A previous director, J.C.A.M. Testers, and a journalist, J.W. Kolkman, had created a network to take Engelandvaarders from Switzerland to Spain, but they had both been arrested at the beginning of December 1942 and later died in concentration camps. De Jong, *Het Koninkrijk* VII, pp. 929-30; IX, pp. 582–8.
47 De Jong, *Het Koninkrijk* VII, pp. 930–1. It is also worthy of note that 'Dutch-Paris' was not purely an escape line, but also acted as a courier route for the *Zwitserse Weg*, an information and espionage network. This makes its survival to the end of the occupation even more surprising. For the story of one family who were taken to Switzerland by this network, see Jenny Gans-Premsela, *Vluchtweg. Aan de Bezetter Ontsnapt* (Baarn, Bosch & Keuning, 1990), pp. 24–45.
48 De Jong, *Het Koninkrijk* VI, pp. 126–9.
49 W. Warmbrunn, *The Dutch under German Occupation 1940–45* (Stanford, Stanford University Press, 1963), p. 189.
50 Warmbrunn, *The Dutch under German Occupation*, p. 189.
51 Warmbrunn, *The Dutch under German Occupation*, p. 189.
52 R.F. Roegholt and J. Zwaan, eds, *Het Verzet 1940–45* (Weesp, Unieboek, 1985), pp. 44–54.
53 Warmbrunn, *The Dutch under German Occupation*, pp. 199–201.
54 Warmbrunn, *The Dutch under German Occupation*, pp. 187–96.
55 RIOD LO-LKP LO/BP2 (Amsterdam, interview with J. Thijssen, district chief LO-Centrum).
56 RIOD LO-LKP LO/BP2 (Amsterdam, interview with J.W.J. Hamerling).
57 De Jong, *Het Koninkrijk* VI, p. 257.
58 RIOD LO-LKP LO/BP2 (Amsterdam, interview with *ds.* Feenstra).

59 RIOD LO-LKP LO/BP2 (Amsterdam, interview with *ds*. Feenstra).
60 RIOD LO-LKP 251a LO-BO4, *Dagboek* Arnold Douwes, 3 November 1943, p. 55.
61 RIOD LO-LKP LO/BP2 (Amsterdam, interview with T. van Leeuwen).
62 RIOD LO-LKP LO/BP1 (Blokzijl, Overijssel).
63 RIOD LO-LKP 251a LO-BO4, *Dagboek* Arnold Douwes, 3 November 1943, p. 54.
64 RIOD LO-LKP LO/BO3 Joure (Friesland).
65 RIOD LO-LKP LO/BP2 (Utrecht).
66 Maurice Ferares, *Violinist in het Verzet* (Amsterdam, Het Bataafsche Leeuw, 1991), p. 139.
67 Presser, *Ondergang* II, pp. 271–2.
68 RIOD LO-LKP LO/BO4 *Dagboek* Arnold Douwes, p. 55.
69 M. Koster, *Ons Leven in onderduiktijd* (Oosterbeek, Meyer R. Siegers, 1983), p. 8.
70 RIOD LO-LKP LO/BO3 (Heerenveen) LO/BO4 (Steenwijk, Ommen).
71 RIOD LO-LKP LO/BO3 (Hoogkerk).
72 RIOD LO-LKP LO/BO3 (Hoogeveen).
73 Koster, *Ons leven*, p. 14.
74 RIOD LO-LKP LO/BP2 (LO II-I Amsterdam).
75 For example, on rescue networks in Limburg, A.P.M. Cammaert, *Het verborgen front. Geschiedenis van de georganizeerde illegaliteit in de provincie Limburg tijdens de Tweede Wereldoorlog* (Leeuwarden, Eisma, 1994).
76 RIOD LO-LKP LO/BP2 (t'Gooi).
77 RIOD LO-LKP LO/BP2 (Het Gooi, LO-werk Oorlog 1940–45, interview with *mr*. Pos).
78 De Jong, *Het Koninkrijk* VII, pp. 463–4.
79 Elma Verhey, *Om het Joodse Kind* (Amsterdam, Nijgh & van Ditmar, 1991), p. 37.
80 RIOD LO-LKP BO/BP2 (Schagen).
81 A.H. Bornebroek, *De Illegaliteit in Twente* (Hengelo, Twentse-Gelderse Uitgeverij Witkam, 1985), pp. 36–40. C. Hilbrink, *De Illegalen. Illegaliteit in Twente en het aangrenzende Salland, 1940–1945* (The Hague, SDU, 1989). T. Wiegman, 'Ds. Overduin helpt onderduikers', *Sliepsteen* III (Autumn 1985), p. 7; IV (Winter, 1985), p. 15; V (1986), p. 7.
82 De Jong, *Het Koninkrijk* VI, p. 348. Corrie ten Boom, *De Schuilplaats* (Hoornaar, Gideon, 1972), pp. 85–145.
83 De Jong, *Het Koninkrijk* VI, pp. 348–51.
84 De Jong, *Het Koninkrijk* VI, p. 350.
85 Presser, *Ondergang* II, p. 264. RIOD LO-LKP LO/BP2 (Amsterdam, *ds*. Feenstra), p. 3.
86 Presser, *Ondergang* II, pp. 274–5.
87 Presser, *Ondergang* II, p. 257.
88 See, most recently, Bloeme Evers-Emden, *Geleende Kinderen. Ervaringen van onderduikouders en hun joodse beschermelingen in de jaren 1942 tot 1945* (Kampen, Kok, 1994) and Bert Jan Flim, *Omdat Hun Hart Sprak. Geschiedenis van de Georganiseerde Hulp aan Joodse Kinderen in Nederland, 1942–1945* (Kampen, Kok, 1996).
89 Flim, *Omdat hun Hart Sprak*, pp. 31, 93, 103.
90 Flim, *Omdat hun Hart Sprak*, p. 32.
91 Flim, *Omdat hun Hart Sprak*, pp. 33–9.
92 Flim, *Omdat hun Hart Sprak*, p. 45.

93 Flim, *Omdat hun Hart Sprak*, pp. 45–6. One of the Jewish paediatricians committed suicide and the other took the earliest opportunity to go underground.

94 Flim, *Omdat hun Hart Sprak*, pp. 52, 54. Her work was not confined to helping children and she had been active in all manner of resistance activities, although she gave up all but the children's work in January 1943.

95 Flim, *Omdat hun Hart Sprak*, pp. 62–3.

96 Flim, *Omdat hun Hart Sprak*, p. 76.

97 Flim, *Omdat hun Hart Sprak*, p. 87. See also, H. Overduin, 'Tante Zus kwam altijd onverwacht. *Opzij* XVI (May 1988), pp. 14-17.

98 Flim, *Omdat hun Hart Sprak*, pp. 93–5. See also Bert Jan Flim, *De NV en haar kinderen, 1942–1945. Geschiedenis van een Nederlandse verzetsorganisatie, gespecialiseerd in hulp aan Joodse kinderen* (Amsterdam, 1990) and A.W. Haverhals-Willemsz, 'Onderduiksperikelen', *Bruggeske* III (1989), pp. 25–31.

99 Flim, *Omdat hun Hart Sprak*, p. 95.

100 Snoek, *De Nederlandse Kerken*, pp. 149–55.

101 Roegholt and Zwaan, *Het Verzet*, pp. 61–2.

102 Flim, *Omdat hun Hart Sprak*, pp. 107–9. Verhey, *Joodse Kind*, pp. 22–5.

103 Ph. A.J. Mees, 'Mieke Louwers-Mees', *Kroniek van de Stichting Geslacht Mees* XXV (July 1976), pp. 3–5.

104 Verhey, *Joodse Kind*, pp. 25–6. Presser, *Ondergang* II, p. 11.

105 Flim, *Omdat hun Hart Sprak*, pp. 133–4.

106 Flim, *Omdat hun Hart Sprak*, p. 121, footnote 4. J. Van der Kar, *Joods Verzet. Terugblik op de Periode Rond de Tweede Wereldoorlog* (Amsterdam, Stadsdrukkerij, 1981), pp. 54–7.

107 Flim, *Omdat hun Hart Sprak*, pp. 138, 163.

108 WL PIIId/840. Herzberg, *Kroniek*, pp. 159–60.

109 De Jong, *Het Koninkrijk* VI, p. 258. Presser, *Ondergang* II, p. 11.

110 John David Morley, 'The Nicest SS Man Imaginable', *Times Magazine*, 4 June 1994, p. 20.

111 For one mention of Zündler's help, see WL PIIIh/836 (Auschwitz).

112 Morley, 'Nicest', p. 20. Saskia Belleman, 'Saviour or Killer from the Waffen SS', *Guardian*, 14 December 1993.

113 J. Houwink ten Cate, *Alfons Zündler en de bewaking van het gevangenkamp aan de Plantage Middelaan 24 te Amsterdam* (RIOD, unpublished, 1994).

114 De Jong, *Het Koninkrijk* VI, p. 352. Flim, *Omdat hun Hart*, pp. 142–7. Van der Kar, *Joods Verzet*, p. 62. Braber, *Zelfs*, pp. 82–3.

115 Flim, *Omdat hun Hart Sprak*, p. 163. He notes that the Utrecht group, Amsterdam group, *Naamloze Vennootschap* and *Trouw* group between them were responsible for saving 385 children from the crèche, with the remaining 215 being taken by individuals or other organisations. These four main organisations were also estimated to have rescued around 1,100 children in total. See also Verhey, *Joodse Kind*, p. 27.

116 Fogelman, *Conscience*, p. 15, quotes Miep Gies as estimating that she was one of around 20,000 rescuers in the Netherlands, but this probably ignores those who were complicit in rescue activities although not directly involved.

9 Persecutors, pursuers and accomplices

1 See, for example, Jeremy Josephs, *Swastika over Paris. The Fate of the French Jews* (London, Bloomsbury, 1989), p. 75.
2 G. Hirschfeld, *Nazi Rule and Dutch Collaboration: The Netherlands under German Occupation, 1940–1945* (Oxford/New York/Hamburg, Berg, 1988), p. 18.
3 Hirschfeld, *Nazi Rule*, p. 26 cites RIOD BDC H1103:7610–14, N. Neidhardt, 'Bericht über meinen Einsatz in Holland', 15 November 1941.
4 Hirschfeld, *Nazi Rule*, pp. 47–8.
5 J. Presser, *Ondergang. De Vervolging en Verdelging van het Nederlandse Jodendom 1940–45* (The Hague, Staatsuitgeverij, 1965), II, p. 170.
6 Presser, *Ondergang* II, pp. 163–4. For another example of her power, see R. Hilberg, *Perpetrators, Victims, Bystanders: The Jewish Catastrophe 1933–45* (London, Secker and Warburg, 1995), p. 135.
7 R. Hilberg, *The Destruction of European Jews*, 3 vols (New York, Holmes and Meier, 1985), p. 407.
8 J. Adler, *The Jews of Paris and the Final Solution: Communal Response and Internal Conflicts, 1940–1944* (New York, Oxford University Press, 1989), pp. 148–50.
9 W. Warmbrunn, *The German Occupation of Belgium 1940-1944* (New York, Peter Lang, 1993), pp. 151–2.
10 Warmbrunn, *Occupation of Belgium*, pp. 120–1, 152, 161–2. M. Steinberg, *L'Etoile et le Fusil*, 3 vols (Brussels, Vie Ouvrière, 1983–86), *Vol. II Les Cent Jours*, p. 203 and *Vol. III La Traque des Juifs*, pp. 222–9. There was one occasion on 28 August 1942 when Belgian police were used on a raid in Antwerp, but their use was not repeated. *Aktion Iltis* on 3–4 September was the only mass raid sanctioned by the authorities.
11 Adler, *The Jews of Paris*, pp. 56–7. Josephs, *Swastika*, p. 43.
12 Adler, *The Jews of Paris*, p. 239.
13 Adler, *The Jews of Paris*, pp. 148–9. Susan Zuccotti, *The Holocaust, the French and the Jews* (New York, Basic Books, 1993), p. 161.
14 Hirschfeld, *Nazi Rule*, p. 153.
15 Hirschfeld, *Nazi Rule*, p. 154, cites broadcast from Radio Oranje, 2 October 1943.
16 Michael Marrus and Robert Paxton, *Vichy et les Juifs* (Paris, Calmann-Lévy, 1981), p. 99. S. Klarsfeld, *Vichy-Auschwitz. Le Rôle de Vichy dans la Solution Finale de la Question Juive en France, 1942* (Paris, Fayard, 1983), p. 20.
17 L.R. de Jong, *Het Koninkrijk der Nederlanden in de Tweede Wereldoorlog*, 14 vols (The Hague, Staatsuitgeverij, 1969–92), V, pp. 446–8. L.R. de Jong, 'Help to People in Hiding', *Delta* VIII (Spring 1965), pp. 41-2.
18 De Jong, *Het Koninkrijk* V, pp. 451–2; VI, pp. 95–6. De Jong, 'Help to People in Hiding', pp. 42–4.
19 De Jong, *Het Koninkrijk* V, pp. 452–3. By 31 December 1941 some 7,177,504 identity cards had been issued. By this stage, registration of the entire population was all but complete.
20 De Jong, *Het Koninkrijk* V, pp. 454–5. De Jong, 'Help to People in Hiding', p. 46.
21 De Jong, 'Help to People in Hiding', pp. 46–7. For details of the specific problems of falsifying identity cards, see De Jong, *Het Koninkrijk* VII, pp. 715–16.
22 De Jong, *Het Koninkrijk* V, pp. 532–4.
23 Warmbrunn, *German Occupation*, pp. 52–3.

24 De Jong, *Het Koninkrijk* V, p. 456.
25 De Jong, *Het Koninkrijk* VI, pp. 714–36; VII, pp. 797–804.
26 De Jong, *Het Koninkrijk* VII, p. 803.
27 Hirschfeld, *Nazi Rule*, pp. 163–5. Cyrille Fijnault, 'The Police of the Netherlands in and between the Two World Wars', in Clive Emsley and Barabara Weinberger, eds, *Policing Western Europe. Politics, Professionalism and Public Order, 1850–1940* (New York/Westport/London, Greenwood, 1991), pp. 240–2.
28 Hirschfeld, *Nazi Rule*, p. 168. Presser, *Ondergang* II, pp. 175–6. J.J. Kelder, *De Schalkhaarders: Nederlandse Politiemannen naar Nationaal-Socialistische snit* (Utrecht/Antwerp, Veen, 1990), pp. 21–4.
29 Hirschfeld, *Nazi Rule*, p. 169.
30 Hirschfeld, *Nazi Rule*, p. 178.
31 Presser, *Ondergang* II, p. 177.
32 A. Vernooij, *Grenzen aan gehoorzaamheid: houding en gedrag van de Utrechtse Politie tijdens de Duitse Bezetting* (Utrecht, Trezoor, 1985), pp. 88–99.
33 Presser, *Ondergang* II, pp. 178–9.
34 Hirschfeld, *Nazi Rule*, pp. 168, 174–6.
35 Vernooij, *Grenzen aan gehoorzaamheid*, p. 67.
36 Guus van Meershoek, 'De Amsterdamse Hoodcommissaris en de deportatie van de joden', in N.D.J. Barnouw *et al.*, eds, *Oorlogsdocumentatie '40–'45. Derde jaarboek van het Rijksinstituut voor Oorlogsdocumentatie* (Zutphen, De Walburg Pers, 1989), p. 13. See also R. Hilberg, *Perpetrators*, pp. 79–80.
37 Meershoek, 'De Amsterdamse hoofdcommissaris', pp. 33–4.
38 Hirschfeld, *Nazi Rule*, p. 177.
39 Hirschfeld, *Nazi Rule*, p. 173.
40 Hirschfeld, *Nazi Rule*, p. 179.
41 Hirschfeld, *Nazi Rule*, pp. 180–1.
42 Steinberg, *Les Cent Jours*, p. 203.
43 Rudi van Doorslaer, 'La police belge et le maintien de l'ordre en Belgique occupée', in Etienne Dejonghe, ed., *L'Occupation en France et en Belgique 1940–1944* (Lille, Revue du Nord, 1987), I, pp. 73–102.
44 Warmbrunn, *The German Occupation of Belgium*, pp. 152, 161–3, 258–9.
45 Warmbrunn, *Occupation of Belgium*, pp. 160–1.
46 Klarsfeld, *Vichy-Auschwitz*, p. 215.
47 John P. Fox, 'How Far Did Vichy France "Sabotage" the Imperatives of Wannsee?' in David Cesarani, ed., *The Final Solution: Origins and Implementation* (London, Routledge, 1994), pp. 198–9.
48 Fox, 'How Far', pp. 201–2.
49 Fox, 'How Far', p. 204.
50 Adler, *The Jews of Paris*, pp. 48, 253 note 69.
51 Adler, *The Jews of Paris*, pp. 148–9. Fox, 'How Far', pp. 205–6.
52 De Jong, *Het Koninkrijk* VI, pp. 362–4. Presser, *Ondergang* II, pp. 179–80.
53 RIOD HSSpF 167/263h, Report by J.N.P. Lam and M. van der Werken, 9 September 1943.
54 De Jong, *Het Koninkrijk* VI, pp. 364–5.
55 RIOD HSSpF 167/263h. Only when those captured made it clear that their hosts knew their true identities were steps taken to apprehend and punish them. See, for example, Report W.C.H. Henneicke and F.J.E. Tak, 4 September 1943.
56 Presser, *Ondergang* II, p. 180. Fifteen of those dismissed were reputed to have been National Socialists.
57 RIOD HSSpF 167/263h, Report, 5 August 1943.

58 RIOD HSSpF 167/262e, Report by H. van Keulen and A Schmidt, 16 September 1943.
59 Presser, *Ondergang* II, p. 181.
60 De Jong, *Het Koninkrijk* VI, pp. 362–4.
61 Presser, *Ondergang* II, p. 261.
62 De Jong, *Het Koninkrijk* VI, p. 366.
63 K. Groen, *Als slachtoffers daders worden. De zaak van joodse verraadster Ans van Dijk* (Baarn, Ambo, 1994).
64 De Jong, *Het Koninkrijk* VI, p. 368. Presser, *Ondergang* II, p. 185.
65 Marrus and Paxton, *Vichy*, pp. 129–31. Zuccotti, *The Holocaust*, p. 161.
66 Zuccotti, *The Holocaust*, p. 199.
67 Josephs, *Swastika*, p. 77.

10 The survival of Foreign Jews

1. J.C.H. Blom, 'De Vervolging van de Joden in Nederland in Internationaal Vergelijkend Perspectief', in *Crisis, Bezetting en Herstel: Tien Studies over Nederland 1930–50* (The Hague, Universitair Pers Rotterdam, 1989), pp. 134–50. As Blom and others have pointed out, the figures for the Netherlands bear more relationship with those for the countries of Eastern Europe and the Soviet Union where the nature of Nazi persecution and the execution of the 'Final Solution' was very different. See especially p. 134.
2 In the case of France, it has to be borne in mind that the Vichy government actively discriminated against foreign Jews. The Pétain regime was perfectly willing to hand over foreign Jews to the Germans but baulked at the prospect of doing the same with French Jews. See S. Klarsfeld, *Vichy-Auschwitz. Le Rôle de Vichy dans la Solution Finale de la Question Juive en France, 1942* (Paris, Fayard, 1983), pp. 179ff.
3 Blom, 'De Vervolging', p. 146.
4 J. Presser, *Ondergang. De Vervolging en Verdelging van het Nederlandse Jodendom 1940–45* (The Hague, Staatsuitgeverij, 1965), II, p. 510.
5 Blom, 'De Vervolging', p. 146, endnote 11.
6 Blom, 'De Vervolging', p. 146, endnote 11.
7 A.J. Herzberg, *Kroniek der Jodenvervolging 1940–45* (Amsterdam, Querido, 1985), p. 323.
8 Blom, 'De Vervolging', p. 135, cites A.J. van der Leeuw, 'Meer slachtoffers dan elders in West-Europa', *Nieuw Israëlitisch Weekblad*, 15 November 1985.
9 J.Th.M. Houwink ten Cate, 'Het Jongere Deel. Demografische en sociale kenmerken van het jodendom in Nederland tijdens de vervolging', *Oorlogsdocumentatie '40–'45, Jaarboeck van het Rijksinstituut voor Oorlogsdocumentatie* I (1989), p. 39.
10 For a more detailed analysis of these trends, see Bob Moore, 'Jewish refugees in the Netherlands 1933–1940: The Structure and Pattern of Jewish Immigration from Nazi Germany', *Leo Baeck Institute Yearbook* XXIX (1984), pp. 73-101.
11 B. Moore, *Refugees from Nazi Germany in the Netherlands, 1933–1940* (Dordrecht/Boston/Lancaster, Nijhoff, 1986), pp. 71–3.
12 The restrictions placed on foreigners taking paid employment in the Netherlands were complex, but domestic service was one sector which did continue to provide some scope for refugee employment – both on an official and unofficial basis.
13 WL-PIIId/197, p. 5.

14 V. Jakob and A. van der Voort, *Anne Frank war nicht allein* (Bonn, Dietz, 1988), p. 69.
15 Moore, *Refugees*, p. 92. Interview with *mevr.* Hoek-Wallach, 16 September 1987.
16 H. Wielek, *De Oorlog die Hitler Won* (Amsterdam, Amsterdam Boek- en Courantmij N.V., 1947), p. 12.
17 Many of the *Ost-juden,* who had come to Germany from Tsarist Russia or Poland had an in-built aversion to the state machinery and all its servants. They were overrepresented among the early exodus of refugees from Germany, forming up to 32 per cent of the total in 1933. In spite of Dutch government attempts to reduce their numbers, they still accounted for 33.5 per cent of the foreign Jews in the country in 1941. G. Hirschfeld, 'Niederlande', in W. Benz, ed., *Dimension des Völkermords. Die Zahl der jüdischen Opfer des Nationalsozialismus* (Munich, R. Oldenbourg Verlag, 1991), p. 137. This last statistic is problematic. By 1941, the listing of people as 'other nationality' may well have included those who had lost or been deprived of their German citizenship. Moreover, not all non-Germans can be assumed to have been *Ost-juden.*
18 G. F. Ferwerda, *Nederlandsche Onderdanen aangetroffen in Duitsche Kampen* (Malmö, Henry Luttrup, 1945). See also, Board of Jewish Deputies Archives, London, Letter from Samuel Cass, Jewish Chaplain, Administrative HQ First Canadian Army, Canadian Army Overseas, to Chief Rabbi's Religious Emergency Council, Board of Deputies, London, 1 May 1945.
19 Jacob Boas, *Boulevard des Misères: Het verhaal van het doorgangskamp Westerbork* (Amsterdam, Nijgh en van Ditmar, 1985), p. 53.
20 Boas, *Boulevard*, p. 56. At this stage, the camp was still nominally controlled by the Ministry of Justice and was under the command of a Dutch officer, Captain Schol.
21 Philip Mechanicus, *Waiting for Death* (London, Calder and Boyars, 1968), p. 32.
22 Mechanicus, *Waiting for Death*, p. 32.
23 Mechanicus, *Waiting for Death*, p. 33.
24 Mechanicus, *Waiting for Death*, p. 34.
25 Mechanicus, *Waiting for Death*, pp. 34–5, 80.
26 Boas, *Boulevard*, p. 14.
27 The stories about Schlesinger's arrival in the Netherlands differ slightly. De Jong says that he arrived legally in the country, while Boas is clear that the couple were arrested and interned, implying that their entry was illegal. However, a large number of legal refugees arriving in the Netherlands after 17 November 1938 were placed in camps, rather than allowed to live freely. L.R. de Jong, *Het Koninkrijk der Nederlanden in de Tweede Wereldoorlog,* 14 vols (The Hague, Staatsuitgeverij, 1969–92) VIII, p. 692. Boas, *Boulevard*, p. 52.
28 De Jong, *Het Koninkrijk* VIII, p. 729, attributes this promotion to the Dutch Commandant Schol, in February 1942, but this seems too early, and is contradicted by his statements in VIII, pp. 741–2.
29 Boas, *Boulevard*, p. 62.
30 De Jong, *Het Koninkrijk* VI, pp. 319, 320–1, 323.
31 Mechanicus, *Waiting for Death*, p. 26.
32 Boas, *Boulevard*, pp. 63–4.
33 Mechanicus, *Waiting for Death*, pp. 251–2.
34 Pisk was also in charge of the so-called '*Fliegende Colonne*' (Flying Column) which was used to 'help' deportees from the station at Hooghalen to Westerbork. This group of approximately 100 people was not averse to ill-

treating or plundering those they were escorting. De Jong, *Het Koninkrijk* VIII, p. 744.
35 De Jong, *Het Koninkrijk* VIII, p. 742.
36 Boas, *Boulevard*, p. 66.
37 WL PIIId/491 (Auschwitz) tells the story of a family who were saved by Spanier from the transports on more than one occasion and of a daughter who was employed as a nurse in spite of her lack of training.
38 Boas, *Boulevard*, p. 68.
39 Mechanicus, *Waiting for Death*, pp. 248–9. De Jong, *Het Koninkrijk* VIII, pp. 765–6.
40 De Jong, *Het Koninkrijk* VII, p. 348.
41 Board of Jewish Deputies Archive, London. Letter from Samuel Cass, Jewish Chaplain, Administrative HQ First Canadian Army, Canadian Army Overseas, to Chief Rabbi's Religious Emergency Council, Board of Deputies, London, 1 May 1945. This includes a list of camp inmates dated 23 April 1945.

11 The last year of occupation and the realities of liberation

1 W. Warmbrunn, *The Dutch under German Occupation 1940–45* (Stanford, Stanford University Press, 1963), p. 119.
2 WL-PIIId/820.
3 H. van der Zee, *De Honger Winter: van Dolle Dinsdag tot Bevrijding* (Amsterdam, Becht, 1979). H.J. Oolbekkink, *Met Lege Handen: Een Hongertocht in Februari 1945* (Amsterdam, Tiebosch Uitgeversmaatschappij, 1979). G.J. Kruijer, *Hongertochten: Amsterdam tijdens de Hongerwinter* (Meppel, Boom, 1951). B.H. Laurens, *Hun Armoe en Hun Grauw Gezicht: Hongerwinter 1944–45* (Rotterdam, Donker, 1985). On the Allied diplomatic and military attempts to send food into the northern Netherlands see, B. Moore, 'The Western Allies and Food Relief to the Occupied Netherlands, 1944–1945', *War and Society* X (1992), pp. 91–118. J. van der Zwan, *De Dag die Manna Viel* (The Hague, Voorhoeve, n.d.). H. Onderwater, *Operatie Manna. De Geallieerde Voedseldroppings April–Mei 1945* (Weesp, Unieboek, 1985).
4 A. Mayer, *One Who Came Back* (Ottawa, Oberon, 1981), pp. 3–6.
5 See for example, B.A. Sijes, *De Razzia van Rotterdam* (Amsterdam, Sijthoff, 1984).
6 E. Verhey, *Om het Joodse Kind* (Amsterdam, Nijgh & van Ditmar, 1991), pp. 57–9.
7 N.K.C.A. in't Veld, *De Joodse Ereraad* (The Hague, SDU, 1989), p. 33. D. Hondius, *Terugkeer: Antisemitisme in Nederland rond de bevrijding* (The Hague, SDU, 1990), p. 55.
8 WL-PIIId/491 (Auschwitz).
9 Connie Kristel, 'De moeizame terugkeer. De repatriëring van de Nederlandse overlevenden uit de Duitse concentratiekampen', *Oorlogsdocumentatie '40–'45* I (1989), p. 78.
10 WL PIIIh/843 (Auschwitz). Hondius, *Terugkeer*, p. 62. J. Presser, *Ondergang. De Vervolging en Verdelging van het Nederlandse Jodendom 1940–45* (The Hague, Staatsuitgeverij, 1965), II, p. 500. Kristel, 'De moeizame terugkeer', p. 83, notes that some 1,200 Dutch citizens were shipped from the Allied prisoner-of-war collection point at Odessa to the West before routes through Germany were reopened.

11 Mayer, *One Who Came Back*, pp. 108–9.
12 WL-PIIIh/125 (Westerbork). Hondius, *Terugkeer*, pp. 79–84.
13 Hondius, *Terugkeer*, p. 84.
14 Hondius, *Terugkeer*, p. 76.
15 Hondius, *Terugkeer*, pp. 74–6. Presser, *Ondergang* II, p. 369.
16 Hondius, *Terugkeer*, p. 46. Kristel, 'De moeizame terugkeer', p. 81.
17 Ferwerda was a former director of Unilever and a former member of the Dutch Shipping and Commerce Commission. Hondius, *Terugkeer*, p. 46.
18 Hondius, *Terugkeer*, p. 47.
19 Hondius, *Terugkeer*, p. 48–9. Kristel, 'De moeizame terugkeer', p. 85.
20 Hondius, *Terugkeer*, pp. 52–3. Kristel, 'De moeizame terugkeer', p. 86.
21 Hondius, *Terugkeer*, p. 54 and cites C. Kristel, 'De Repatriëring van de Nederlandse overlevenden uit de concentratiekampen' (Doctoraalscriptie, University of Amsterdam, 1987).
22 Hondius, *Terugkeer*, p. 69–70.
23 Hondius, *Terugkeer*, p. 74.
24 Kristel, 'De moeizame terugkeer', pp. 90–1.
25 Kristel, 'De moeizame terugkeer', p. 91.
26 Kristel, 'De moeizame terugkeer', p. 92.
27 R. Friedman and R. van der Heide, *Het Joodse Oorlogspleegkind: Contact Commissie der Joodse Coördinate Commissies* (Amsterdam, Amsterdam Boek- en Courantmij N.V., 1946), notes the royal decree which created the Commission, KB 137, 13 August 1945. F. C. Brasz, 'Na de Tweede Oorlog', in J.C.H. Blom et al., eds, *Geschiedenis van de Joden in Nederland* (Amsterdam, Balans, 1995), pp. 367–8. Joel S. Fishman, 'The War Orphan Controversy in the Netherlands: Majority–Minority Relations', in J. Michman and T. Levie, eds, *Dutch Jewish History* (Jerusalem, Tel Aviv University/Hebrew University of Jerusalem, 1984), p. 424. Verhey, *Joodse Kind*, pp. 40–51, 72–80.
28 Fishman, 'War Orphan Controversy', p. 425. J. Michman, H. Beem and D. Michman, eds, *Pinkas. Geschiedenis van de joodse gemeenschap in Nederland* (Ede/Antwerp/Amsterdam, Kluwer/Nederlands–Israëlitisch Kerkgenootschap/Joods Historisch Museum, 1992), p. 219 notes that of the 25 members of the OPK, only 11 were Jews and of them 4 were avowedly assimilationist.
29 Michman et al., *Pinkas*, p. 218.
30 Joël Fishman, 'De joodse oorlogswezen. Een interview met Gesina van der Molen, voorzitter van de Commissie Oorlogspleegkinderen', in Barnouw et al., eds, *Oorlogsdocumentatie '40–'45*, VII (1995), p. 58.
31 Fishman, 'De joodse oorlogswezen', p. 54.
32 M.G. van Haperen van Beurden, 'Conflict van overlevenden om overlevenden. Het vraagstuk van de joodse oorlogspleegkinderen, juli 1942–september 1949' (Doctoraalscriptie, Catholic University of Nijmegen, 1989), pp. 176–8. Fishman, 'De joodse oorlogswezen', p. 58.
33 Joel S. Fishman, 'Jewish War Orphans in the Netherlands – The Guardianship Issue 1945–1950', *Wiener Library Bulletin* XXVII (1973–74) nos. 30–1, pp. 31–6.
34 E.C. Lekkerkerker, 'Oorlogspleegkinderen', *Maandblad voor de Geestelijke Volksgezondheid* VII (October 1946).
35 RIOD LO/BO3, Typed copy of an article, 'Een Speurtocht naar 'n Jodenjongetje' in *Vrij Nederland* (n. d).
36 Lekkerkerker, 'Oorlogspleegkinderen', p. 6.
37 Michman et al., *Pinkas*, p. 220.
38 Michman et al., *Pinkas*, p. 220 argues that the OPK position was contrary to Dutch family law and tradition.

39 Lekkerkerker, 'Oorlogspleegkinderen' p. 3.
40 Verhey, *Joodse Kind*, pp. 115–24.
41 J.J. Kalma, *Redt de Joden. Wat Gebeurd er met de Joodse Oorlogspleegkinderen* (Lekkum [Leeuwarden], Joachimsthal, 1946), pp. 8–10.
42 Kalma, *Redt de Joden*, pp. 12–13.
43 Kalma, *Redt de Joden*, p. 10. Brasz, 'Na de Tweede Oorlog', p. 370. Fishman, 'War Orphan Controversy', p. 431.
44 Fishman, 'De joodse oorlogswezen', p. 59.
45 Michman *et al.*, *Pinkas*, p. 221.
46 Brasz, 'Na de Tweede Wereldoorlog', p. 371. Michman *et al.*, *Pinkas*, p. 221, argue that the new procedures were often ignored with the OPK majority finding it easy to establish psychological or educational grounds for not placing an orphan with a Jewish family. Moreover, the judges who had the final say often ignored OPK advice when they recommended that a child be placed with a Jewish family.
47 Michman *et al.*, *Pinkas*, p. 221.
48 Fishman, 'Jewish War Orphans', p. 32.
49 Joel S. Fishman, 'The Ecumenical Challenge of Jewish Survival; Pastor Kalma and Postwar Dutch Society, 1946', *Journal of Ecumenical Studies* XV (1978), pp. 461–76. See pp. 464–7.
50 Fishman, 'Jewish War Orphans', p. 32. The organisation was founded by the JCC in August 1945 in the hope that it might eventually replace the OPK. Verhey, *Joodse Kind*, p. 99.
51 Joel S. Fishman, 'The Anneke Beekman Affair and the Dutch News Media', *Jewish Social Studies* XL1 (1978), pp. 3–24.
52 Fishman, 'Anneke Beekman', p. 5. Verhey, *Joodse Kind*, pp. 177–89.
53 Fishman, 'Anneke Beekman', pp. 8–9.
54 Professor I. Kisch, 'Concerning the Jewish War Foster Child', *Nieuw Israëlietisch Weekblad*, 18 February 1949, cited in Fishman, 'Jewish War Orphans', p. 35.
55 Het Nederlands-Israëlitisch Kerkgenootschap en Het Portugees-Israëlitisch Kerkgenootschap, *De Verdwijning van Anneke Beekman en Rebecca Meljado: Witboek* (Amsterdam, 1954).
56 Fishman, 'Anneke Beekman', p. 14.
57 Fishman, 'Jewish War Orphans', p. 35. Presser, *Ondergang* II, p. 514; *Ashes in the Wind* (London, Souvenir Press, 1968), p. 542, gives more precise figures for spring 1947. Of 3,481 children handled by the OPK, 1,540 had been reunited with their parents, a further 472 had been allocated to Jewish guardians and 36 non-Jewish guardians. Of the remainder, Presser estimates that a third grew up in non-Jewish homes. A.J. Herzberg, *Kroniek der Jodenvervolging 1940–45* (Amsterdam, Querido, 1985), p. 318, gives a total of 2,440 Jewish orphans. Brasz, 'Na de Tweede Wereldoorlog', p. 371, notes the final total of Jewish children placed with non-Jewish households was 358 – or about 25 per cent of those whose position was determined by the OPK. Van Haperen van Beurden, 'Conflict van overlevenden', pp. 151, 177 cites 79 per cent of orphan children dealt with by the OPK 1945–49 returning to a Jewish *milieu*.
58 A.J. van Schie, 'Restitution of Economic Rights after 1945', in Michman and Levie, eds, *Dutch Jewish History*, pp. 403–5.
59 L.R. de Jong, *Het Koninkrijk der Nederlanden in de Tweede Wereldoorlog*, 14 vols (The Hague, Staatsuitgeverij, 1969–92), XII, pp. 676–7.
60 De Jong, *Het Koninkrijk* XII, p. 679.
61 De Jong, *Het Koninkrijk* XII, p. 677.
62 De Jong, *Het Koninkrijk* XII, p. 676.

63 De Jong, *Het Koninkrijk* XII, pp. 680–1. Presser, *Ondergang* II, p. 222.
64 Van Schie, 'Economic Restitution', p. 412.
65 De Jong, *Het Koninkrijk* XII, pp. 690–1.
66 Van Schie, 'Economic Restitution', p. 409.
67 De Jong, *Het Koninkrijk* XII, p. 706.
68 Van Schie, 'Economic Restitution', p. 419.
69 In't Veld, *Joodse Ereraad*, pp. 34–5.
70 In't Veld, *Joodse Ereraad*, pp. 37, 43–4.
71 J. Houwink ten Cate, 'De justitie en de Joodsche Raad', in E. Jonker and M. van Rossem, eds, *Geschiedenis en Cultuur. Achttien Opstellen* (The Hague, SDU, 1990), pp. 149–50.
72 In't Veld, *Joodse Ereraad*, pp. 43–4. Michman, 'Jewish Council', pp. 827–8.
73 J. Michman, 'The Controversy Surrounding the Jewish Council of Amsterdam. From its Inception to the Present Day', in M.R. Marrus, *The Nazi Holocaust* (Westport/London, Greenwood, 1989), p. 829.
74 Hans Knoop, *De Joodsche Raad. Het Drama van Abraham Asscher en David Cohen* (Amsterdam, Elsevier, 1983), pp. 221-2. Houwink ten Cate, 'De justitie', p. 152.
75 Houwink ten Cate, 'De justitie', p. 152–3.
76 Houwink ten Cate, 'De justitie', p. 153.
77 Houwink ten Cate, 'De justitie', p. 154.
78 Knoop, *Joodsche Raad*, pp. 234–5.
79 Knoop, *Joodsche Raad*, p. 233.
80 In't Veld, *Joodse Ereraad*, pp. 66–7. De Jong, *Het Koninkrijk* XII, p. 474.
81 Brasz, 'Na de Tweede Wereldoorlog', p. 373–4.
82 In't Veld, *Joodse Ereraad*, p. 67.
83 In't Veld, *Joodse Ereraad*, p. 62. Houwink ten Cate, 'De justitie', pp. 160–1. Michman *et al.*, *Pinkas*, p. 223.
84 David Cohen, *Zwervend en Dolend* (Haarlem, Bohn, 1955). Manuscript memoirs held by the RIOD, dictated 1956. Extracts published in a special edition of the *Nieuw Israelietisch Weekblad*, May 1982, pp. 1–27.
85 Lehmann Papers (Columbia University, New York) James G. McDonald Papers G. 70 'C'. Cohen to McDonald, 27 December 1953.
86 Michman, 'Jewish Council', p. 830, cites A.J. Herzberg, *Om een Lepel Soep* (Amsterdam, Querido, 1976), pp. 82–7. Sikkel's father had apparently been a missionary among the Jews. Houwink ten Cate, 'De justitie', p. 155.
87 Houwink ten Cate, 'De justitie', pp. 163–4.
88 Hondius, *Terugkeer*, pp. 131–2.
89 Hondius, *Terugkeer*, pp. 132–3.
90 Jacques Gulwirth, 'Antwerp Jewry Today', *Jewish Journal of Sociology* X (1968), p. 123.
91 M. Steinberg, *L'Etoile et le Fusil,* 3 vols (Brussels, Vie Ouvrière, 1983–86), *Vol. III La Traque des Juifs 1942–44* II, pp. 211–13, 246. Brasz, 'Na de Tweede Wereldoorlog', p. 373.
92 Brasz, 'Na de Tweede Wereldoorlog', p. 367.

12 Conclusion

1 P. Griffioen and R. Zeller, 'Jodenvervolging in Nederland en België tijdens de Tweede Wereldoorlog: Een Vergelijkende Analyse', *Oorlogsdocumentatie* VIII (1997), n.p.
2 Griffioen and Zeller, 'Jodenvervolging', n.p.

Glossary and abbreviations

Afdeling Effectenregistratie van de Raad voor het Rechtsherstel
Securities Registration Department of the Council for Legal Restitution.
Afdeling Rechtspraak
The Department for the Administration of Justice the Dutch Ministry of Justice.
Altreich
Term used to describe Germany within its 1937 borders (i.e. before annexations).
Anschluss
The German annexation of Austria in March 1938.
Auswärtiges Amt
German Foreign Office.
Beauftragte
Representative of the *Reichskommissar*. Thus Senator Böhmcker was Seyss-Inquart's representative for Amsterdam.
Bevolkingsregister
The Dutch Population Registry.
Comité voor Bijzondere Joodse Belangen (CBJB)
The Committee for Special Jewish Interests, created in 1933 to oversee the secular interests of the Jewish Communities in the Netherlands.
Comité voor Joodse Vluchtelingen (CJV)
The Committee for Jewish Refugees. The organisation created in 1933 by the Jewish communities to meet the welfare needs of refugees from Germany.
Commissie voor Oorlogspleegkinderen (OPK)
The Commission for War Foster-Children. A Dutch government commission created in 1945.
Communistische Partij Nederland/Holland (CPN/H)
Communist Party of the Netherlands/Holland.

Dolle Dinsdag

Mad Tuesday, 5 September 1944, the day on which reports of an allied breakthrough led to premature celebrations of imminent liberation in the northern Netherlands.

Endlösung

Final Solution.

Ereraad

Jewish Court of Honour established under the aegis of the post-war *Joodse Coördinatie Commissie* (q.v.) in 1946 to investigate the conduct of the Jewish Council leadership.

Expositur

The office of the Jewish Council of Amsterdam wholly responsible for liaison with the German authorities. Its head was Dr Edwin Sluzker.

Gemeentepolitie

The Dutch Municipal Police, originally under the control of local mayors and the Ministry of the Interior, they were transferred to the jurisdiction of the Ministry of Justice by the Germans.

Generalkommissar

Commissioner-General. Title given to the four immediate subordinates of the Reich Commissioner: Dr Friedrich Wimmer (Administration and Justice), Dr Hans Fischböck (Finance and the Economy), Hanns Albin Rauter (Security) and Fritz Schmidt (Special Affairs).

Generalkommissariat

Chancellery of the Commissioner(s)-General.

Gereformeerde Kerk

Dutch Orthodox Calvinist Church.

Grüne Polizei (groene politie)

Name used to describe the German *Ordnungspolizei* (order police) operating in the Netherlands and derived from their green uniforms.

Hausraterfassungsstelle

A department of the *Zentralstelle* (q.v.) charged with the registration of property left in Jewish houses after the occupants had been arrested and deported.

Hervormde Kerk

Dutch Reformed Church.

Höhere SS- und Polizeiführer

Higher SS and Police Leader. The supreme regional commander for all SS and police officers. Directly responsible to Himmler for the implementation of policies related to the security of the state. Office held by Hanns Albin Rauter in the Netherlands.

Hollandse Schouwburg

See *Joodsche Schouwburg.*

Hongerwinter

The hunger-winter of 1944–45 when the German occupiers prevented foodstuffs and fuel from reaching the towns and cities of western and north-western Netherlands.

Jodenvervolging

The persecution of the Jews.

Joodsche Invalide

The largest Jewish hospital in Amsterdam.

Joodsche Schouwburg

The 'Jewish' Theatre, used as a collection point for Jews captured during raids in Amsterdam. Formerly the Hollandse Schouwburg.

Joodse Coördinatie Commissie (JCC)

The Jewish Co-ordination Commission. A body originally established in 1940 to co-ordinate the response of the Jewish Communities to the German occupation. Led by Lodewijk Visser, the JCC operated in opposition to the Jewish Council of Amsterdam but was wound up on 10 November 1941. A successor organisation with the same name was founded in Eindhoven on 5 January 1945, initially to oversee the welfare of Jews and rebuild Jewish life.

Joodse Raad voor Amsterdam (JR)

The Jewish Council for Amsterdam. Founded under the joint-presidency of Abraham Asscher and David Cohen in February 1941, the Council ultimately took on responsibility for Jews in the whole of the Netherlands.

Judenräte

Jewish Councils.

Judenreferent

'Jewish experts' appointed by Himmler and Eichmann (IVB4) to oversee the organisation of deportation for the countries of occupied Europe. In the Netherlands, the post was held by Willi Zöpf.

Kindertransporten

Children's Transports. The evacuation of children from German cities and Vienna between November 1938 and September 1939 organised by Gertrude Wijsmuller-Meijer.

Knokploeg (KP)

Action group. Originally a name for street gangs, it was applied to resistance groups operating in Amsterdam during February 1941, and later to all underground groups involved in direct actions.

Kommunistische Partei Deutschlands (KPD)

The German Communist Party.

Koninklijke Marechaussee

The Dutch State Police, originally under the control of the Ministry of Defence, they were transferred to the Ministry of Justice by the Germans and centralised with other Dutch police forces as from 1 January 1941.

Kriegsmarine

The German Navy.

Landelijke Knokploegen (LKP)
National action groups. Formed in 1943 primarily to attack rationing offices and population registries to secure ration books and identity cards for the activities of the *LO* (q.v.).

Landelijke Organisatie voor Hulp aan Onderduikers (LO)
National Organisation for Assistance to those Underground. Founded at the end of 1942, it grew into one of the largest resistance organisations and by the summer of 1944 had 15,000 members and sheltered between 200,000 and 300,000 people.

Landstorm Nederland
The Territorial Guard. A Dutch militia formed by the Germans to defend the country from Allied attack.

Le Ezrath Ha Jeled
The guardianship organisation of the post-war *Joodse Coördinatie Commissie* (q.v.).

Lippmann-Rosenthal
A bank, originally Jewish-owned, which was taken over by the Germans to administer the collection of Jewish assets and the financing of the Jewish communities prior to their deportation. Its employees often worked alongside those of the *Zentralstelle* (q.v.).

Luftwaffe
The German Air Force.

'Mischlinge'
Term used to describe people who had a mixture of Jewish and non-Jewish antecedents.

Nationaal-Socialistische Beweging (NSB)
The Dutch National Socialist Movement and the largest National Socialist party in the Netherlands. Led by Anton Mussert.

Nationaal Socialistische Nederlandse Arbeiders Partij (NSNAP)
The Dutch National Socialist Workers' Party. A small splinter group which attempted to imitate the workings and ideology of the NSDAP in Germany.

Nationaal Steunfonds (NSF)
The National Assistance Fund, a secret fund created to finance resistance and underground activities.

Nederlandse-Israëlietische Kerkgenootschap
The central organisation of the Dutch-Jewish (Ashkenazi) communities in the Netherlands. Its main concerns were religious rather than secular matters.

Nederlandse SS
The Netherlands' section of the SS.

Nederlandse Unie
Netherlands Union. A political organisation created in the summer of 1940 to oppose the NSB. At first welcomed by the Germans as a means

for increasing collaboration from the Dutch civil population, it was
eventually banned when it was realised that most people had joined to
express their patriotic (i.e. anti-German) sentiment.

Nederlandse Verbond van Vakvereenigingen (NVV)
The Dutch Association of Trade Unions, affiliated to the Dutch Social
Democratic Party.

Niederländische Grunstückverwaltung
Dutch Landed-Property Administration. The selling agency used by the
Germans to dispose of land and buildings owned by Jews.

Onderduikers
Term used to describe those who went underground, although this
encompassed a wide range of activities and circumstances. The term
literally means 'divers' or 'those who dive under'. The term *fietsers*
(cyclists) was also used to describe these people.

Oorlogspleegkinderen
War foster-children.

Orde Dienst (OD)
1. Name given to the police force which operated inside Westerbork
   transit camp and which was recruited from the inmates.
2. The Order Service, a quasi-military organisation set up by the resistance
   towards the end of the occupation to maintain order as the German
   withdrawal took place and to liaise with the incoming Allied forces.

Ordnungspolizei
The German order police in the Netherlands, often referred to as the
Grüne Polizei (q.v.).

Ost-juden
Jews from Eastern Europe (primarily from Poland and Russia)
differentiated from most German Jews by cultural origins and orthodox
observance.

Persoonsbewijs (PB)
Identity Card. Compusory for all Dutch civilians during the German
occupation.

Politieke Recherche Afdeling
The Political Investigation Department of the Dutch police.

Procureur-Generaal
Attorney-General. The chief law officer in each legal-administrative
district.

Puls
The name of the removal firm (Abraham Puls) used by the Germans to
empty dwellings vacated by Jews. It also gave its name to a verb
'pulsen', to have the contents of one's house removed.

Razzia
A raid. Name given to German raids in Amsterdam and other large
Dutch cities to capture Jews and, later, forced labour.

Referat IVB4
A subdivision of the Gestapo (and thus of the RSHA). Led by Adolf
Eichmann, this organisation was primarily responsible for the
deportation of Jews from Europe to the extermination camps. It had a
branch office in The Hague run by Willi Zöpf.

Referat Innere Verwaltung
Division of the Generalkommissariat for Administration and Justice
concerned with internal administration and led by Dr Hans Calmeyer.

Reichskommissar für die besetzten Niederländischen Gebiete
Civilian Reich Commissioner for the Netherlands, a post held by Dr
Arthur Seyss-Inquart.

Reichskommissariat
The Chancellery of the Reich Commissioner.

Reichskristallnacht
(lit., 'Night of Broken Glass') The pogrom carried out by the Nazis against
Jews in Germany and Austria on the night of 9–10 November 1938.

Reichssicherheitshauptamt (RSHA)
Reich Security Main Office established in September 1939. An SS and
government organisation which controlled offices responsible for
intelligence, security and criminal police work, and including the
Gestapo and SD. Under the overall command of Heinrich Himmler, it
was run by Reinhard Heydrich until his death and then by Ernst
Kaltenbrunner.

Reichssippenamt
Organisation established by Heinrich Himmler for genealogical and
racial research.

Rijksinstituut voor Oorlogsdocumentatie (RIOD)
The Netherlands State Institute for War Documentation.

Rüstungsinspektion (Niederlande)
Armmaments Inspectorate of the Netherlands. The Office for German
Military-Economic Affairs.

Schutzpolizei
German municipal police.

Schutzstaffel (SS)
Originally the security organisation of the NSDAP, under Heinrich
Himmler, it became the most powerful single organisation in the Nazi
State.

Sicherheitsdienst (SD)
The security and intelligence service of the SS and inextricably linked to
the Gestapo and German police organisations.

Sicherheitspolizei (Sipo)
The German security police.

Sociaal-Democratische Arbeiders Partij (SDAP)
The Dutch Social Democratic Party.

Sozialdemokratische Partei Deutschlands (SPD)
The German Social Democratic Party.

SS – comparative officer ranks

SS	German army	British army
SS-Untersturmführer	Leutnant	Second Lieutenant
SS-Obersturmführer	Oberleutnant	Lieutenant
SS-Hauptsturmführer	Hauptmann	Captain
SS-Sturmbannführer	Major	Major
SS-Obersturmbannführer	Obersleutnant	Lieutenant-Colonel
SS-Gruppenführer	Generalleutnant	Major-General
Reichsführer-SS	Generalfeldmarschall	Field Marshal

Strafgeval
Punishment case. A term applied to Jews who had committed 'crimes', such as failing to report for labour service. More serious misdemeanours were punished by incarceration in gaol at Amersfoort.

Vermögensverwaltung und Rentenanstalt (VVRA)
The Property and Revenue Administration Organisation used by the Germans to seize Jewish businesses, property and life insurance policies.

Verordnung (VO)
Orders and decrees issued by the German occupying power through the Dutch civil service.

Vertrauensmann (V-mann)
Undercover agent or informer working for the German authorities.

Waffen-SS
Term introduced in 1940 to describe militarised units of the SS.

Weerafdeling (WA)
The uniformed but unarmed defence section of the Dutch National Socialist movement.

Weeskinderen
Orphans.

Wehrmacht
The German armed forces.

Wiener Library (WL)
The Wiener Library, London.

Wirtschaftsprüfstelle
The German Bureau for Economic Investigation in the Netherlands.

Wirtschaftsverwaltungshauptamt (WVHA)
Economic-Administrative Central Office of the SS. Formally established in early 1942, but Oswald Pohl controlled the management of most SS construction and economic activities before that date. The WVHA also oversaw economic activities at concentration and extermination camps.

Zentralauftragsstelle
The 'Central Contract Office'. The Office for German Civilian Economic Affairs in the Netherlands.

Zentralstelle für jüdische Auswanderung
   The Central Agency for Jewish Emigration. The office run by the
   German Sipo and SD in Amsterdam to oversee the deportation of the
   Jews from the Netherlands and run by Ferdinand Hugo Aus der Fünten.

Sources

Richard Breitman, *The Architect of Genocide: Himmler and the Final
   Solution* (London, The Bodley Head, 1991), pp. 311–13.
G. Hirschfeld, *Nazi Rule and Dutch Collaboration: The Netherlands under
   German Occupation, 1940–45* (Oxford/New York/Hamburg, Berg,
   1988), *passim.*
W. Warmbrunn, *The Dutch under German Occupation, 1940–45*
   (Stanford, Stanford University Press, 1963), pp. 312–15.

Bibliography

BOOKS

Abma, G. *et al.* (eds), *Tussen Goed en Fout: Nieuwe gezichtspunten in de geschiedschrijving 1940–45* (Franeker, T. Wever, 1986)

Ader-Appels, J.A., *Een Groninger Pastorie in de Storm* (Amsterdam, Kirschner, 1949)

Adler, J., *The Jews of Paris and the Final Solution: Communal Response and Internal Conflicts, 1940–1944* (New York/Oxford, Oxford University Press, 1989)

Adler-Rudel, S., *Ostjuden in Deutschland 1880–1940* (Tübingen, Mohr, 1959)

Adriani Engels, M.J. and Wallagh, G.H., *Nacht over Nederland* (Amsterdam, Ons Vrije Nederland, 1946)

Appel, L., *Het Brood der Doden: Geschiedenis en ondergang van een joods meisjes weeshuis* (Baarn, Bosch en Keuning, 1982)

Baalen, C.C. van, *Paradijs in Oorlogstijd: Onderduikers in de Noordoostpolder, 1942–45* (Zwolle, Waanders, 1986)

Baert, J., *De Vluchtelingen in Nederlanden* (Assen, Van Gorcum, 1938)

Barnouw, D. and Stroom, G. van der (eds), *The Diary of Anne Frank: The Critical Edition* (London, Viking, 1989) published in Dutch as *De Dagboeken van Anne Frank* (The Hague, Staatsuitgeverij, 1986)

Bazuin, J.E., *Herinneringen en Hoop: Uit het Leven van een Joods Gezin in Sneek voor de Tweede Wereldoorlog* (Sneek, Gemeentebestuur, 1980)

Beem, H., *De Verdwenen Mediene* (Amsterdam, Amphora, 1950)

Beloff, M., *On the Track of Tyranny* (Freeport, N.Y., Books for Libraries Press, 1971)

Benz, W. (ed.), *Dimension des Völkermords. Die Zahl der jüdischen Opfer des Nationalsozialismus* (Munich, R. Oldenbourg Verlag, 1991)

Bergh, S. van den, *Deportaties. Westerbork Theresiënstadt Auschwitz Gleiwitz* (Bussum, van Dishoeck, 1946)

Berghe, G. van den, *Met de Dood voor Ogen: Begrip en Onbegrip tussen Overlevenden van Nazi-kampen en Buitenstanders* (Berchem, EPO, 1987)

Berghuis, C.K., *Joodse vluchtelingen in Nederland, 1938–1940. Documenten betreffende toelating, uitleiding en kampopname* (Kampen, Kok, 1990)

Berkley, K.P.L., *Overzicht van het Ontstaan, De Werkzaamheden en het Streven van den Joodsche Raad voor Amsterdam* (Amsterdam, n.p., 1945)

Bieshuizen, J. and Werkman, E., *De Magere Jaren: Nederland in de crisistijd 1929–1939* (Alphen a/d Rijn, Sijthoff, 1980)

Blom, J.C.H., *Crisis, Bezetting en Herstel: Tien Studies over Nederland 1930–1950* (The Hague, Universitair Pers Rotterdam, 1989)

Blom, J.C.H., *De Muiterij op de Zeven Provinciën. Reacties en Gevolgen in Nederland* (Bussum, HES, 1975) (2nd edn, Utrecht, HES, 1983)

Blom, J.C.H. *et al.* (eds), *Geschiedenis van de Joden in Nederland* (Amsterdam, Balans, 1995)

Boas, J., *Boulevard des Misères: Het verhaal van het doorgangskamp Westerbork* (Amsterdam, Nijgh en van Ditmar, 1985)

Boas, H., *Herlevend Bewaard: Aren Lezen in Joods Amsterdam* (Amsterdam, Keesing, 1987)

Boas, H.J., *Religious Resistance in Holland* (London, George Allen and Unwin, 1945)

Boekman, E., *Demografie van de Joden in Nederland* (Amsterdam, Hertzberger, 1936)

Bolhuis, J.J., *et al.* (eds), *Onderdrukking en Verzet. Nederland in Oorlogstijd*, 4 vols (Arnhem, van Loghum Slaterus, 1947–55)

Boom, B. van der, *Den Haag in de Tweede Wereldoorlog* (The Hague, SeaPress, 1995)

Boom, C. ten, *The Hiding Place* (Washington, DC, Chosen Books, 1971) translated as *De Schuilplaats* (Hoornaar, Gideon, 1972)

Bornebroek, A.H., *De Illegaliteit in Twente* (Hengelo, Twentse-Gelderse Uitgeverij Witkam, 1985)

Braber, B., *Passage naar Vrijheid. Joods Verzet in Nederland 1940–45* (Amsterdam, Balans, 1987)

Braber, B., *Zelfs als wij zullen verliezen. Joden in Verzet en Illegaliteit 1940–1945* (Amsterdam, Balans, 1991)

Bregstein, P., *Gesprekken met Jacques Presser* (Amsterdam, Atheneum-Polak & van Gennep, 1972)

Bregstein, P. and Bloemgarten, S., *Herinnering aan Joodse Amsterdam* (Amsterdam, Bezige Bij, 1978)

Brilleman, L., *The Story of My Life* (unpublished, Wiener Library)

Browning, C., *The Final Solution and the German Foreign Office* (New York, Holmes and Meier, 1978)

Browning, C., *The Path to Genocide: Essays on Launching the Final Solution* (Cambridge, Cambridge University Press, 1993)

Brugmans, H., and Frank, A., *Geschiedenis der Joden in Nederland* (Amsterdam, n.p., 1940)

Burrin, P., *Hitler and the Jews: The Genesis of the Holocaust* (London, Edward Arnold, 1994)

Buskes, J.J., *Waar Stond de Kerk?* (Amsterdam, De Volkspaedagogische Bibliotheek, 1947)

Caestecker, F., *Ongewenste Gasten. Joodse vluchtelingen en migranten in de dertiger jaren* (Brussels, VUB, 1993)

Cahen, J., *Een Hoofdstuk uit de Nieuwste Geschiedenis van de Haagse Joden* (The Hague, Izak Zadoks Stichting, 1979)

Cammaert, A.P.M., *Het verborgen front. Geschiedenis van de georganizeerde illegaliteit in de provincie Limburg tijdens de Tweede Wereldoorlog* (Leeuwarden, Eisma, 1994)

Caransa, A., *Verzamelen op het Transvaalplein: ter Nagedachtenis van het Joodse Proletariaat van Amsterdam* (Baarn, Bosch & Keuning, 1984)

Caransa, A., *'Van School Verwijderd, Jood'. Documenten betreffende de verwijdering van joodse leerlingen van de Amsterdamse Ambachtschool en in 1941* (Haarlem, Tuindorp, 1990)

Casutto, E., *The Last Jew in Rotterdam* (Monroeville, Pa., Whitaker House, 1974)

Cesarani, D. (ed.), *The Final Solution: Origins and Implementation* (London, Routledge, 1994)

Citroen, S., *Duet Pathétique. Belevenissen van een Joods Gezin in Oorlogstijd 1940–45* (Utrecht, Veen, 1988)

Cohen, D., *Zwervend en Dolend* (Haarlem, Bohn, 1955)

Cohen, E.A., *De Negentien Treinen naar Sobibor* (Amsterdam, Sijthoff, 1985)

Cohen, R.I., *The Burden of Conscience. French Jewish Leadership during the Holocaust* (Bloomington, Indiana University Press, 1987)

Colijn, G.J. and Littel, M.S. (eds), *The Netherlands and Nazi Genocide: Papers of the 21st Annual Scholars' Conference* (Lewiston, N.Y., Edwin Mellen Press, 1992)

Courtois, S., and Rayski, A., *Qui savait Quoi? L'extermination des Juifs 1941–1945* (Paris, Éditions la Découverte, 1987)

Czapski, G., *Die Judengesetzgebung der deutschen Verwaltung während der Besetzung der Niederlande im zweiten Weltkrieg* (Berlin, George Weis, 1955)

Dahl, R.A. (ed.), *Political Oppositions in Western Democracies* (New Haven, Yale University Press, 1966)

Dam, C. van, *Jodenvervolging in de Stad Utrecht: De Joodse Gemeenschap in de Stad Utrecht 1930–50* (Zutphen, De Walburg Pers, 1985)

Dawidowicz, L., *The War against the Jews 1933–45* (Harmondsworth, Penguin, 1975)

Dejonghe, E. (ed.), *L'Occupation en France et en Belgique 1940–1944*, 2 vols (Lille, Revue du Nord, 1987)

Delleman, Th. (ed.), *Opdat wij niet vergeten* (Kampen, n.p., 1949)

Dien, Ab van, *Opgejaagden: Herinneringen van een joodse onderduiker in het Valther bos* (Valthe, Welzijnswerk Valthe, 1982)

Dittrich, K. and Würzner, H. (eds), *Nederland en het Duitse Exil* (Amsterdam, van Gennep, 1982)

Dobschiner, J-R., *Te Mogen Léven: Een Nederlandse Jodin vertelt haar geschiedenis* (Franeker, T. Wever, 1974) translated as *Selected to Live* (Glasgow, Pickering and Inglis, 1974)

Doorn, B. van, *Vught. Dertien Maanden in het Concentratiekamp* (Laren, A.G. Schoonderbeek, 1945)

Dov Kulka, O. and Mendes, P.R., *Judaism and Christianity Under the Impact of National Socialism* (Jerusalem, Historical Society of Israel, 1987)

Durlacher, G.L., *Strepen aan de Hemel: Oorlogsherinnering* (Vianen, ECI, 1986) translated as *Stripes in the Sky* (London, Serpent's Tail, 1991)

Durlacher, G.L., *Drowning: Growing up in the Third Reich* (London, Serpent's Tail, 1993)

Eckardt, A.L. (ed.), *Burning Memory: Times of Testing and Reckoning* (Oxford/New York, Pergamon, 1993)

Elsendoorn, J., *De Vermorzeling: Het verhaal van een overlevende* (Amsterdam, Querido, 1979)

Emanuel, W., *Underground in Holland* (Amsterdam, 1979) mimeograph RIOD, Amsterdam

Emsley, C. and Weinberger, B. (eds), *Policing Western Europe: Politics, Professionalism and Public Order, 1850–1950* (New York/Westport/London, Greenwood, 1991)

Evans, M.R., *Lest We Forget* (Berrien Springs, Mich., Andrews University Press, 1991)

Evers-Emden, B., *Onderduikouders en hun Joodse 'kinderen' over de onderduikperiode* (Utrecht, Stichting ICODO, 1988)

Evers-Emden, B., *Geleende Kinderen. Ervaringen van onderduikouders en hun joodse beschermelingen in de jaren 1942 tot 1945* (Kampen, Kok, 1994)

Evers-Emden, B. and Flim, B.J., *Ondergedoken Geweest* (Amsterdam, Kok, 1995)

Fein, H., *Accounting for Genocide: National Responses and Jewish Victimization during the Holocaust* (New York, Free Press, 1979)

Ferares, M., *Violinist in het Verzet* (Amsterdam, Het Bataafsche Leeuw, 1991)

Ferwerda, G.F., *Nederlandsche Onderdanen aangetroffen in Duitsche Kampen* (Malmö, Henry Luttrup, 1945)

Fleming, G., *Hitler and the Final Solution* (Oxford, Oxford University Press, 1986)

Flim, B.J., *Omdat Hun Hart Sprak. Geschiedenis van de Georganiseerde Hulp aan Joodse Kinderen in Nederland, 1942–1945* (Kampen, Kok, 1996)

Flinker, M., *Dagboek 1942–43* (Amsterdam, Amphora, 1985)

Fogelman, E., *Conscience and Courage. Rescuers of Jews during the Holocaust* (London, Victor Gollancz, 1995)

Frank, C., *Alsof er niets gebeurd was* (Haarlem, In de Knipsheer, 1985)

Frenkel, F.E., *Identiteitskaart, Persoonlijkheid: Een Kwestie van Wisselwerking* (Amsterdam, De Beuk, 1988)

Friedman, P., *Their Brother's Keepers. The Christian Heroes and Heroines who Helped the Oppressed Escape the Nazi Terror* (New York, Crown, 1957)

Friedman, P. and Heide, R. van der, *Het Ooorlogspleegkind: Contact Commissie der Joodse Coördinatie Commissies* (Amsterdam, Amsterdam Boek- en Courantmij N.V., 1946)

Gans, M.H., *Memorboek* (Baarn, Bosch & Keuning, 1971)

Gans-Premsela, J., *Vluchtweg. Aan de Bezetter Ontsnapt* (Baarn, Bosch & Keuning, 1990)

Garfinkels, B., *Belgique: Terre d'Accueil: Problème du Réfugié, 1933–1940* (Brussels, Editions de L'Institut de Sociologie de l'Université Libre de Bruxelles, 1974)

Gescher, F.M., *Het Helse Einde van Vucht. Duitse Methoden op Nederlandse Bodem* (Wassenaar, H.J. Dieben, 1945)

Gies, Miep, *Anne Frank Remembered: The Story of the Woman who Helped Hide the Frank Family* (New York, Simon and Schuster, 1987)

Gilbert, M., *The Holocaust. The Jewish Tragedy* (London, Collins, 1986)

Gilthay Veth, D. and Leeuw, A.D. van der, *Rapport door RIOD inzake Activiteiten van drs. F. Weinreb gedurende 1940–45,* 2 vols (The Hague, Staatsuitgeverij, 1976)

Goldberger, L. (ed.), *The Rescue of Danish Jews: Moral Courage Under Stress* (New York, New York University Press, 1987)

Groen, K., *Als slachtoffers daders worden. De zaak van joodse verraadster Ans van Dijk* (Baarn, Ambo, 1994)

Grossmann, K.R., *Emigration* (Frankfurt-am-Main, Europäische Verlagsanstalt, 1969)

Gutman, Y. and Zuroff, E. (eds), *Rescue Attempts during the Holocaust* (Jerusalem, Yad Vashem, 1977)

Harari, J. (J. Pick), *Die Ausrottung der Juden im Besetzten Holland. Ein Tatsachenbericht* (Tel Aviv, n.p., 1944)

Helman, A., *Milljoenen Leed: De Tragedie der Joodsche Vluchtelingen* (1940)

Herzberg, A.J., *Brieven aan mijn Grootvader* (Amsterdam, Querido, 1983)

Herzberg, A.J., *Brieven aan mijn Kleinzoon. De Geschiedenis van een Joodse Emigrantenfamilie* (The Hague, Bakker/Dammen, 1964)

Herzberg, A.J., *Kroniek der Jodenvervolging 1940–45* (Amsterdam, Querido, 1985)

Herzberg, A.J., *Om een Lepel Soep* (Amsterdam, Querido, 1976)

Hilberg, R., *The Destruction of European Jews*, 3 vols (New York, Holmes and Meier, 1985)

Hilberg, R., *Perpetrators, Victims, Bystanders: The Jewish Catastrophe 1933–1945* (London, Secker and Warburg, 1995)

Hilbrink, C., *De Illegalen. Illegaliteit in Twente en het aangrenzende Salland, 1940–1945* (The Hague, SDU, 1989)

Hillesum, E., *Letters from Westerbork* (London, Cape, 1987)

Hillesum, E., *Etty: De Nagelaten Geschriften van Etty Hillesum* (Amsterdam, Balans, 1986)

Hillesum, E., *Het verstoorde leven. Dagboek van Etty Hillesum, 1941–1943*, 12th edn (Bussum, De Haan, 1983) translated as *Etty: A Diary 1941–43* (London, Cape, 1983)

Hillesum, E., *In Duizend Zoete Armen. Nieuwe Dagboekaantekeningen van Etty Hillesum* (Weesp, De Haan, 1984)

Hillesum, E., *Men zou een Pleister op Vele Wonden willen zijn. Reacties op de Dagboeken en Brieven van Etty Hillesum* (Amsterdam, Balans, 1989)

Hirschel, L., *1939–43: Kroniek* (n.p., 1986)

Hirschfeld, G., *Nazi Rule and Dutch Collaboration: The Netherlands under German Occupation, 1940–1945* (Oxford/New York/Hamburg, Berg, 1988)

Hondius, D., *Terugkeer: Antisemitisme in Nederland rond de bevrijding* (The Hague, SDU, 1990)

Houwaart, D., *Kehillo Kedousjo Den Haag. Een Halve Eeuw Geschiedenis van Joods Den Haag* (The Hague, Omniboek, 1986)

Houwaart, D., *Mijn Jodendom* (The Hague, Voorhoeve, 1980)

Houwaart, D., *Verduisterde Bevrijding* (The Hague, Omniboek, 1982)

Houwaart, D., *Weinreb: Een Witboek* (Amsterdam, Meulenhoff, 1975)

Houwaart, D., *Westerbork: Het Begon in 1933* (The Hague, Omniboek, 1983)

Houwink ten Cate, J., *Alfons Zündler en de bewaking van het gevangenkamp aan de Plantage Middelaan 24 te Amsterdam* (RIOD, unpublished, 1994)

Hoyos, L. de, *Klaus Barbie: The Untold Story* (London, W.H. Allen, 1985)

Huizing, B. and Aartsma, K., *De Zwarte Politie 1940–1945* (Weesp, De Haan, 1986)

Hulst, J.W. van, *Treinen naar de Hel: Amsterdam, Westerbork, Auschwitz* (Amsterdam, Buijten en Schipperheijn, 1983)

Jakob, V. and Voort, A. van der, *Anne Frank war nicht allein: Lebensgeschichten deutscher Juden in der Nederlanden* (Berlin/Bonn, Dietz, 1988)

Jong, L. de, *The Netherlands and Nazi Germany* (Cambridge, Mass., Harvard University Press, 1990)

Jong, L.R. de, *Het Koninkrijk der Nederlanden in de Tweede Wereldoorlog,* 14 vols (The Hague, Staatsuitgeverij, 1969–92)

Jong, S. de, *Joodse Oorlogsherinneringen 1940–45* (Fraeneker, T. Wever, 1975)

Joods Historisch Museum, *Documenten van de Jodenvervolging in Nederland, 1940–1945* (Amsterdam, Athenaeum-Polak & van Gennep, 1979)

Josephs, J., *Swastika over Paris. The Fate of the French Jews* (London, Bloomsbury, 1989)

Kalma, J.J., *Redt de Joden. Wat Gebeurd er met de Joodse Oorlogspleegkinderen* (Lekkum [Leeuwarden], Joachimsthal, 1946)

Kar, J. van de, *Joodse Verzet. Terugblik op de Periode Rond de Tweede Wereldoorlog* (Amsterdam, Stadsdrukkerij, 1981)

Kaspi, A., *Les Juifs Pendant L'Occupation* (Paris, Éditions du Seuil, 1991)

Keith, J., *A Friend Among Enemies. The Incredible Story of Arie van Mansum* (Richmond Hill, Ontario, Fitzhenry and Whiteside, 1991)

Kelder, J.J., *De Schalkhaarders: Nederlandse Politiemannen naar Nationaal-socialistische snit* (Utrecht/Antwerp, Veen, 1990)

Kempner, R.M.W., *Twee uit Honderdduizend. Anne Frank en Edith Stein* (Bilthoven, H. Nelissen, 1969)

Kershaw, I., *The Nazi Dictatorship: Problems and Perspectives of Interpretation,* 3rd edn (London, Edward Arnold, 1993)

Klarsfeld, S., *Memorial to the Jews Deported from France 1942–1944. Documentation of the Deportation of the Victims of the Final Solution in France* (New York, Beate Klarsfeld Foundation, 1983)

Klarsfeld, S., *Vichy-Auschwitz. Le Rôle de Vichy dans la Solution Finale de la Question Juive en France, 1942* (Paris, Fayard, 1983)

Klinken, G.J. van, *De Joodse Gemeenschap in het Groninger Westerkwartier, Pieze en Roden* (Groningen, Vrienden v/h Rijksarchief Groningen, 1987)

Knoop, H., *De Joodsche Raad: Het Drama van Abraham Asscher en David Cohen* (Amsterdam, Elsevier, 1983)

Kohner, H. and Kohner, W., *Hanna and Walter – A Love Story* (New York, Random House, 1984) translated as *Hanna en Walter: Een Liefdesgeschiedenis* (Amsterdam, H.J.W. Becht, 1985)

Koker, D., *Dagboek Geschreven in Vught* (Amsterdam, G.A. van Oorschot, 1977)

Koning, B., *Bevrijding van Nederland 1944–1945*, 2nd edn (Nijkerk, G.F. Callenbach, n.d.)

Kossmann, E.H., *The Low Countries 1780–1940* (Oxford, Clarendon, 1978)

Koster, M., *Ons Leven in onderduiktijd* (Oosterbeek, Meyer R. Siegers, 1983)

Kruijer, G.J., *Hongertochten: Amsterdam tijdens de Hongerwinter* (Meppel, Boom, 1951)

Kruskal, H., *Two Years Behind Barbed Wire* (unpublished, Jerusalem 1945)

Kulischer, E.M., *Europe on the Move: War and Population Change 1917–1947* (New York, Columbia University Press, 1948)

Laquer, R., *Dagboek uit Bergen-Belsen, Maart 1944 – April 1945* (Amsterdam, Querido, 1965)

Laurens, B.H., *Hun Armoe en Hun Grauw Gezicht* (Rotterdam, Donker, 1985)

Leeuwen, E. van, *Klein in Memoriam: Late Herinneringen* (The Hague, BZZTÔH, 1983)

Leiden, *Joden en Leiden* (Leiden, Gemeentelijk Archiefdienst, 1980)

Leydesdorff, S., *Wij Hebben als Mens Geleefd: Het Joodse Proletariaat van Amsterdam 1900–40* (Amsterdam, Meulenhoff, 1987)

Liepman, A.J., *Westerbork en Theresienstadt* (Boxtel, Bogaert, 1945)

Lier, C. van, *Schroeiplekken. Ervaringen uit Vught, Westerbork, Auschwitz, Ravensbrück en Malchow* (Amsterdam, Sara, 1978)

Lijphart, A., *The Politics of Accommodation* (University of California, 1968)

Linden, R.R., *Making Stories, Making Selves: Feminist Reflections on the Holocaust* (Columbus, Ohio, Ohio State University Press, 1993)

Lindwer, W., *De Laatste Zeven Maanden: Vrouwen in het Spoor van Anne Frank* (Hilversum, Gooi en Sticht, 1988)

Lindwer, W. (ed.), *Het Fatale Dilemma. De Joodsche Raad voor Amsterdam, 1941–1943* (The Hague, SDU Uitgeverij, 1995)

Maass, W.B., *The Netherlands at War 1940–1945* (London, Abelard-Schuman, 1970)

Marchand, C., *Door het Oog van de Naald* (Amsterdam, Loeb, 1981)

Marrus, M.R., *The Holocaust in History* (Toronto, Meckler, 1987)

Marrus, M.R., *The Nazi Holocaust* (Westport/London, Greenwood, 1989)

Marrus, M.R., *The Unwanted: European Refugees in the Twentieth Century* (Oxford, Oxford University Press, 1985)

Marrus, M.R. and Paxton, R., *Vichy et les Juifs* (Paris, Calmann-Lévy, 1981) (*Vichy France and the Jews* (New York, Basic Books, 1982))

Mayer, A., *One Who Came Back* (Ottawa, Oberon, 1981)

Mayer, A.J., *Why did the Heavens not Darken?* (London/New York, Verso, 1990)

Mechanicus, Ph., *In Depôt. Dagboek uit Westerbork* (Amsterdam, Polak & van Gennep, 1964) published in English as I.R. Gibbons (trans.) *Waiting for Death* (London, Calder and Boyars, 1968)

Mechanicus, Ph., *'Ik Woon, zoals je weet, Drie Hoog'. Brieven uit Westerbork* (Amsterdam, Balans, 1987)

Meijer, J., *Hoge Hoeden, Lage Standaarden: De Nederlandse Joden tussen 1933 en 1940* (Amsterdam, Het Wereldrenster, 1968)

Meijer, J., *Jood en Jodendom in Stad en Ommelanden* (Heemstede, Meijer, 1984)

Meijer, J., *'Moeder in Israël' Een Geschiedenis van het Amsterdamse Asjkenazische Jodendom* (Haarlem, n.p., 1964)

Meyer, J., *Het Jonas Daniël Meijerplein. Bezinning op Drie Eeuwen Amsterdams Jodendom* (Amsterdam, n.p., 1961)

Michman, D. *Het Liberale Jodendom in Nederland 1929–1943* (Amsterdam, Van Gennep, 1988)

Michman, J. (Melkman), *Met Voorbedachten Rade: Ideologie en Uitvoering van de Endlösung der Judenfrage* (Amsterdam, Meulenhoff, 1987)

Michman, J. and Levie, T., *Dutch Jewish History: Proceedings of the Symposium on the History of the Jews in the Netherlands* (Jerusalem, Hebrew University Institute for Research on Dutch Jewry, 1984)

Michman, J., Beem, H. and Michman, D. (eds), *Pinkas. Geschiedenis van de joodse gemeenschap in Nederland* (Ede/Antwerp/Amsterdam, Kluwer/ Nederlands-Israëlitisch Kerkgenootschap/Joods Historisch Museum, 1992)

Miert, J. van (ed.), *Een gewone stad in een bijzondere tijd: Utrecht 1940–1945* (Utrecht, Het Spectrum, 1995)

Minco, M., *Bitter Herbs. The Vivid Memories of a Fugitive Jewish Girl in Nazi-Occupied Holland* (London, Penguin, 1991) originally published as *Het Bittere Kruid* (n.p., van Daamen, 1957)

Moore, B., *Refugees from Nazi Germany in the Netherlands, 1933–1940* (Dordrecht/Boston/ Lancaster, Nijhoff, 1986)

Nederlands-Israëlitisch Genootschap *et al., De Verdwijning van Anneke Beekman en Rebecca Meljado: Witboek* (Amsterdam, Nederlands-Israëlitisch Genootschap, 1954)

Neuman, H.J., *Arthur Seyss-Inquart: Het Leven van een Duits onderkoning in Nederland* (Utrecht, Ambo, 1967)

Noakes, J. (ed.), *The Civilian in War: The Home Front in Europe, Japan and the USA in World War II* (Exeter, Exeter University Press, 1992)

Oliner, S. and Oliner, P.M., *The Altruistic Personality: Rescuers of Jews in Nazi Europe* (New York, Free Press, 1988)

Onderwater, H., *Operatie Manna. De Geallieerde Voedseldroppings April–Mei 1945* (Weesp, Unieboek, 1985)

Oolbekkink, H.J., *Met Lege Handen: Een Hongertocht in Februari 1945* (Amsterdam, Tiebosch Uitgeversmaatschappij, 1979)

Paape, A.H. (ed.), *Studies over Nederland in Oorlogstijd* I (The Hague, Martinus Nijhoff, 1972)

Paldiel, M., *The Path of the Righteous. Gentile Rescuers of the Jews during the Holocaust* (Hoboken, N.J., Ktav, 1993)

Piper, F., *Auschwitz: How Many Perished, Jews, Poles, Gypsies ...* (Krakow, 1991)

Polak, L.Ph., *Zó verging het ons Nederlandse Joden* (n.p., 1945)

Pos, H.J. (ed.), *Antisemitisme en jodendom* (Arnhem, 1939)

Presser, J., *Ondergang. De Vervolging en Verdelging van het Nederlandse Jodendom 1940–45* (The Hague, Staatsuitgeverij, 1965) abridged English edition, trans. A. Pomerans, *Ashes in the Wind: The Destructions of Dutch Jewry* (London, Souvenir Press, 1968)

Raatgever, J.G., *Van Dollen Dinsdag tot de Bevrijding* (Amsterdam, De Telg, n.d.)

Ravine, J., *La Résistance Organisée des Juifs en France 1940–1944* (Paris, Juillard, 1973)

Reijnders, C., *Van 'Joodsche Natiën' tot Joodse Nederlanders* (Proefschrift, Rijksuniversiteit Utrecht, 1969)

Reitlinger, G., *The Final Solution* (London, Sphere, 1971)

Rittner, C. and Myers, S., *The Courage to Care: Rescuers of Jews during the Holocaust* (New York: New York University Press, 1986)

Roegholt, R.F., *Ben Sijes: Een Biografie* (The Hague, SDU, 1988)

Roegholt, R.F. and Zwaan, J. (eds), *Het Verzet 1940–45* (Weesp, Unieboek, 1985)

Rose, L., *The Tulips are Red* (New York, A.S. Barnes, 1981)

Ryan, M.D. (ed.), *Human Responses to the Holocaust: Perpetrators and Victims, Bystanders and Resisters* (New York/Toronto, Edwin Mellen Press, 1981)

Sannes, H.W.J., *Onze Joden en Duitschland's Greep naar de Wereldmacht* (Amsterdam, n.p., 1946)

Santen, E., *Aan Twee Minuten heb Ik niet genoeg: Op zoek naar mijn Joodse Oorsprong* (Amsterdam, Sara, 1983)

Schelvis, J., *Vernietigingskamp Sobibor* (Amsterdam, De Bataafsche Leeuw, 1993)

Schloss, E., *Eva's Story: A Survivor's Story by the Step-Sister of Anne Frank* (London, Allen, 1988)

Schloss, E., *Herinneringen van een Joodse Meisje* (Amsterdam, Sua, 1989)

Sijes, B.A., *De Februari-staking: 25-26 Februari 1941* (Amsterdam, Meulenhoff, n.d.)

Sijes, B., *Studies over Jodenvervolging* (Assen, van Gorcum, 1974)

Sijes, B.A., *De Razzia van Rotterdam*, 2nd edn (Amsterdam, Sijthoff, 1984)

Sluyser, M., *Amsterdam, Je hebt een zoute smaak* (Amsterdam, n.p., 1964)

Sluyser, M., *Er Groeit Gras in de Weesperstraat* (Amsterdam, n.p., 1962)

Sluyser, M., *Voordat Ik het Vergeet* (Amsterdam, n.p., 1957) published in English as *Before I Forget* (New York, n.p., 1962)

Smelik, K.A.D. (ed.), *Jodendom* (The Hague, Nederlands Bibliotheek en Lectuur Centrum, 1983)

Snoek, J.M., *The Grey Book* (Assen, Van Gorcum, 1969)

Snoek, J.M., *De Nederlandse Kerken en de joden 1940–1945* (Kampen, Kok, 1990)

Stam, C. van, *Wacht binnen de dijken – Verzet in en om de Haarlemmermeer* (Haarlem, De Toorts, 1986)

Stanford, J.C., *Tagebuch eines deutschen Jude im Untergrund* (Darmstadt, Darmstädter Blätter, 1980)

Stegeman, H.B.J. and Vorste-veld, J.P., *Het Joodse Werkdorp in de Wieringermeer 1934–1941* (Zutphen, De Walberg Pers, 1983)

Stein, A., *Quiet Heroes. True Stories of the Rescue of Jews by Christians in Nazi-occupied Holland* (New York, New York University Press, 1988)

Steinberg, L., *Le Comité de défense des Juifs en Belgique* (Brussels, Editions de l'Université de Bruxelles, 1973)

Steinberg, M., *L'Etoile et le Fusil*, 3 vols (Brussels, Vie Ouvrière, 1983–86), *Vol. I La Question Juive 1940–42* (1983); *Vol. II Les Cent Jours de la Déportation* (1984); *Vol. III La Traque de Juifs 1942–44* (1986)

Steinberg, M., *De Ogen van het Monster. Volkerenmoord dag in dag uit* (Antwerp/Baarn, Hadewijch, 1992)

Stokman, S., *Het Verzet van de Nederlandsche Bischoppen tegen Nationaal-Socialisme en Duitse Tyrannie* (Utrecht, Het Spectrum, 1945)

Stroom, G. van der, *Duitse Strafrechtspleging in Nederland en het lot der Veroordeelen* (The Hague, Staatsuitgeverij, 1982)

Stoutenbeek, J., *Joods Nederland: Een Cultuurhistorische Gids* (Amsterdam, Querido, 1989)

Taubes, I., *Persecution of the Jews in Holland 1940–44: Westerbork and Bergen-Belsen* (London, 1945)

Thomas, G. and Morgan-Witts, M., *Voyage of the Damned* (London, Coronet, 1976)

Tijn, M. van, *Een Boom in de Vlagte* (Bloemendaal, n.p., 1975)

Tijn, M. van, *Ik Leef Nog* (Bloemendaal, n.p., 1974)

Tjepkema, A., and Walvis, J., *'Ondergedoken': Het Ondergrondse Leven in Nederland tijdens de Tweede Wereldoorlog* (Weesp, De Haan, 1985)

Touw, H.C., *Het Verzet der Hervormde Kerk* (The Hague, Boekcentrum N.V., 1946)

Tricht, C. van, *Onderduikers en Knokploegen: Het Verzet van de Landelijke Organisatie voor Hulp aan Onderduikers en de Landelijke Knokploegen* (Amsterdam, De Bataafsche Leeuw, 1991)

Trunk, I., *Judenrat. The Jewish Councils in Eastern Europe under Nazi Occupation* (New York, Macmillan, 1972)

Valkhoff, Z., *Leven in een niet-bestaan. Beleving en betekenis van de joodse onderduik* (Utrecht, ICODO, 1992)

Veld, N.K.C.A. in't, *De Joodse Ereraad* (The Hague, SDU, 1989)

Veld, N.K.C.A. in't, *De SS en Nederland* (Amsterdam, Sijthoff, 1987)

Verduner, Y. and F., *Signs of Life: The Letters of Hilde Verduner-Sluizer* (Washington, D.C., Acropolis, 1990)

Verhey, E., *Om het Joodse Kind* (Amsterdam, Nijgh & van Ditmar, 1991)

Verhoeven, R., *Een zomerdag in 1942. 14 Juli 1942, de dag voorafgaand aan de eerste deportatie van joden uit Amsterdam* (Amsterdam, Piramide, 1995)

Vernooij, A., *Grenzen aan gehoorzaamheid: houding en gedrag van de Utrechtse Politie tijdens de Duitse Bezetting* (Utrecht, Trezoor, 1985)

Visser, A., *Onderduikers op de Veluwe* (Wezep, Bredewold, 1990)

Visser, F., *De Pensionhoudster en de Onderduiker* (Baarn, Bosch & Keuning, 1980)

Vogel, L., *Dagboek uit een Kamp* (The Hague, n.p., 1946)

Warmbrunn, W., *The Dutch under German Occupation 1940–45* (Stanford, Stanford University Press, 1963)

Warmbrunn, W., *The German Occupation of Belgium 1940–1944* (New York, Peter Lang, 1993)

Weinreb, F., *Der Krieg der Römerin: Erinnerungen 1935–43,* 2 vols (Munich, Thauros, 1981–82)

Weinreb, F., *Das Wunder vom Ende der Kriege: Erlebnisse im Letzten Krieg* (Weiler im Allgau, Thauros, 1985)

Weinreb, F., *Collaboratie en Verzet. Een poging tot ontmythologisering,* 3 vols (Amsterdam, Meulenhoff, 1969)

Wesselink, E.H., *Kom vanavond met verhalen* (Eibergen, Eibergen-Historisch Kring, 1990)

Westerweel, W., *Verzet zonder geweld. Ter herinnering van Joop Westerweel* (n.p., n.d.) mimeograph, RIOD

Wielek, H., *De Oorlog die Hitler Won* (Amsterdam, Amsterdam Boek- en Courantmij N.V., 1947)

Wijsmuller-Meijer,T., *Geen Tijd voor Tranen* (Amsterdam, n.p., 1961)

Wildt, A. de, *Het is maar voor een nacht* (Amsterdam, Verzetsmuseum, 1990)

Wind, E. de, *Eindstation ... Auschwitz* (Amsterdam, n.p., 1946)

Wolf, H., *De Gespijkerde God* (Nijmegen, SUN, 1995)

Wolff, S. de, *Geschiedenis der Joden in Nederland. Laatste Bedrijf* (Amsterdam, n.p., 1946)

Wyers, S. (ed.), *Als ik wil kan ik duiken. Brieven van Claartje van Aals, verpleegster in de joods psychiatrische inrichting Het Apeldoornsche Bosch 1940–1943* (Amsterdam, Thomas Rap, 1995)

Zee, H. van der, *De Honger Winter: van Dolle Dinsdag tot Bevrijding* (Amsterdam, Becht, 1979)

Zee, N. van der, *Jacques Presser* (Amsterdam, Balans, 1988)
Zee, N. van der, *De Kamergenoot van Anne Frank* (Amsterdam, Lakeman, n.d.)
Zomeren, D. van, *Geschiedenis van de Joodse Gemeenschap in Weesp: Ze waren gewoon ineens weg* (Weesp, Ark/Heureka, 1983)
Zuccotti, S., *The Holocaust, the French and the Jews* (New York, Basic Books, 1993)
Zuylen, L.F. van, *De Joodse Gemeenschap to Enschede 1930–45* (Hengelo, Twents-Gelderse Uitgeverij Witkam, 1983)
Zwan, J. van der, *De Dag die Manna Viel* (The Hague, Voorhoeve, n.d.)

Articles

Ariel, J., 'Jewish Self-Defence and Resistance in France During World War II', *Yad Vashem Studies* VI (1967), pp. 221–50.
Avni, H., 'Zionist Underground in Holland and France and the escape to Spain', in Y. Gutman and E. Zuroff (eds), *Rescue Attempts during the Holocaust* (Jerusalem, Yad Vashem, 1977), pp. 555–90.
Barnouw, D., 'Vijftig jaar na de inval', *Bijdragen en Mededelingen betreffende de geschiedenis der Nederlanden* CVII (1992), pp. 287–95.
Baron, L., 'The Dynamics of Decency: Dutch Rescuers of Jews during the Holocaust', *Frank P. Piskor Faculty Lecture*, St Lawrence University, May 1985.
Bauer, Y., 'The *Judenräte* – Some Conclusions', in M.R. Marrus (ed.), *The Nazi Holocaust* VI (Westport/London, Greenwood, 1989) pp. 165–77.
Blom, J.C.H., 'Nederland onder Duitse bezetting 10 Mei 1940–5 Mei 1945', in D.P. Blok *et al.* (eds), *Algemene Geschiedenis der Nederlanden* XV (Haarlem, Fibula-van Dishoeck, 1982), pp. 55–94.
Blom, J.C.H., 'The Persecution of the Jews in the Netherlands: A Comparative Western European Perspective', *European History Quarterly* XIX (1989), pp. 333–51.
Boas, H., 'The Persecution and Destruction of Dutch Jewry 1940–1945', *Yad Vashem Studies* VI (1967), pp. 359–74.
Braber, B., 'De Rol van het joodse verzet in de tweede wereldoorlog', *Ter Herkenning* XIII (1985), pp. 227–37.
Bruijn, W. de, 'Ongewenschte vreemdelingen', *Skript* XIV (1992), pp. 92–100.
Caron, V., 'Prelude to Vichy: France and the Jewish Refugees in the Era of Appeasement', *Journal of Contemporary History* XX (1985), pp. 157–76.
Cohen, Y., 'French Jewry's Dilemma on the Orientation of its Leadership. From Polemics to Conciliation: 1942–44', *Yad Vashem Studies* XIV (1981), pp. 167–204.

Daalder, H., 'Dutch Jews in a Segmented Society', *Acta Historiae Neerlandicae* X (1977), pp. 175–94.

Doorslaer, R. van, 'La police belge et le maintien de l'ordre en Belgique occupée', in E. Dejonghe (ed.), *L'Occupation en France et en Belgique 1940–1944,* I (Lille, Revue du Nord, 1987).

Dunk, H.W. von der, 'The Shock of 1940', *Journal of Contemporary History* II (1967), pp. 169–82.

Farjeon, A., 'The Dutch Journal: The Sadler's Wells Ballet in Holland, May 1940' Parts 1–3, *Dance Chronicle* X (1987), pp. 330–66; XI (1988), pp. 84–115; XI (1988), pp. 274–312.

Fijnault, C., 'The Police of the Netherlands in and between the Two World Wars', in C. Emsley and B. Weinberger (eds), *Policing Western Europe. Politics, Professionalism and Public Order, 1850–1950* (New York/ Westport/ London, Greenwood, 1991)

Fishman, J.S., 'The Anneke Beekman Affair and the Dutch News Media', *Jewish Social Studies* XLI (1978), pp. 3–24.

Fishman, J.S., 'The Jewish Community in Post-War Netherlands, 1944–1975', *Midstream* XXII (1976), pp. 42–54.

Fishman, J.S., 'Jewish War Orphans in the Netherlands – The Guardianship Issue 1945–1950', *Wiener Library Bulletin* XXVII (1973–74) nos 30–1, pp. 31–6.

Fishman, J.S., 'The Ecumenical Challenge of Jewish Survival; Pastor Kalma and Postwar Dutch Society, 1946', *Journal of Ecumenical Studies* XV (1978), pp. 461–76.

Fishman, J.S., 'The War Orphan Controversy in the Netherlands: Majority–Minority Relations', in J. Michman and T. Levie (eds), *Dutch Jewish History* (Jerusalem, Tel Aviv University/Hebrew University, 1984), pp. 421–32.

Fishman, J.S., 'De joodse oorlogswezen. Een interview met Gesina van der Molen, voorzitter van de Commissie Oorlogspleegkinderen', *Oorlogsdocumentatie '40-'45* VII (1995), pp. 51–66.

Fox, J., 'How far did Vichy France "Sabotage" the Imperatives of Wannsee?', in D. Cesarani (ed.), *The Final Solution: Origins and Implementation* (London, Routledge, 1994)

Gellman, I., 'The St Louis Tragedy', *American Jewish Historical Quarterly* II (1971), pp. 144–55.

Graaff, B.J.G de, '"Strijdig met de tradities van ons volk". Het Nederlandse beleid ten aanzien van vluchtelingen in de jaren dertig', *Jaarboek van Buitenlandse Zaken* (The Hague, 1988), pp. 169–87.

Griffioen, P. and Zeller, R., 'Jodenvervolging in Nederland en België tijdens de Tweede Wereldoorlog: Een Vergelijkende Analyse', *Oorlogsdocumentatie '40-'45* VIII (1997).

Gulwirth, J., 'Antwerp Jewry Today', *Jewish Journal of Sociology* X (1968), pp. 121–37.

Gutman, Y., 'The Concept of Labor in Yudenrat Policy', in M.R. Marrus (ed.), *The Nazi Holocaust* (Westport/London, Greenwood, 1989), VI, pp. 521–50.

Haverhals-Willemsz, A.W., 'Onderduikersperikelen', *Bruggeske* III (1989), pp. 25–31.

Hess, S., 'The Disproportionate Destruction: The Annihilation of the Jews in the Netherlands 1940–45', in G.J. Colijn and M.S. Littel (eds), *The Netherlands and Nazi Genocide: Papers of the 21st Annual Scholars' Conference* (Lewiston, N.Y., Edwin Mellen Press, 1992), pp. 63–76.

Hilberg, R., 'The Judenrat: "Conscious or Unconscious Tool"', in M.R. Marrus (ed.), *The Nazi Holocaust* VI, (Westport/London, Greenwood, 1989), pp. 162–4.

Hirschfeld, G., 'Der "freiwillige" Arbeitseinsatz niederländischer Fremdarbeiter während des Zweiten Weltkrieges als Krisenstrategie einer nichtnationalsozialistischen Vervaltung', in H. Mommsen and W. Schulze (eds), *Vom Elend der Handarbeit. Probleme historischer Unterschichtenforschung* (Stuttgart, Klett-Cotta, 1981), pp. 497–513.

Hirschfeld, G., 'Niederlande', in W. Benz (ed.), *Dimension des Völkermords. Die Zahl der jüdischen Opfer des Nationalsozialismus* (Munich, R. Oldenbourg Verlag, 1991).

Houwink ten Cate, J.Th.M., 'Het Jongere Deel. Demografische en sociale kenmerken van het jodendom in Nederland tijdens de vervolging', *Oorlogsdocumentatie '40-'45, Jaarboek van het Rijksinstituut voor Oorlogsdocumentatie* I (1989), pp. 9–66.

Houwink ten Cate, J.Th.M., 'De Justitie en de Joodsche Raad', in E. Jonker and M. van Rossem (eds), *Geschiedenis en Cultuur. Achttien Opstellen* (The Hague, SDU, 1990) pp. 149–68.

Houwink ten Cate, J.Th.M., 'Heydrich's Security Police and the Amsterdam Jewish Council (February 1941–October 1942), *Dutch Jewish History* III (Jerusalem 1993), pp. 381–93.

Houwink ten Cate, J.Th.M., 'De Joodse Raad voor Amsterdam 1941–1943', in W. Lindwer (ed.), *Het Fatale Dilemma. De Joodsche Raad voor Amsterdam 1941–1943* (The Hague, SDU Uitgeverij, 1995).

Jong, L. de, 'Help to People in Hiding', *Delta* VIII (Spring 1965), pp. 37–79.

Jong, L. de, 'Jews and Non-Jews in Nazi Occupied Holland', in M. Beloff (ed.), *On the Track of Tyranny* (Freeport, N.Y., Books for Libraries Press, 1971).

Jong, P. de, 'Responses of the Churches in the Netherlands to the Nazi Occupation', in M.D. Ryan (ed.), *Human Responses to the Holocaust: Perpetrators and Victims, Bystanders and Resisters* (New York/Toronto, Edwin Mellen Press, 1981).

Kleerekoper, S., 'Het joodse proletariaat in het Amsterdam van de 19e eeuw', *Studia Rosenthaliana* Ii (1967), pp. 97–108.

Kopuit, M., 'Herinneringen Prof. Dr. David Cohen', *Nieuw Israëlitisch Weekblad* (May 1982) (special issue).

Kristel, C., 'De moeizame terugkeer. De repatriëring van de Nederlandse overlevenden uit de Duitse concentratiecampen', *Oorlogsdocumentatie '40-'45, Jaarboek van het Rijksinstituut voor Oorlogsdocumentatie* I (1989), pp. 77–100.

Kristel, C., 'A Sacred Duty. The Holocaust in Dutch Historiography', *Low Countries Yearbook*, II (1995), pp. 186–94.

Leeuw, A.J. van der, 'Meer Slachtoffers dan elders in West-Europa', *Nieuw Israëlitisch Weekblad* (15 November 1985).

Lekkerkerker, E.C., 'Oorlogspleegkinderen', *Maandblad voor de Geestelijke Volksgezondheid* VII (October 1946).

Levin, D., 'The Fighting Leadership of the Judenräte in the Small Communities of Poland', in M.R. Marrus (ed.), *The Nazi Holocaust* (Westport/London, Greenwood, 1989), VII, pp. 73–89.

Maga, T., 'Closing the Door: The French Government and Refugee Policy, 1933–1939', *French Historical Studies* XII (1982), pp. 424–42.

Marrus, M.R. and Paxton, R.O., 'The Nazis and the Jews in Occupied Western Europe 1940–1944', *Journal of Modern History* LIV (1982), pp. 687–714.

Mason, H.L., 'Testing Human Bonds within Nations: Jews in the Occupied Netherlands', *Political Science Quarterly* XCIX (1984), pp. 315–43.

Meershoek, G. van, 'De Amsterdamse Hoodcommisaris en de deportatie van de joden', in D. Barnouw *et al.* (eds), *Oorlogsdocumentatie* III (Zutphen, De Walburg Pers, 1992), pp. 9–44.

Mees, Ph.A.J., 'Mieke Louwers-Mees', *Kroniek van de Stichting Geslacht Mees* XXV (July 1976), pp. 3–5.

Michman, D., 'De oprichting van de "Joodsche Raad van Amsterdam" vanuit een vergelijkend perspectief', in D. Barnouw *et al.* (eds), *Oorlogsdocumentatie* III (Zutphen, De Walburg Pers, 1992), pp. 75–100.

Michman, J., 'Gothische Torens op een Corinthisch Gebouw', *Tijdschrift voor Geschiedenis* LXXXIX (1976), pp. 493–517.

Michman, J., 'Planning for the Final Solution against the Background of Developments in Holland in 1941', *Yad Vashem Studies* XVII (1986), pp. 145–80.

Michman, J., 'The Controversial Stand of the Joodse Raad in the Netherlands: Lodewijk E. Visser's Struggle', *Yad Vashem Studies* X (1974), pp. 9–68.

Michman, J., 'The Controversy Surrounding the Jewish Council of Amsterdam. From its Inception to the Present Day', in M.R. Marrus, *The Nazi Holocaust* (Westport/London, Greenwood, 1989), VI, pp. 821–43.

Moore, B., 'Jewish Refugees in the Netherlands 1933–1940: The Structure and Pattern of Jewish Immigration from Nazi Germany', *Leo Baeck Institute Yearbook* XXIX (1984), pp. 73–101.

Moore, B., 'Jewish Refugee Entrepreneurs and the Dutch Economy in the 1930s', *Immigrants and Minorities* IX (1990), pp. 46–63.

Moore, B., 'Occupation, Collaboration and Resistance: Some Recent Publications on the Netherlands during the Second World War', *European History Quarterly* XXI (1991), pp. 109–18.

Moore, B., 'The Western Allies and Food Relief to the Ocupied Netherlands, 1944–1945', *War and Society* X, 2 (1992), pp. 91–118.

Moore, B., 'British Economic Warfare and Relations with the Neutral Netherlands during the "Phoney War", September 1939–May 1940', *War and Society* XIII (1995), pp. 65–89.

Munnick, B. de, 'Uitverkoren in uitzondering? Het Verhaal van de Barneveldgroep, 1942–1943', *Skript Historisch Tijdschrift* XII (1990), pp. 67–78.

Ommeren, A., van and Scherphuis, A., 'De Creche, 1942–43', *Vrij Nederland* 18 (January 1986).

Overduin, H., 'Tante Zus kwam altijd onverwacht', *Opzij* XVI (May 1988), pp. 14–16.

Paldiel, M., 'The Altruism of the Righteous Gentiles', *Journal of Holocaust and Genocide Studies* III (1988), pp. 187–96 reprinted in Y. Bauer (ed.), *Remembering for the Future*, I (Oxford, Pergamon, 1989), pp. 517–25.

Paldiel, M., 'To the Righteous among the Nations Who Risked Their Lives to Rescue Jews', *Yad Vashem Studies* XIX (1988), pp. 403–25.

Peet, A.W., 'De Jodenvervolging', *Kronijck Voorst* XIII (1990), pp. 23–31.

Piper, F., 'Estimating the Number of Deportees to, and Victims of Auschwitz-Birkenau Camp', *Yad Vashem Studies* XXI (1991), pp. 49–103.

Poznanski, R., 'La résistance juive en France', *Revue d'Histoire de la Deuxième Guerre Mondiale* CXXXVII (1985), pp. 3–22.

Reuvekamp, A., 'Sommige mensen krijgen levenslang', *Opzij* VII (May 1979), pp. 26–7.

Roon, G. van, 'The Dutch Protestants, the Third Reich and the Persecution of the Jews', in O. Dov Kulka and P.R. Mendes (eds), *Judaism and Christianity Under the Impact of National Socialism* (Jerusalem, Historical Society of Israel, 1987).

Schie, A.J. van, 'Restitution of Economic Rights after 1945', in J. Michman and T. Levie (eds), *Dutch Jewish History* (Jerusalem, Tel Aviv University/Hebrew University, 1984), pp. 401–20.

Schmitt, H.A., 'How I Fled Nazi Germany', *Virginia Quarterly Review* LXII (1986), pp. 499–518.

Schöffer, I., 'Een geschiedenis van de vervolging der Joden in Nederland 1940–1945', *Tijdschrift voor Geschiedenis* LXXIX (1966), pp. 38–63.

Schöffer, I., 'Weinreb, een affair van lange duur', *Tijdschrift voor Geschiedenis* XCV (1982), pp. 196–224.

Schogt, H., 'Motives and Impediments in Describing War Memories: The Tragedy of the Jew', *Revue Canadien Etudes Néerlandaises* XI (1990), pp. 3–7.

Shapiro, L. and Sapir, B., 'Jewish Population of the World', *American Jewish Yearbook* L (1948–49), pp. 691–724.

Sijes, B.A., 'The Position of the Jews during the Occupation of the Netherlands: Some Observations', *Acta Historiae Neerlandicae* IX (The Hague, Nijhoff, 1976), pp. 170–92.

Singer, B., 'France and its Jews in World War II', *Contemporary French Civilisations* II (1977), pp. 1–23.

Steinberg, L., 'Jewish Rescue Activities in Belgium and France', in Y. Gutman and E. Zuroff (eds), *Rescue Attempts during the Holocaust* (Jerusalem, Yad Vashem, 1977).

Steinberg, M., 'Faced with the Final Solution in Occupied Belgium. The Church's Silence and Christian Action', in Y. Bauer *et al.* (eds), *Remembering for the Future* (Oxford, Pergamon, 1990).

Steinberg, M., 'The Trap of Legality: The Association of the Jews of Belgium', in M.R. Marrus (ed.), *The Nazi Holocaust* (Westport/London, Greenwood, 1989), VI, pp. 797–820.

Strauss, H.A., 'Jewish Emigration from Germany. Nazi Policies and Jewish Responses (I)', *Leo Baeck Institute Yearbook* XXV (1980), pp. 313–61.

Strauss, H.A., 'Jewish Emigration from Germany. Nazi Policies and Jewish Responses (II)', *Leo Baeck Institute Yearbook* XXVI (1981), pp. 343–409.

Stuhldreher, C.J.F., 'De Nederlandse Staat en de opsporing van de gedeporteerde joden', *Oorlogsdocumentatie '40-'45, Jaarboek van het Rijksinstituut voor Oorlogsdocumentatie* I (1989), pp. 67–76.

Weiss, A., 'Jewish Leadership in Occupied Poland – Postures and Attitudes', in M.R. Marrus (ed.), *The Nazi Holocaust* (Westport/London, Greenwood, 1989), VI, pp. 440–70.

Wiegman, T., 'Ds. Overduin helpt onderduikers', *Sliepsteen* III (Autumn 1985), p. 7; IV (Winter 1985), p.15; V (Spring 1986), p. 7.

Yahil, L., 'Methods of Persecution: A Comparison of the Final Solution in Holland and Denmark', *Scripta Hierosolymitana* XIII (1972), pp. 279–300.

Theses and dissertations

Braber, B., 'De Activiteiten van Barbie in Nederland in de jaren 1940–1945' (Doctoraalscriptie, University of Amsterdam, 1984)

Haperen van Beurden, M.G. van, 'Conflict van overlevenden om overlevenden. Het vraagstuk van de joodse oorlogspleegkinderen, juli 1942–1 september 1949' (Doctoraalscriptie, Catholic University of Nijmegen, 1989)

Kristel, C., 'De Repatriëring van de Nederlandse overlevenden uit de concentratiekampen' (Doctoraalscriptie, University of Amsterdam, 1987)

Moore, B., 'Refugees from Nazi Germany in the Netherlands: The Political Problem and Government Response, 1933–1940' (Ph.D. thesis, University of Manchester, 1983)

Williams, I., The Role of the Jewish Council of Amsterdam under Nazi Rule, February 1941–September 1943' (Dissertation, Bulmershe College of Higher Education, 1985)

Unpublished

Boom, B.E. ten, 'The Deportation of the Jewish Community in Den Haag', Conference: Deportation Management and Resistance in (Western) Europe, RIOD, 23–24 November 1992.

Houwinck ten Cate, J.Th.M., 'The *Sicherheitspolizei* and SD in Western Europe', Conference: Deportation Management and Resistance in (Western) Europe, RIOD, 23–24 November 1992.

Meershoek, G. van, 'The Amsterdam Municipality, its Police Force and the Persecution of the Jews', Conference: Deportation Management and Resistance in (Western) Europe, RIOD, 23–24 November 1992.

Romein, P., 'Local Government in the Netherlands and the Deportation of the Jews', Conference: Deportation Management and Resistance in (Western) Europe, RIOD, 23–24 November 1992.

Index